The Boiled Frog Syndrome

"A *tour de force* combining in-depth analysis of the pernicious health effects of much of our modern built environment with a passionate plea for a renaissance of perennial principles of life and architecture that can be expressed in a new built environment that is both healthy and beautiful. The book is both visionary and immensely practical, giving advice from which we can all benefit."

David Lorimer, Project Director, Scientific and Medical Network

"In our modern world there are a number of raw nerves. Thomas Saunders touches on arguably the most important of these in his book *The Boiled Frog Syndrome*. The impact on the subtle energies of organic life from modern technologies as far apart as architecture and electricity has been brought between one set of covers for the first time. This achievement needed the broadest and sharpest of intellects, a simultaneous and detailed knowledge of those technologies combined with a deep understanding of the subtle energies of our planet, two talents rarely found in one person. This book demands the reader's attention from first to last page, and will undoubtedly prove to be a formative and informative influence on every reader."

Roger Coghill, Director, Coghill Research Laboratories

"Thomas Saunders' book could not come at a more relevant moment when events remind us that we must have respect for the environment in which we live – otherwise we will cease to live. A complex, fascinating, always open-minded attempt to show us how to challenge the Establishment."

Maureen Lipman, actress

"Thomas Saunders shows how life on Earth is part of a universal vibratory system. He takes a sober and authoritative look at the risks and proven harm accompanying neglect of the laws of this system, in the modern architectural and electromagnetic environment. He then takes us on an inspiring journey illustrating that early cultures had profound understanding of how to co-operate with natural energies, and showing how great architecture reflects the grand design of the universe. *The Boiled Frog Syndrome* is an eye-opening, life-enhancing book."

Neville Hodgkinson, formerly medical and science correspondent to
The Sunday Times and author of *Will to Be Well* and *AIDS:
The Failure of Contemporary Society*

"This is a fascinating book. Whatever your views, prejudices or assumptions, Thomas Saunders brings new perspectives to important global environmental and design issues affecting the future of our planet. He suggests that the way we live now has, within it, the seeds of long-term corrosion. His detailed research into 'sick building syndrome' and the possible effects of what he describes as the electro-magnetic 'fog' surrounding us, shows a disturbing picture. He asks whether we are continually adjusting our lives in such a way that we are becoming complicit to irreversible change and damage.

His is a spiritual book, in a non-theological sense. He seeks to find pointers to the way people must live together in the future, if we are to survive, from the understandings, mysteries and philosophies of the ancient past. The book challenges us to care for harmony, balance and proportion (in architecture and in lifestyle) as much as we care for our material wellbeing. He explores the arcane and mathematical relationships between music and sound, numbers and structures in the natural world as well as the man-made world. He argues that the pace of change has snapped our intellectual inheritance, and he makes a powerful and intriguing case."

Robert Rowland, former Editor of the BBC's 'Money Programme'
and 'Panorama' and Head of BBC Open University Production Centre

"Thomas Saunders' fascinating new book offers us all a wake-up call for the way we are living our lives. He convinces us that we can play a part, however small, in changing both our personal and global environments. *The Boiled Frog Syndrome* is a book that can truly make a difference."

Les Dennis, entertainer

"Thomas Saunders has written a remarkable book. His findings at once generate interest, concern and outrage in equal measure. He effectively links the seemingly mutually exclusive worlds of ancient arts and skills, modern sciences, humanity and design to weave a compelling story that makes these arcane subjects accessible to all. More importantly he describes in detail how people, the natural world and our technologies interact with a disturbing potency with the potential to create both harmony and harm.

Like the parabolic boiled frog, we tolerate the intolerable until it's too late. This is one of the key messages. It's always later than we think and unless we understand and act on the facts presented in this book, then we will deserve to enter the age of ignorance. This book is suitable for general reading and should also become a standard text for architecture and design students and other professionals. Everyone should be aware of the need to look beyond the obvious and have the ability to ask informed questions of those who shape our world. Thomas gives us the tools to do this. Those who create our environments need to be aware of the subtle (and not so subtle) forces that make the difference between places that promote wellbeing and delight, and those which act to defeat these qualities.

This book has two parts. The first introduces us to a diverse range of natural and artificial phenomena, and the effect that each has on humanity: sunspots, the sub-atomic universe, the nature of 'sacred' sites, radio waves, and geopathic stress are some of the many topics covered. However, Thomas is an architect and in the second part he proposes an important set of ideas related to design that are rooted in history which are important for us today. He discusses the revival and uses of low technology and natural effects to offer a gentler and more humane design response. His explanation of the mystical language of numbers and of divine harmony is important and readily understandable. Thomas is no reactionary academic; he continually seeks to explain how these quiet sciences can be used by everyone, not just the design professionals.

Not long ago, Thomas might have been burnt at the stake for his research. Thankfully we live in an enquiring world which is richer for this immensely readable and comprehensive book. After reading *The Boiled Frog Syndrome* we will never look at the world in the same way again."

Peter Ullathorne, JP RIBA AADipl. FRSA AAIA,
Vice President, HOK International, London

The Boiled Frog Syndrome

Your Health and the Built Environment

THOMAS SAUNDERS

⟨⟩WILEY-ACADEMY

First published in Great Britain in 2002 by WILEY-ACADEMY
A division of JOHN WILEY & SONS

Copyright © 2002 John Wiley & Sons Ltd, The Atrium, Southern Gate, Chichester,
West Sussex PO19 8SQ, England
Telephone (+44) 1243 779777

Email (for orders and customer service enquiries): cs-books@wiley.co.uk
Visit our Home Page on www.wileyeurope.com or www.wiley.com

This publication is designed to provide accurate and authoritative information in regard to the
subject matter covered. It is sold on the understanding that the Publisher is not engaged in
rendering professional services. If professional advice or other expert assistance is required, the
services of a competent professional should be sought.

Other Wiley Editorial Offices

John Wiley & Sons Inc., 111 River Street, Hoboken, NJ 07030, USA

Jossey-Bass, 989 Market Street, San Francisco, CA 94103-1741, USA

Wiley-VCH Verlag GmbH, Boschstr. 12, D-69469 Weinheim, Germany

John Wiley & Sons Australia Ltd, 33 Park Road, Milton, Queensland 4064, Australia

John Wiley & Sons (Asia) Pte Ltd, 2 Clementi Loop #02-01, Jin Xing Distripark, Singapore
129809

John Wiley & Sons Canada Ltd, 22 Worcester Road, Etobicoke, Ontario, Canada M9W 1L1

ISBN 0-470-84553-8

Typeset in Baskerville by Deerpark Publishing Services Ltd, Shannon, Ireland
Printed and bound in Great Britain by TJ International, UK
This book is printed on acid-free paper responsibly manufactured from sustainable
forestry in which at least two trees are planted for each one used for paper production.

*This book is dedicated to my wife Janet,
an inspiring, generous and loving spirit*

Contents

Acknowledgements

Without the encouragement, patience and support of my wife Janet, it is unlikely that this book would have been realised.

Particular thanks are due to John Baldock for all his editorial skills and words of wisdom.

I also thank Alasdair Philips, Editor and Publisher of *Powerwatch Network Newsletters*, and Simon Best, Editor and Publisher of *Electromagnetics News, Electromagnetics and VDU News* and *Electromagnetic Hazard and Therapy* (www.em-hazard-therapy.com) for kind permission to quote extracts from these magazines. (Since May 2000, *Electromagnetic Hazard and Therapy* has incorporated *Powerwatch News* and the Powerwatch Helpline www.powerwatch.org.uk.)

I would also pay tribute to Alasdair, Simon and Roger Coghill for their dedicated and tireless work over the years to bring to our attention the whole range of electromagnetic field hazards we now encounter in our daily lives.

The Gibran National Committee is also thanked for giving permission to quote from Kahlil Gibran's play *Iram that al Imad (Iram of the Columns)*.

Finally, I give my special thanks to Professor Keith Critchlow and the work of the Kairos organisation which has been the inspiration and foundation of Part II of this book. I invited Professor Critchlow to comment on relevant sections of the texts attributed to his lectures, and he requested that the following note be included in the Acknowledgements:

Keith Critchlow, acting as a representative of the aural tradition has conducted 'closed' summer schools in both the UK and the US over the past 20 years or so. In these, of which I have attended many, he has given out material that is unpublished based on the principles of the venerable aural tradition that a printed word cannot be questioned, and may even transmit both a fraction of the deeper meanings as well as be 'frozen' in the printed word. Thereby in danger of being commented on by another who may direct a reader/hearer into only a single interpretation. Plato wrote clearly on this matter in his most important seventh letter (or epistle), which the reader is referred to. However, I have been given permission to pass on my understanding of the words I 'heard' at these lectures by K.C. as our times are urgently in need of whatever light can be shed on the cardinal questions that awaken all people, the questions of:

(a) Who am I?
(b) From whence did I come?
(c) What am I doing here?
(d) To where am I going?

Good architecture embodies these questions by the very principles of beauty, proportion, and intrinsic integral cosmology.

The summer schools referred to above are run by Kairos. For contact details see Appendix I.

Illustrations

Thanks must also go to the sources given below for their kind permission to reproduce the following images:

Dover Publications Inc. New York for the dynamic/static rectangles and the Parthenon, harmonic analysis from *The Geometry of Art and Life* by Matila Ghyka.

Research Into Lost Knowledge Organisation (RILKO) Publications for the diagrams of the Constellation of Virgo and the Notre Dame Cathedrals of France from *The Mysteries of Chartres Cathedral* by Louis Charpentier and the Lambdoma from the *Rilko Journal* no. 57 by Robert Cowley.

Kairos Worksheet number 19 for the Proportional rectangles based on musical notes.

Oxford University Press for Plate II (p. 38) from *Geometry, Proportion and the Art of Lutherie* by Kevin Coates (1985).

Introduction

Since the beginning of time, we human beings have striven to create the perfect social and physical environment, a Utopia that fulfils all our needs – physical, emotional, intellectual, and spiritual.

Our search to create the ideal environment is illustrated through our cities and buildings, which are manifestations of the prevailing political, social, economic and spiritual values of the period. Paradoxically, the war against fascism in the 1940s caused the obliteration of vast tracts of cities in Europe and Asia, which subsequently have been rebuilt with futurist bleak glass and concrete jungles that have since proved to be the cause of many of the social problems of our time – a dire warning that a sterile 'Brave New World' is upon us wherein nature and the natural world have no place.

Worldwide population expansion makes increasing demands on land use for building new towns that may be significantly less than suitable for human habitation. The shortage of appropriate development sites has been further reduced by planning laws and government restrictions. Land shortages, overcrowding and economics have resulted in the building of houses on land polluted with toxic industrial waste, landfill sites used for dumping refuse where the waste has been compressed and covered over with a thin layer of topsoil in the forlorn hope that it will prevent the emission of noxious gases. Inevitably, this has brought illness and strange allergies to the new inhabitants. Currently, there are thousands of hectares of toxic land earmarked for future homes, workplaces, even hospitals, and in many cases the polluted soil will not be thoroughly eradicated. We have assumed that the Earth can be treated as a lifeless, harmless commodity that will absorb and neutralise the poisonous substances being dumped.

New towns and cities built on virgin land may be less of a potential physical health hazard, but so many have proved to lack the 'spirit' or 'soul' so necessary for human habitation because their location and planning have been based on 'logical' social engineering concepts. Brasilia, the capital of Brazil, built in the 1950s, is a prime example of what can happen when little or no account is taken of the qualities and characteristics of climate, topography, geography or geology. The siting of Brasilia was determined solely by measurements on a map.

A year after Brazil became a republic in 1889, one of the founders of independence, José Bonifácio, proposed the building of a new capital city. For strategic defence reasons it was to be established equidistant from all frontiers in the geographical centre of the country.

The Brasilia region is characterised by desert-like terrain, and the geophysical and environmental conditions of the site are less than ideal. In addition, vast distances have to be travelled to get to Brasilia from the established coastal towns such as Rio de Janeiro, the 'organically' established centre of commerce and one of the great cities of the Western world with its hedonistic cosmopolitan population, spectacular scenery, magnificent beaches and climate. Nobody, especially those who lived in Rio at the time, wished to move to the new capital, which prompted the government into resorting to coercion and the imposition of penalties to press banks, commercial enterprises and embassies to relocate their headquarters in Brasilia. This could be compared to a Londoner or New Yorker being deported to Siberia.

Those who drew up the plans for Brasilia designed a city not for human beings but for the movement and convenience of traffic. Residential zone 'villages' were cut off from one another by the main roads, as if under siege from the motor car. Perhaps even more devastating to the Latin psyche, there were no piazzas or places where young men and women could promenade in the hope of eyeing a likely mate. No doubt the ingenuity of the young has since devised alternative ways to meet friends, but the 'soft' human needs of society were certainly not addressed here. Sunlight, wind direction, orientation and the aspirations of human beings were no longer the basic factors determining the planning and layout of streets in a twentieth-century new town or estate. Brasilia, the manifestation of a modern architectural idealisation, became a Shangri-La for the motor car, but no Utopia for human beings. How could this have been hailed as an architectural triumph?

Twentieth-century Western culture has bred a scepticism of anything not 'scientifically proven': materialism and social conditioning have tended to sever or suppress that part of us which has an innate sense and awareness of nature and our natural surroundings. We scar the landscape to construct buildings, roads and cities, such as the new satellite towns of Cumbernauld in Scotland and Harlow and Milton Keynes in England, treating the Earth as an inert, lifeless mass of rock and soil (which may even be a reflection of the same scant respect we have of ourselves). But, at a subconscious level, our body, mind and psychic super-sensitivities remain highly attuned and expressed through the supreme intelligence of the cells in our body. We are a sensitive organism, constantly reacting to the most minute external vibrations that influence our actions, thought processes and every other aspect of our daily life.

At a subconscious level, we interact with the full spectrum of the Earth's energy fields, cosmic radiation, electromagnetic fields (EMFs) and every other stimulus in the external environment. Our cells, organs, glands, neurotransmitters and our subtle body sensors translate the signals into sensations ranging from discomfort, fatigue, illness and depression to pleasure, comfort, vitality, uplifted spirits and even transcendence. Whatever the external stimuli, it creates apparently inexplicable, often hardly discernible feelings whenever we arrive at a particular place or building. Our intuitive sensors feed us important information that should not be lightly dismissed. Colours, lighting, textures, the flow of air and the actual proportions and shapes of the interior rooms have a sum total impact on the mind, body and spirit.

Generally, buildings both old and new provide us with most, if not all, the conveniences of living we have come to accept and demand, yet it appears that many of us prefer to be in older buildings rather than the so-called modern 'glass and concrete boxes'. Some of the architecture of today is undeniably elegant and imaginative, so is our seeming preference for the past simply a form of nostalgia common to all ages? Or do many of these older buildings possess certain intrinsic, positive qualities not present in modern architecture? Whether or not we have a personal taste for a traditional style and décor, intuitively we can indeed sense the effect. Of course not all churches will lift our spirits and not all modern office buildings, blocks of flats or houses will make us feel depressed or offend our taste, but whatever the age, style or function, there is a reason why some places make us perturbed, or even ill, whereas other locations or buildings have a magical 'aura' where we feel we are in touch with a natural vitality or essence of harmony and well-being.

The needs of human beings extend beyond the material dimensions of physiology and biology: we are conditioned by our psychology, our perceptions, instincts, intuitions and an awareness of nature itself, all of which transcend our basic requirements for simple bodily comforts and shelter from the weather. Buildings can be likened to our third skin. The first skin is our flesh, the second skin our clothing, while the third is the protective sheath provided by the buildings in which we spend most of our lives.

Naturally, we want our buildings to be at least benign and disease-free, and preferably to be life enhancing. We want them to have a 'soul', to be user-friendly and to cause the least possible damage to the global and local environment. The majority of people are highly receptive to innovative, avant-garde modern architecture. We want our architects to be original and inventive, but at the same time we want them to ensure that modern technology and its short-term improvements do not have a negative impact on our long-term health and quality of life.

Today, planners, architects and engineers appear to focus on high-tech, eye-catching 'contemporary' buildings that provide watertight sheaths to protect our material comforts without addressing the impact their creations may have on our physical and spiritual health. Our relationship with nature and the interconnectedness with the human psyche have not been understood. This has had an affect on our everyday lives: a few years ago we became aware of the effects on the environment and the ecology of the planet, but we are now witnessing the effect on our immediate personal environment and our health. The root cause is one-dimensional ideology and the belief that materialism and the physical body are the only 'realities', excluding the mind and spirit as concepts that have no place in the modern world where anything – disease, natural disasters, food production, global warming and environmental disasters – can be overcome and cured by advanced technology. However, many, if not all these problems have come about because we are constantly at war with nature.

Professor James Lovelock, an independent British scientist and Fellow of the Royal Society who cooperated with NASA on its space programme, proposed a new theory of life and the evolving planet. Lovelock hypothesised that the Earth, rocks, oceans, the atmosphere and all living things are part of one boundlessly intelligent organism, continually evolving over a vast span of geological time. In 1988 his book *The Ages of Gaia*[1] supported the age-old tradition that Gaia (the Greek earth goddess) is not always benign as she will protect her own health and well-being rather than any individual species. This controversial view appears, at last, to have achieved political respectability. Ministers and officials of the British Government, including Demos (the government's 'think tank'), are taking seriously the idea that everything is interconnected and the planet is a holistic living organism. The Gaia theory has survived the science establishment's ridicule over the years but they too have now accepted Lovelock's hypothesis, which could form the basis of future government policy on environmental matters.[2]

This is in accordance with the ancients' view that the Earth's energy fields and rhythms had to be respected in order to preserve the essence and integrity of nature. Furthermore, the planet and its living organisms had to be supported in a state of balance and harmony to sustain our own physical and spiritual health. Any alterations to the landscape, for example deforestation, the over-farming of crops, mining and other earth or river works, and especially the siting of a building or structure, had to be carefully evaluated before the energy fields were disturbed. The ancients also recognised that the spiritual energies of a place could be affected by the emotional/ psychological charge created by particular human activity occurring at that location. Hence the building of a temple of worship or healing could enhance the positive vibrations associated with a specific location already possessing certain natural 'magical' qualities, so resulting in a sacred site.

The 'freedom of spirit' (interpreted by some as 'anything goes') in modern art and architecture is an abandonment of the soul – a dismissal of the sacred in favour of the profane and the deconstruction of nature.

The modern diseases of civilisation, from fatal cancers to various forms of debilitating, chronic sicknesses and allergies, have multiplied over the past one hundred years or so, and the source of the majority of these can be traced to the West's concentration of new development on polluted land, the actual buildings themselves, our insatiable demand for artificially generated electricity and our exploitation of nature. We lack understanding of the harmful effects of negative Earth energies. The built environment must be considered as a significant contributor to the cause of the diseases of Western civilisation.

Although we wring our hands in despair knowing that we are plunging headlong into an abyss, we still refuse to forego the latest electronic gadget and must have the next high-tech device or system that we believe will enhance our pleasure, personal comfort and convenience. We demand the same of the pharmaceutical companies and the medical profession, expecting them, without question, to keep discovering wonder drugs and new ways to cure our largely self-induced ills. The dangers are becoming more apparent day by day, but we turn a blind eye. Are we in silent collusion with architects and doctors because the majority of us are prepared to suffer the gradual deterioration of health – even when it may end in an early demise – rather than allow anything to interfere with our current or hoped-for lifestyles? This condition is known as the *Boiled Frog Syndrome*.

A frog jumps into a pot of water which is gradually being heated. As the water gets warmer, the frog adjusts its body temperature and continues to adjust to the increasing water temperature until, ultimately, the frog gets boiled alive.

Like the frog, we keep adjusting and reacting to the increasing health hazards to satisfy our expectations and demands for more comforts, greater convenience and easier living. But despite Western materialism, few people seem satisfied and content.

We have encouraged architects, industrial producers and property developers to meet our demands for buildings and goods almost completely without question, complaint or active criticism, and past records show that there has been little or no political will to eliminate or reduce the hazards. Timely and effective control are not exercised by either government authorities or the medical and architectural professions who often choose to ignore epidemiological and anecdotal evidence. Perhaps if doctors and architects communicated with each other, using a common language, there could be a breakthrough in understanding the worsening effect.

This said, there does appear to be a growing reaction in the field of medicine. We are now more sceptical of orthodox allopathic treatments that do not recognise human beings as holistic entities as well as being a body of flesh and bone. The necessity for certain types of radical surgery and the prescription of drugs that may cause more harm than good are now being questioned, and we are also becoming more consciously aware of the detrimental effects that certain environmental conditions – both inside and outside buildings – can have on our general health and sense of well-being. Instinctively we know the zealots and high priests of advanced technology need to balance their blinding logic and rationalisation with an understanding of the basic tenets – so vital for human existence – that have been known, taught, written about and practised for many thousands of years.

Ancient seers respected our planet as an intelligent living organism, and believed that everything in the universe, including human beings, has a common interconnecting bond: the patterns and movement of the heavenly bodies are a macrocosmic mirror image of life on Earth down to the microcosmic level of the sub-atomic world. In other words, the natural patterns, rhythms and proportions or geometry found in nature are repeated throughout the universe.

Those initiated into these teachings not only had a deep sense of the subtle play of energies by which the cosmos functions as a harmonious whole, but also knew how to replicate these vibrations in a manifested form so that the buildings they designed would have a resonance with human beings and the natural world to create and sustain healthy living conditions that would feed our soul. Vitruvius, who lived two thousand years ago, emphasised that architectural values are human values. Consciousness, self-awareness and a profound understanding of the mystical essence of human nature and the cosmos should be the qualities demanded of anyone who professes to be an architect – or indeed, a medical practitioner. How do our modern buildings match up to these fundamental principles?

The design of any building, whatever its style or age, and including our modern

architecture, can produce these resonating, harmonious, healthy and satisfying qualities providing the architect has been educated and trained to practise the principles
handed down by the masters of ancient wisdom. Ironically, we have now reached a
stage in this present cycle when the critical circumstances have created a positive
opportunity for the architect to become, once again, the 'master builder'.

Western society's emerging reawakening to a way of life that reacts against pure
materialism will force architects to take advantage of the new-found freedom created
fortuitously by the technical experts in lifting some of the burdens of day to-day and
mundane matters. Instead, they can now focus on the essence and fundamental
principles of architecture.

The challenge for the twenty-first century is to synthesise and bring together the
wonders of modern technology with the integrity of ancient spiritual wisdom and the
understanding of the eternal laws of nature and the universe. The confrontation arises
from the way we perceive the world; for example our senses lead us to believe that the
Earth is standing still and that the Sun moves across the heavens, yet intellectually we
know that the Earth moves around the Sun. These conflicting 'realities' can only be
reconciled when our consciousness and understanding can fuse the paradox into one,
undivided unity. How can the resolution of this dilemma be manifested in the quality
of the built environment? We can begin by avoiding distractions from the essence of
our being.

This book explores the legacy of the twentieth century's repudiation of ancient
wisdom and sets out to heighten our awareness by examining some of the root causes
of the problems and offering guidance on practical solutions to prudently avoid some of
the current health hazards. It provides the 'ammunition' to challenge those in authority
who appear to take a one-dimensional materialistic view of humanity and nature. But
before we, the consumer – the end-user – can demand a hazard-free, healthy soul-
enriching environment fit for human habitation we must also change our attitudes and
rediscover our holistic nature – that we are physical, mental *and* spiritual beings.

References

1. Lovelock, J. (1989) *The Ages of Gaia*, Oxford: Oxford University Press.
2. Woods, R. 'Meacher comes out as guru of Mother Earth', *The Sunday Times*, 7 May 2000.

Suggested further reading

Carey, J. (1999) *The Faber Book of Utopias*, London: Faber & Faber.
Day, C. (1990) *Places of the Soul*, Northants: The Aquarian Press.
Russell, P. (1982) *The Awakening Earth*, London: Routledge & Kegan Paul.

Part I
Health Hazards of Today

1.
Your health and the built environment

Health is a state of complete physical, mental and social well-being and not merely an absence of disease or infirmity.

The World Health Organization

The average Western person – homemakers, businesspeople, homeworkers, children and the elderly – spend up to 85 per cent of their lives either inside a building or inside a vehicle conveying them from one building to another. Gradually it is being acknowledged that the prevailing site conditions and the actual siting, design, construction, and maintenance of a building can have a profound effect on the health of the occupants, whether that building is an office, school, hospital, shopping centre or one's own private residence where electronic equipment and business machines have become commonplace. Sick building syndrome (SBS) and other health hazards, usually associated with the workplace are now being experienced in households since 30 per cent or more of the employed population now operate from their home base. It would be unwise to imagine that your home is as 'safe as houses'.

Sick building syndrome is a general 'malaise' but there are other serious, life-threatening environmental illnesses known as the 'diseases of civilisation'. In the UK, of the 90,000 deaths before the age of 65, there will be 32,000 from cancer and 25,000 from heart failure. Before 1950 cancer was a relatively rare disease, mostly afflicting old people. Since then the disease has increased by 1 per cent per year, and varying estimates suggest that within 50 years everyone will suffer some form of cancer.[1] Current official statistics predict that one in three of us will be afflicted, and children are becoming ever more prone despite the billions spent on research throughout the world. Twentieth-century Western industry and commerce has produced approximately 70,000 new synthetic materials and chemicals, many of which have been derived from oil by-products. Less than 2 per cent have been tested for their effects on human health and more than 70 per cent have not been tested at all.[2] About a thousand more come into general circulation every year. The upsurge of cancers has been attributed mainly to our exposure to toxins and a wide range of industrial chemicals, gasses and other substances in the air we breathe inside the workplace and our home. Other sources are contaminated water and food.

According to an extensive study of nearly 90,000 identical and non-identical twins by the Karolinska Institute in Stockholm, published in the *New England Journal of Medicine*: 'On average, environmental factors were associated with twice as many cancers as in born genetic factors…and even an identical twin had only a 10% chance of contracting the same cancer as his or her sibling'.[3] Ultimately, all cancers are genetic diseases caused by damaged genes, however, the study demonstrated that the environment rather than genetic factors poses the greatest risks. Radiation and pollution were among the prime culprits. Just because we now have the technology to map the human genome, claims that this will enable diseases such as cancer to be a thing of the past within the next 50 years seem most unlikely unless more is done to identify and deal with the avoidable environmental hazards. While we cannot choose the genes we inherit from our parents, it is in our hands to control our environment.[4]

How fresh is the air we breathe?

Since the eighteenth century's 'Age of Reason', Western civilisation has treated the Earth as an inert benign provider of resources to be exploited at will for the sole benefit of human beings in the belief that however much we polluted the environment, the land, sea and air would absorb and neutralise it. The idea that one tract or region of land could possess unique beneficial features, or that another could be harmful and detrimental to health, has been dismissed as irrelevant and superstitious nonsense: one location or site was assumed to be as suitable for human habitation as any other. We are now beginning to realise that certain areas of land and many of our new buildings can also be a source of illness and disease. Until the late nineteenth century, London was a city concentrated along the north bank of the Thames, leaving the south side, especially around Southwark, as undeveloped low-lying marshland notorious for mosquitoes and rats. Over the last hundred years or more, this area has become a densely populated part of the London urban sprawl. In the spring of 1994 a research programme known as the Middlesex Report published results showing that where houses have been built in the vicinity of such waterlogged land, the infant mortality rate is 31.9 per cent higher than for dry land areas. Scientific studies have eliminated other statistical variables such as social classifications and it is clear that both young babies and adults are at risk. In Chapter 3 we discuss the harmful effects of generated electromagnetic fields (EMFs). In this and the next chapter we examine other sources of health hazards in the built environment, such as:

- Contaminated land
- Natural gas emissions (radon)
- Asbestos and lead poisoning
- Contaminated water
- Volatile organic compounds (VOCs)
- Poor architectural and engineering design and specification
- Inadequate facilities management.

Any one or combination of these sources can be a direct cause of disease or debilitating illness, or a contributory factor in the breakdown of the body's immune system.

Modern lifestyles, methods of working and standards of comfort have increased our demand for warm, draught-free buildings. Double-glazing, sealed windows and doors, the replacement of ventilated larders with refrigerators, central heating (making the open-fire chimney flue redundant), and building codes demanding efficient insulation to conserve energy have created virtually airtight homes. (The building codes do also require some form of ventilation to allow a trickle of air to flow, but often these vents are sealed up by the house-owner in order to save heating costs.) It is now unusual to find a commercial building that is not air-conditioned and, in order for an air-conditioned building to operate efficiently, it too must be completely sealed up except where the air is mechanically drawn in and extracted. The interior air quality of all types of buildings, both old and new, can be a most significant health risk factor.

We like to believe the air in the countryside and by the sea is 'fresh', however, scientists at the Norwegian Institute for Air Research who collected samples of air from inside their laboratory, from out of doors in Oslo and at a remote coastal station, found traces of perfume chemicals in all the samples. The artificial perfumes used in fragrances, synthetic scents, soaps, air fresheners and other household products were detected in the atmosphere and especially indoors. Traces of synthetic musks have been found in the North Sea, rivers, fish, human fat and breast milk. Musk Ambrette, now banned in the European Union, has been found to cause testicular atrophy, and musk Xylene has been linked to carcinogens in rats. The long-term toxic effects on living organisms is unpredictable.[5]

During the last decade or so, Western governments have made efforts to control the dangers from radon gas, asbestos and lead poisoning, legionnaires' disease and, to a limited extent, have continued their attempts to reduce the menace of toxic gasses and leachates from polluted land and waste dumps. However, many other, equally hazardous sources such as volatile organic compounds (VOCs) are among the common, everyday materials and equipment found in most households and other types of buildings.

Contaminated land

Worldwide population expansion makes increasing demands on land use for building new towns that may be significantly less than suitable for human habitation. The increasing shortage of appropriate development sites has been reduced further by planning laws, government restriction and a policy of rural land conservation. Land shortages, overcrowding and economics have led to the demolition of derelict or unwanted industrial buildings for reuse for other purposes, but without enforcement of the removal and disposal of any highly polluting toxic chemicals and heavy metal waste products from the original manufacturing processes. Houses have been allowed to be built on landfill sites used for dumping refuse where the waste has been compressed and covered over with a thin layer of topsoil in the forlorn hope that it will prevent noxious gasses from rising. Inevitably, the outcome has been illnesses and strange allergies suffered by the new inhabitants. Industrial waste has polluted other sites being recycled for housing, and in our ignorance or greed we have assumed that the Earth can be treated as a lifeless, harmless commodity that will absorb and neutralise the dumped poisonous substances. The detoxification of polluted land can be a very high cost factor and not all land owners or property developers are prepared to ensure that their site is properly treated and cleared of health hazards.

One official definition of 'contaminated land' is: land sustaining a substance or substances in quantities or concentrations potentially harmful to human health, animals, plants, buildings, building services or other environmental receptors. 'Land' includes any structures, surface material, top soil, subsoils, surface water, groundwater and aquifers.

Many landfill and disused industrial sites that have been developed for new housing, schools and hospitals were heavily contaminated. Both national governments and local authorities have not been enforcing proper safeguards to permanently clean up and safeguard development land. In many cases in Europe, the US and Japan, well-publicised major test cases appear to have had little impact on local authorities who have the power but often lack the political will to enforce the Town Planning and other regulations at their disposal. Why is it that those who govern show such reluctance to listen to the knowing, common sense of the so-called ordinary people?

In 2000, the British Environment Agency was strongly criticised by a House of Commons Select Committee for failing to take action and not enforcing prosecution against polluters such as waste tippers and sewage disposal and industrial firms. Conservative estimates suggest that in the UK there are about 100,000 contaminated sites representing more than 50,000 hectares (125,000 acres) of 'brownfield' (previously contaminated) land, 8,000 waste dumps and 463 high-risk hazardous dumps. However, there may be many more uncharted and unregistered locations.[6]

The Internet company www.homecheck.co.uk claims to be able to publish information about possible contaminated land, pollution risks and waste sites within half a kilometre of any given post code in the UK. According to its estimates there are two million people in the UK who are at risk from toxic poisoning due to living near to one of the 46,000 sites that emit pollutants, such as landfill sites with toxic substances or radon gas areas. There are another 400,000 old industrial sites and 275,000 abandoned waste tips.[7]

When a site used for compacted household refuse is completely filled it is usually covered with a layer of topsoil and sold on as land suitable for development. Organic waste materials generate methane and other noxious gasses: sooner or later the local air will be polluted on a continuing basis. Illegal dumping of dangerous substances such as asbestos, heavy metals, pesticides, solvents, clinical waste and even radioactive materials has rendered some municipal sites, normally used for domestic refuse only, as hazardous as those classified as high-risk locations.

The soil and local groundwater becomes, in effect, a live organic ecosystem. Land once used for a gas works, sewerage plant, steelworks or other industrial purposes can leave in the soil a legacy of heavy metals, solvents, acids and other pollutants. The contaminants leaching out into the groundwater, polluting the rivers and water supply, will affect human beings, animals and plant life. We can ingest toxins through the foodstuffs grown in polluted soil, breathe in microscopic particulates of asbestos, solvents and noxious gasses from the contaminants buried on the land and suffer skin allergies or worse caused by corrosive substances and hazardous clinical waste pollution. Contamination sources, be they methane or carbon monoxide gases from compressed decomposing organic matter or heavy metals and toxic chemicals – lead, cadmium, mercury, arsenic and polyaromatic hydrocarbons (PAHs) – can cause explosions, asphyxiation and toxic poisoning to both human, animal and plant life as well as decomposing the structural elements of buildings.

Each year in Britain alone, around 600 million drugs and medications are prescribed.[8] Complex drugs – heart pills, sex hormones, antibiotics, anti-cancer vitamins and hormone replacement treatments – are surviving the human digestive system, passing through sewage works and entering rivers and the sea. Tons of antidepressants and other toxic drugs are polluting our rivers, threatening fish life and getting into our drinking water. Researchers now believe the waterborne drug pollution may account for the deaths of small aquatic organisms, low sperm counts and changing spawning patterns. Even accumulated traces of suntan lotion and synthetic chemicals used in perfume have been found in fish.

The availability of land for development in the UK decreases year by year. Fierce protection of the countryside, rural areas, greenbelt land and public open spaces in and around our towns and villages has been a strong government policy for decades. Demographic changes, the loss of manufacturing processes, the ever expanding population and the breakdown of the family unit have created, according to government estimates, a need to build over 4 million new homes by 2016. To avoid conflict with the Town Planning restrictions on greenfield site development, the government is actively encouraging property developers to build on brownfield sites, however, several major issues remain unanswered: who will be responsible for identifying the locations and contaminant hazards, and who will pay the costs of detoxification?

Landowners of disused industrial sites have no incentive to clean up their mess yet still expect unrealistic prices to be paid for the site by would-be developers who in turn are reluctant to accept the often unquantifiable financial risks of detoxification as there is no method that guarantees an absolutely safe decontamination.

The government is as guilty as others who fail to properly and effectively decontaminate polluted sites: the Millennium Dome fiasco has cost the British taxpayer an estimated £200 million (in addition to the other three-quarters of a billion pounds) because the ministry officials in charge of the project decided it would take too long and cost too much money to carry out a complete clean-up job. The site had been used as a gas works – one of the largest in Europe – and a chemical factory. Although the heavily polluted soil was said to have been removed to a depth of 15 metres (50 feet), it emerged some eighteen months after the Dome was completed that a 4-metre (13-feet) layer of contaminated soil had been left 3 metres (10 feet) below ground level and 'sealed' with a 20-centimetre (eight-inch) layer of concrete and top soil.

Understandably, no-one wanted to buy the Dome or remove it to develop the site for other purposes because the cost liability of properly decontaminating the land could not be assessed. In the meantime, until a developer/investor could be persuaded to take it off the government's hands, the taxpayer had to pay several more millions a year just to keep the building closed.[9]

Removal of the toxic soil is one remedy but the contaminated material will have to be disposed of elsewhere; encapsulation is more or less a cosmetic and largely ineffective method because it still leaves the dangerous contaminants in-situ and eventually gasses can rise up and chemicals can leach out. A biotechnology technique using organisms to neutralise the toxic waste is a promising solution but this course of action will take a long time.

The Environmental Protection Act's (1990) proposal to create a detailed register of potentially contaminated land was abandoned after intense lobbying on the basis that such a register would blight the development of certain brownfield sites. Had this legislation become law it could have saved a lot of people from unknowingly living on contaminated land. Instead, under the later Environmental Act (1995) a number of government agencies were required to compile information on pollution, categorise the risks, produce guidelines to minimise the impact and recommend the type of remedial work that needed to be carried out.

The long-term health hazards and environmental damage have been underestimated by government agencies, landowners and property developers. The International Society of Soil Mechanics and Geotechnical Engineering (ISSMGE) is of the opinion that in the future the issue of contaminated land will become even more complicated and more costly. Medical evidence, media interest and public concerns highlighting an awareness of the health risks have mounted pressure on the government to resolve the problem of how contaminated brownfield land can be made safe and who will pay the cost. The dilemma became newsworthy some time after a new private housing estate was built in the 1980s on land previously used as a dump for industrial waste in the docklands area of East London, less than 8 kilometres (5 miles) from the City. Not long after the purchasers had moved into their new houses they began to suffer skin rashes and other strange maladies including bites from a type of tropical mosquito hitherto unknown in the locality. None of the inhabitants had a previous medical history of these symptoms and illnesses. Site investigations proved the land had not been properly decontaminated and surveys reported the buildings were showing signs of cracking, subsidence and chemical attack.

The British medical journal, *The Lancet*, published a report in 1998 entitled 'Risk of congenital anomalies near hazard-waste landfill sites in Europe'. Data collected from Belgium, Denmark, France, Italy and the UK focused on sites in areas covered by registers of congenital anomalies and that were known to contain hazardous waste of non-domestic origin. Of the 21 sites investigated, 9 were closed before the start of the study period and 10 were in operation for more than 20 years before the end of the study. The results showed that the chances of having babies with defects – spina bifida, hole in the heart and artery malfunction – increased by as much as 33 per cent for women living within a 3-kilometre (2-mile) radius of a toxic waste landfill dump. There was also a significant overall increased health risk to residents living near the sites: these included neural tube defects, malformation of the cardiac septa, arteries and veins, as well as the risk of breathing anomalies, asthma and vomiting. Also the increased risk of hypospedias (an abnormality in the penis or perineum) was of particular concern regarding male reproductive abnormalities related to endocrine disrupting chemicals. Those who lived within a 3- to 7-kilometre (2-to 4-mile) radius were only somewhat less susceptible to the health hazards.[10]

In 1999, a *Sunday Times* investigative team uncovered a cluster of birth defects among children living near a network of toxic waste dumps in Corby, Northampton-shire, where the incidence of limb deformities was more than 10 times higher than would be normally expected in a town of about 60,000 people. A number of steel-works sites disused since the 1980s were still contaminated with significant levels of arsenic, zinc and nickel. The subsequent illegal dumping of chemical waste, asbestos and hospital waste had added to the high toxicity of the land and one of the waste dumps had been contaminated by anthrax. Further investigations by the Health and Safety Executive found another one of the sites to be a likely source of several outbreaks of legionnaires' disease in the locality.[11]

Despite the medical evidence, a group of residents in Lancashire who formed Action to Reduce and Recycle our Waste had to campaign against a proposal to allow a landfill waste site to be located less than 200 metres (650 feet) from a school.

Now that the European Union restrictions require rubbish dumps to be phased out, forcing local councils to reduce the volume of rubbish disposed of in the ground, the only alternative for the UK is to burn its annual 28 million tons of household waste. (The problem is exacerbated because serious attempts to encourage people to reduce and recycle their waste has generally proved to be unsuccessful and, as time goes on, the waste mountain will get higher.) Currently, the UK government has planned up to 130 incinerator plants with a capacity to deal with 200,000 tons of waste annually, or up to 94 plants with a larger capacity of 0.25 million tons. Although the incinerated waste could also generate electricity, this does not assuage the vociferous objections from environmental groups and the residents who will be living in the vicinity of an incinerator plant. Opponents believe that incinerated by-products such as dioxins and other toxic substances in the waste gases are known to be carcinogenic. Indeed, activists from a North London group closed down Britain's biggest incinerator at Edmonton and, surprisingly, a jury cleared them of criminal damage.[12]

Whether we bury or burn it, our rubbish will create one form of pollution or another. The potential health hazard depends largely on how close you are to the source.

Imperial Chemical Industries (ICI), the massive chemical company based in Cheshire, was forced to evacuate a complete community and offered to buy the 470 houses at full market value after admitting the company was responsible for poisoning the homes with fumes from a toxic dump. The village, near Runcorn, was built on an 8.5-acre sandstone landfill quarry that had been used by ICI for around 50 years to dump millions of tons of dangerous waste, including hexachlor-obutadiene (HCBD) – a by-product of the manufacture of chlorine. The dumping stopped in the 1970s but HCBD had seeped through the rock strata and into some of the houses. Instances of kidney disease in Runcorn are twice the national average, and one mother lost five children.Other families have experienced miscarriages and child deformities, and the incidences of cancer are high. In addition, plants withered and pets died prematurely. An ICI spokesperson admitted that the high concentrations of HCBD were, undoubtedly, due to the dumping of toxic waste.[13]

Both local and national government authorities have been made all too aware over recent decades that granting permission to develop landfill and toxic waste dump sites that have not been properly and adequately decontaminated can result in serious health hazards to the occupants of the new buildings. The regulations, considered by independent experts to be far too lax, are often not adequately enforced. The original polluters are allowed to get away with a cursory clean-up of the site and developers are only interested in doing the barest minimum to conform to the already low standard demands of the present regulations.

An example is the Royal Small Arms factory at Enfield, in Greater London, which has produced guns such as the Enfield rifle and ammunition over a 200-year period. The site, sold to a firm of house-builders to develop a 'village' of 1,300 houses, is known to have been contaminated over the years by the manufacturing processes, leaving the land polluted with cadmium, lead, mercury, copper, nickel, zinc, chromium, arsenic, phenols, cyanide and asbestos fibre. The local authority granted Town Planning consent for the development in April 2000 before the significant issues of decontamination were resolved, and the builders were allowed to start work on the site. Local residents, environmental groups and the media – the BBC and the London *Evening Standard* newspaper – were highly critical of the council, which eventually decided to set up a panel of inquiry into the affair.Two local newspapers were invited to attend the inquiry meeting, but all other interested parties, journalists and campaigners were barred, despite being challenged by an *Evening Standard* legal team. The outcome was that the council and the developers insisted they had cleaned up the site according to government standards. However, if it materialises that the land has not been adequately decontaminated, the building operatives could be at risk, the foundations of the new houses could deteriorate and the people who will buy the properties could suffer health hazards in much the same manner as those in similar circumstances already cited.[14]

Suggested prudent avoidance

If you are living, working, attending school or hospital in close proximity to land contaminated by a previous industrial user or a landfill waste site it is likely the local atmosphere may be polluted. If you are concerned, you must take action: make enquiries with your local authority to establish what type of waste or contaminants may have been dumped or seek the advice from one of the several independent environmental consultants rather than rely on the opinions of the previous land-owner, developer or estate agent. Friends of the Earth has published a guide to waste dumps entitled *Toxic Tips,* and the report by Paul Symmes, *The Redevelopment of Contaminated Land for Housing Use* (1997) may be useful. Alternatively, a comprehensive bibliography can be found at www.ContaminatedLand.co.uk/gov-guid. You can now also visit the website of www.homecheck.co.uk which provides initial location data. In addition you need to check the Town Planning register and local strategic plans for any proposal to build a waste incinerator.

On a brighter note, scientists working at Aberdeen University's Institute of Medical Sciences over a seven-year period have developed the world's first bacterial sensor to detect and decontaminate polluted land. They have inserted a gene that creates bio-luminescence into bacteria which thrives on soil. The small bacterium emits a glowing light if it is in clean soil. The light goes out if there are toxins present and the lights come on again when the site has been cleaned. The effect has been likened to the use of canaries in underground mines to detect carbon monoxide. The biosensor will give a response within minutes indicating whether a soil sample is toxic or not and what type of toxins are present. It is claimed that this technique will be a far more reliable and comprehensive test than conventional technology.[15]

Radon gas

Radon (Rn), the heaviest noble gas produced by the decay of radium, thorium and actinium, is one of the 92 naturally occurring chemical elements in the Earth's crust. It is radioactive and the longest-lived isotope, having a half life of just under four days: the gas continually diffuses through several metres of strata before it decays. The level of radon throughout the world is dependent on the amount of uranium in the geological strata of a region and the degree of fissures in the rock formation. It can also be waterborne and increased levels have been found in groundwater shortly before earthquakes. It is colourless, odourless, tasteless and present in the air we all breathe, accounting for about half our exposure to natural radiation. Once radon reaches fresh air it rapidly and harmlessly diffuses, but high levels of concentration can be the source of a serious health hazard if the gas becomes trapped in a confined, poorly ventilated space such as a cave, mine or building. Radon permeates into a building by osmosis, penetrating concrete, brickwork and seeping through cracks in the foundations and pipework. Even some ordinary building materials in everyday use, such as plasterboards, building blockwork and crushed granite bricks all exhale low levels of radon as well as gamma rays. If the gas cannot disperse in a building, particles of dust and minute droplets of moisture can become contaminated, and the radioactive polluted air breathed in by the occupants will irradiate lung tissue causing cell deterioration, which may result in the onset of cancer.

The first written account of the effects of what we now know to be radon gas appeared in 1556 in a book, *De Re Metallica,* by Georgius Agricola, a German physician and mineralogist.[16] His systematic study of mining and minerals in several mining towns of central Europe showed that many miners were dying a painful death from rotting lungs caused by breathing in the pestilential air. Improved ventilation shafts and the use of lace face masks helped to reduce the death rate, but 300 years later over half the miners working in the uranium mountain areas of Czechoslovakia were still suffering an early death.

Current estimates suggest the annual death toll due to lung cancer caused by exposure to radon gas is between 2,500 and 3,000 people in Britain alone, and between 5,000 and 20,000 in America where 10 per cent of homes exceed the safe limits. British researchers in the 1920s highlighted the dangers of radon poisoning, but this was ignored by the Establishment. Some fifty years later the Swedish authorities carried out studies which eventually became government legislation in 1981 to control exposure limits. A 1992 survey studied nearly a quarter of a million dwellings in Sweden and found 15,000 houses were contaminated.[17] The World Health Organization (WHO) and other European and US governments have followed the earlier Swedish example.

The high-risk areas in the UK are the counties of Devon, Cornwall, Somerset, Derbyshire, Northamptonshire and the granite regions of Scotland and Ireland. In the US the high-risk areas include Ohio, Colorado, Pennsylvania, Washington, New Jersey and, perhaps somewhat surprisingly, central Florida where there are large deposits of phosphates and extensive groundwater. Generally, the low-risk regions are where the substrata is unbroken rock and heavy clay.

In January 2001, UK government ministers told all local authorities to test private water supplies – wells, springs and boreholes – for radon and uranium, as levels in seven wells in West Devon were found to exceed safety limits. In the worst case, scientists measured radon at five times the accepted level. Private water supplies in other areas of high radon gas, such as Derbyshire, Cornwall and Northampton, could also be affected.[18]

In 1985 the UK introduced formal building code and bylaw legislation to control radon penetration into buildings. Seven years later the Royal Institute of British Architects (RIBA) published practice guidance notes for its members recommending methods for dealing with the prevention of radon gas permeation in existing buildings and construction techniques for new buildings. The paper, which mainly focused attention on the likely claims of negligence against architects who failed to take appropriate action, stated: '...radioactive gas being emitted by the ground is a relatively new phenomenon to most architects'.[19] This was an astonishing admission when it had been estimated that at least 250,000 homes in Britain are affected, as well as a significant number of other buildings, including schools and hospitals located in high-risk areas, and that over 100,000 households in the UK are known to be above the safety level threshold.

The dangers of high levels of radon poisoning in buildings was brought home to the general public in the UK when the consumer magazine *Which?* produced a detailed report on the health risks and the regions most affected, with advice on what to do and what preventive or remedial action was available.[20]

Radon pollution came to prominence in the US in the mid-1980s when the Wattrus House story was made public. A Mr Wattrus, a nuclear power station worker, lived on the Reading Prong, a granite region stretching from New Jersey to the coast in Pennsylvania. Every morning when he reported for work the radiation test alarm recorded high levels. In the evening when leaving the plant his radiation levels were much lower. Obviously his home was more polluted than the power station and subsequent investigations into Mr Wattrus's case led to the Radon Gas and Indoor Air Quality Research Act 1986. A year later the Environmental Protection Agency (EPA) set up a research programme that estimated that over 2 million homes were at risk. However, funding dried up about seven years later and while the EPA Air and Energy Engineering Establishment remains active, all the original programmes for testing and remedial action have been transferred to the private sector.

Although the EPA provides ongoing support, there is no formal legislation. In an attempt to avoid the increasing number of cases of litigation against house-builders and selling agents, the US home property industry has become self-regulatory and carries its own system of testing and implementing remedial and preventive construction methods. In the meantime, the European Commission has attempted to coordinate the radon research work of 26 different countries, especially those in uranium-mining areas, with Germany and Sweden leading the investigation. However, Eire is probably the only pro-active country in Europe to devise a programme to 'solve' the problem by 2002. Canada is thought to be one of several countries where the rules appear to be rather lax.

In high-risk areas the occupants of all types of buildings – not just houses – are vulnerable to radon poisoning. When our buildings had open-fire chimney flues, poorly fitting windows and doors, and the timber-joisted floors were raised above ground level, the concentration of gas was dispersed by draughts and the freer flow of air within the building and under the floor. In regions where radon levels are high, and energy-efficient, well-insulated, draught-proof buildings with solid concrete floors are built directly on the ground, the occupants can be extremely vulnerable. Additionally, the central heating system in a house will slightly reduce the inside air pressure, which will tend to draw in the outside air through unblocked vents and gaps in loose fitting windows and doors. In high-risk areas this negative pressure can accelerate the intake of the gas.

Suggested prudent avoidance

The construction of a new building in a radon region can readily incorporate a number of techniques to combat gas penetration and accumulation: for example the floor can be raised above the outside ground level to allow the air space below to be either mechanically or naturally ventilated. Alternatively, solid floors built directly on to the ground can be protected with a form of mechanical barrier to prevent gas from rising. In both cases, any gaps in the foundations or the pipework into the building from below ground must be sealed to close up joints where the gas could seep through. Groundwater in the vicinity of the building should be drained and any building materials specified for the project should be carefully selected to avoid those known to be in the highly radioactive category. While each case presents its own, often challenging, special circumstances, the principles are the same: create good ventilation, seal the gaps below the floor and form barriers where possible. In addition there are techniques for tunnelling under the building to exhaust the gas by mechanical suction or installing a system of ducts into all the rooms to allow the gas to be exhausted at roof level.

Remedial action to existing buildings can be costly. However, most countries offer government grants to pay for expert advice and the cost of remedial treatment to existing buildings, and radon detection equipment and testing apparatus are generally available for local authority or private use (see 'Contacts' at the end of this book).

Asbestos

Asbestos is a natural mineral fibre commonly found in rock formations in many parts of the world. The material has been used since prehistoric times and its peculiar properties – its flexibility and durability, and being chemically inert and thermally resistant – were ideally suited to the industrial developments taking place in the late nineteenth century. Since the 1900s, about 6 million tons of asbestos has been imported into the UK for use as a building material for insulation products, ceiling and floor tiles, roofing, cements, fire protection, lagging, rope and pipe gaskets and many other industrial uses. Protective clothing, brake linings, battery and electrical insulation and domestic appliances – such as hairdryers and ironing boards – are among a wide range of asbestos-based products still to be found in the home, in buildings in general, vehicles, railway rolling stock and ships. The three main types of asbestos fibre are:

Chrysotile (White) fibre:	white, soft and pliable used for textiles and weaving
Crocidolite (Blue) fibre:	soft and strong used for insulation and sprays
Amosite (Brown) fibre:	spiky and elastic used for building boards and ceiling tiles

Other types of asbestos mineral fibre – for example anthophyllite, tremolite and acinolite – were not so commonly used, but all came under the general heading of asbestos.

A major health hazard occurs when the damaged, frayed brittle material releases the minute, lightweight fibres into the air we breathe. Miners of asbestos rock, the factory workers making asbestos products and the builders and domestic appliance manufacturers who had to cut, fit, drill or spray the material were exposed to inhaling the microscopic dust. When a severe fire breaks out in a building containing asbestos, the exploding fibres spread over a wide area.

Those who lived and worked near asbestos manufacturing factories were equally vulnerable to the airborne fibres. The asbestos brake linings used for decades in our cars and trucks have deposited on the streets, parking areas and garages, lethal fibres that we pick up on our shoes and walk into our buildings. A man who worked at an aluminium processing factory near Banbury, Oxfordshire, died of mesothelioma in 1995. Unwittingly he had been bringing home asbestos dust fibres in his work clothing, which caused his wife Ann to contract the same disease. In 1998 she took action against the company and was awarded £110,000 in damages.[21]

The diseases associated with asbestos are:

Asbestosis:	a fibrosis of the lung parenchyma causing respiratory difficulties or leading to cardio-respiratory failure
Mesothelioma:	a tumour of the chest cavity which can develop some 20 or more years after exposure; usually the patient dies within two years of diagnosis
Lung cancer:	bronchial carcinoma (a tumour on the lung airways); heavy smokers are particularly vulnerable

The authorities now recognise that there is no 'safe threshold' exposure for any type of asbestos. In the 1920s it was common knowledge that airborne asbestos fibres were harmful and regulations to protect factory workers were introduced. Inexplicably those who worked with asbestos in shipyards and railway rolling stock factories, building operatives, other manufacturers of appliances using asbestos products and the public at large were not included. The UK prohibited the importation of the blue and brown variety in 1980, followed by the introduction of a number of licensing regulations and codes of practice controlling the use and removal of asbestos, and eventually culminating in the 1999 prohibition of all types of asbestos. The ban included Chrysotile, which hitherto had been considered to be relatively 'harmless'. Asbestos has been virtually banned in the US since the 1960s and 1970s when successful lawsuits effectively prevented companies from continuing to manufacture asbestos-based building products. The WTO has banned countries from exporting asbestos, but Canada continues to send the product to ten other countries and argues that it poses no health risk if used according to instruction.

Recent epidemiological studies have indicated that the hoped-for reduction in cases of asbestos-related diseases due to Health and Safety Executive measures taken two decades ago has not materialised. Instead, current forecasts suggest that the disease will continue to rise because so many buildings still contain asbestos and operatives working with the material have not been protected. A survey carried out by *The Lancet* found that more than one person in a hundred aged 50 years will die of asbestosis or lung cancer, which will account for between 5,000 and 10,000 deaths a year for the next 40 years.[22] This is in accordance with a 1999 estimate that around 250,000 people in Western Europe will die from asbestos-related diseases over the next 35 years. The largest group of workers currently at risk are those in the building trades who are liable to disturb asbestos during the course of their work: this does not include those who are licensed asbestos removal contractors. The majority of deaths occurring today are due to exposures that took place between 15 and 60 years ago when asbestos was not strictly controlled. Those who continue to be at risk are maintenance and repair operators working on older buildings, the cable, telecommunications and IT engineers and the small-time handyman or DIY enthusiasts working in their own homes.

Current estimates by the TUC suggest that about 1.4 million commercial and residential properties still contain asbestos.[23]

There is no safe way of knowing whether or not a building is asbestos-free unless it has been thoroughly investigated by expert surveyors. The problem has become so acute that the Health and Safety Executive will introduce even more stringent regulations under the Control of Asbestos at Work Regulations 2002. Under the new regulations, any person who has, to any extent, control of the premises or means of access, or is responsible for repair or maintenance, will be forced to have a comprehensive survey carried out on the basis that asbestos will be presumed to be present in a building unless there is evidence to prove otherwise. The regulations clearly define what must be carried out to conform to the new rules.

Despite worldwide publicity, stringent restrictions and severe penalties, the dangers are still treated with impunity by building workers and even some of the licensed removal specialists. Careless handling of the material is typified by the scandal of the 3,000 tons of asbestos inside the star-shaped Brussels headquarters of the European Commission, known as Berlaymont. The building was scheduled for renovation in 1991 to be ready to rehouse the bureaucrats in 2001. Due to the bungling over the removal of the asbestos in the building, some of which had escaped into the atmosphere, been illegally dumped or not removed under properly controlled conditions, the completion date is now in doubt.[24]

There is also the ever present threat of contamination caused by damaged asbestos fibres escaping into the atmosphere from the thousands of tons of asbestos cladding and roofing on existing buildings. In 1999, a fire broke out at a 10,000-square-metre (108,000-square-feet) paper factory in Kent, which was partly constructed of asbestos. Clouds of asbestos fibre spread over a 20-kilometre (12-mile) area contaminating orchards, fields and gardens. Thousands of people in the vicinity were warned to stay indoors. Police sealed off roads and the Environment Agency had to arrange an extensive emergency clean-up. It may take years before the extent of the damage to health can be assessed.[25]

Compensation costs for victims of asbestos-related diseases is expected to exceed £145 billion, making it the most expensive category of insurance claim in history. Insurance companies that, so far, have not been forced out of business due to the increasing number of claims have had to revise upwards their reserves. Equitas, the insurer set up to handle claims for the Lloyds of London market, has told US policy-holders that it will not pay out claims unless some form of physical injury can be proven because there is not enough money to compensate everyone in the US who claims to have been exposed.[26]

In summary, even governments at 'superpower' level seem to be as guilty of care-lessness as the impatient building operative who refuses to take the appropriate precautions to call in the bona-fide expert asbestos removers rather than disrupt the work. It will be decades before all our buildings are cleared.

Suggested prudent avoidance

If you suddenly come across asbestos in your building, report it immediately to the local authority which will inspect and advise where to contact bona-fide licensed contractors to carry out the removal work, deep-clean the space to remove all traces of asbestos dust and then dispose of the toxic materials at a licensed site.

Lead poisoning

Lead is highly toxic even in low concentrations. It can make up as much as 25 per cent of our body weight, and less than half that amount in the blood can cause dementia, brain damage, renal and heart failure. Once in the body it cannot be leached out. The most vulnerable are growing foetuses and children who more readily absorb lead, and who as a result can develop behaviour problems and learning difficulties.

The significant sources from which we may ingest or inhale lead are drinking water pipes, roofing materials, food grown in contaminated soil, car exhaust fumes, lead paint in old buildings, glazed pottery, old lead toy soldiers and fumes from heated soldered joints in plumbing and electronic equipment. (Lead contamination in the soil can remain a pollutant for 200 years whereas the same quantity of DDT (dichlorophenyl trichloroethane) pesticide will become neutralised after only 6 months.)

As early as 500 BC it was known that inhaling lead fumes and particles was a serious danger to health: miners of silver, which has a lead content, wore pig bladders over their heads as a primitive respiratory mask. It has been suggested that the fall of the Roman Empire was partly due to the lead water pipes and the use of lead drinking goblets and water vats. They even used lead pellets to adulterate the wine to accelerate fermentation. It may also be that the high incidence of artists going insane was caused by the traditional practise of mixing their own paint pigment with lead.

Until the 1920s, when technical changes in paint manufacture reduced the lead content, lead paint was used extensively on walls, woodwork and metal. Although the danger was common knowledge, the paint was not prohibited in buildings until 1965 in the UK and 1978 in the US, where legislation now ensures that all households are tested and treated. Despite the ban, it is estimated that about half the older 28 million homes in the UK are decorated in lead-based paint. Old lead paint can be chipped off by a vacuum cleaner bumping into the skirting or crumble off windowsills and flake on to the floor. Children, especially crawlers, swallow the lead-laden particles of paint picked up on their fingers, and this may account for the number of young people suffering from the effects of lead poisoning. Fine paint dust accumulating under floorboards, getting into carpet piles and furniture presents a health hazard to all occupants. Another group most vulnerable are professional painters, decorators, plumbers and the home improvement DIY enthusiast.

Suggested prudent avoidance

Disturbing old lead paint can be extremely hazardous: removing the paint by dry sanding or the use of blow torches creates dangerous lead-laden dust and fumes; wet sanding or hot air tools are less harmful. The use of an appropriate and approved chemical stripper may be marginally better only where the space is very well ventilated and the operative wears a protective breathing mask. Alternatively, the old paint can be left intact and carefully encapsulated with a modern paint.

Although buildings that are less than 20 years old are relatively low in lead because paint and the soldering work on copper pipes are lead free, the wiring to the TV, computer and other electronic components may be soldered with a lead-based material that can give off fumes as the equipment heats up. Modern cars now use lead-free petrol but it may be many decades before we are free of lead-polluted land and buildings.

Legionnaires' disease

Thirty-four American Legionnaires attending a convention in Philadelphia in 1976 died from a source of bacteria found in the air-conditioning ducts of the hotel. The life-threatening disease became known as *Legionnella Pneumophila*. Thirty-seven other types of legionnella have now been identified, including a relatively short-lived illness without the symptoms of pneumonia known as Pontiac Fever. Lochgoilhead Fever, yet another form of legionnellosis, was named after an outbreak in Scotland in 1988. The disease attacks the lungs, and those who are susceptible to lung and chest complaints – especially heavy smokers – are the most vulnerable. Symptoms include high fever, muscle pain, respiratory difficulties and vomiting. The fatality rate is about 18 per cent: those who do survive can take several months to reach full recovery.

The legionnella organism is found in rivers, lakes, ponds, streams, mud and various sources of water systems in buildings. The microbes thrive in any warm, non-sterile or stagnant water contaminated with algae, amoeba, sludge, rust, scale, sediments or other organic material. Water temperatures below 20°C and above 60°C do not encourage growth of the organism but it will proliferate in a range between 20°C and 45°C. In cooler water it can remain dormant until the temperature rises.[27]

Uncovered water storage tanks, water softeners, calorifiers, little-used water appliances, long, dead-leg plumbing runs and intermittently used pipes will provide an ideal legionella breeding environment. Another potential incubator is any water system that can create droplets of water such as air-conditioning water towers, certain types of humidifiers, condensers, jacuzzi baths, showers, spray taps and fountains. The bacteria become a health hazard when we inhale airborne, aerated particles of contaminated water.

A chance observation in 1988 led to the discovery of the source of a serious outbreak of the disease in London. Two people were admitted to the same hospital in Essex where they lived – one patient was thought to be suffering from pneumonia and the other suspected of having food poisoning. Within a few days both cases were finally diagnosed as legionnaires' disease and at the same time it was discovered that both patients worked at the BBC in Portland Place, London. Soon after, a further 58 cases were diagnosed, 18 of whom also worked at the BBC, and the remainder either regularly passed by or lived near the building. Eventually three patients died. The source of the outbreak was traced to the air-conditioning water cooling tower on the BBC roof, which had not been maintained or cleaned during the shut-down period of about three months in the autumn of 1987. The sludge allowed to accumulate in the base of the cooling tower provided an ideal environment for the legionella bacteria to multiply. When the air-conditioning plant was recommissioned, a fine aerosol spray of contaminated water from the tower showered down from the roof on to the street and the building below.

It has become a criminal offence, carrying a fine of up to £2,000 with two years' imprisonment for any owner, manager or person who is responsible for the maintenance of the building where legionnaires' disease breaks out.

Although the causes of legionnaires' disease and good preventive practice are now well documented worldwide for design engineers and building facilities managers, outbreaks are still fairly frequent. In Melbourne, Australia, 60 people caught legionnaires disease and at least 3 people died subsequently. All were visitors to the new £33 million Aquarium. The source was traced to the aquarium's water cooling towers (similar to the BBC outbreak mentioned above). A BBC1 news bulletin two days later reported that the Australian authorities believed up to 3,000 aquarium visitors from many other parts of the world could also have been infected.[28] Three days later a British tourist died from legionnaires' disease while on holiday in Thailand. It was reported that one-third of the public buildings inspected – including several unnamed five-star hotels, hospitals, and offices in Bangkok and other tourist cities – had already been found to be a source of the deadly bacteria.[29]

Suggested prudent avoidance

Good architectural and engineering design can control legionnellosis by avoiding the obvious pitfalls of specifying outdated types of water cooling towers, certain spray humidifiers and planning well-considered layouts of pipework. Prevention can be achieved by regular maintenance, not using recirculated water and paying attention to cleaning out tanks and changing filters, and any new or repair work to plumbing runs should be chlorinated or pasteurised to cleanse the pipework. At home, occasionally run water through the infrequently used shower heads and taps.

Advice on water sampling, treatment and suitable materials for construction is readily available from water companies, health and safety authorities and building research organisations.

Indoor air contaminants

'Air pollution' conjures up scenes of the people of London, Los Angeles, Calcutta or Mexico City choking under a blanket smog of car exhaust fumes and poisonous industrial smoke. However, studies begun in the US and followed up by British scientists in 1998 found that the quality of air inside our homes and work places poses long-term health risks and fell below the minimum standards set for outdoor air by the World Health Organization (WHO). The problem is often exacerbated in buildings that are air-conditioned. Tests carried out by the Buildings Research Establishment (BRE) in more than a thousand homes found the air inside was ten times more polluted than the smog-laden city air outside! Dr Jeff Lewellyn, an indoor pollution expert at the BRE, found that levels of noxious gasses were far higher in new homes built after 1980 due to the modern materials used.[30]

A separate study in Australia found that one-year-old houses were up to twenty times above the safety levels. The sources were formaldehyde used for treating floor boards and furniture, toxic compounds from paints and solvents, and hormone disrupting chemicals found in carpets and vinyl flooring.

The indoor air we breathe contains a mass of microscopic particulates. In addition to the asbestos fibres, lead flakes, perfumes and air fresheners mentioned earlier there are many other sources: bacteria and viruses, animal and dust mite dander, saliva and perspiration, pollen, dust, tobacco smoke, moulds and mildew, as well as the gasses nitrogen dioxide, carbon monoxide, sulphur dioxide and hydrocarbons from heating and cooking. Other carcinogens and toxic volatile organic compounds (VOCs) include benzene, formaldehyde, chloride found in everyday household products such as solvent-based cleaning fluids, pesticides, synthetic-fibre furnishings, PVC products and photocopier ink toner. A variety of building products such as solvent-based paints and wood preservatives, insulation foam, certain decorative materials and formaldehyde-based adhesives used in building boards and furniture are other sources of harmful VOCs. Carpets can be laden with dust contaminated with heavy metal particles, and asbestos dust and toxic chemicals walked in from the street. NASA tested the crew cabin of the Skylab III mission and found the construction materials, fabrics and electronic wiring produced over 300 VOCs, of which 107 were a serious health hazard.

Exposure to these modern toxic chemicals has developed another form of illness known as multiple chemical sensitivity (MCS), which can be as debilitating and as difficult to live with – let alone cure – as electromagnetic sensitivity (EMS) (see Chapter 3).

Pollutants can damage cells, cause premature ageing and will progressively degenerate the body's natural resistance to disease. Some compounds can be carcinogenic or mutagenic. Generally, dependent upon the degree of contamination, VOCs are seldom lethal but chronic exposure can produce debilitating allergic reactions such as skin diseases, asthma and general vulnerability to infectious diseases. Symptoms often experienced include breathing difficulties, eye infections, headaches and liver damage.

A team of US government scientists carried out extensive toxicology tests on phthalates: these artificial, chemical, oily solvents used to soften PVC are often found in many common plastics and household products including children's toys. Dr Earl Gray, the research team leader of the investigation, was especially concerned that the phthalates used in babies' soft rattles and teething rings should be severely restricted. Other studies on rats showed significant sexual deformities and warped sexual development, which may account for the peculiar and unexplained sexual changes in animals and fish and the falling sperm count in human males. Further research was also undertaken to examine exposure in the home where phthalates occur not only in PVC products but also as pollutants found in foods and dust.[31]

Serious indoor air contamination can exist even before a building is occupied. Unless the supervising architect, engineer or construction manager witnesses the thorough cleaning of all the ducts and voids in the floors, ceilings and walls, the building will be a permanent health hazard to the occupants. The inevitable building contractor's rubbish, rubble, dust and débris often already contaminated with vermin, free-floating fibres, fungi, bacteria and decaying scraps of sandwiches need to be eradicated under strict supervision before the building is handed over. Even an immaculately cleaned job will not stay that way for long. Dust, débris and other pollutants will accumulate from the usual piles of papers, books and the usual wear-and-tear usage of the building. Without regular deep cleaning of all ducts, voids and furnishings, the health hazards will develop.

Ongoing good housekeeping, management, maintenance and repair are major factors influencing the quality of healthy air in a building. Poor or non-existent housekeeping and maintenance standards can result in respiratory illness, allergies and other debilitating medical conditions or, in extreme cases, can lead to more serious outbreaks such as legionnaires' disease. Poor housekeeping standards had reached a critical stage when the Royal College of Nursing, supported by other nursing organisations, demanded improvements to cleaning and hygiene methods in British hospitals as more patients were contracting difficult-to-treat infections such as the bacteria 'methicillin resistant *Staphylococcus aureus*' (MRSA), which lives on the skin and survives in dust containing dead skin cells. The nursing organisations said the reason that MRSA outbreaks had soared by some 80 per cent over a two-year period from 1995 to 1997 was the reduction in domestic housekeeping services and the trend towards poorer hygiene in hospitals.[32]

Medical experiments in Sweden attributed the high incidence of asthma in the winter months to houses being kept virtually airtight. When a house is draught-proof and sealed, the build-up of natural body perspiration and vapour from bathing, cooking and heating raises the humidity level well above 45 per cent. One of the known causes of asthma is the breathing in of the faeces of the common house dust mite. These microscopic creatures, abundant in any household (however clean it may be), have no lungs. Instead they breathe through their skin; however, the atmosphere must be relatively moist to keep the body pliable, otherwise in dry conditions the mite will die or lie dormant. Simple trickle ventilation to achieve a minimum of three air changes an hour to keep the moisture content below a critical level of about 35 to 40 per cent will reduce the incidence of asthmatic attack.

Lack of good ventilation in any building will also increase our chronic exposure to indoor toxic gasses, chemicals and other contaminants. Therefore we must become more discerning about the type of household products – aerosols, pesticides and cleaning fluids – we use in the home and at work. We should also be aware that the building professions continue to use untried, untested materials and technologies, or worse they specify products that are known for their potential toxicity. This is now inexcusable as all product manufacturers are required by Health and Safety Executive law to provide detailed data sheets known as Control of Substances Hazardous to Health (COSHH) reports. These state the chemicals used, the level of toxicity, the precautions to be taken and the type of protective clothing to be worn by building operatives when using any given product. Most other countries in the West have their equivalent counterparts to the Health and Safety Executive agency in the UK to control all aspects of building industry working practices, protective clothing, the categorisation and use of building materials and products and accident procedures. However, while the Health and Safety Executive's rules are strict and enforceable in safeguarding employees, the legislation does not cover the amateur DIY enthusiast who may also use potentially hazardous materials, though every product's COSHH report containing important information and guidelines is available to everyone and the instructions should be carefully followed.

Suggested prudent avoidance

Whether you engage professional painters, plumbers and carpenters or you carry out the work yourself, be aware of the serious health hazards of inhaling paint and soldering fumes, sawdust from building boards and toxic gasses given off from a variety of adhesive materials. Debilitating fumes can hang around the house for several days or weeks, therefore paint jobs should be carried out in unoccupied, well-ventilated areas. Wherever possible use water-based rather than solvent-based products.

There are other ways to help ourselves to keep the air as fresh and pollutant-free as possible: for example, remove the sources of contaminants by choosing non-toxic cleaning fluids, ventilate well rather than use synthetic air fresheners, eliminate tobacco smoke, furnish with natural materials rather than synthetic carpets and fabrics to lessen the quantity of harmful fibres in the air, and where possible maintain low temperatures and good humidity levels appropriate to your comfort zone. In addition to taking all these precautions it is still necessary to thoroughly 'deep' clean everywhere at least once a year.

Recommendations published by the Clean Air Council (a division of the Associated Landscape Contractors of America) and conclusions reached by experiments carried out by NASA suggest a strategy for using indoor plants for air pollution abatement (provided of course, the leaves are kept dust free). The planet was enveloped in primeval toxic gasses for a few billion years until primitive plant life evolved from the swamps. Green plants began the process of cleaning up the atmosphere and increased the oxygen content to a level where complex organisms could develop. Plants, trees and rainforests still perform the same function. Although indoor landscape planting will not 'purify' the air to an acceptable level, certain species can, to a limited extent, reduce some of the pollutants. For example, a spider plant can remove 96 per cent of carbon monoxide from a sealed chamber. Plants such as the rubber plant (to detoxify and remove formaldehyde), dracaena, areca palm (a good humidifier) and Boston fern sited near office workers significantly improved general humidity levels and air quality.[33] A simple technology and the most effective plants to use can be found in several books such as the American publication *Environmental Interiorscapes*.[34] Plants will also improve the general ambience and create a visual interest much needed to combat some of the symptoms of sick building syndrome, which is the subject of the next chapter.

References

1. Adriaane Pielou, *The Mail on Sunday* 'You' magazine, 11 June 2000.
2. Snyder, Stuart D. (1997) *Environmental Interiorscapes*, New York: Whitney Library of Design.
3. Richard Alexander, 'Environmental exposure to toxical chemicals causes cancer', *New England Journal of Medicine*, vol. 343, no. 2, 13 July 2000.
4. Geraint Smith, *Evening Standard*, 13 July 2000.
5. Richard Woods and Mark Macaskill, 'Perfumes that linger may be a health hazard', *The Sunday Times*, 3 May 1999.
6. Nick Nuttall, 'Ministers order inquiry into the poison tips', *The Times*, 8 August 1998.
7. Environment Agency, *The State of the Environment of England and Wales: The Land*, February 2000. ISBN 0-11-3101660-x.
8. Steve Farrar, 'Plastics linked to sex mutation', *The Sunday Times*, 18 April 1999, p. 30.
9. Nicholas Hellen, 'Hidden dome pollution hits sell off price', *The Sunday Times*, 3 June 2001.

10. 'Risk of congenital anomalies near hazardous-waste landfill sites in Europe: the Eurohazcon study by Dr Helen Dolk et al.', *The Lancet*, vol. 352, 8 August 1998.

11. Stephan Bevan and Graham Hind, 'Birth defects cluster formed near toxic dump', *The Sunday Times*, 11 April 1999.

12. Michael McCarthy, 'In Toxic Town the fires of protest burn brightly, *The Independent*, 27 August 2001, p. 6.

13. Alan Hart, Charles Bagley and Terinia Taras, 'Village in shadow of death', *News of the World*, 6 February 2000, p. 12.

14. Stuart Payne and Deepa Shah, 'Enfield gives polluted site green light in "cover-up"', *Evening Standard*, 18 October 2000.

15. *The Magazine of the Institution of Planning Supervisors*, vol. 3, June 2000, p. 7.

16. Agricola, G. (1556) *De Ra Metallica*, Basel: Froben & Episcupius.

17. Clavensjo, B. and and Akerblom, G. (1994) The Radon Book – Measures Against Radon, The Swedish Council for Building Research, D4:1994. Stockholm, Sweden. p.129.

18. Mark Henderson, 'Water from private wells poses risk of radiation', *The Times*, 10 January 2001.

19. *RIBA Practice* 87, July/August 1992, p. 1.

20. *Which?*, July 1992, pp. 3869.

21. BBC Ceefax, 31 August 1998.

22. Gregory R. Wagner MD (Division of Respiratory Disease Studies, National Institute for Occupational Safety and Health, Centres for Disease Control and Prevention, Morgantown, WV26505 USA), 'Asbestosis and Silicosis', *The Lancet*, vol. 349(9061), 1997, pp. 1311–15.

23. BBC Ceefax, 30 March 2001.

24. Marcus Warren, 'Eurocrats office dust prompts poison alert across Belgian capital', *Sunday Telegraph*, 2 November 1997.

25. Peter Griffiths, 'Alert as mill fire showers asbestos ash for 12 miles, *Evening Standard*, 29 July 1999.

26. Lisa Buckingham, '£145 bn record bill for asbestos claims', *Financial Mail on Sunday*, 24 June 2001.

27. Health and Safety Executive, (1991) *The Control of Legionnellosis*, Health & Safety Series booklet HS 98 (G) 70.

28. BBC1 Ceefax, 2 May 2000.

29. Colin Anderson, 'Major health alert as tour Briton dies', *Evening Standard*, 5 May 2000.

30. Steve Connor, 'Air pollution in homes more dangerous than city smog', *The Sunday Times*, 15 March 1998.

31. Steve Farrar, 'Plastics linked to sex mutation', *The Sunday Times*, 18 April 1999.

32. Lorraine Fraser, 'Nurses' fear on hygiene', *The Mail on Sunday*, 30 August 1997.

33. Kate Rew, *Evening Standard*, 31 August 1999.

34. Snyder, Stuart D. (1997) *Environmental Interiorscapes*, New York: Whitney Library of Design.

Suggested further reading

Health & Safety Executive Regulations at Work, Her Majesty Stationery Office Publications.
The Rosehaugh Guide: Buildings & Health, RIBA Publications, London, 1990.

2.
Sick building syndrome

A general malaise

Our body is an exquisitely tuned, sensitive organism, constantly reacting to the most minute external vibrations that influence our actions, thought processes and every other aspect of our daily life. Like everything else in the universe, it is holistically integrated and part of the unified whole. According to the paradoxical Laws of Chaos, the infinitesimal beat of a butterfly's wings in the Arctic can cause a gale in the Bay of Biscay. As the planet's atmosphere can range from a terrifying tornado to a gentle breeze, so, on a microcosmic level, we respond to the external and internal phenomena that unknowingly determine our moods, emotions, energy levels and sense of well-being. Current evidence of sick building syndrome (SBS) suggests the great majority of our architects and indeed others engaged in the building industry have little or no understanding of the adverse physiological, biological and psychological impact of their designs, specifications, even their choice of colour and lighting, on human beings.

SBS has been defined as a 'general malaise'. Though not life-threatening, it can be seriously debilitating and chronically disabling. The symptoms are usually a combination of fatigue, poor concentration, general lethargy, headaches, a runny nose and eyes, dry or sore throat and eyes, aching limbs, skin rashes, tight chest and allergy fevers. When it was first recognised about thirty years ago, the syndrome was believed to have affected only office workers but since then it has become clear that the occupants of all types of buildings, including private places of residence, can also be afflicted.

Despite the evidence backed by statistics and government research, there is still a body of opinion among die-hard doctors, architects, engineers, property developers and facility managers who remain deeply sceptical that SBS exists other than in the minds of either psychologically disturbed or work-shy people. Some employers continue to disregard the range of complaints suffered by their staff and stoically accept the resulting high absenteeism and low productivity. In most cases the symptoms persist only while the person occupies a sick building environment, however, if your own house is affected, long-term exposure can become a chronic and serious health hazard.

The syndrome came to the fore in the 1960s when office workers found that their various symptoms became more acute as the working week progressed and then cleared at weekends or during vacation periods. This was not a problem of 'Monday morning' depression but more a 'Friday afternoon' condition when distress and discomfort was at its peak. Early studies suggesting that about 50 per cent of the staff susceptible to the malaise, the majority of whom were either women or low-paid employees, led office managers and the medical profession to conclude that the health problems were attributable exclusively to a phantom 'malingerer's complaint' rather than anything to do with the building environment, especially as, in most cases, the buildings were new. The establishment's reaction is not so surprising since, as will be shown later, similar accusations have been levelled against workers who developed the more serious symptoms of myalgic encephalomyelitis (ME – or chronic fatigue syndrome) as well as repetitive strain injury (RSI), upper limb disorders and chemical and electrical sensitivities.

Absenteeism in the UK costs industry £10.2 billion a year, mainly through minor illnesses, stress and family duties. A survey covering more than 530 firms estimated that 200 million days were lost through sickness in 1998, representing 8.5 days per worker, or 3.7 per cent of working time.[1]

A slightly less biased view was taken in the 1980s after independent research and World Health Organization (WHO) studies suggested that SBS could be traced to the oil crisis ten years earlier when Western governments imposed restrictions on the temperatures normally maintained in air-conditioned buildings. Oil consumption had to be reduced, resulting in less cooling and fewer fresh air changes. Higher temperatures, low humidity levels and the increased recirculation of used air laden with bacteria, dust and organic contaminants seemed to be a likely cause. However, it later became apparent that low-grade air-conditioning was not the only cause as people who worked in hospitals, industrial plants, staff and pupils of schools and the occupants of hotels and private dwellings – whether the buildings were air-conditioned or not – were suffering identical symptoms as those in offices. Furthermore, SBS had become a worldwide malaise affecting many post-1950 new buildings and refurbishments.

A more recent malaise suffered by airline passengers and crews could be called 'sick plane syndrome'. The symptoms, quite distinct from jet-lag, are described as mild forms of influenza or a non-specific illness that can last up to several days after a flight. This is caused by the policy of several airlines to economise on fuel by reducing the quantity of pressurised, treated fresh air mixed with the already used, and therefore contaminated, recirculated air in the cabins. Highly infectious diseases such as tuberculosis can be continually recycled in addition to poisonous organophosphates leaking from faulty oil seals into the air-conditioning system, which can produce symptoms similar to Gulf War syndrome. (Organophosphates are chemicals used for the highly toxic sheep dip and weed killer on farms, and head-lice shampoos and fly sprays in the home.) Lack of proper filtration maintenance increases the hazards. The pilot's flight deck is served with 150 cubic feet (4 cubic metres) of fresh air per minute, the first-class cabin gets 50 cubic feet (1.5 cubic metres) per minute, and economy class gets as little as 7 cubic feet (0.1 cubic metres) of fresh air per minute. Cabin staff say the problem can be so severe that they have to take oxygen canisters on long-haul flights. British Airways' confidential files, claimed to have been seen by *The Sunday Times*, reveal that more than 150 air crew have suffered nausea, nosebleeds, dizziness, disorientation and flu-like symptoms over the past year.[2] Current Federal Aviation Authority (FAA) regulations that set the standards for aircraft ventilation require a minimum of 10 cubic feet per minute of fresh air per person, however aircraft manufacturers are now trying to persuade the FAA to revise the rules to only 5 cubic feet per minute to make their planes more competitive on running costs. The sick plane syndrome phenomenon has been around for years because for some time airlines have instructed their pilots to turn down the intake of fresh air delivered into the cabins unless a passenger complains.[3] The problem is that by the time you are languishing in your bedroom or hotel room feeling decidedly unwell it is too late to complain to the pilot. However, when you recover you can tell the airline why you will not be using their services in the future.

Leaked reports have shown that after the *Discovery* shuttle docked at the International Space Station, astronauts spent several hours installing new equipment and then suffered a series of complaints – nausea, headaches and vomiting – similar to those of SBS. The problem occurred after they had removed some of the wall panel linings in the Russian module *Zarya* and toxic gasses were released.[4]

A high-volume of recycled contaminated air is only one of several other sources of SBS, all of which can be traced back to aspects of the siting and the architectural or engineering design, specification and construction of the original building or refurbishment. If the quality of the subsequent management, housekeeping and maintenance of the completed building is also low grade, the health hazards will be exacerbated.

Most Western governments now recognise that a very large number of buildings – not just offices, but also houses, schools and even hospitals built since the 1950s – are the direct cause of either chronic illnesses or the malaise known as sick building syndrome suffered by occupants. The general deterioration in health of those who occupy such buildings is attributable to a combination of a number of factors including the siting, the choice of materials, and the actual design and configuration of interior spaces. Even the acoustic properties and colour schemes are known to trigger adverse mental and physical reactions.

Poor ventilation systems, synthetic materials exuding toxic gasses, tinted glass windows, and electromagnetic fields (EMFs) are just a few of the modern innovations causing stress, depression, fatigue, or even more serious illnesses – the so-called 'diseases of civilisation' – such as cancer. Government agencies and generally those in the building professions – both teachers and practitioners – have shown a stubborn reluctance to accept that the choice of location, design and construction of their buildings, and the careless exposure to electromagnetic fields, can be hazardous to occupants.

The 'conditioned' air we breathe

A mechanically ventilated building, whether the air is chilled or not, sets up artificial conditions that need to be finely tuned and balanced. In essence, the windows are sealed so that all the air in the building is drawn through filters to remove outside airborne pollutants, dust and bacteria before being circulated to the occupied areas.

There are three main types of air-conditioning systems: variable air volume (VAV); fan coil unit (FCU); and chilled ceiling or chilled beam. VAV is where the whole of the void above the ceiling is used to distribute the conditioned air into the spaces below. The FCU, is a piece of equipment mounted above the ceiling or under a window which receives filtered air through ducts and then passes it over either refrigerated water or hot water pipes to control the desired temperature of air being blown by a fan convector into the room. Here, a certain proportion of 'old' air is recirculated to save the cost of filtering, cleaning and heating or cooling the total volume of air needed to provide adequate ventilation to the building. Finally, the chilled ceiling or chilled beam system uses air delivered into a void under the floor which enters the room via vents and, by natural heat convection due to warm bodies and electrical equipment, rises up and flows over exposed refrigerated pipes in the ceiling. The advantage with this type of air-conditioning is that there are no moving parts, and windows can be opened without unbalancing the system. However, although chilled ceilings have been successfully installed in many owner-occupied and government buildings for over three decades, hidebound property developers have been reluctant to use the system despite the low cost and efficient working advantages.

Suggested prudent avoidance

The efficiency and healthiness of any standard air-conditioning system depends on its proper maintenance – frequent changing of air filters and keeping the main ducts cleaned to remove dust, bacteria and gasses, some of which may have been left in place by the original building contractors. In any case, over time the dust and dirt will accumulate and must be thoroughly removed by deep-cleaning methods to maintain a healthy environment. In 1992, the UK Health and Safety Executive reported some three hundred toxic substances had been found in offices and stated that air-conditioned buildings with sealed windows and an abundance of electrical equipment created an unhealthy working environment aggravated by low humidity levels.

Good management can eliminate or greatly reduce the sources of pollution by banning smoking and separately exhausting photocopier machines, and good housekeeping can keep down the accumulation of dust, floating fibres, fumes and other contaminants already in the building. However, more often than not, the fundamental cause of an unhealthy air-conditioned building is due to cost cutting in its basic design and planned performance standards demanded by the developer or proposed by the architects and engineers to trim construction budgets.

Theoretically, provided that the number of fresh air changes per hour is adequate, that the volume of recirculated air is relatively low and the whole system is efficiently maintained and kept clean, a well-engineered mechanical air-conditioning system should not create a serious health hazard. Nevertheless, however well designed and maintained the system may be, there may still be sick building syndrome side-effects. Occupants can suffer high levels of stress because they have no control over their immediate environment: they cannot open the sealed windows to give them the sense of being connected to the outside world; they cannot feel a 'fresh air' breeze or at least experience some air movement; and they cannot control the temperature and humidity to suit their own level of comfort. As will be shown later, modern air-conditioned office buildings designed with low ceilings, tinted glass windows and deep floor plans create an oppressive environment that adds to the distress, depression and stress of the workers.

A degree of prudent avoidance can be taken by airline passengers and cabin crews. Although the airlines deny it, evidence suggests that some pilots do adjust the air-handling units drawing in fresh air (as mentioned above), but if passengers complain they return the controls to normal. If you are sitting towards the rear of the cabin you are more likely to breathe in a greater proportion of polluted air than those at the front who are nearer to the air intakes. The chances of contracting infectious, airborne diseases from other passengers sitting in front of you have increased to the extent that now people are being advised to wear an Aviation Health Institute (AHI) face mask which has been specifically designed to screen out 98 per cent of the germs. The manufacturers say that the masks have become so popular that soon they will be commonplace.[5]

Negative ion depletion

The past decade or so has seen the expansion of high-heat-output electronic and electrical equipment installed in our workplaces and our homes (a computer will generate ten times more heat than a human body). The older air-conditioning systems were designed mainly for people rather than machines, and even the more recent but low-grade systems where the heat load has been underestimated and there is no provision to regulate humidity in the mechanical plant, will produce an over-warm, very dry environment depleted of negative ions and high in static electricity.

There appears to be no scientifically acceptable agreement on the precise nature of ions and yet no living organism can survive without them. Russian scientists experimented with animals and plants in an environment void of ions and within a few days neither the animals nor the plants had survived. One theory is that natural radioactivity from the Earth's core, cosmic radiation and water droplets in the atmosphere create an electrical charge of positive and negative ions. The ions are positive in the ionosphere and negative at the Earth's surface. In the relatively 'fresh' air of the open countryside of woodlands, mountains and waterfalls, the volume of negative (most beneficial) ions are plentiful and in balance with the positive (non-beneficial) ions. Almost the only 'clean' air in the world, where negative ions are in abundance, is at the foot of a glacier where pollutants condense out on the ice.

Ions are thought to be electrically charged molecules of air gasses. If an electron is added to or removed from a gas molecule, this produces a negative ion and the removal of a positive ion. Substantial amounts of negative ions induce a sense of calmness, alertness, quick recovery from illness and a general sense of well-being. Most of us have experienced feelings of depression when a thunderstorm is brewing but, as soon as the lightning flashes and the thunder cracks, the air feels cleaner and fresher, and suddenly we feel energised and revitalised. The more abundant positive ions continually 'gobble up' negative ions to achieve a balanced state. Once they have used up all the available negative ions in the air they automatically go for the negative ions that naturally occur in our bloodstream. In an air-conditioned building, the air flowing through metal ventilation ducting dislodges electrons in the same manner as a stream flowing along a river dislodges small pieces of earth and stones from the banks. The dislodged electrons create a positive ion charged atom.

A lack of negative ions produces chemical changes in the body, affecting our libido, muscles, adrenals, eyes, heart, kidneys, white blood cells and the reproductive system. The biological reaction causes us to feel fatigued and suffer other sick building symptoms such as skin disorders and aching joints. Negative ion depletion can also affect the calcium ions binding brain tissue and impair our immune system.

In a dry, overheated, 'airless' urban building, whether air-conditioned or not, the indoor environment will have large numbers of positive ions. Several years ago there was a fad for installing negative ionisers in the home. Unfortunately, these early machines gave off a toxic ozone gas and in 1961 they were banned in the US. The new generation of ionisers are greatly improved and the self-filtering types do not leave a smudge of black dust around the unit. These ionisers have been subjected to extensive testing, and are capable of counterbalancing negative ion depletion without creating harmful side-effects. Modern ionisers will absorb pollutants such as cigarette smoke, pollens, allergens and fumes, whereas an air purifier will filter the stale and blow out the clean air without necessarily improving the negative ionisation. Unless the air purifier filters are frequently changed they will do more harm than good.

When the air is too dry, the furniture will crack, the piano will go out of tune, your contact lenses will irritate and eczema and psoriasis may develop. On the other hand, if the air is too damp, the furniture will develop mould, the piano will still go out of tune, you will feel lethargic and asthma may develop. Good relative humidity is essential to maintain a healthy environment. Ideally, a level of between 40 per cent and 55 per cent humidity should be maintained, however some offices have been found to be as low as 23 per cent, which leads to serious dehydration. Negative ion depletion can be overcome to some extent by installing plants, flowers in water, fountains or aquaria to keep the humidity levels in balance, but the effects of this are limited. The ancient Chinese wisdom gave clear instructions about the need for a good air flow (*Feng*) and the beneficial effects of moving water (*Shui*) to create a healthy, prosperous environment. These ancient principles will be looked at further in Chapter 7.

Another, secondary cause of negative ion depletion is static electricity. Touching a static charged door handle or filing cabinet can be painful and even though there is no electrical current it can still cause biological damage. The crackling and hissing sounds on a radio, TV or computer screen are created by static electricity: sometimes this can be the cause of electronic equipment breakdown and the source of serious fires. Again, low humidity and high temperatures will build the level of static which in turn, apart from depleting the negative ions, will attract dust and fibre contaminants in the air. Carpets, furnishings and clothing made of synthetic materials will add to the electrical charge in the immediate environment.

Suggested prudent avoidance

Everyone has a natural static electrical charge. Our body has a relatively high conductivity and being located between the Earth's crust and the atmosphere we are like an electrode that distorts the electrical field until it becomes uniform or homogeneous. Walking generates static, but as one foot is left on the ground, the charge becomes earthed or grounded. However, a person wearing rubber- or synthetic-soled shoes will not be earthed to the ground, and in this case the static voltage generated on the skin will cause a mild electrical shock. Natural fibre carpets can reduce static only if they are on a non-synthetic underlay, and anti-static treatments on synthetic materials may help neutralise the effect of static.

Computers produce high levels of static derived from the electrical power, the cathode ray tube gun and the flyback transformer. Antistatic screens can be fitted but they must be properly earthed and cleaned with antistatic materials. Antistatic mats can also be fitted under the screen, keyboard and printer but again, these must be earthed.

The field of static around a computer screen will attract positive charged dust particles laden with chemical pollutants. The dust deposited on the operator's skin can block the pores and cause skin rashes, dryness, allergies and sore eyes. The incidence of repetitive strain injury among computer operators may be due in part to their hands and fingers on the keyboard being in close proximity to the screen's static and radiation fields.

Noise

Noise is disturbing, unwanted sound. 'Noise pollution' is a general health hazard and another contributing factor to sick building syndrome. Burglar and car alarms, police sirens, traffic, trains, aircraft, building and road works, a neighbour's stereo, shouting, music blasting from dance clubs, theatres and sporting events are dangerous sources of noise. Equally disturbing are the almost inaudible noises from badly fitting fans, drumming from the air-conditioning plant, the buzz from ageing fluorescent tubes, laser printers and photocopiers, or the throbbing drone from faulty equipment. Noise has become such an acute social problem that we now have 'sound police' who have powers to confiscate stereo equipment from people who continually and uncaringly disturb their neighbours with loud music.

On the other hand, too little sound can also be stressful to those who may feel they are constantly being overheard or unable to enjoy isolation when they need time to think and concentrate. Young people envelope themselves in loud music to create a form of privacy. The hard, resonating surfaces in an Italian restaurant that amplify the sound are welcomed by diners who do not want their conversations overheard in a crowded space, and the high buzz of conversation and telephones ringing in large open-plan offices can have the same effect.

Inhabitants of large cities are bound to suffer high levels of noise pollution during the day and night but even suburban or countryside dwellers will be disturbed by barking dogs and the home improvement enthusiasts who insist they can only do their building or repair work at weekends. Power tools, hedge trimmers and lawn mowers have become such a nuisance that the European Union (EU) has issued directives to manufacturers to reduce the noise made by their equipment. Germany has already banned noisy mowers between noon Saturday and Monday, and no doubt other countries will now follow suit.[6] In the home, the vacuum cleaner, washing machine, loud music and the TV can build up the stress of daily life.

The intensity of sound is measured by a unit called a decibel (dB). For example, on the top of a mountain or in the middle of the night in the countryside, away from traffic and airport noise, the very quiet sound level would be in the range of up to 20dB. A church might be anything up to 50dB and a small office up to 70dB. When the levels rise to between 70dB and 80dB the sound begins to be uncomfortable, such as in a busy restaurant, pub or along a street in a town. At 90dB, for example where there is heavy traffic, a police siren or near a building site, and you have to raise your voice to be heard, the noise has reached a level to which prolonged exposure can damage the ears. Noise becomes painful and harmful when the decibel level exceeds 100dB. The sound in a night club can reach 120dB, and explosions or jet aircraft taking off will record even higher levels.

The spectrum of sound audible to the human ear ranges between the frequencies of 20 Hertz and 20,000 Hertz (Hz). The characteristics of sound are its *pitch* (the frequency of the soundwave), its *loudness* (the amplitude of the wave) and its *timbre* (the extent of the harmonics of the fundamental frequency). Sound intensity is dependent on the relationship between pitch and loudness. Soundwaves below the 20Hz threshold of human hearing are in the range of *infrasonics*. Earthquakes, tidal waves and other natural phenomenon produce infrasound frequencies that can be heard by animals, birds and insects. Their disturbed patterns of behaviour can be accurate predictions that seismic activity is occurring in some other part of the world far away from their habitat. Whales use infrasound to communicate over distances exceeding 1,000 kilometres (620 miles) by using a 'conduit' or channel where the ocean's varying temperature layers meet. Nuclear submarines using the same channel may be responsible for whale signals being jammed or confused. Dolphins use sound for hunting food, communicating and finding a mate: indeed, conservation groups believe that seismic oil exploration soundwaves and offshore drilling work are driving dolphins away from the seas around the British Isles.[7]

Although ultrasound wave frequencies are above human audibility, subconsciously we can 'hear' sounds above and below our normal threshold. *Ultrasonics* has a number of applications, for example the use of its rapid vibrations to destroy bacteria in milk, clean surfaces and to break up large molecules. Sound engineers overlay CD recordings with sound above our normal threshold to improve our enjoyment of the music. Although we are not consciously hearing these higher frequencies, they affect the brain's limbic system which releases the endorphin compounds that relieve pain and make us feel happy. Playing the high-frequency music of Mozart to disruptive, dysfunctional children has achieved remarkable results: ten minutes after entering the classroom, blood pressures and pulse rates were significantly reduced, with the pupils becoming more calm and therefore more receptive to learning. French researcher Dr Tomatis has pioneered the therapeutic effects of varying sound frequencies to heal physiological and psychological illnesses and disabilities.[8]

It is not unusual for small-boat sailors to 'hear' submerged whales and dolphins. On several occasions on long transatlantic trips, when the weather has been relatively calm, I have sat in the cockpit of my boat, quietly reading, when suddenly there is a nudging 'vibration' in the air. Within moments, a whale or a pair of dolphins will surface around the boat. Of course, it is naturally exciting to be with these wonderful creatures and to feel that one is not alone, but there is also a noticeable sense of enjoyment and pleasure.

Some of the subsonic or ultrasonic sounds we 'hear', such as the noise caused by erratic voltages and vibrations affecting the flyback unit on a computer, can be insidiously disturbing. However, excessive noise can cause temporary deafness and be extremely painful: long-term exposure can result in permanent ear damage, loss of balance, and may even reduce life expectancy. Dr Deepak Prasher of the Royal National Ear, Nose and Throat Hospital, and head of the EU sponsored Protection Against Noise Study, reported that chronic exposure to noise induces stress, leads to changes in hormones and specific conditions such as ulcers and heart disease. A German study found that children living around Munich airport, monitored over a three-year period, had significant changes in blood pressure and showed cognitive and memory impairment.[9]

The Royal Society for the Protection of Birds (RSPB) believes song birds in the UK are losing their tune. Indeed, studies have shown that traffic noise has rendered them tone deaf, reducing their songs to a harsh crackle. The birds cannot hear one another and have difficulty in learning their unique songs.[10] Other research has shown that birds are imitating the sounds they hear most frequently in urban areas – mobile phones, car alarms and horns. Dutch studies have also indicated that traffic and other sources of excessive noise in the environment have so disrupted the birds' hearing that many native populations have become significantly depleted. Destruction of their natural habitat as well as the use of pesticides and chemicals killing off plants and insects have also contributed to the decline.

Government health and safety regulations are designed to protect all employees or self-employed persons who are employed at an office, building site or any other place of work – including disco clubs and theatres (ship and air crews and members of the armed forces are among the few exemptions). Every employee is legally safeguarded under the Health and Safety at Work Act and the Noise at Work Regulations, which came into effect on 1 January 1990. When the 'daily personal noise exposure' reaches 85dB (equivalent to standing on the corner of a very busy roundabout) the employer must provide the employee with ear protectors; when the level rises to 90dB and above, the employee is obliged to use them.

The Musicians Union mailed all its members to make them aware of the possible health risks if exposed to excessive noise, also advising them that they are protected under the Health and Safety rules. In answer to the question 'does classical music damage your hearing?', the union's consensus view is 'potentially yes – particularly for bass players'. The information pack states that 'high sound levels are an integral part of a musician's life but, in all probability, will permanently damage your hearing. The risk depends on how loud the sound is and how long you are exposed to it'. Damage can occur at levels as low as 80dB if sustained on a regular basis. The pamphlet cites two programmes: Berio's opera *La Vera Storia* producing a noise level measured at 92.2dB, and Bruckner's *Symphony No.5,* which recorded a higher exposure of 94.2dB. Union members were advised of the possible irreversible damage and it was recommended that, at certain performances, some form of ear protection should be used.[11]

So are the sound engineers for pop concerts and theatre musicals responding to the public's demand for louder and louder music because general noise pollution is making us all hard of hearing, or is it because we confuse volume with the quality of sound? Alternatively, maybe the DJs, sound engineers and bar staff who spend hours every night in such a noisy environment need to keep turning up the volume because their own hearing has become so impaired due to chronic exposure. In 1999, the London theatre production of *Rent* was so loud that local residents complained and environmental officers were called in to take court action.

However, it seems that we object to other people's noise but willingly subject ourselves to potential ear problems and pain provided it is *our* sort of music and entertainment.

Suggested prudent avoidance

Modern lightweight building techniques, framed construction systems and all the essential mechanical, electrical plant and equipment have produced health hazards linked to noise not previously encountered. A relatively new breed of expert, the acoustic engineer, has become an important specialist in the professional building team whose job is to deal with the noise problems and create an environment where sounds are balanced. Reverberation from reflective surfaces creates a liveliness, whereas space overloaded with absorbent material can deaden the sound so much it becomes a strain on the voice and hard work to speak.

A major problem is how to deal with the people who live and work in high-rise sealed air-conditioned buildings, far above the street noise and other external sounds where it is so quiet that the only noise may be the faint but incessant hum of the ventilation system or the buzz of a high-voltage lamp. These stressful and disturbing sounds can be overcome to some extent by introducing machines producing 'white noise' to compensate for the unsettling quietness. Active noise control as a method of reducing or cancelling out sound by artificially introducing a second sound of equal amplitude but in reverse phase has been known for the past 50 years or more. Such measures can go some way towards counterbalancing the drawbacks of modern, high-rise sealed buildings but do not overcome the distressful claustrophobia often experienced when the external environment cannot be sensed or heard. The condition is exacerbated when the building's windows are glazed in tinted glass.

Light and colour

> God created the heavens and the Earth in the very beginning...(and) God said 'Let there be light'
>
> (Genesis 1:1, 3)

We shall do well then to consider this potential and beautiful principle of light and its concomitant colours, for the more deeply we penetrate into its inner laws, the more would it present itself as a marvellous storehouse of power to vitalise, heal, refine and delight mankind. Few realise that they are walled in by the limitations of the sense perceptions. Not only is there a great deal more to life than anyone has ever seen, but there are also unknown forms of light which no optical equipment will ever register. There are unnumbered colours which cannot be seen as well as sound which cannot be heard, odours which cannot be smelled, flavours which cannot be tasted and substances which cannot be felt. We are thus surrounded by a super sensible universe of which we know nothing because the centres of sense perception within ourselves have not been developed sufficiently to respond to the subtle rates of vibration of which that universe is composed.[12]

Light is a primary source of energy and a form of electromagnetic radiation to which the human eye is supersensitive. In his book *Colour Me Healing*, Jack Allanach writes that Professor Popp, the German 'father' of the emerging science of photobiology, has now established that our cells communicate by low level light transmission.[13] Colour is the sensation produced when light of different wavelengths falls on the retina. Seeing is a chemical reaction driven by light.

Physicists have disputed the nature of light since the earliest times, but Sir Isaac Newton (1642–1727) was the first to recognise that white light is a mixture of coloured light that can be separated by refraction: this led to his corpuscular theory that light was a stream of bullet-like particles. Another British physicist and physician, Thomas Young (1773–1829), who opposed Newton's theory, demonstrated that the interference of light indicated that light is transmitted by waves. (Young spoke 12 languages before he was 20 years old and helped to decipher the Egyptian Rosetta Stone). The present view, that of Niels Bohr (1885-1962), the Danish atomic physicist, expresses the concept that light is both a wave and an energy quanta – photons. A photon is a quantum of electromagnetic radiation regarded as a particle with no mass that travels at the speed of light. Quantum theory says that everything in the universe – from living organisms to solid rocks – is a varying, condensed form of sunlight. Each of the

60 billion cells in our body that emits light in the form of ultra-weak photoradiation were discovered by Russian scientists in the first half of the twentieth century.[14]

The visible spectrum is split into seven major colours – red, orange, yellow, green, blue, indigo and violet – in an order of decreasing wavelengths, and when mixed in equal proportions they produce white light. Other colours are produced by varying the proportions or omitting certain prime colours. Coloured pigments and dyes absorb certain wavelengths and reflect others, for example a blue shirt illuminated by white light absorbs all the components of white light except the reflected colour blue. In other words, the colour of something is that which remains after all the other colours have been absorbed.

White light is a mix of all the colours of the spectrum or a mix of the three primary additive colours – red, green and blue – in equal proportions. We sense colours of the rainbow by seeing different proportions of red, green and blue light, and this is how we get colour TV. Human beings have only three receptors; birds have up to six receptors and other animals see infrared, ultraviolet (UV) and other colours more than we can imagine beyond our relatively limited range of the visual spectrum. Incidentally, the sky is blue because small particles of dust and droplets of water scatter light in the same manner as the particles scatter and turn the Moon red when there is an eclipse.

Light and human biology

The ancients described our eyes as 'the windows of the soul'. Our life processes are regulated by the light penetrating our eyes and getting through to the endocrine glands: the pineal, pituitary, thyroid, hypothalamus and adrenals. These glands and receptors disseminate all of our physical, mental and psychic processes including our behavioural responses and perceptions of the myriad of stimuli at every moment of the day. The subliminal mind filters out what we need to consciously hear, see, smell and think. It also registers all bodily processes and retains the memory of every experience in its entirety. Subliminal advertising, now illegal, could flash a message on a TV screen for a minute fraction of a second, which is too fast for the conscious eye to see, though the subliminal mind can still 'read' the message and respond accordingly. As we can 'hear' the beat and rhythm of inaudible sounds, so we can 'see' the invisible geometric constructs of an object or building: we are able to assimilate all external phenomena but to avoid becoming overwhelmed with this constant barrage of information the mind filters the data input allowing us to integrate ourselves into the world.

The pineal gland, the 'brain' within the brain, is pea-sized, shaped like a pine cone and located in the centre of the skull at the lines of intersection between the ears and the eyebrows. This master gland controlling all the other endocrine glands secretes the flow of hormones through the body via the autonomic nervous system – the brain's electrical pulses operating the 'on-off' switches controlling the release of a cocktail of chemicals affecting our metabolism, emotions and moods of elation or depression. The two most important secretions, serotonin and melatonin, govern a wide range of energy levels, mental activity, sleep patterns, hallucinations and dreams. The pineal gland is ultra-sensitive to light and extremely faint electromagnetic fields. (Traditionally, monks shaved the top of their heads to allow more light to impinge upon the pineal gland as a means of accelerating their spiritual development – 'enlightenment'.)

The pineal gland is a biological clock and is highly sensitive to Moon phases and sunspot activity. When in our normal habitat the body operates on a 24-hour clock basis regulated by the sunlight controlling the day/night rhythmic secretion of serotonin and melatonin. The release of melatonin is essential for the replenishment of our immune system, hence the healing process through sleep, whereas a lack of melatonin leads to immune system deficiencies. (As darkness approaches the release of serotonin ceases and melatonin is released to make us feel drowsy, calm and ready for sleep.) Deprivation of light for any length of time will cause our biorhythms to change to a 25-hour cycle to coincide with the Moon rather than the Sun cycles. When a person is subjected to a permanently light environment their serotonin secretions will intensify to the point where they may become hyperactive, overstressed and emotionally overwrought. Contraction of the intestinal muscles, overexcitement – butterflies in the stomach or the 'gut' reaction – are other symptoms caused by the release of serotonin.

In periods of daylight the pineal gland's release of serotonin and cortisol boosts our energy levels, intensifies emotions and induces a feeling of vitality. (We produce more cortisol in the summer than the winter months.) During the autumn and winter periods we are more likely to feel ill, depressed or succumb to colds, 'flu and other ailments due to the lack of sunlight. People who live in darker countries far away from the equator are more prone to depressive illnesses and suicide. Between 6 and 10 per cent of the North American population suffer seasonal affective disorder (SAD) – a syndrome coined in 1992 by Dr Norman Rosenthal, a research scientist at the National Institute of Mental Health in Bethesda, Maryland. Apparently, 80 per cent of SAD patients will respond to light treatment, however, a person subjected to extremely long periods of either lightness or darkness will become disorientated and manic.

The release of vital secretions from the endocrine glands are controlled by the brainwave patterns. When we feel drowsy our electrical brainwave patterns change from beta – the normal level when we are awake – to alpha. As we fall asleep, begin dreaming and then move into deeper hypnotic and psychic subconscious experiences, so the electrical pulse rate changes further to delta and gamma frequency levels that control the release of essential secretions from other endocrine glands. Relatively weak shifts in the strength of natural electromagnetic fields radiating from the Earth and outer space, or from artificially generated electromagnetic fields, can set up interference patterns with the brain's minute electrical wave activity.

Such disturbance to the brain's release mechanism of the endocrine secretions affects our biological rhythms, mood swings, stress levels and reproduction cycles, and depletes our immune system. Any form of sleep deprivation, such as sleeping in a room which is not dark, will suppress the production of melatonin resulting in clinical depression or non-clinical depression such as jet lag. Shift work can have the same effect. When we are seriously ill, part of nature's cure is to keep us asleep for long periods to allow melatonin and other secretions to replenish and boost the immune system. Recent research has found that long periods of darkness are essential for the healthy development of the eyes in young children: sleeping with the light on at night during the first two years is likely to cause short-sightedness.[15]

Clinical trials of blind women have shown that they have a significantly lower risk of developing breast cancer than fully sighted women. Doctors are now convinced that breast cancer is a disease of industrialised civilisation where rates are five times higher than in Third World countries, and research suggests the cause may be our '24-hour society' – the use of artificial light which prevents people in the West from experiencing total night-time darkness when the natural production of melatonin takes place. Our immune system also depends on melatonin to regulate the levels of the hormone oestrogen, which is linked to breast cancer. Artificial light, jet lag and shift work (including flight crews) disrupts the production of melatonin.[16]

During the past twenty or thirty years there has been increasing concern regarding the quality of the physical and social environments to which pre-term infants are exposed in neonatal intensive care units (NICUs). A report on infant behaviour and development claims that: 'The hazards associated with medical care such as inappropriately applied medical interventions, electromagnetic hazards, noise levels and intense continuous lighting are all potential environmental stressors which can negatively effect infant health and development'. The continuous bright general lighting conditions usually found in hospitals were linked to a number of health problems in animals and humans, including retinal pathology, disruption of circadian rhythms, reduced melatonin secretion, sleeplessness, fatigue, cognitive difficulties and behavioural patterns. Intermittent cyclical lighting that accords with normal daylight and night-time periods induced prolonged sleep states in infants which increased the release of the growth hormone, reduced the levels of cortisol (necessary to overcome stressful situations) and increased weight gain and heart beat rates. A reduction in noise levels as well as cyclical lighting in day/night nurseries also facilitated the general restoration to normal growth and development.[17]

Light therapy

The therapeutic value of light and colour, known for thousands of years, is based on the specific properties of the different wavelengths of each colour of light to stimulate the natural healing ability within the body. Red light, the longest wavelength, is used for deep penetration, and at the other end of the visible spectrum is violet, the shortest wavelength used to stimulate a quickening sense of the higher, spiritual aspects of being and self-healing.

The treatment rooms of ancient Egypt were designed to use sunlight to refract light into the separate colours of the spectrum so that each patient could be bathed in the appropriate coloured light. Light and colour therapy was also well-known in Persia, and the Greeks used various materials in their solaria to change the sunlight colour most appropriate to a specific healing process. Orthodox Western medicine has tended to ignore this powerful, naturally therapeutic healing technique, preferring instead to rely on drugs and radical surgery. Sunlight therapy to kill off tuberculosis (TB) bacteria was used at a clinic founded by Swiss doctor Auguste Rollier in 1903. Two years later when he presented his findings at a medical conference in Paris, the entire audience walked out in disbelief.

In 1985, Swedish architect Erik Asmussen designed a unique 74-bed hospital – Vidar Kliniken, at Jarna on the Baltic – based on the philosophy of Rudolf Steiner who founded the Anthroposophical Society in 1912 (better known in the US as the Waldorf School Movement). The hospital walls were painted in the Steiner *Lazure* technique to produce a 'living' atmosphere of colours to create varying 'temperatures' to suit the nature of the illnesses: for example, patients with fevers or inflammations were given rooms painted in shades of blue, and warm pink rose tints were used for patients with 'cool' diseases like cancer.[18]

A major milestone was reached in 1998 when a conference on light held at Reading University in the UK brought together delegates, lecturers and practitioners from many parts of the world to disseminate their latest studies. They exchanged information and techniques on light, photo medicine, the use of lasers, polarised light, strobes for bio-stimulation and a 'colour puncture' system using selected colours beamed on to acupuncture meridian and pressure zones. Colour puncture is hardly a new 'medicine' as it had been pioneered over the past 30 years by German scientist Peter Mandel to successfully treat so-called 'terminal' patients suffering from cancer as well as other severe diseases and psychological ailments. Mandel's work and the development of colour puncture is the subject of Jack Allanach's book *Colour Me Healing* (see page 40). Another pioneer, Dr Jacob Liberman, tells us in his book *Light: Medicine of the Future* that as light is our essence, it is a therapy for healing ourselves.[19]

A technique using UV and visible lightwaves to irradiate about 2 per cent of a patient's blood and then reinfuse it into the bloodstream has been successfully practised by Russian professor Kira Samoilova to decontaminate viral infections. Full colour spectrum light can lower blood pressure and control cholesterol levels, and the UV component can stimulate production of Vitamin D, which aids absorption of calcium, magnesium and phosphorus – essential for osteoarthritis and repair of bone damage.

Gradually, medical opinion is beginning to understand and appreciate the therapeutic values of light and colour as alternatives to a number of standard allopathic treatments. London's Hammersmith Hospital has used a device called a light mask, developed by Dr David Norton, which produces red flickering lights to treat women suffering from severe menstrual conditions. At the same hospital, leading dermatologist Dr Tony Chu has developed a light machine to cure acne. The patient is exposed to a blue light treatment to kill off the bug and a red light to heal the skin. This appears to be a successful therapy with no side-effects.

Researchers at Tokyo University have now produced a titanium dioxide chemical coating for wall and floor tiles that reacts with UV light to break down dirt, grime and bacteria. Could this mark the end of toxic cleaning fluids?

Light and the built environment

Physiologically, biologically and psychologically we are profoundly affected by the quality and quantity of light and colour determined by a building's location, orientation and interior spaces. A room with windows on different elevations varies the interplay of colour, texture and reflected direct light: gentle rhythmic daylight can change our thought patterns and mood. Being able to see the sky and landscape through clear glass windows keeps us connected with the natural environment and avoids sensory deprivation and the feeling of being trapped. Working in large, open-plan offices with regimented rows of desks where the ceiling heights are oppressively low, the lighting scheme is bland and the décor is dull and visually uninteresting, can induce feelings of claustrophobia, lethargy and boredom. Staff who have to spend their working day permanently under artificial light because the floor plans are so deep (greater than 7 metres/24 feet) will tend to suffer greater fatigue than those sitting near the windows.

Not being able to see the external environment, at least from time to time during the day, is stressful enough, but tinted-glass windows, enveloping the whole of the interior with a gloomy, near-dark atmosphere, play tricks with our perceptions of time and sense of what is going on outside the building – is it noon or approaching home-time in the early evening? At a subtle level, the unsettling and disconcerting 'discrepancy' adds to the stress of sensory confusion.

Working – or living – under tinted glass and artificial light inhibits the pineal gland's flow of serotonin, which reduces our sense of vitality and aliveness to the point where, after a time, we feel drowsy and fatigued. Dark tinted glass or mirrored glass have produced dramatic façades and are effective against solar heat gain, however glass manufacturers have now developed a virtually clear glass to filter out the radiant heat from the Sun. Another option in contrast to the sheer, shiny opaque-glass box characteristics of late-twentieth-century office buildings is to design façades with projections to shade the interior without reducing the quality of daylight. Master architects of the past used these techniques to create comfortable, well-lit imaginative and distinctive buildings well before the arrival of artificial air-conditioning and tinted glass.

Inadequate natural daylight levels demand continuous, unvaried artificial lighting usually in the form of fluorescent tubes. The mechanism of a fluorescent lamp is an electrical spark flashing across the tube at about 100 times a second – somewhat similar to the dot on a TV screen travelling 625 times a second to create the images produced. We are not conscious of the flash across the screen or the flicker across the lamp, but at a subliminal level the electrical pulse of 100 times a second is registered in the brain. This 'unseen' pulse can produce a disturbing interference pattern with the brain's normal electrical wave pattern causing nausea, tiredness, eye strain, and what is known as techno-stress – also caused by the subliminal flicker from computer and TV screens. Even the body's temperature and women's ovulation cycles can be affected. The pulse of the flash has a similar effect to strobe lighting, which is known to cause epileptic fits.

Interference with brainwave patterns can be overcome by installing high-frequency ballast controls to increase the flash from 100 times a second to 200 times a second.

Full colour spectrum fluorescent lamps that simulate natural daylight, including infra-red and UV frequencies, will also help to reduce the inherent health hazard.

Later we shall see how the power centres (chakras) in the body correspond to a colour code according to the vibrational frequencies that relate to the endocrine gland secretions, which determine how we are feeling. Humans respond to the vibrations of colour as they do to the vibrations of sound and music: strong colours can be manipulative and demanding but most useful when reserved for counterpoint and accent. Large expanses of 'solid' colours can be depressing whereas the *Lazure* (see page 44) and similar techniques of painting or spraying translucent 'veils' of colour over a white background create a vibrancy and aliveness. Rectilinear rooms painted white can even 'sound' louder than when painted in a different colour. Colours, lighting, textures, the flow of air and the actual proportions and shapes of the interior rooms have a sum total impact on the mind, body and spirit of all those who enter the building.

Ideally, an overall lighting scheme should aim to counter the lack of daylight to provide good colour rendition, low brightness and a system of polarisation to reduce glare. Uplighting and walls washed with light create visual interest and a gentle contrast to enhance the interplay of colour and texture. Individual workstation task lighting to suit the type of activity being carried out can add to the general lighting environment. Highly reflective surfaces, glare and over-brightness should be avoided to reduce visual fatigue and eye strain. Low-grade computer software producing poorly defined images is another source of disturbing visual stress.

Architectural interior features of colour and texture will modify the overall quality of light. Bland, vanilla colour schemes may be soporific and will tend to dull the senses. Dark muddy colours absorbing too much reflective light can create a feeling of gloom and depression; strong, intense primary colours can be visually too demanding, which will contribute to the symptoms of stress, fatigue and eye strain. When viewing the internal and external colour schemes in some of our modern buildings, the impression is that the architect selected the colours on the basis of subjective preferences or current fashion rather than a profound basic understanding of the effect of colour on our body, spirit and mind.

The subconscious eye is constantly seeking to counterbalance any one predominant colour. For example a green room demands a small splash of red, orange requires blue, yellow needs violet – these are pairs of 'contrasting colours', so called because they are directly opposite each other on the colour circle. If you stare at, say, a blue-coloured disk and after a few seconds transfer your gaze to a sheet of white paper you will see the exact image replicated but in the colour orange. The same will happen with a shape of any colour – the transferred image will always appear in the contrasting colour because the eye needs to 'adjust' to neutral grey. (All the pigment colours of the rainbow mixed together will make neutral grey, whereas all the seven rainbow colours of light will make white light). Operating-theatre staff wear green gowns because the surgeons and staff are subjected to looking at amorphous patterns of blood. If they wore white gowns, whenever they averted their eyes from the area of the bloody incision on to their clothing they would experience a temporary visual confusion because the same image of blood would appear as a contrasting green colour. Green gowns neutralise the blood image thus avoiding temporary 'blindness'.

This colour also induces a calmness and balance – why else do theatres have a 'green room' where actors wait before going on stage?

So what influences our choice of favourite colours for clothing or interior décor, and are these preferences purely subjective? When we choose to wear a yellow dress, a blue tie or a pink shirt, do we select a garment for that day because it is the only one clean or most readily to hand, or are we intuitively 'knowing' that we need that colour's particular vibrational frequency to match our mood or to boost our vitality? Every colour, as with every sound, has its own unique wavelength that we can sense and distinguish through the subliminal receptors in the body. The subtle energy field surrounding our body radiates colour vibrations that fluctuate and change in intensity depending on our state of health and emotions. Whether one can actually see this array of colours – the 'aura' – surrounding the physical body or perhaps intuitively sense its presence is not important, however, some highly tuned sensitive people are in fact able to 'read' these bands of radiating colours. In *The Cosmic Serpent,* Jeremy Narby suggests that DNA emits photons that correspond exactly to the narrow band of visible light. The intensity of the light is equal to 'that of a candle at a distance of about 10 kilometres (6 miles), but is highly coherent' and acts like 'an ultra-weak laser'. Narby links DNA photon emissions to consciousness, which 'could be the electromagnetic fields constituted by the sum of these emissions'.[20] Could this be a possible scientific explanation for the phenomenon of the aura? (see Chapter 7, 'Subtle bodies', page 153).

Geopathic stress

Phases of the Moon, solar flares, magnetic storms and other planetary movements and the Earth's relative position to the Sun create variations in the rise and fall of the magnetic field that affect the biological rhythms in all living organisms. These natural fields are extra or very low frequencies and relate closely to the same frequencies as human brainwaves.

The Earth's magnetic force-lines emanate from the North to the South Pole like the meridians of longitude. The great circles of horizontal meridian lines around the Earth like straight patterns of latitude are known as the 'solar net'. These meridians are between a few metres to over 2 kilometres apart; they cannot be detected after sundown and are considered to be alignments sometimes known as 'ley-lines'. It is believed that this network pattern also covers the oceans and provides a magnetic reference grid for navigation by all sea creatures.[21]

An English solicitor, Guy Underwood, born in England in 1883, turned to researching genealogical trees and building electrical apparatus: in later life he became a well-known archaeologist and dowser (water diviner). In his book *Patterns of the Past,* Underwood points out that deer, mice and pheasants, among other creatures, prefer to move along certain tracks and pathways, which suggests that ley-lines are a concentration of subtle earth currents of electromagnetic or electrostatic fields.[23]

Eminent ophthalmologist and Fellow of the Royal Society of Medicine, Ann Silk (see also pages 64, 91, 114 and 122), believes that the existence of Earth energy fields has the support of the scientific work of geophysicists and seismologists worldwide since the nineteenth century. She quotes NASA satellite images of energy waves from earthquakes and fault movements that travel vertically and horizontally along and through the plates: the planet is circled with measurable magnetic waves. She also suggests that science supports these views, as set out under 'Geoelectricity' in the McGraw Hill *Encyclopaedia of Science and Technology*, 1995.[23]

Further evidence from a 1993 paper by Professor Zaffanella, *Survey of Residential Magnetic Field Sources*,[24] suggests that electric or telluric Earth currents can be either natural or caused by buildings, quarrying, reservoir loading and electric trains, which can reactivate faults to generate piezoelectricity. The cause may be due to high electrical conductivity deposits in the earth, such as certain metallic sulphides and graphites, and the oxidation processes associated with groundwater.[25]

It is believed that the network of energy fields that cover the Earth's crust is like the fine pattern of pores on our skin. At a more subtle level, the network can be likened to the invisible veins of energy in the human body – known in acupuncture as 'meridians' – for it connects the focal points of positive and negative earth energies in much the same way as the meridians connect the human body's power centres or chakras (see pages 128, 148 and 154). Probably the most often quoted networks are the Hartmann Grid and the Curry Net.

The Hartmann Grid and the Curry Net

Born in Mannheim, Germany, in 1915, Dr Ernst Hartmann studied medicine in Heidelberg. He was a prisoner during the Second World War and afterwards began intensive studies of geobiology. In 1961 he founded the research centre Forschungskreis Fuer Geobiologie to promote lectures, seminars and carry out research to show how human well-being (the mind, body and soul) interacts with the cosmos, the atmosphere, the weather and characteristics of the environment. Other factors such as the interplay of culture, civilisation, the earth energies and the actual location of one's own home were also included in the comprehensive studies. In addition to his medical practice and research work in 1968 he began editing a magazine, *Wetter-Boden-Mensch* (Weather-Ground-Human). His book, *Illness as a Problem of Location*[26] deals with the biophysical forces of the earth energy fields, their impact on the body's organs and their contribution to triggering illnesses and the degeneration or mutation of cells. Hartmann expressed deep concern that the inter-relationship of all natural and artificially generated electromagnetic fields with all living organisms needed to be addressed, evaluated and brought into our conscious awareness for the safeguard and benefit of evolution and ecology.

Before his death in 1992, Hartmann wrote '*Yin Yang: On Constitution and Reaction Types*,[27] in which he set out his research on global grid patterns and geopathic stress zones.

The Hartmann Grid, rediscovered in 1950, is a global pattern of North–South and East–West axes crossing about 2 metres apart on the North–South line and 1.5 metres apart on the East–West line in temperate latitudes. The North–South axis converges towards the magnetic poles and the length of the East–West axis varies accordingly. Hartmann described the lines as the Earth's aura.

His forty years of research and extensive medical records led Hartmann to conclude that the Hartmann Grid was governed by the phases of the Moon, sunspot activity, the local weather and the influence of environmental pollution. The effect of the grid energy pattern will penetrate the full height of an entire building, and there is strong evidence to suggest that long-term work or sleeping positions over points located where the axes intersect can be hazardous to health. (Numerous well-attested cases of illness are included in Hartmann's *Illness as a Problem of Location*.) In Germany it is usual practice for geobiologists (dowsers) to check the site where a patient lives and sleeps. The recommended remedy is to detect the grids and then relocate the working or sleeping positions in the neutral zones within the grid patterns.[28]

Other independent research carried out by Dr Whitmann and Dr Manfred Curry (1900–1953) at the Medical and Bio-Climate Institute in Southern Germany, resulted in the rediscovery of a 4.5-metre (15-feet) grid pattern diagonal to the Hartmann lines. Known as the Curry Net, this grid has Northeast–Southwest and Southeast–Northwest axes.

Curry's Irish-American parents emigrated from Boston, New England, to Munich, Bavaria, where he studied medicine. While still a student he invented the 'land skiff' (a bicycle driven by rowing movements); a weather watch; the 'Curry clamp'; the 'Curry brake' and various types of sails still used in boats today. An accomplished Olympic sailor, he became a doctor of medicine when he was thirty, and five years later began research into the environmental factors influencing our health. He wrote a number of books and directed several films.

The Hartmann and Curry network bands have both a negative and positive charge. Where similar charges of the two grids intersect, the disturbance or interference magnifies the contamination effect, especially where they coincide with underground water crossings.

Geopathic stress zones are most likely to be found where there are geological fault lines, fissures in the rock formation, mineral seams and varying strata and subterranean streams flowing in sand or silicone where there will be varying degrees of pressures and geophysical perturbations. All these factors can affect the thermic radiation and magnetic field characteristics of a particular place. Therefore, at certain times and in certain locations, the energy-field strength or vibrations will change. This unique effect determines whether the 'spin' of a location's energy field is positive or negative and thus creates either benign 'zones of resonance' or malign 'interference patterns', which impact upon all matter and living organisms. The affected area can vary in size from a few square metres to a large region. Areas which have a negative spin – that is, are malign – are known as 'geopathic stress zones'.

Modern infrared thermometers can detect and measure the changing spectrum of a location's energy field and whether it is either a positive or negative spin. Where geological fault lines occur, a clockwise spin will have a positive resonance with the human body. This would enhance a sense of well-being, tending to make us feel connected with the spirit of the natural world, and the release of certain endocrine gland secretions could induce psychic and spiritual experiences. Sites and buildings recognised as being sacred and beneficial, including notable religious temples such as the cathedrals at Chartres and Bourges, are built precisely over a well or crossing underground streams, or, as in the case of Aachen, over beneficial, positive hot springs. On the other hand, at a location where there is an anti-clockwise or negative spin the interference pattern of the energy field will create the opposite effect.

Underground streams, even those flowing sluggishly, generate a weak electromagnetic field: the current build-up concentrates the thermic neutron radiation from deep within the Earth and generally sets up a negative, anti-clockwise spin. Some researchers believe negative 'earth rays' are secondary radiations caused by cosmic rays striking subterranean water. Others maintain that the rays are diffuse emanations from inside the Earth which have become concentrated and directed upward by subterranean water currents. At the Academy of Agriculture in Warsaw, Poland, Professor Jerzy Mazurckak developed an apparatus to measure the spontaneous photon emission of biological organisms, and discovered that plants, animals and even minerals reacted to geopathic stress radiation with increased photon activity.[29]

Geopathic stress can perhaps best be described as naturally occurring meandering bands or veins of energy, in the form of a faint electrical charge, that have a noxious or detrimental effect on the extremely subtle electrical balance in the human body. Long-term exposure to geopathic stress can be seriously detrimental to health and could be responsible for up to 50 per cent of the damage to the immune system, along with other health hazards such as radon gas, the effects of electromagnetic fields, stress, poor diet, smoking and excessive drinking. The prolific American inventor Thomas Edison (1847–1931), known especially in the field of generated electricity, the light bulb and radio transmission, issued warnings that alternating electrical currents – that is, artificially generated electromagnetic fields – and their interaction with geopathic stress lines could be linked to the incidence of cancer. Extensive research and certain medical opinion confirms that a connection exists between geobiological earth radiation and chronic illness. Although certain diseases are not necessarily directly attributable to the location of grid zones and subterranean water, such harmful rays can trigger the start of the illness by weakening the immune system. The symptoms associated with geopathic stress include:

- Sense of apathy and lack of energy even after a long sleep
- Restless sleep
- Depression
- Muscular pains
- Headaches
- Rheumatism and arthritis
- Muscular Sclerosis
- Cancer
- Poor response to medical treatment.

The effect of geopathic radiation on biological organisms became the subject of a Polish state financed central research programme coordinated by the Polytechnic in Szczecin (Stettin). The scientific investigation into the harmful effects of subterranean water veins and global grids included various tests to examine the position of the beds of patients who had died of cancer. At one hospital, where a patient's bed was located over the crossing of interference zones, the tests showed a steep rise in the magnetic field. After the removal of the spring mattress and the iron bed frame with wire netting, the magnetic radiation was reduced by one sixth. The results, published in 1989, formed the basis of new guidelines for Polish town planners, architects and construction engineers.[30]

An investigative report into the high incidence of cancer in the town of Bilbiburg in Bavaria was published by Baron Von Pohl.[31] Von Pohl's investigations, carried out in 1928 under strict test conditions, showed that all the dwellings where cancer deaths had taken place were located over strong earth rays. With amazing accuracy he was able to predict the actual room in the house and even the position of the bed used by the cancer patients. A later study, published in 1992 by Dr H. A. Nieper, President of the German Society of Oncology, showed that about 90 per cent of all cancer patients had been found to be sleeping over geopathic stress zones. In July 1993, Dr Dubrov, a Russian biophysicist, and author of *The Geomantic Field of Life*, was one of the speakers at the British Society of Dowsers' International Diamond Jubilee congress in York when he confirmed similar findings and conclusions.[32]

Von Pohl extended his research to include the effect of geopathic stress on animals, plants and insects. He concluded that with the exception of cats, who tend to seek out and enjoy geopathic zones, all other domesticated and farm animals, including poultry, birds and fish, are highly sensitive to and react strongly against negative earth rays. Insects, parasites, viruses and bacteria are geopathic stress ray seekers; bees are also attracted and the radiation in honey output will give a clear indication as to which hives are located over zone lines. Oak trees grow best and thrive over subterranean water crossings. In a forest of 11 per cent oaks and 70 per cent beech trees, of all lightning strikes 58 per cent were on the oaks and only 6 per cent struck the beech trees. As lightning is naturally attracted to underground water streams, this suggests that strikes against oaks are neither random nor haphazard. If apple and pear trees bloom but do not fruit, or a tree has cankerous or poor, twisted growth, it is likely they are growing over a line of geopathic stress. Rural folklore has it that when selecting a piece of land for a building site, sheep were driven into the field: if they were peaceful and stayed calm overnight it was considered to be a good place to build. The likelihood that the siting of any barn, livestock shed or stable could affect the health and output of farm animals was borne out by a report from the former USSR where, in one case, of the 35,000 cows suffering from mastitis 78 per cent were confined to barn areas affected by geopathic stress.[33]

Another researcher, Kathe Bachler, a dedicated teacher and educational leader from Austria who trained in mathematics and science, was deeply concerned about whether the poor academic performance of certain children could be attributed to geopathic stress zones. She was given a grant from the School of Education, Salzburg, to devote herself full time to this work. Her studies, supported by many teachers, physicians, psychologists and parents, covered 11,000 cases in over 3,000 homes in 14 countries, all carefully catalogued, cross-referenced and well documented. Her findings were published in 1988[34] and clearly showed that schools built over certain earth rays and global grids had a measurable influence on the health and academic achievements of both children and adults. Further research led her to believe that the environmental factors of climate, weather conditions, materials used in buildings, electrical appliances as well as geopathic stress have a far greater effect than is generally recognised. She also believed that even malicious thoughts and emotional stress can contribute to our illnesses, whereas good, loving and non-judgemental thoughts will have a healing, beneficial effect.

German organisation Internationaler Arbeitskreis fuer Geobiologie e.V held its first congress in Andernach in May 1990. The following is a translation by Ilse Pope (12 July 1990) from a report by the Chairman of its Working Party on Geobiology and Building Ecology, Hofrat Professor Dr Emil Worsch:

> Regarding the geobiological connection between earth radiation and chronic disease, in particular cancer, it could be shown, as already reported two years ago, but now with even greater precision, that at least the starting cause of these diseases is very closely connected with the radiation complex habitually found in cancer zones and at cancer points. Here it was found again and again that the so-called double Curry zones, in connection with radiation from water, but sometimes also without this, were the main cause. Of approximately 600 cancer cases which I investigated, there were less than 5% which had no connection with the radiation situation outlined above.

In addition, infrared aerial photography carried out over the medieval town of Regensberg in Sweden in 1981 has shown that the ancient meandering streets follow precisely the lines of underground water courses. Was it coincidental or by accident that all the buildings were located away from the potentially harmful geopathic stress rays created by the subterranean streams?

What to do

Initially, you should trust your own intuition: if you are suffering from low energy, restless sleep or recurring health problems it could well be that the position of your favourite chair or your bed is located over a geopathic stress line. Often we are attracted to geopathic zones in the same manner as we can become allergic to the foods we enjoy the most. Cats are prone to seek out geopathic lines: their favourite place to sleep at night or curl up during the day may be an indication of a potentially harmful position.

A geopathic vein may be a very narrow band snaking across the corner of a room: here it is relatively easy to move the chair or bed into a neutral area. If the arrangement of wardrobe cupboards, a window or the door prevent the bed from being repositioned there are other ways to reduce the impact of the harmful rays: change the metal bed frame or springs to a wood construction; line the underside of the mattress with aluminium foil or board out the frame with a cork lining. Sometimes the strategic placement of a quartz crystal in the room can be effective.

In his book *The Secret of Life* (1925), the Russian-born French radio engineer Georges Lakhovsky put forward the view that all living organisms emit and receive radiations and are capable of detecting them.[35] During the First World War, carrier pigeons often became confused or lost when operating in areas where the first wireless transmitters were being used. Lakhovsky discovered canals in the pigeon's head that function like an aerial antennae with an extremely weak oscillating electrical circuit. When a pigeon was released it circled three times before setting off. This led him to believe that the brain canals were activated by flight, and as the bird flew through varying electric and magnetic areas in space these provided the navigational information to guide it home. (The early type of wireless effectively jammed the natural electromagnetic signals over a several-mile radius.) Lakhovsky deduced that these canal structures radiating and resonating electromagnetic wavelengths were part of the physiology of all living organisms and that the oscillations determine the quality of health or 'life field'. He believed that exposure and intake of pollution and toxins due to lifestyle, diet and environmental conditions, including certain locations of rock attracting high-energy cosmic radiation where conductivity was confused, would weaken the life field and trigger disease and death.

Based on his understanding that living cells are structures with oscillating circuits that both radiate and resonate with electromagnetic radiation of varying wavelengths he invented the Lakhovsky Coil – a single spiral of copper wire designed to act as a shield to protect the wearer against adverse geopathic stress by means of induction of out-of-phase radiations that cancelled them out. This oscillating circuit was shown to be successful for plants and animals as well as human beings. Lakhovsky also found that multiple-frequency broadband ultra-short radio waves could stimulate plant growth and health. Lakhovsky fled Paris for New York in 1941 and died a year later. It was not until the 1970s, when his other invention, the 'multiple wave oscillator' (MWO) was unearthed in New York, that his genius became known.

An American researcher into biological communication systems based on electromagnetic radiation, Professor Philip Callahan, served in the US Military on radio beam stations in Northern Ireland in 1943 and later in Japan, and unknowingly worked on almost parallel lines to Lakhovsky in his book *Tuning into Nature*.[36] Callahan discovered that healthy, well-oxygenated plants do not attract overwhelming insect attacks provided a natural diversity of insect control organisms and their support vegetation is present. He concluded that as insects are genetically programmed to respond to mainly infrared stimuli, their behaviour could be controlled by electronic means that are non-polluting. His other work concerned the properties of soils. Callahan pointed out that fertile soils are paramagnetic and all infertile soils are diamagnetic. (The magnetic susceptibility of materials to applied magnetic forces is a measure of the conductivity of these materials to magnetic and electromagnetic energies.) Igneous rocks such as granite and basalt are usually the most paramagnetic types of soil. As diamagnetic materials have no magnetic field, they weaken an applied magnetic field and so have a negative susceptibility. On the other hand, ferromagnetic materials, due to their crystalline structures, strongly enhance an applied magnetic field.[37]

A number of devices for protecting the wearer or their property are now available, claiming to rebalance and neutralise the effects of geopathic stress and generated electromagnetic fields. There is no known scientific proof that any of these products are effective, but personal testimonies indicate that they may possibly have a beneficial influence on our biological functions.

Dowsing

Experienced dowsers offer a geopathic survey service, whereby they will mark up a drawing of the room, the building or the site to show where any harmful lines are located. Depending on the situation, a dowser may prescribe the use of steel spikes, copper coils, magnets, metal rods or stones being staked into the ground to divert the veins away from the areas where the occupants are most vulnerable. Alternatively, you could become a dowser yourself, starting with some of the various courses offered to beginners by the many reputable dowsing organisations such as the British Society of Dowsers.

To maintain a healthy, prosperous environment it is necessary to discover the presence of any harmful energy fields in our intended place of residence or work, or where we keep livestock or plant crops, and then take action to avoid or neutralise them. Modern science has developed an array of specialised techniques such as infrared photography, terrestrial radar, geomagnometers, Geiger counters, seismic meters, ultrasonic and microwave detectors, however, this equipment is expensive, generally needs highly trained operators, and can detect only a fairly limited range of frequencies. The simplest method for detecting and evaluating earth energies and geognostic properties of the land is the age-old art or science of dowsing – sometimes called 'divining' – described by dowsers as 'the art of knowing'. Positive and negative lines, underground springs, subterranean streams, geological faults, mineral deposits, pipes and archaeological remains can all be detected by an experienced, well-trained dowser with surprising accuracy. Experiments comparing a scientist operating electronic equipment and an expert dowser using a pair of rods or a pendulum to detect a magnetic earth energy ray or an underground stream have shown that the dowser was not only as accurate as the scientist but also carried out the work and produced the results in a fraction of the time and at a fraction of the cost.

Prehistoric cave paintings, ancient Egyptian hieroglyphics and sculptures, biblical writings, medieval woodcuts and other historical documents show dowsing as a usual means to find sources of water and track earth energy fields. Before we developed the technology for building aqueducts, transcontinental conduits, desalination plants and installed a vast underground network of piped water, the responsibility for guaranteeing adequate and good quality water to supply a new town or rural community depended solely on the expertise of dowsers. Two thousand years ago, Vitruvius, the Roman architect and engineer, wrote detailed instructions on the various methods he used for dowsing a site for water. However, in the sixteenth century Martin Luther denounced dowsing as the work of the devil, since when the Western world has treated it with caution. (The French translation of 'water spring' is 'La Source' or

'*Eau de Source*', and a dowser is known as a *sourcier* or *sorcier*. This word is repatriated across the English channel as 'sorcerer' – one who dabbles in black magic.)

In the rural areas of many parts of the world it is still commonplace for farmers, builders and architects to use the services of a dowser, or indeed practise dowsing themselves. In his talk given at the International Diamond Jubilee Congress in York in July 1993 (reported in the British Society of Dowsers magazine, September 1994), Dr Alexander Dubrov spoke of the long history of dowsing in Russia and the Commonwealth of Independent States where dowsing (referred to as 'biolocation') continues to be used extensively for finding water, mineral deposits, archaeology and detecting leaks in underground pipework and transcontinental pipelines. In the nineteenth century Empress Katerina II issued a proclamation that a dowsing rod must be included in the Coat of Arms of the City of Petrozavodsk, and in 1960 the USSR government set up a Ministry of Geology to provide a foundation for the official recognition of dowsing. Dr Dubrov listed the continuing wide-ranging research work, practical operations and training programmes to highlight the increasing level and widespread dowsing activity being pursued in Russia.

Many Western farmers and most water boards continue to use dowsers. UK and US oil and gas companies extensively and very successfully use dowsers to find new drilling locations both on land and at sea. Although few of the major companies are willing to admit to the use of dowsers, some of the larger fields have been discovered by this method. Roche Pharmaceuticals used a dowser to locate water for its new industrial plant, and Honda brought dowsers from Japan to identify the most favourable siting of its new factory in Swindon, UK.[38]

During the Vietnam War, dowsers were trained to find Vietcong tunnels and hidden arms; dowsers were used in the Falklands War to detect 'undetectable' plastic mines; the Ministry of Defence used dowsers to search for anthrax-infected horses during the Second World War; the Ministry of Agriculture used dowsers to find swine fever corpses hidden by a farmer; police forces in several countries, including the US and Europe, use dowsers to assist their detective work; and many important archaeological finds have been discovered by dowsing. Sir Geoffroy Tory, a British naval intelligence officer, used map dowsing to locate nuclear submarines. It sounds very bizarre but it appears these exploits met with a considerable degree of success.

German, French and Austrian medical practitioners use dowsers in their healthcare programmes and architects and engineers from those countries are trained to locate harmful earth rays on building sites. The Municipal Authorities in Russia and Poland also have regular training programmes to teach dowsing to student architects and engineers.

But generally speaking, our modern urban architects and engineers do not concern themselves with the qualities of the land, and the only geognostic exploration deemed necessary is to drill for samples of the subsoil to determine its load-bearing capacity for foundations. They also rely exclusively on the records kept at the local municipal or utility company's offices to find the location of water mains and other underground services. No wonder the ancient skill of dowsing has been largely abandoned.

Scientists and researchers have put forward several hypotheses in an attempt to explain how dowsing works. One theory well supported by a number of scientific experiments suggests that the wide spectrum of electric and magnetic fields and electromagnetic radiation can be picked up by the nervous system in the human body, and the experienced dowser has learned to identify particular signals according to a personal set of codings and physical responses. In other words, dowsing is a combination of physical (material) and mental (psychic) responses registered by a natural, neurological reaction in the body. All of us are constantly reacting involuntarily to the most subtle information received from natural phenomena, but we do not necessarily consciously register the signals. Dowsers, however, are trained to become aware of the faintest response and use tools such as bent rods, a pendulum, forked hazel or willow twigs to 'amplify' the information. The tools can be made of any material because all they do is respond to the minutest movement of the dowser's hand or wrist caused by the nervous system in the arm muscles. Some dowsers experience a gripping sensation in the solar plexus, a twitch in the forearm, or some other indication in the body. Undoubtedly the brain and all the neurophysiological sensors come into play, particularly the pineal gland as the main receptor.

Where water flows through a pipe or in an underground conduit, minute electrical vibrations are discharged in the range of between 1 and 12Hz. Our brainwaves, operating on a similar frequency, set up a resonance with the flow of water. When dowsing for geological faults, the piezoelectrical discharge caused by the Earth's plates squeezing against each other can also be registered in the brain. How dowsing works when searching for archaeological remains and other static inert material such as a buried pipe may be difficult to accept but, as we have seen earlier, everything has a vibrational quality and evidence backed up by personal experience indicates that if we focus our attention the mind can achieve the most remarkable insights. In *Dowsing: New Light on an Ancient Art*, Tom Williamson, a geological consultant, wrote about German researchers who suggest that experienced dowsers can detect the low frequency vibrations produced by the geological murmurings of the Earth often found near water-bearing features such as fault lines.[39]

Until relatively recently, the idea that humans may be sensitive to weak magnetic fields was not accepted, but American scientists have now found tiny magnets inside the human brain, and other research at Manchester University suggests that we do indeed have the faculty for navigation by magnetic fields. The ancient art/science of acupuncture has used magnets in healing practices, and the idea that whales and other creatures, including insects, use their equivalent of the pineal gland to navigate the Earth's magnetic radiation is a well-established science.[40]

Another theory based on parapsychology, psychic phenomenon and our 'sixth sense' or 'third eye' faculties may go some way towards explaining how map dowsing – that is, 'knowledge at a distance' – works. For example, those dowsers who have successful track records for locating oil and gas fields at sea or in vast tracks of land, initially use maps to 'traverse' an area before pinpointing the actual drill rig positions on-site. Sometimes even the pinpointing is done from a helicopter or high-flying aircraft. This seems to defy all logic and reasoning but there is no doubt that it works and to a high degree of accuracy. In his *The Electric Shock Book* Michael Shallis refers to map dowsing thus: 'Map dowsing is no different from field dowsing. The map is a symbolic representation of the landscape, the landscape is a symbolic representation of a non-material and higher reality. The mystery of map dowsing is removed once it is recognised that all forms of dowsing, including radionics and radiesthesia are a means of tapping into the ethereal world, which itself is expressed in physical reality and then further represented by visual symbols. Dowsing is a means of connecting the human dowser to the subtle forces of nature'.[41]

In *Beyond Supernature*, marine biologist and zoologist Dr Lyall Watson provides a biophysical explanation to the many examples of animals having extraordinary sensitivity to water and their ability to dowse for underground sources at times of drought.[42] This was highlighted in a TV documentary showing elephants walking for miles in dried up scrubland. After several days they came to a dusty patch of land, skirted around the area and then began to pound the dirt. They dug to a depth of about 2 metres (6 feet) and suddenly water began to seep into the hole. Soon the elephants and other animals were drinking and bathing in a deep pool in the middle of the most arid terrain.

Dowsing brings to us an awareness of the subtle earth energies and heightens our respect for the natural environment and the subtle forces that can affect our health and sense of well-being. The past decade has seen the developing interest in dowsing, which may be a small milestone marking our return journey to the ancient wisdom of learning how to live in harmony with nature.

Everyone has the natural ability to dowse: in fact we are 'dowsing' all the time except we are not consciously registering the minute fluctuations in the body that influence our reactions to a given situation, for example when we walk over a subterranean stream or geopathic stress line. In everyday life we naturally filter out the subtle signals, otherwise we would be overwhelmed by a constant barrage of 'information', but we can re-learn how to tune into the subtle signals of natural phenomena provided we focus our attention on the specific details we need to know. Even though you may not be conscious of your innate dowsing ability, when you next go into a building or walk over the land, become aware of the 'feeling' of the minute reactions in your body. Initially it does not take long to learn the bare rudiments of dowsing, though it does take a long time of dedicated practice to become a reliable, expert dowser.

We live in an age when logic and materialistic rationality tend to downgrade or dismiss outright the inestimable value of our innate awareness. Today we would rather refer to 'gut feelings' or something 'not smelling right' rather than our intuitive sense. Dowsing is a personal experience of intuition at work. It needs training and practice as well as a degree of trust in one's own intuitive sense. The more we encourage the development of our intuition (our sixth sense) we begin to listen more carefully to the 'quiet inner voice' and regain our awareness of nature's natural forces. Whether you want to dabble in dowsing as a game of harmless fun just to experience the phenomenon of the intuitive mind at work, or whether you want to become a professional dowser, it has the value of increasing our conscious awareness of the natural unseen world about us. At the very least, if your body becomes sensitive to the Earth's energy fields you will be able to detect and avoid any harmful geopathic stress lines that may be present in your home or place of work

References

1. BBC Ceefax, 30 July 1999.
2. Stephen Bevan and Kevin Dowling, 'Boeing tries to cut fresh air on planes', *The Sunday Times*, 11 July 1999.
3. Jon Ungoed-Thomas, 'Altitude sickness', *The Sunday Times*, 7 May 2000, p. 22.
4. Robert Uhlig, *The Daily Telegraph*, 29 July 1999.
5. Nichola Gill, 'Breathe easy', *The Sunday Times* 'Style' magazine, 25 June 2000.
6. Stephan White, 'No power noise: EU set to tackle loud machinery', *The Mirror*, 24 May 1999.
7. Simmonds, Mark, Senior Lecturer, Environmental Studies, University of Greenwich.
8. Tomatis International Headquarters, 144 Avenue des Champs Elysées, Paris 75008, France.
9. Peter Gruner, 'Now hear this: noises of the city can cause heart failure', *Evening Standard*, 9 October 1998. See also Deepak Prasher, 'New strategies for prevention and treatment of noise-induced hearing loss', *The Lancet*, 352 (9136), 17 October 1998, pp. 1240–42; and Deepak Prasher, 'Protection against noise; a European Commission concerted action', *International Journal of Occupatonal Environmental Health*, 12(1), 1999, pp. 93–95.
10. Trushar Bardot, 'Songbirds forget their tunes in cacophony of road noise', *The Sunday Times*, 10 January 1999.
11. The Musicians Union Noise Awareness for Orchestral Musicians, November 1998.
12. Hall, Manly P. (1997) *The Secret Teachings of All Ages*, Los Angeles: The Philosophical Research Society, p. LXXXiii–iv.
13. Allanach, Jack (1997) *Colour Me Healing*, Dorset: Element Books.
14. Niggli, Hugh (1998) 'Biophotons: Our body produces light', *Scientific and Medical Network Review*, no. 68, December 1998, pp. 16–17.
15. *Daily Telegraph*, 5 May 1999. Report on research by Professor Richard Stone of the Scheie Eye Institute, Pennsylvania Clinic, Philadelphia.
16. Mark Rowe, 'Artificial light "may cause cancer"', *The Independent on Sunday*, 1 August 1999, p. 5.
17. Miller, Cynthia L. *et al.* (1995) *Infant Behaviour and Development* 18, 87–95, University of Notre Dame, Indiana.
18. David O. Webber, 'Life enhancing design', *Color Luminosity & Color Perspective*, The Health Care Forum, p. 6, para. 6 (undated).
19. Liberman, J. (1991) *Light: Medicine of the Future*, Santa Fe: Bear & Co.
20. Narby, Jeremy (1999) *The Cosmic Serpent*, London: Phoenix.
21. Downer, John (1999), *SuperNatural*, London: BBC Worldwide.
22. Underwood, Guy (1968), *Patterns of the Past*, London: Museum Press.
23. *McGraw Hill Encyclopaedia of Science and Technology* (1995) McGraw Hill Publishing.
24. Zaffanella, *Survey of Residential Magnetic Field Sources*, vol. 1, 'Goals, Results, Conclusions', EPRI Research Project 3335-02 EPRITR-102759-VI.
25. A. Silk, 'Earth energies – the facts', *The Journal of the British Society of Dowsers*, vol. 39. no. 270 (December 2000), p. 9.
26. Hartmann, E. (1964) *Illness as a Problem of Location*, Heidelberg: Karl F. Haug Verlag.
27. Hartmann, E. (1991) *Yin Yang: On Constitution and Reaction Types*, Munich: Forschungskreis Fuer Geobiologie e V.
28. Hartmann, E. (1976) *Geobiologisher Arbeitskeis Kassel*, Verlag Haug.
29. Prof. J. Mazurckak, 'Earth Radiation in the Laboratory', trans. Ilse Pope, *Zeitschrift Fuer Radiaesthesie*, no. IV, October–December 1998, p. 13.
30. Ibid.
31. Von Pohl, Baron (1932) *Earth Currents, Causative Factor of Cancer and Other Diseases*, Stuttgart: Frech-Verlag.
32. Dubrov, A. (1998) *The Geomantic Field of Life*, trans. Frank L. Sinclair, New York: Plenum Press.
33. Gordon, R. (1989) *Are You Sleeping in a Safe Place?*, London: The Dulwich Health Society.
34. Bachler, K. (1989) *Earth Radiation*, Manchester: Wordmasters.
35. Lakhovsky, G. (1986) *The Secret Life*, trans. L. Reiper, Society of Metaphysicians.

36. Callahan, P. (1975) *Tuning in to Nature*, US: Devin-Adair.
37. Sangster, Hugh, 'The electricity of life', *Rilko* 45, pp. 8-12. First published in *Nexus* magazine, 1993.
38. *The Scientific and Medical Newsletter* 1997.
39. Williamson, T. (1993) *Dowsing: New Light on an Ancient Art*, London: Robert Hale.
40. Roger Highfield, 'A butterfly with built-in compass', reporting on a study by Professor Orley Taylor and colleagues at the University of Kansas, published in the *Proceedings of the National Academy of Sciences, The Daily Telegraph*, 23 November 1999.
41. Shallis, M. (1988) *The Electric Shock Book*, London: Souvenir Press.
42. Watson, Lyall (1986) *Beyond Supernature,* London: Hodder & Stoughton.

Suggested further reading

Publications on BREEAM reports, Building Research Establishment, Garston, England.
Thurnell-Read, J. (1996) *Geopathic Stress*, Dorset: Element Books.

3.
Electromagnetic radiation

The cosmic energy field

Life on Earth is a constituent part of an integrated universal radiation system in which terrestrial energy fields interact with fields of cosmic energy – alpha, beta, gamma and neutron rays with light, infrared, microwave radiation – originating from the Sun, Moon, planets and the Milky Way. All these forms of radiation create 'zones of resonance', or 'patterns of interference', which affect all physical matter, including rocks, soil, plants, animals and human beings. Without these interacting, unseen and extremely weak fields of subtle energy we would not exist, plants could not survive, birds and animals could not navigate, turtles could not return after 30 years at sea to the beach where they were hatched, and the tides of the oceans would not rise and fall.

Modern physics has defined the principal cosmic forces as gravitation, electromagnetism, the weak electric force, and the strong force. Although modern electronic equipment, radio telescopes and space probes have enabled us to discover and evaluate the cosmic energies generated by the Sun, Moon, planets and stars, at present the source of these fundamental forces of nature remains a mystery. Gravity and geomagnetism are the two forces exerting direct influences on both animate and inanimate objects: gravity is attraction, magnetism is both attraction and repulsion. (Sir Isaac Newton, famous for his discovery of gravity, put forward a little-known interpretation of attraction and magnetism: he concluded that stones and indeed all other matter possessed a 'soul'.)

An energy field is emitted from everything regardless of size or substance, and modern electronics equipment can measure the wavelength and frequency radiated from each object. At a fundamental level, everything on our planet – rocks, metals, plants, animals and human beings – emits its own life-sustaining electromagnetic field (EMF). When two or more objects are in close proximity their respective energy fields become modified by interaction to produce one combined, larger energy field. In the case of the heavenly bodies, the cosmic fluctuations and energy fields vary as their relative positions constantly change, in turn affecting the global energy field of the Earth. The geological structure and the variations to the natural landscape also interact and create modifications to the Earth's energy field. Therefore at certain times and in certain places the vibrations or field strengths will be irregular. The uniqueness of every location is determined by trees, mountains, hills, rivers, underground streams, rock formations, stones and other changes in the environment such as buildings.

The Earth's natural electromagnetic field

The Earth is a huge bar magnet. As it rotates around its polar axis the planet's molten core acts like a dynamo, producing an electrical current around the globe, thus creating a natural electromagnetic field. The interaction of the Earth's *geomagnetic* field with solar activity creates the *magnetosphere*, which shields us from the bombardment of harmful cosmic radiation. The magnetosphere does not rotate with the Earth: as the same side is always facing the Sun the geomagnetic field at the Earth's surface constantly changes during the course of a 24-hour period. The Earth's position relative to the Sun, the phases of the Moon, the movement of other planets, solar flares and magnetic storms also create variations in the Earth's magnetic field. The path of the solar wind deflected by the Earth streams out into space like the tail of a comet, setting up variations in the cosmic force fields that again change the strength of the magnetic field as the Earth rotates, thus affecting, at a subtle level, the biological systems of all living things. These natural electromagnetic fields are extremely low and relate closely to the same frequencies as human brainwaves.

The Earth's geomantic field – the subtle energy field patterns on the Earth's surface – also changes with the phases of the Sun and Moon and because the north and south poles are inclined at an angle of 23.5° to the horizontal plane, the seasonal changes and magnetic field fluctuations all add to the matrix of these subtle forces causing unique variations and degrees of concentrations from one location to another, which affect the biological rhythms in all living organisms.

Russian Professor Chezhevsky made a lifetime study of sunspots, collating data from records over 2,400 years. He claimed his research showed that the world's mass movements such as wars, uprisings and revolutions (1789, 1830, 1848, 1870, 1905 and 1917) and the outbreak of the Second World War were significant sunspot dates. Since his death in 1964 we have witnessed worldwide student unrest in 1968; the invasion of Afghanistan in 1979; the Falklands War; the turmoils in Eastern Europe and the USSR; and the Gulf War in 1989/90. All these dates are consistent with the 11-year sunspot cycles.

Lunar phases modulating the Earth's geomagnetic field over a 29.5-day cycle peak at full Moon. In 1954, Professor Frank Brown transported oysters in light-proof containers from the harbour in New Haven, Connecticut, to a dark room in his laboratory in Evanston, 1,600 kilometres (1,000 miles) and one time zone away in the middle of a land mass. At first the oysters opened and closed their valves according to the high and low tide rhythms at New Haven. After two weeks, the rhythm slipped and re-phased to the exact times of lunar zenith and nadir at Evanston – that is, when the Moon would have caused high and low tides at that location. Brown's other experiments with plants and animals showed the effects of weak radiation emanating from cosmic and terrestrial sources, indicating that various organisms, mammals and other marine life are indeed influenced by pervasive weak geomagnetic fields. (Plants seem able to sense the small geomagnetic changes originating in the ionosphere when the Sun rises at dawn.) Brown concluded that a clear boundary does not exist between an organism's metabolic electromagnetic field and those of its physical environment.

Each autumn about 100 million butterflies migrate 4,000 kilometres (2,500 miles) from breeding grounds in the US to central Mexico. Despite being weak fliers and strong winds blowing them off course, they still arrive at the same destination as their ancestors. They make the round trip only once. Research by Professors Orley Taylor *et al.* at the University of Kansas (published in the *Proceedings of the National Academy of Sciences*) has established that migratory insects navigate by the Earth's magnetic field rather than by the Sun, using the magnetic sensors in their head and thorax.[1]

Energy fields are in the form of waves: each wave has its own frequency, amplitude and wavelength and can be likened to an ocean wave or a ripple of water on a lake. When the energy waves emitted from two separate objects are 'in phase' (that is, they are compatible), the resultant energy output is positive, in sequence and 'beneficial'; when the waves are 'out of phase' the combined energy is incoherent, negative and detrimental. Not all living organisms have an adverse reaction to negative energy fields but human beings and many other species need a positive and coherent energy input to maintain health and vitality. A negative signal can set up an interference pattern causing a malfunction to the extremely weak electromagnetic field effects on the brainwaves and cells of the body (see Chapter 2, 'Geopathic stress').

One form of energy, known as the Schumann Wave, was identified in 1952 by German Professor W. O. Schumann, who hypothesised that the interaction between the Earth and the ionosphere created a magnetic radiation resonating at the same, or similar frequencies to human brainwaves. Ten years later the US National Bureau of Standards confirmed the detection of these signals of frequencies around 8 Hertz (Hz), which vary over a 24-hour period due to the phases of the Moon, sunspot activity and relative planetary positions (see 'The electromagnetic field spectrum', page 72, for a definition of Hertz). It is well established that 8Hz is vital and beneficial to all living organisms and coincides with the human brain's alpha rhythm of 8Hz to 12Hz: experiments with animals shielded from the waves have shown disturbed and deteriorated patterns of behaviour. Schumann Waves diminish to zero strength at about 10,000 metres (33,000 feet) above the Earth's surface. Commercial aircraft cruise above this level and later research at NASA found that jet lag distress can be avoided by introducing Schumann Wave stimulators into aircraft cabins. Such devices producing waves at 7.83Hz have been installed in manned spacecraft.

The subatomic universe

Everything in the universe is composed of millions of infinitesimally small atoms. At the centre of each atom is a nucleus which consists of positively charged particles called protons, and neutrons which are electrically neutral, as the name implies. The electrons are negatively charged particles that orbit the nucleus in the form of a wave. The nucleus has the same number of protons as there are electrons outside, making the atom neutral overall. Until the discovery of the electron by J. J. Thomson in 1898, it was thought that the atom was a minute, indivisible 'billiard ball' but the electron, and later the discovery of the proton by Ernest Rutherford in 1914, showed that the atom had an internal structure. When the neutron was discovered by James Chadwick in 1932 it seemed that the universe was built of these three particles; since then physicists have found even smaller components such as the massless photons, hadrons, leptons, quarks, anti-quarks, neutrinos and anti-neutrinos. The neutrino, produced from nuclear reactions lying deep in the centre of the Sun, can travel through everything, including the Earth. Nothing can block the path of a neutrino and about 100 million pass through our body every second, even at night on the dark side of the planet. Solar neutrinos account for about one-fiftieth of the Sun's energy.

It is difficult to imagine the bizarre subatomic world where particles can be in more than one place at the same time, are able to travel through space and yet have no substance. It may be even more difficult to contemplate a solid object of the material world not only being made up of tiny atoms in constant movement with more space than matter between one atom and the next, but also that each atom has even smaller elements moving around the nucleus. The imagination is stretched further by the photon, an elementary particle with spin that travels at the speed of light but has no mass. In other words, it is not made of anything! Colour, like the photon, has no mass either. What makes an object red, another yellow or violet is only the varying electromagnetic frequencies of different wave bands or vibration acting upon the three sensors in our eye registering combinations of red, blue and green.

Although subatomic physics has opened the window on to a phenomenal, almost incredible universe, many areas of modern science repeatedly seem to confirm the view held by the ancient seers: 'As above, so below'. Written thousands of years ago, the basic tenet of the ancient Hindu scriptures known as the *Vedas* (a Sanskrit word meaning 'divine knowledge') is that everything in the universe – the galaxies, stars, planets and all living organisms – has a life force, a consciousness, and that everything interacts with everything else. The ancients respected the Earth as an intelligent living entity, as much alive as every cell in our body, and Jeremy Narby suggests that although a plant may not talk, it has a spirit in it that is conscious, that sees everything, which is the essence of the plant – its essence – that makes it alive.[2]

Electromagnetic fields and paranormal phenomena

The Earth's crust is rich in quartz, the most common form of crystal. Quartz rock formations such as granite have high magnetic and piezoelectric properties. When a weak electrical current is applied to quartz it will expand slightly. When quartz is struck or squeezed under pressure it will emit negative ions that create an electromagnetic field causing the crystal to act as a transducer of energy, converting the electrons into other forms such as ultrasound and light. When strong pressure is applied, the rocks can give off high-voltage piezo discharges. Crystalline rocks forming the continental plates are constantly under pressure due to gravitational pull, the phases of the Moon, the effects of solar wind and other outer-space activity, which sets up positive ionisation and creates fluctuating levels of energy.

'Fault lines' occur where the pressure on the strata of the Earth's surface is relieved, causing piezoelectrical discharges to be squeezed out from the rocks, ionising the air to create luminous rays, 'eerie lights' and fireballs. Eyewitness accounts of these ghostly nocturnal lights range from 'will-o-the-wisp' and 'curious flames' to UFOs. Sceptics are convinced that because many UFO sightings have been located where natural fault lines occur, the blazing lights associated with the phenomenon are actually earth lights or flashes of energy erupting from geological piezoelectrical activity. Sites associated with magical, psychic activities and other phenomena such as haunted houses also seem to occur in locations along geological fault lines.

Ann Silk (see also pages 47, 91, 114 and 122) was deeply interested in ghost sightings and the tricks our eyes can play on us. About one in ten people admit to having seen a ghost with accompanying reports of strange sounds, smells, touch, temperature changes and other psychic phenomena. On the Isle of Wight there are many haunted houses, each of which lies on the geological fault line running roughly east–west along the length of the island. Strange lights, ghostly knockings, footsteps and door openings could be due to the piezoelectric activity generated by the rocks grinding against each other; hair standing on end can also be caused by high levels of this type of static electricity.

A feeling of being icy cold in a haunted room, despite the thermometer recording normal temperatures, may be due to a rogue electromagnetic field reacting on the hypothalamus – the gland regulating our body temperature controlled by the pineal gland. A weak electromagnetic energy field can also enhance psychic processes and induce altered states of consciousness due to the interaction with the pineal and pituitary gland secretions. The pituitary gland governs the onset of puberty when hormonal changes affect the degree of calcification in the body and our teeth and bones begin to harden. Hair, bone, feathers and horn – often used in occult shamanic practices – produce faint electromagnetic pulses that interact with external electromagnetic fields. When we are frightened our hair stands on end! Even the most minute and extremely weak shifts in the natural geomantic field strength, or an artificially generated electrical field, can interfere with the brain's wave patterns causing a trigger release mechanism of the endocrine gland secretions that affect us biologically and emotionally.

Astrophysicist Dr Percy Seymour of Plymouth University believes he has an explanation for the paranormal. In his book *The Paranormal: Beyond Sensory Science*[3] he argues that all matter in the universe leaves an indelible trace in the form of a 'world line', like a permanent wave left by a ship. These permanent tracks of energy leave an imprint on the place where, for example, a person of strong habits and personality had lived. Strong emotion or a violent death may be 'imprinted' on the walls of a house by some electromagnetic field energy. For example, we know an electron can be a wave (energy) or a particle (matter or mass). A particle has an intelligence and can be in two places at the same time and two particles can 'know' what each one is doing as if there is some connecting link between them. Therefore, all atoms and molecules impose different sets of vibrations and patterns on the 'world line' and depending upon a person's sensitivity they can 'tune' in like a radio receiver to all the broadcast wavebands. Seymoure's 'world line' may go some way toward explaining clairvoyance, telepathy and other psychic or 'paranormal' phenomena.

Modern science may convince us that we are closer than ever before to discovering the innermost secrets of the universe, but our understanding of pure energy is still in its infancy. For example, the weird phenomenon known as 'ball lightning' or 'plasma fire' continues to elude scientific explanation and has yet to be reproduced in a laboratory. This extraordinary phenomenon was witnessed by a couple from Norwich in the UK several years ago when they were struck by a blinding flash of lightning. The explosion seemed to come from nowhere, temporarily paralysing them. When the man and his wife recovered after the severe shock, they saw hovering before their eyes a glowing ball of light the size of a tennis ball, floating through the window, across the kitchen, out of the door and down the hall before it glided into a bedroom. Their next-door neighbour had also seen the ball of light in the kitchen before it exploded and blew out the electrics in the house.[4]

A similar incident was reported in North Wales by Gladys Hughes. Gladys was driving home when she ran into a bank of mist rolling off the river and saw a glowing ball of green light, 'the size of a football', spinning forwards like a wheel with four spikes of radiating light. It came within a few centimetres of her side window and as she slowed the car, the ball slowed with her; as she accelerated the ball kept pace. She could not shake it off until she emerged from the mist and the ball suddenly shot up and away out of sight. Others in the locality had also witnessed the strange green light rocketing into the sky. Professor Roger Tennison, an electrical engineer at the University of Kent, confirmed that he and others had witnessed a glowing ball of light aboard a Pan Am flight between New York and Washington: it floated down the aisle from the cockpit and disappeared through the rear toilets. Fear of derision generally prevents such observations from being openly talked about, but there are thousands of similar accounts from around the world.

Usually, ball lightning causes very little damage and appears to be attracted to electrical equipment, especially in confined spaces. Ghostlike, it can even travel through solid matter. Scientists have proffered many theories, but the most likely explanation may be that it is related to the mass of spinning positive and negative charges in the invisible electric field that occurs when we get thunder storms and lightning, or it may be a mass of plasma. Whatever it is, ball lightning, like so many other natural or so-called 'paranormal' phenomena, has yet to be fully understood and explained.

Energy fields and 'sacred' sites

Why do some locations have a magical 'aura' that puts us in touch with a natural vitality or gives us a sense of harmony and well-being, whereas other places can make us feel perturbed, uncomfortable, or even ill?

Prehistoric people were acutely aware of the benign locations where positive energy fields could be used for healing, fertility, food production and good health. They carefully avoided those areas where negative energies were present. In the same manner as their distant ancestors, the so-called 'primitive' societies that still exist today in remote regions or even in some Third World countries are aware of these natural forces and co-exist respectfully with them. Although the local geology may be somewhat different now, it is clear that through the ages, from the Megalithic peoples to the present day, settlements were sited at locations where positive energy fields existed. The ancient shamans, priests and 'magicians' were relied on to dowse for the beneficial sites as well as to neutralise a location or cleanse a site of the 'bad vibes' perhaps due to natural elements or where a violent battle or accident had taken place. This highly developed intuitive knowledge and sensitivity of energy fields evolved into a spiritual reverence and 'Sacred Earth' culture that persisted well into medieval Europe. For example, a network of round stone towers, built by the early Christian monks between the fourth and twelfth century AD, has been found in Ireland. According to American Professor Philip Callahan, researcher on biological communication systems and author of *Tuning in to Nature*,[5] these hollow structures, about 28 metres (100 feet) high were built as antennae to receive cosmic or magnetic energy to improve the quality of soil, to act as pest control and to detoxify the ground.[6]

Megalithic settlements and the 'sacred' sites of stone circles and alignments were carefully located where positive energy fields were found. Where negative energy fields existed – for example global grid crossings, geopathic stress zones, blind springs and certain underground water courses (see Chapter 2) – standing stones were partially sunk into the ground to 'pin' the energy down like an acupuncture needle as a safety valve to stabilise the earth energy networks reacting to cosmic rays from outer space.

Megalithic monuments including single stones, circles, dolmens, barrows and tumuli are found throughout Europe, Scandinavia, the Middle East and even further afield in Japan, Africa, Easter Island and Central America. An Anglican priest, the Reverend Gordon Strachan, discovered a group of Megalithic standing stones in Israel, orientated in a north–south direct straight line in Tel Gezer on the coast near Tel Aviv. He found references in the Bible associated with the stones where alone there are some 10,000 Megalithic remains on the hillsides of the River Jordan.

Britain has 286 Megalithic stone circles; of these, 235 are located within a mile of a geological fault or earth fissure. Other structures acted as boundary markings, calendars and perhaps as instruments for influencing the weather as well as being a focal point for religious practices. The precise location of the stones suggests that the ancient Megalithic builders understood the presence of unique earth energies. This highly evolved stone technology was developed to harness the terrestrial and cosmic forces as well as provide extremely accurate structures to chart and predict the movement of the heavenly bodies.

The Rollright Stones

British zoologist Don Robbins used ultrasonic detector equipment to monitor the high-frequency sounds emitted by bats. One day, about 20 years ago, as he was passing a Megalithic stone circle in Oxfordshire known as the Rollright Stones, he was surprised to find the stones were emitting a strong signal. (The Rollrights is a group of about 73 stones with a single 'king' stone located in a nearby field.) Robbins formed a group of physicists, geologists, a chemist and electrical engineers to scientifically investigate the phenomenon. This became known as the Dragon Project and was the subject of his book *Circles of Silence.*[7] Over a number of years the group used devices such as sensitive, wide-band ultrasonic equipment, Geiger counters, geomagnometers, infrared cameras and gaussmeters to measure the ultrasonic and radioactivity. At dawn they could monitor a consistent pulsing sound but as the day progressed the pulse increased to an ultrasonic screech lasting several hours, especially on the mornings coinciding with the feasts of the equinox. Regular patterns varied according to the time of day, phases of the Moon and seasons of the year. According to Robbins, the stones appeared to be creating an ultrasonic barrier to the inner circle. He found Geiger counter readings of 22 cycles per minute with unusually high spots in areas around some stones where readings would rise to twice the background levels in five-minute flares of beta radiation. Sometimes the Geiger counter registered exceedingly high counts as if it had been placed less than a metre from a radioactive isotope. Similar readings recorded by investigators at other Megalithic stone sites confirm that the lunar phases from full to new Moon do indeed influence the energy field levels emanating from the ground. They too found the fluctuations occurred several times during the course of a twenty-four hour period, but the variations were particularly pronounced at the times of the full Moon and the eclipses.

The Rollright Stones and other Megalithic structures were carefully designed to a length of unit of the Megalithic yard (82.966 centimetres or 2.72 feet) to produce a geometry and alignment having remarkable astronomical correspondences. When Robbins built his own stone circle, applying the same geometry and arrangement according to ancient principles, he found the ultrasonic energy so intense that it damaged some of his instruments. The Dragon Project established that the stones shielded the circle interior from certain energy fields. This implied that the circle was a device to create an 'umbrella' form of protection using the stones to store static electricity and act as condensers to directly reduce the electromagnetic field strength. In his book on Chartres Cathedral, Louis Charpentier suggests that a church built of natural stone is more conducive to the spiritual experiences of worshippers as the stone would provide a shield against external electromagnetic fields, whereas a concrete construction will tend to magnify such radiation.[8] As will be shown later, the effect of the stone would also be amplified by the geometry of the building and its precise location.

Harmful earth energies such as global grid patterns and negative geopathic stress zones are now becoming recognised and more readily understood. Today, instead of planting standing stones to neutralise the negative effects, metal spikes can be hammered into the ground, or crystals or copper coils can be buried. The several alternative modern products now available may be effective, however they are rather more expensive than using simple iron bars (these remedies are discussed later).

Generated electricity

We have evolved on Earth over three million years but in one single generation – the past 50 years – we have exposed ourselves to extraordinarily and unnaturally high levels of a wide range of artificially generated electromagnetic radiation. Suddenly, this unbelievably powerful force has become available but without any guidelines or precedents to help us fully understand it, monitor it or regulate its use. Instead we continue to exploit it to gain economic and political power, often at the expense of nature, our own health and well-being and the quality of the environment.

Fundamentally, all biological and cosmic processes are electrical. The function of every cell, organ, tissue, muscle, bone and the central nervous system, including the brain, depends on complex, extremely subtle, electrical frequencies. Life on Earth has always been subjected to the electromagnetic variations determined by changes in cosmic radiations and activity affecting the whole spectrum of energy vibrations, from light to microwaves to radio and to colour and smell.

Marine life such as whales depend on extremely low electromagnetic fields for navigation and long wavelength frequencies to communicate with each other over extraordinary distances, said to be as great as up to a thousand miles. Our own body sensitivity to the most subtle and faint vibrations has been likened by one American researcher to suggest that if the terminals of a 1.5-volt battery torch were connected to wires dipped in the Pacific Ocean – one at San Diego and one at Seattle – the cells of a surfer at Long Beach or a fish off Monterey could still detect the electromagnetic field (about one-ten-millionth volt per inch!). (Since the use of strategic defence underwater low-frequency transmitters for communication with nuclear submarines have increased, we have heard more about whales stranding themselves on beaches).

As mentioned earlier, cosmic rays from the Sun and outer space interact with the Earth's electrical and magnetic fields creating a constant interaction between the natural electricity in the atmosphere and all biological systems. The extremely subtle frequency changes caused by the interaction of the heavenly bodies influence our biorhythms and may give some credibility to the art and science of astrology. Physicists long held the view that while animals are able to detect minute electrical and magnetic fields used for navigation and hunting prey, human beings did not possess sense organs to detect electromagnetic fields other than the eye and feeling the effects of heat. This opinion has been superseded. Now there is no doubt that biological systems not only interact with external electromagnetic fields at a cellular level but that the extremely low frequency in the region of 300Hz has a far greater effect than generated power. In his conclusions on electromagnetic radiation, set out in *Indoor Air Pollution*, L. H. Hawkins, said:

> Human beings have evolved in an environment in which natural non-ionising (non-heating) electromagnetic fields have become incorporated into basic physiological control systems. Fundamental control of cellular organisation, membrane function, cell reproduction and growth may all be dictated by electromagnetic forces. Artificial electromagnetic fields, to which we are now exposed at an increasing power and frequency spectrum, may in certain circumstances interfere with these basic control

mechanisms. Our evidence so far is that cellular responses occur at critical frequencies or 'windows' and that many of these windows occur in the ELF (extremely low frequency) region. It is of interest that the Earth's natural EM field (outside the visual spectrum) consists largely of extremely low frequencies.

Cellular effects may be related to an increased risk of behavioural dysfunction (depression and suicide for example), heart disease and other illnesses. The majority of epidemiological evidence however points to a significant association between exposure to EM fields and an increased risk of cancer. The effects of EM fields on cellular growth and suppression of cellular immunity can be postulated to explain an association between exposure to ELF electromagnetic fields and cancer.[9]

The pioneering work of Dr Rupert Sheldrake on the unseen enveloping morphogenetic field (the etheric shield – see Chapter 7, 'Subtle bodies') of an organism that determines the actual form, shape and size of a living entity illustrates the effect electromagnetic energy has upon nature. Even the weakest electromagnetic field can easily penetrate the body via the natural ions in the blood. The chemical nutrients in the food we eat, such as protein, are broken down by an electromagnetic interaction and continuous electrical brain signals activate the release of the endocrine gland secretions, including the production of lymphocytes and antibodies, to surge through the body to combat bacteria, viruses and cancer cells.[10]

No other invention or discovery has had such a profound impact on life on Earth as generated electricity. It is the foundation of modern science, high technology, nuclear energy and space travel. We can certainly feel electricity but we cannot see, hear, smell or taste it. So what exactly is it? Electricity has two forms: *static electricity* and *current electricity*. Static electricity – known to the ancient Greeks – depends on stationary charges. It occurs when materials such as amber or straw are rubbed together or when we pass a comb through our hair, but there is no current. The crackle or hiss on a TV or computer screen is created by static. Lightning is caused by static electrical charges in a cloud creating friction between the particles. Current electricity consists of a flow of electron charges artificially generated.

Who were the early pioneers whose astounding discoveries led to the harnessing of the power of electricity? The word 'electricity' – from *elektron*, the Greek for amber – was coined by William Gilbert (1544–1603), physicist and physician to Queen Elizabeth I. Gilbert's extensive experiments with magnets also led him to coin the phrase 'magnetic pole' and to suggest that the Earth is a spherical magnet and the planets are held in orbit by magnetic attraction.

The distinction between positive and negative electricity was made in the early part of the eighteenth century but the electromagnetic revolution began in earnest with Luigi Galvani (1737–98), an obstetrician and anatomist, who pioneered research into the electrical properties of living things. The process of galvanising is named after him.

The first practical battery – the electrophorus, a device used to accumulate electrical charge – was invented by Count Alessandro Volta (1745–1827), Professor of

Physics at Pavia University, who gave his name to the unit of electromotive force, the volt.

Our modern awareness of electromagnetism began in the 1820s when Hans Christian Oersted (1777–1851), Danish physicist and professor at Copenhagen University, discovered the magnetic effect of an electric current and established the relationship between electricity and magnetism. The oersted, the unit of magnetic field strength, is named after him.

André Ampère (1775–1836), the French physicist who gave his name to the ampère (the unit of current) is remembered for his fundamental work on the physics and mathematics of electricity and electromagnetism. He drew the distinction between electrostatics and electric currents, and between current and voltage. Ampère also demonstrated that wires carrying current exert a force on each other and explained magnetism in terms of electric currents.

The concept of the electromagnetic field – one of the greatest scientific achievements of the nineteenth century – was introduced by the Scottish physicist, James Clerk Maxwell (1831–79). In 1873 Maxwell published his equations unifying the phenomena of electricity, magnetism and light into one set of equations. Known as 'Maxwell's equations', these are fundamental to modern telecommunications.

Maxwell also predicted the existence of electromagnetic radiation over a wide spectrum of frequencies, but it was Heinrich Hertz (1857–94), the German physicist, who first produced and detected radiowaves in 1888. Until Hertz's discovery, radio frequency radiation (RFR) was unknown. The Hertz (Hz), the unit of frequency, is named after him.

The possibility of electromagnetic induction was discovered by Michael Faraday (1791–1867), the British chemist and physicist. Faraday, who made the connection between electricity and magnetism, is credited with the invention of the dynamo, which led to the generation of electrical power. In 1887 the first power station was opened in Brighton, Sussex, and within 20 years power stations were being built throughout the world. Faraday also discovered the process of electrolysis and invented the 'Faraday Cage', a box or other container (sometimes even room-sized) lined with a metal to insulate the interior from external electric and magnetic fields.[11]

Another major breakthrough occurred in 1897 when the electron was discovered by British physicist J. J. Thomson, thereby overturning the ancient belief that the atom was indivisible.

In the early days of power generation in the 1880s, there were disputes over the advantages of distributing by direct current (DC) or alternating current (AC). For example, a car battery supplies direct current electricity flowing in one direction from a negative to a positive terminal. However, a problem arises when this is translated into distributing electricity from a power station because a significant amount of energy is lost in the transmission cables. The higher the voltage – that is, the power needed to drive the current – the lower the loss. It was not only easier to build an AC generator; it was also easier to reduce down the power through transformers to a lower voltage for the end user.

The merits of distributing electricity as alternating current rather than direct current were recognised by Nikola Tesla (1856–1943), an American electrical engineer born in Croatia, and it was his prodigious work that made it feasible. Tesla also challenged some of the accepted laws of electricity and magnetism, and put forward many advanced, even 'futuristic', theories. In *The Man Who Invented the Twentieth Century*, Robert Lomas used Tesla's own writings, record documents and FBI files to acknowledge the true extent of the brilliant genius of the man and how some of his inventions and discoveries were officially suppressed and obscured by US government agencies and are still held as 'top secret'. Lomas suggests that the electric light and domestic electricity supplies credited to Thomas Edison, radio credited to Marconi, and the first hydroelectric power station credited to George Westinghouse, were in fact the original ideas and inventions of Tesla, as were fluorescent light, seismology, a global communication network, and a 'death ray' gun.[12] Despite his considerable contribution to modern electronics, Tesla died a poor and disillusioned man after a long period of illness, thought to have been caused by his life-long exposure to electromagnetic fields. The tesla, the unit of magnetic flux density, is named after him.

Global radio communications began in 1901 when Italian electrical engineer Guglielmo Marconi (1874–1937) successfully transmitted signals across the Atlantic from England to Newfoundland. Within 40 years a radio telegraph system covered the planet. In the 1930s, Scottish physicist Sir Robert Watson-Watt (1892–1973) pioneered the development of RADAR – an abbreviation of **Ra**dio **D**etection **A**nd **R**anging – a radio location system sending out high-frequency radiowave pulses from a powerful rotating transmitter and receiving the signals reflected back from any object encountered. (The signals are displayed on a cathode ray tube.) The first radar system was built in Britain in 1935, and a year later the BBC began TV transmissions from London.[13]

The exponential growth in electrical home appliances began in the 1950s. Ten years later satellite broadcasting had become a commercial reality. However, in the 1960s, concerns began to be expressed regarding the effect of electromagnetic fields on our health.

What are electromagnetic fields?

The electrical current in a wire is like water passing through a pipe. In the same way that a head of water is needed to apply the pressure or force to make the water flow through the pipe, an electrical current needs a *voltage* to be applied before it can flow through the wire. The higher the voltage the stronger the electric field, and the stronger the current the higher the magnetic field. When a 'live' cable is connected to the electricity supply, an electric field will be generated, radiating out from the cable but reducing in strength as the distance from the source increases. When an appliance such as a table lamp is switched off but remains plugged into the mains, an electric field continues to radiate but there is no magnetic field until the appliance is switched on and the current flows. The magnetic field also radiates outward and diminishes in strength as the distance from the source increases.

The electric field and associated magnetic field are considered to be independent at low frequencies. As the frequency increases to the kiloHertz range and beyond, the fields interact and combine into one electromagnetic field. The power of an electromagnetic field is determined by its wavelength and its frequency (the rate at which it oscillates). The relationship of wavelength to frequency can be likened to the ripples on the water when a stone is thrown into a lake: the distance between the ripples is the wavelength or cycle, and the number of waves occurring in a given time period is the frequency or vibration. Frequencies are measured in Hertz, and the full cosmic spectrum of electromagnetic fields runs from zero to lightwave frequency.

The electromagnetic field spectrum

The Earth's natural electromagnetic fields and the electromagnetic fields of all biological systems operate at extremely low frequencies between 1Hz and 30Hz. The band up to 300Hz is designated extremely low (ELF) and voice frequency (VF). Mains power in the home varies between 50Hz in the UK and Europe and 60Hz in the US and Canada.

A kiloHertz (kHz) is one thousand times stronger than a Hertz. The range from 3kHz to 300kHz extends from very low frequency (VLF) and low frequency (LF) up to medium frequency (MF). These bands of the spectrum are used for heating, radiotelegraphy and medium-wave broadcasting. Human hearing is in the range between 20Hz and 16kHz.

A megaHertz (mHz) is one million times stronger than a Hertz. The range from 3mHz to 300mHz includes high frequency (HF) and very high frequency (VHF). These bands of the spectrum are used for radiofrequency and VHF broadcasting.

A gigaHertz (gHz) is one billion times stronger than a Hertz. The range from 3gHz to 300gHz includes ultra high frequency (UHF), super high frequency (SHF) and extra high frequency (EHF). These bands are used for satellite and military purposes, TV broadcasting, hi-tech medicine, mobile phone transmission and microwave ovens. Generally speaking, communication systems operate in a wide band from 3kHz to 300gHz, but some underwater radio transmissions use frequencies below the 1kHz level.

A terahertz (tHz) is one trillion times stronger than a Hertz. This band of the spectrum includes infrared light, visible light (the colours red, yellow, green, blue, violet), ultraviolet (UV) light, x-ray and gamma ray frequencies.

Light, an electromagnetic radiation travelling at a velocity of 301,700 kilometres (187,500 miles) per second in free space is, according to the physics and quantum theory, the highest attainable velocity in the universe. Relative to the vast array of the cosmic spectrum, the band of colour visible to humans is infinitesimally small. Each colour has its own unique frequency – for example, red has a slow 'vibration' compared to the faster frequency of violet. The eye responds to these vibrations and the brain interprets the electromagnetic signals enabling us to see colour. In addition we have built-in mechanisms that enable us to respond unconsciously to the frequencies outside our range of sight, smell and taste – for example, the body can be burned by UV, infrared and microwaves.

Sensitivity to electromagnetic fields

All living organisms are sensitive to electromagnetic energies. Without the system of extremely weak electrical currents in our bodies, we would not be 'alive'. Every human cell operates like a battery, sending out signals to activate the constant interchange of biochemical and bioelectrical processes. An overdose of radiation – such as solar flares or artificially generated electromagnetic fields – can produce, to a lesser or greater degree, abnormal biological changes affecting our genetic response to stress and our ability to resist disease.

The function of many of our physical, biological and thought processes are controlled by the release of the chemical secretions produced by our endocrine gland system. These hormonal secretions are vital to maintaining an efficient immune system and their effective and efficient release is triggered by the extremely low electromagnetic fields in the body. Our levels of vitality, sleep patterns and dreaming are dependent upon the secretions of serotonin, melatonin and dopamine released by the pineal gland (known as the 'governor' of the system, and in earlier times called the 'seat of the soul' and the 'third eye'). As mentioned in Chapter 2, the pineal gland is extremely sensitive to light and electromagnetic fields: daylight and high levels of brightness will trigger the release of serotonin; as it gets dark in the evening, melatonin takes over. The efficient function of the system can be impaired when a person is chronically exposed to an environmentally low-level magnetic field. People who are clinically depressed can have significantly lower levels of serotonin. Melatonin is known as an anti-cancer, life-enhancing hormone. Sleep problems, lethargy, moodiness, depression and immune deficiency diseases are attributed to reduced levels of melatonin released in the body.

In *Melatonin: Your Body's Natural Wonder Drug,* Dr Russell Reiter, Professor of Neuroendocrinology, University of Texas Health Science Centre and co-author Jo Robinson produced evidence that exposure to low-frequency electromagnetic fields can reduce melatonin level secretions by as much as 50 per cent.[14] Also, the April 1992 edition of *Electronics World and Wireless World* reported that considerable evidence indicates that low-frequency electronic and magnetic fields coinciding with natural ion magnetic resonances can have a biological effect on the pineal gland. Human blood contains ions that have a range resonance with the Earth's geomagnetic field and an alternating field ranging between 1Hz and 500Hz. If an electrical or magnetic field is applied near this resonance frequency it can impact upon the lymphocyte cells which, in turn, will affect the immune system response and may well explain many cases of lymphatic leukaemia and other diseases.

The ambient electromagnetic fields in an average urban environment are relatively low, but in standing in close proximity to everyday electrical household equipment such as washing machines, hair dryers, shavers, TV sets and computers, our exposure is substantially higher. This is greatly increased by apparatus using radio frequency and microwave devices. Our natural ions, tissues, blood cells and whole body movement can be affected by the electrical charges caused by high-frequency electromagnetic fields. An adverse reaction reduces the ability of white blood cells to kill tumour cells and in turn can also affect reproduction glands, inhibit cell growth and impair our natural extremely low-frequency electrical brainwave activity that controls the hormone efficiency of the immune system and the central nervous system.

For the first time in the history of the planet we are now exposed to unnatural stresses on the function of all living systems imposed by exceptionally high, artificially generated voltages and the all-pervading extremes of high and low frequencies. Other than visible light our environment is now saturated, many million times more, by the amount of electromagnetic radiation, than we experienced just a hundred years ago.

Since the beginning of the twentieth century we have seen the proliferation of power stations, pylons marching across the landscapes carrying high-tension cables and transformer stations to supply the phenomenal worldwide demand for electricity. This first gathered momentum when public radio broadcasting began in 1920, and then significantly increased over the past 40 years with the development of radar and microwave technology, which largely evolved from the inventions of weapons and defence equipment. Radar and satellite dishes, TV, radio and mobile phone transmission masts now add to the electromagnetic smog blanketing many parts of the planet. In the home or workplace there is an abundance of cables, wires, appliances and gadgets – all generating electromagnetic fields to the point where, awake or asleep, it is almost impossible to find a place of refuge. There is also circumstantial evidence to suggest that artificially generated electromagnetic fields reinforce the harmful effects of the geopathic stress radiation emanating from the Earth's natural magnetic field.

Although the supply of electricity has been available for a comparatively short period, no other invention has ever had such an impact upon human beings. But how can we now live without it? This new form of energy has enhanced every aspect of our life, lifestyle and convenience but it will continue to exact a price. We pay in terms of our health – the so-called 'twentieth-century diseases of civilisation' – and environmental pollution.

The invisible electromagnetic smog often referred to by scientists as 'noise' is otherwise known as electromagnetic interference (EMI) and radio frequency interference (RFI). Distorted patterns created by this noise can randomly activate equipment, jam communications and even compromise national security defence systems. Lightning, solar flares and other atmospheric disturbances are a natural source of EMI. Artificial sources include power lines, heavy industrial transformers, welding equipment, mobile phones, radar and radio masts. Just about any piece of electrical apparatus can generate a stray electromagnetic signal. When you switch on the light and you hear a 'click' on the radio it means there is an electrical incompatibility caused by EMI. Even wires (other than optic fibre) carrying data can be affected by electrical mains cables. Stray data emissions from a computer can be picked up by an espionage agent using a simple radio antenna, and terrorists could use a strong radio signal to jam the controls of, say, a nuclear power plant. EMI-sensitive electronic equipment installed in an office building in the vicinity of a port, airport, military facility or an electrified railway system will be vulnerable to breakdown or occasional malfunction. To improve the situation a European directive was issued in 1996 to test prove the EMI resistance of all electrical equipment.

Undoubtedly we are sensitive to the full electromagnetic spectrum, including radio and microwave frequencies. Now, in our modern world, the incessant and daily increase in the global proliferation of generated electromagnetic fields continues to subject us to exposure levels we were not designed to withstand. In addition to cancers, birth defects, skin allergies, chronic fatigue syndrome (ME), Alzheimer's and AIDS – some of the so-called 'diseases of civilisation' – the incidence of electromagnetic sensitivity (EMS) has become another plague of modern living, gathering momentum and frequency over the past twenty or so years.

Early pioneering work on electromagnetic sensitivity by Dr Jean Munro and Dr Cyril Smith began in 1980 at the Breakspear Hospital in Hertfordshire,[15] which has since become one of Europe's leading authorities on environmental illnesses. Studies suggest that an overdose of, or long-term exposure to electromagnetic fields can, somehow, set off a biochemical reaction, and once a person becomes sensitised, symptoms intensify and in some cases can persist for many years. Many private groups and associations have now been formed by fellow sufferers and gradually, worldwide, the medical establishment no longer regards hypersensitivity as a psychological aberration. However, there are very few specialised clinics with experts in this field. Awareness of the potential hazards and knowing how to avoid unnecessary exposure is the best prevention against becoming oversensitised, but you do not necessarily have to live under overhead high-tension cables or be a prolific user of the mobile phone to develop the condition.

A move from the city to a rural area where the electromagnetic smog may be less dense can help, but for those with extreme hypersensitivity it is virtually impossible to find an EMF smog-free environment other than the middle of the Amazon jungle, and even there the radio frequencies cannot be escaped. An alternative is to live in a building encased in the type of shielding material used in military facilities to protect the radar and guided weapon systems from enemy attack by electromagnetic radiation. Unfortunately, as soon as the person goes outside the shielded area the symptoms return. The house or protected room must be virtually free of all electrical apparatus – even the telephone. In such extreme cases, life is painful and miserable, but the condition itself is not life threatening.

Some people can consciously sense very low and extremely low frequency radiation as a faint tingle on the skin, although it may register as a stronger reaction. These frequencies are emitted from ordinary, everyday equipment such as TVs, electrical tools, fluorescent lighting as well as radar transmissions. In the workplace – and increasingly in the home – computers, laser printer, photocopiers, lighting transformers and electronic communications systems further increase exposure to the body.

Is generated electricity a serious health hazard?

Cancer develops in normal, healthy people when their immune system fails to control the cells in the body developing abnormal growth patterns. Smoking, drinking, stress and other causes can trigger the development of cancer and if the body's natural electrical pulses, which control the normal function of the immune system, are impaired or disturbed for long periods by an adverse electromagnetic field the effect can be a major contributor to the incidence of immune deficiency diseases. The intervention of the Earth's geomantic field with the magnetic fields produced from industrial, commercial and household electrical appliances can produce an erratic on-off effect in our normal biological processes and this might explain the high incidence of breast cancer in both women and men in the developed countries of the world.

Government 'watchdog' agencies such as the US Environmental Protection Agency (EPA) and in the UK the National Radiological Protection Board (NRPB) take the official line that there is no clear evidence of a cancer or other health hazard from the 'normal' levels of electromagnetic radiation found in the vicinity of overhead power lines, substations and household appliances and equipment. (But what is 'normal' compared to a hundred years ago?) However, in a leaked draft report the EPA concluded that all these were *probable* human carcinogens, while radio frequency and microwave electromagnetic fields were a *possible* risk. The report also said studies of leukaemia, lymphoma and brain cancer in children exposed to magnetic fields from residential electrical power distribution systems show a consistent pattern. But in 1990, after a two-year study, the published report deleted the conclusions and blandly suggested that uncertainties remained about the effects of electromagnetic radiation![16] Meanwhile the UK NRPB somewhat grudgingly acknowledged that 'there are several possible areas of biological interaction which have health implications and about which our knowledge is limited.'

Since the mid-1970s the rate of new cases of childhood leukaemia in the US has steadily increased. The most common form of acute lymphoblastic leukaemia has risen by 20 per cent from 1973 to 1991 and this was particularly noticeable among white children. In the age range 1 to 4 years, new cases of the disease in the UK have also risen by about the same rate. Officially, the causes are said to be unknown.[17]

Many of the world's research scientists, such as Dr Ross Adey, Professor of Medicine (Neurology), Lorna Linda University School of Medicine, California, have dedicated their lives to work on epidemiological studies or laboratory tests with animals and tissues. They have discovered specific interactions between artificially generated electricity, the natural static geomantic field, the magnetic fields and the Schumann field with the Earth's crust and the ionosphere. In February 1997 at the Ninth International Montreux Congress on the changing electromagnetic environment, Dr Adey claimed that all industrial societies have modified the electromagnetic environment many thousands of times over the natural levels. Referring to power-line magnetic fields, extremely low frequency and electromagnetic fields, he suggested there was little doubt as to the significance of his findings in four main areas:

1. The effect on the immune system reduces white blood cells to kill tumour cells.
2. The evidence of epidemiological studies link abnormal foetal development and miscarriages with electrical blankets and other appliances such as home heating or night storage heater systems.
3. The effect on the control and regulation of cell growth.
4. The effect on the central nervous system and the brain controlling the hormonal mechanisms.[18]

Dr Robert Becker, once tipped as a Nobel prize winner and an eminent American authority on biological defects associated with EM fields, concluded after 30 years of research that the exposure of living organisms to abnormal electromagnetic fields can result in significant abnormalities.[19] As early as 1963 he linked psychiatric illness with magnetic storms. In 1973 he was appointed by the Navy to a secret civilian advisory committee to assess the environmental impact of Project Sanguine – a planned, extremely low frequency (ELF) submarine communications system. The data produced indicated that there were biological effects potentially hazardous to human health. After considering the evidence the committee unanimously felt that major segments of the US population were 'currently at risk' from power-line fields and went on record to recommend that the White House be advised of their findings. The report was suppressed and Dr Becker's research grants were withdrawn.

At about the same time researchers in the USSR, Eastern European and America were studying the effect on animals exposed to the range of electromagnetic fields normally found in most office and home environments. The results showed increased levels of stress and severe weakening of the immune system. Later, other researchers in Europe and North America were studying the incidence of leukaemia suffered by people who either lived close to power lines or were power-line workers. In each case the death rate was double – and in some cases treble – the statistically expected number, which suggested a connection between electromagnetic fields and the incidence of cancer, leukaemia, stress-related illnesses and other ailments, such as fatigue, allergies, depression and HIV, associated with the twentieth-century environment.

Cases of malignant diseases such as breast cancer, melanoma and brain tumours are on the increase and the conclusions from so many epidemiological studies show a clear relationship and link to environmental electromagnetic fields. The growing evidence points to very weak electromagnetic fields interacting with free radicals – naturally occurring chemicals linked to cancerous changes and the ageing process – to produce ongoing reactions in chemicals found in everyday products such as paint sprays and indoor pesticides.

Giving evidence at a public enquiry on the proposed new pylons in Yorkshire, Professor Gerald Scott, Professor Emeritus in chemistry at Aston University, described 'free radicals' thus:

(The)…situation is exacerbated by the chemical pollutants found in the industrial environment. Of particular importance are the atmospheric pollutants such as sulphur dioxide, ozone and oxides of nitrogen. Other environmental agents, such as chlorinated solvents found in the domestic as well as the industrial environment, all increase free radical concentrations in cells. This means that the biological antioxidants are already working near the limits of their effectiveness and any additional oxidative stress, such as that caused by electromagnetic fields, may reduce their concentrations beyond the limit at which they are effective within the cell. In these circumstances, there may be a sudden change from a steady state condition in the cell chemistry to a chain branching situation leading to the onset of diseases, such as cancer, which are known to be associated with lack of cellular antioxidants. It is an unfortunate fact that different oxidative stress factors often occur together. For example, ozone and, to a lesser extent, oxides of nitrogen are known to be formed by electrical discharges at overhead power lines and the combination of EM fields and toxic gaseous pollutants are more likely to cause the switch from controlled cell reactions to explosive destruction and disease. Even the 'healthy' rural environment may not be free of this hazard since the short wavelengths of the Sun's spectrum cause very powerful photo-oxidation of the cells in the surface of the skin with subsequent development of skin cancers. An additional oxidative stress caused by magnetic fields could exacerbate this effect in people exposed to both.[20]

The professor went on to criticise the NRPB, suggesting it pays little attention to the mass of scientific papers on the effects of weak magnetic fields on cell chemistry. The official view is that DNA genetic damage is not caused directly by electromagnetic radiation, but this is strongly refuted by biochemists.

Professor of Physics Denis Henshaw, of Bristol University, found a link between the electrical fields surrounding overhead power lines and their interaction with pockets of radon gas, other air pollutants and radioactive particles included in the atmosphere, which may account, to some extent, for the apparent association with childhood cancer. After 3 years and a further 2,000 field samples, in 1999 his Human Radiation Group studies both supported and confirmed his earlier theories.[21] Similar work also carried out in laboratories in other countries indicated that certain known chemical promoters are significantly enhanced in their action by the presence of power-line frequency magnetic fields, suggesting that the clustering of cancer cases may have common chemical as well as magnetic field factors.

Biologist and long time researcher Dr Roger Coghill suggested that many cellular processes depend on the synthesis of adenosine triphosphate (ATP) and electron transportation to move muscles, pump blood and to influence our thinking and breathing activities. Symptoms of muscle pain, asthma, memory loss and an inability to concentrate implicate a faulty synthesis and supply of ATP. Studies have shown that cancers can arise when cells revert from respiratory to fermentational pathways of ATP synthesis, which could also explain the high incidence of cancers and tumours near power lines.[22]

Electronics researcher and geophysicist Anthony Hopwood, based in Worcester, claimed that power lines appear to double the concentration of gamma rays or charged particles striking the Earth from outer space. Hopwood made this discovery while experimenting to measure the change in the number of particles that reach the Earth's surface after a solar flare eruption. Charged particles are a known cause of cancer, and doubling their number would tie in with the increased risk found by researchers around some cancer cluster sites. It is believed that symptoms of ill health could also be induced by the effect of EM fields on the chemical reactions inside cells causing a boost in the levels of free radicals resulting in cell damage. Similar tests carried out by the Swedish Radiation Protection Institute appear to confirm Hopwood's findings and other Russian research has linked an 11-year solar cycle (when solar storms reach their peak) with the incidence of breast cancer.[23]

The Swedish National Board for Industrial and Technological Development is now convinced that power line radiation is hazardous, and new legislation has been introduced to prevent unnecessary exposure. The National Regulatory Research Institute in the US is also convinced of the hazards. The American National Institute of Environmental Health Sciences (NIEHS) published a working group study in 1998 assessing the health effects from exposure to power-line frequency electromagnetic fields. The report concluded, by a majority vote, that EM fields should be considered a *possible* human carcinogen, but it pulled back from the brink of classifying EMFs as a *known* or *probable* human carcinogen.

The National Academy of Sciences (NAS) report *Possible Health Effects of Exposure to Residential Electric and Magnetic Fields* stated that: 'No conclusive and consistent evidence shows that exposures to residential electric and magnetic fields produce cancer'. However, the working group reported that the data 'support an association between exposure to calculated magnetic fields and the incidence of childhood leukaemia', and 'there is limited evidence that EMF is carcinogenic to children'.[24] While these findings are not conclusive nor indisputable evidence, they represent a major breakthrough after decades of pioneering work.

Bioelectromagnetic research has expanded over the past decade from a thousand or so to the current number of more than 20,000 studies worldwide. In fact, much of the research is carried out by independent scientists who, in the main, are attached to universities and are dependent for financial support from the industries producing electricity and mobile phones. While the source of the grants does not deter them from producing unbiased scientific evidence, some may tend to give the benefit of the doubt to the hand that feeds them. Despite the sponsorship by the manufacturers, the already abundant evidence clearly indicates mounting health hazards over a wide spectrum of electromagnetic fields.

The British government, the Secretary of State for Health and the Health and Safety Executive (HSE) take advice and implement laws and regulations to work within the limits of exposure recommended by the NRPB. As a government watchdog, the NRPB is supposed to conduct its own research, provide technical services and give advice in the field of the whole range of radiation, including the possible adverse effects of both ionising radiation (radioactive material, UV and X-rays) and non-ionising radiation (radio frequencies) to protect the general public from any health hazards associated with electromagnetic fields. How independent this service can be is questionable when it is funded partially by the industry it is supposed to be monitoring, and partially by a government whose main political interests are to stimulate and maintain economic development and growth. It is also significant that the UK limits set by the NRPB are higher than those in the US and other European and Scandinavian countries, and seven times greater than the recommendations by the International Commission on Non-Ionising Radiation Protection (ICNIRP). Even China and Russia have lower exposure limits.

Generally, throughout the Western world, electricity supply companies such as Britain's National Grid have vigorously and successfully defended all attempts to prove that high-tension cables cause, or indirectly trigger immune deficiency diseases such as cancers, Alzheimer's and Parkinson's. The argument used by those scientists working for the electricity supply industries and the government agencies is based on their non-acceptance of anecdotal evidence. They also ignore or dismiss independent epidemiological studies and the increasing numbers of people experiencing disease, disabilities and other health problems due to a range of electromagnetic fields, including radio frequency and microwave radiation. But how else are new diseases discovered other than by anecdotal evidence? Repetitive strain injury (RSI), sick building syndrome (SBS), bovine spongiform encephalopathy (BSE), acquired immune deficiency syndrome (AIDS) and myalgic encephalomyelitis (ME), all came to be recognised through anecdotal evidence. In the case of ME – considered by many employers and the medical profession to have been a complaint invented by lazy shirkers to avoid doing an honest day's work – a breakthrough came eventually when the cause was diagnosed as a brain disorder after modern techniques for measuring electrical activity indicated that organic changes in the brain may be biochemical. It appears that all biological cell functions are controlled by a form of weak electrical circuitry. Cells communicate or 'whisper' together in a language that appears to be shaped by physics (electromagnetic energy) rather than chemistry. The type of brain-wave form – an abnormal negative voltage produced when people await a stimulus to which they must respond – was found to be different in ME patients. In other words, it is now accepted that it is an electrical brainwave malfunction. The paradox is that the medical establishment does not accept the view that weak, generated electromagnetic fields can be hazardous to health!

British, American and other Western governments have also sheltered behind the advice of their respective agencies and have not only gone to great lengths to reassure the public that electromagnetic fields, including radio frequency and microwave radiations, are not a health hazard but have also actively encouraged and promoted the expansion of generated electricity pylons and TV, radio broadcasting and mobile phone transmission masts. These attempts at bland reassurances to pacify public concerns not only contradict or ignore good, independent scientific research – they cover up the more sinister government-funded secret weapons establishments where, for the past three or more decades, electromagnetic fields have been developed for lethal and non-lethal armaments, counter-intelligence and crowd control. (It has been claimed that such non-lethal weapons were used against women protesters at Greenham Common, a US airforce base in England.)

The following article published in *Powerwatch Network Newsletter* (November 1996) may help to convince any reader who remains sceptical about the effect of electromagnetic fields on the mind and body:

New World Vistas – Air & Space Power for the 21st Century, was a major undertaking by the USAF Scientific Advisory Board. They produced 14 volumes of papers on a variety of topics and have just published a 15th volume. This includes 1000 word essays requested by the Chairman, Dr Gene McCall, setting out individual specialist members' visions of what the next 50 years will bring. Biological Process Control is the third essay, and it deals with the physical regulation of biological processes using electromagnetic field:

We are at the start of an explosion of knowledge in the field of neuroscience. We will have achieved a clear understanding of how the human brain works, how it really controls the various functions of the body, and how it can be manipulated (both positively and negatively). One can envision the further development of electromagnetic energy sources, the output of which can be pulsed, shaped and focused, that can couple with the human body in a manner to prevent voluntary muscular actions, control emotions (and thus actions), produce sleep, transmit suggestions and interfere with both short-term and long-term memory. New weapons to control an adversary without leading to a lethal result would offer significant improvements in the capabilities of special operations forces.

The prospect of weapons to use against individual targets is reasonable; the prospect of such weapons being effective against massed forces seems more remote, although use in a multiple hostage situation would probably be feasible.

It should be possible to create speech in the human body, for covert suggestion and psychological direction. When powerful microwaves in the gigaHertz range enter the human head, tissue expands fast enough to produce an acoustic wave. If a pulse stream is used, it will be possible to create a high quality audio 'sound' inside the head. Thus, it should be possible to 'talk' to selected adversaries in a fashion that would be most disturbing to them.[25]

The author, a leading member of the military research fraternity in the US, chose to remain anonymous. The full essay was sent to Powerwatch by the International Committee for the Convention Against Offensive Microwave Weapons, Philadelphia. A taped transcription from US scientist Eldon Byrd, who worked on classified projects for the Naval Surface Weapons office, described the findings thus:

We can alter the behaviour of cells, tissues, organs and whole organisms...alter the levels of hormones in living creatures, alter the reaction time of irreversible chemical processes as well as the chemistry itself in a living cell, we can alter time perception in humans and animals, we can make animals go to sleep, we can make bone grow and we can stop bone growing, we can start and stop cell de-differentiation – what that means is that we can make a cell that's programmed to do one thing, do something else. We can inhibit and enhance what messenger RNA does in a cell. We can regulate immune processes and affect calcium ion binding on cells. That is important because most of the chemical processes in the human brain seem to be mediated by calcium ions. We can entrain brainwaves – this has been proven and replicated many, many times now. We can turn the DNA transcription process on and off at will. We can cause profound alterations and defects in embryos in the gestation period by directly enacting fields with the growing organism. We can cause up to six times higher foetus mortality and birth defects in laboratory animals with fields so weak that you can hardly detect them. You can slow down or speed up the ageing processes of cells to the point where you can slow down to extend cell life. These are only some of the results of interactions of weak, pulsed, usually ELF, magnetic fields and living systems.[26]

Where artificially generated electromagnetic fields are concerned, it is clear that we are all caught up in a socio-political conflict between our demand for cheap, ample electricity for our personal and business prosperity and the imperative global need to reduce environmental risks and health hazards to a minimum. The situation is exacerbated because politicians find it difficult to resist the pressure by lobbyists representing powerful business interests who produce persuasive arguments to sway the balance in favour of continuous economic growth. But measures to improve public awareness and minimise the risks need not necessarily mean over-restrictive controls and regulations which could retard business development and prosperity. The general public's concern over job losses, dearer food, water and electricity or the rising costs of running a business, encourages politicians to turn a blind eye to potential hazards – the Boiled Frog Syndrome – until such time as they are challenged by a large enough group of voters who are no longer prepared to tolerate the risks, whether these are actual or perceived.

It is not surprising that the general public's confidence in politicians, government-sponsored agencies, multinational companies, the medical and legal professions is in serious decline. It took over 60 years after the 1920 scientific studies identifying the health hazard of radon gas before safeguarding regulations came into force. The chronic lung disease caused by the inhalation of asbestos fibres has been known to medical science for many decades; the manufacturers, public health authorities and successive governments were aware of the extreme health risks as early as the 1920s but it was not until 1968 that legislation came into force – and even then to only partially control the use of asbestos.

X-rays, discovered by Wilhelm Roentgen in 1895, are used as a medical diagnostic tool and radio therapy treatment. Less than 50 years ago, adults and children could go into a shoe shop and use a machine to x-ray their feet to test whether the new shoes were fitting properly or not. Now, worldwide control has limited modern-day radiographers to x-ray exposure doses several times smaller than that of the child in the shoe shop.

Radium, a metallic element discovered by Pierre and Marie Curie in 1898, is also used in radiotherapy. In the 1920s radium was thought to prolong life and to be so highly beneficial it was added to cosmetics, toothpaste, creams and drinks. People bought meters to ensure they were getting their adequate daily intake; watch dials were painted with luminous paint to 'glow in the dark' and the painters would happily lick their paint brushes to take in this new elixir. We now know that radium is not only extremely destructive to DNA molecules and chromosomes, it is also a potential killer and is the source of radon gas.

The pesticide DDT (dichloro diphenyl trichloroethane) was first used in 1939 and continued to be extensively sprayed on crops throughout the world for 30 years until it was banned due to its high toxicity. It was never properly tested, as was the case with the genetically modified (GM) food products brought on to the market in 1997. These products are now firmly established in the food chain despite a strong warning from Cologne University in 1994 that GM foods could cause a genetic change in our bodies through the DNA system.

The US government gave solemn assurances to its soldiers, used as guinea pigs in the atom bomb experiments, that the fall-out from a nuclear explosion test was 'harmless'. The sedative drug Thalidomide, prescribed to pregnant women between 1959 and 1962, caused severe foetal abnormalities of the hands and feet. The drug was not adequately tested before studying the long-term effects. The designers of the *Titanic* were so sure it was unsinkable that the ship carried only enough life boats for half the passengers – yet it sank on its maiden voyage with the loss of over 1,500 lives.

Exposure to electromagnetic fields is another instance, similar to the other cases noted above, where we, the general public, are used for live experiments and like laboratory-tested animals we are not even asked whether or not we wish to cooperate.

The generation of electricity, power lines and pylons has been with us for a hundred years. It was not until 1972 that the Central Electricity Generating Board (now known as the National Grid) made any attempt to carry out research into the possible health hazards of electromagnetic fields, and even this innovation was largely created to defend the power-generation companies from the growing concerns voiced by the independent international scientific community and epidemiological research.

Worldwide, during the past 30 years, reputable scientists, medical researchers and epidemiologists have been studying the possible harmful effects of both extremely low and high electromagnetic fields including radio and microwave radiation. Their experiments and studies have progressively become more detailed, sophisticated and ultra-scrupulous to ensure they will stand up to scrutiny by their peers but, principally, in anticipation of the strongest opposition from the interested parties such as the power-generating companies and mobile phone manufacturers. Throughout this long period the ever-widening evidence showing adverse and damaging health effects has never diminished: in fact it continues to gather momentum.

The difficulties surrounding the link between health hazards and electromagnetic field radiation is, on the one hand, the demand by government agencies and power-generating and mobile phone companies for the scientific proof to be *conclusive* and, on the other hand, the culture of scepticism and suspicion that developed out of the public's lack of confidence in the opinions and information offered by the scientists employed by the government agencies and interested business organisations.

The known science of today may not be able to produce conclusive scientific proof that certain electromagnetic fields can affect the human organism. (Another difficulty may be the compartmentalised system of teaching biology, medicine and physics as separate sciences, which affects the common validation of results of research because there is a lack of mutual understanding of each other's discipline.) Nevertheless, despite the earlier lack of scientific 'proof' as to how smoking, asbestos fibres and DDT cause cancer, the successful legal actions against the tobacco companies were based entirely on statistical evidence: the scientific proof of biochemical links between cancer and smoking arrived only several years later. Therefore, in the case of electromagnetic radiation exposure it seems inconsistent not to accept the strong anecdotal, statistical, epidemiological and scientific evidence.

There is no doubt that smoking and other excesses can trigger the development of cancer, but if the electrical pulses controlling the normal function of the immune system are impaired or disturbed for long periods by an adverse electromagnetic field, the effect could be a major contributor to the incidence of immune deficiency diseases. The magnetic fields produced from industrial, commercial and household electrical appliances can create an erratic 'on-off' effect in our normal biological processes, and this might explain the high incidence of breast cancer in both women and men in Western industrialised countries. Dr Leif Floberg, a former lecturer at Lund University in Sweden, claimed that power frequency magnetic fields interacting with natural radiation will eventually cause almost everyone to get some form of cancer due to 'natural chronic vibrational fatigue'.

Whatever the warnings, we are not going to stop using electricity. However, as we shall see, the potential hazards can be minimised by understanding the likely dangers and taking prudent action to avoid unnecessary exposure.

References

1. Roger Highfield, 'A butterfly with built-in compass', *The Daily Telegraph*, 23 November 1999.
2. Narby, Jeremy (1999) *The Cosmic Serpent*, London: Phoenix.
3. Seymore, Percy (1992) *The Paranormal: Beyond Sensory Science*, London: Penguin.
4. John Cribbin, 'Sparks of Genius', *The Guardian*, 22 October 1992, pp. 14–15.
5. Callahan, P. (1975) *Tuning in to Nature*, US: Devin-Adair.
6. Sangster, H. (1995) 'The electricity of life', *Rilko* no. 45, p. 10.
7. Robbins D. (1985) *Circles of Silence*, London: Souvenir Press.
8. Charpentier L. (1972) *The Mysteries of Chartres Cathedral*, London: Research Into Lost Knowledge Organisation (Rilko).
9. Leslie and Lassau (eds) (1992) *Indoor Air Pollution*, Cambridge: Cambridge University Press.
10. Sheldrake, R. (1983) *A New Science of Life*, London: Granada.
11. *The Macmillan Encylopedia* (1984), London: Macmillan.
12. Lomas, R. (1999) *The Man Who Invented the Twentieth Century: Nikola Tesla, Forgotten Genius of Electricity*, London: Headline.
13. *The Macmillan Encyclopedia* (1984), London: Macmillan.
14. Reiter R. and Robinson, J. (1996) *Melatonin: Your Body's Natural Wonder Drug*, New York: Bantam.
15. 'Electrical sensitivity', *Powerwatch UK Network Newsletter*, Issue 1, February 1995, p. 1.
16. US scientists vote 50/60 Hz electromagnetic fields as "possible human carcinogens", *Electromagnetic Hazard & Therapy*, vol. 9, no. 3, 1998, pp. 1 and 3.
17. Draper, G. J., Kroll, M. E., Stiller, C. A. (1995) 'Childhood Oxford', *Surveys*, vol. 19.
18. Professor Ross Adey, 'Speaking out', BBC Radio Scotland, 10 January 1992. *Electromagnetic News*, vol. 3, no. 3–4, p. 7
19. Becker, R. (1990) *Cross Currents*, Los Angeles: Tarcher.
20. Professor Gerald Scott, 'Free radicals provide a mechanism for EMFs to promote cancer', *Electromagnetic News*, vol. 3, nos 5 and 6, December 1992, pp. 7–8.
21. TV Channel 4, 'Dispatches': Electricity and Cancer, 14 February 1996 and further reporting by Tom Wilkie, Science Editor.
22. Article by Dr Roger Coghill in *Structural Survey Magazine*, no. 6, 1993/94.
23. 'Powerline cancers may be due to focusing on solar radiation by live fields in 11-year cycles', *Electromagnetic & VDU News*, April/June 1993, pp, 8–9.
24. National Academy of Sciences (NAS) (1997) *Possible Health Effects of Exposure to Residential Electric and Magnetic Fields*, National Academy Press, pp 2 and 186.
25. 'Biological process control', *Powerwatch Network Newsletter*, Issue 11, October/November 1996, p. 3.
26. *EM Fields Information Sheet No 1* (11/93), published by Electro Magnetic Fields in conjunction with Powerwatch UK and Scientists for Global Responsibility, Power Watch Suffolk UK (undated), p. 51.

4.
The evidence

Overhead power transmission lines

A significant proportion of the population of the Western world lives in 50Hz or 60Hz electromagnetic fields (EMFs), which exceed the acceptable level of 100 nanoteslas (nT) due to the electrical equipment, gadgets, computers, TVs and radios commonly used in the home or workplace. In 1999, the National Grid planned an additional 1,000 pylons to the 21,000 already striding across the countryside and towns of Britain in order to meet the demand, especially in the southeast of England. Those who live in close proximity to overhead power lines, TV, radio and mobile phone transmission masts can be subjected to fields of up to 25,000nT. In the UK approximately 60,000 people live under or very near high-voltage cables. Does this abnormally high electromagnetic environment create a serious health hazard?

According to the National Radiological Protection Board (NRPB), there is no evidence of a cancer risk. This same stance is taken by the electrical engineering industries, and at public enquiries the government inspectors and high court judges tend to favour such establishment opinions. However, many eminent, internationally renowned scientists, epidemiologists, medical practitioners and researchers believe their overwhelming evidence and studies should be sufficient to convince the authorities and power-line companies that electromagnetic fields can indeed be a serious health hazard. Findings have shown an unmistakable correlation between the degree of exposure to power-line electromagnetic fields and the risk of childhood leukaemia and brain cancer.

An early pioneer was epidemiologist Dr Nancy Wertheimer. In 1974, assisted by physicist Ed Leeper, Dr Wertheimer collected data in the greater Denver area of Colorado on the location of every child who had died of leukaemia between 1950 and 1969. The addresses coincided with the proximity to the pole-mounted transformers on the last leg of the local power distribution system. The leukaemia incidents occurred in clusters along the path of the overhead wires corresponding to the high current levels flowing along the line where the greatest low frequency alternating current fields were present. Epidemiologists Maria Feychting and Anders Ahlbom of

Sweden's Karolinska Institute studied nearly 500,000 people who lived within 300 metres (1,100 feet) of a high-tension power line from 1960 to 1985. The findings showed an unmistakable correlation between the degree of exposure to power-line electromagnetic fields and the risk of childhood leukaemia. By restricting their analysis to a set distance from high-power transmission lines the researchers could calculate the field strength for each household and be confident that the power lines were the main source of electromagnetic radiation and not some other environmental factor. The evidence also indicated that children seemed to be more vulnerable than adults. The cancer risk grew in proportion to the strength of the EM field.[1]

A more recent study of adults by the same group of researchers and published in *Epidemiology* in 1997, covered around 400,000 people who again lived within a 300-metre (1,100-feet) range of high-voltage power lines. This identified 325 leukaemia cases and 223 cases of tumours. In the same edition, a study of 870 cases of adult leukaemia by Dr Chung-Yi Li in Taiwan formed a strong link with residential proximity to powerlines.[2]

Chemical engineer Rodney Girdlestone, whose main interest is diagnosing electromagnetic stress, mentions several cases of health hazards attributable to overhead power lines.[3] The small English village of Fishpond in Gloucester was surrounded by high-tension cables. The increase in illness coincided with the grid company's dramatic increase in voltages carried by the lines. In Dalmally, a small village in Scotland, 275kV cables pass over a local authority housing estate, police station, post office and within 100 metres (330 feet) of a school. In the 36 houses, 8 people had died from cancer over a period of 5 years, and a further 3 residents had died of motor neurone disease. All lived in houses lying close to the high-voltage transmission line connecting Cruachan – the UK's largest hydroelectric scheme – to the national grid. Girdlestone also highlighted a British Channel 4 programme shown in 1984 – 'The Good, the Bad and the Indefensible' – which illustrated the case of the American farmer across whose land a powerline was erected. Shortly after the installation, his hens started laying 'scrambled' eggs, his cattle aborted and milk production fell dramatically.

Another example was a cancer cluster found in the triangle north of Bournemouth, Dorset, at a point where the 400,000-volt national grid bifurcates, straddling the villages of Ferndown and West Moors with pylons carrying 132,000 volts. One researcher into the cluster also established a link with the layout of the domestic water supply to the area.[4]

A number of local authorities, backed by informed pressure groups, including environmentalists and conservationists, are refusing to grant permission for electricity power lines to be run over or near houses, schools and hospitals, as well as restricting the building of properties close to or under existing overhead cables. Unfortunately, not all local councils have either the political will to resist, or the funds to match the financial resources at the disposal of property companies and the electricity producers who can rely on the comparatively lax limits of exposure set by the NRPB to support their case.

As recently as 1996, a large new private housing estate was completed in the small town of Chippenham, Wiltshire, about 30 kilometres (20 miles) from Bristol. A line of pylons carrying high-voltage cables ran the length of the site on one of the long bound-

aries. The developer was granted permission to build many houses parallel and immediately in line with the overhead cables. Without the aid of any recording instruments,
the high-tension voltage 'buzz' from the wires could be felt and heard for about 50
metres (160 feet) or so at right angles to the line of the nearest cable where the buzzing
sound enveloped all the houses. In the village of Pilning, just north of Bristol, pylons
have been built just 80 metres (300 feet) away from a school playground.

In the centre of Moscow, a street lined with blocks of flats and offices has high-
tension cables festooned above the footpath not more than 3 metres (10 feet) or so
from the windows of the upper storeys, yet, officially, Russia has one of the lowest
limits of exposure levels in the world. In May 1995 the people of Hong Kong opposed
the routing of a new 400kV power line alongside high-rise housing with pylons
immediately outside apartment windows. The following day, China Light and
Power took a full-page advertisement in the *Eastern Express* in an attempt to dismiss
the health hazard issue.[5] However, gathering worldwide public awareness has
achieved positive outcomes: in the early 1990s there were successful court cases in
North America, such as the Texan power company that was ordered to re-route its
cables away from a school, and the Canadian British Columbia Hydro Company that
bought up houses in the path of its new high-voltage lines to avoid possible costly
litigation.

Strong opposition to the Eastlink scheme for a power line between New South
Wales and Queensland resulted in the Australian Senate setting up a special inquiry
into the effects of electromagnetic fields. Where the proposed line crossed important
ecological areas it required the uprooting of between one and two million trees in a
location already requiring the planting of millions more trees to hold salinity at
sustainable levels. Protesters claimed that the proposed power line was not required,
and called on their government to adopt the principles of full cost accounting and
show commitment to socially, environmentally and economically responsible energy
policies.[6]

The UK has seen the growth of REVOLT (Rural England Against Overhead Line
Transmission), which was formed in 1992 to oppose the new Yorkshire (Lockenby to
Shipton) power line. At the public inquiry the inspectors concluded that National
Grid did in fact need the new line, however, its report included some positive guide-
lines:

27-8. Clearly overhead lines are a form of development and they should be considered against the background of planning policies.
27-10. It is not disputed that the installation of overhead lines has a severe visual
impact on almost all landscapes and environments. Therefore the installation of
such lines is clearly at odds with the underlying aims of the relevant development
plan policies designed to protect or improve the environment, and thereby stimulate the economy, in both urban and rural areas.
27-11. Therefore, we conclude that the establishment of need is a necessary prerequisite to the grant of any consent of overhead lines.
27-12. Where need is established it is clearly right to seek to identify the least
harmful route and to assess whether further mitigation measures are necessary.[7]

Highlighting the environmental impact and the visual intrusion of pylons marching across town and countryside has had a far greater influence on the results of inquiries than simply the possible health hazards. In certain cases, based more on aesthetic and environmental grounds, cable routes have been either directed away from buildings and protected areas or the high-tension lines have been installed underground. Whilst buried cables avoid ugly steel pylons the magnetic field is just as strong unless expensive materials are used to insulate the cables. In most suburban, built-up areas where the cables are underground they are generally laid under the footpath, running close to buildings. This generates an even higher magnetic field level already present in most interiors due to in-house wiring and electrical appliances creating an electromagnetic polluted home environment well in excess of the acceptable levels noted earlier. For some people, especially children, these levels can be critical to their overall health and well-being.

Either unofficially, or officially, in some US states adopted policy has set out guidelines based on preventive avoidance to reduce the exposure hazard. However this does not resolve the problem of the existing power cables strung over or immediately close to buildings where people live, work, play and convalesce. The increasingly insatiable demand by the public and the military for more electrical power throughout the world means that power companies have to continually upgrade the voltages carried by their cables. At one stage 100kV was considered adequate to satisfy demand; then 275kV became the norm, and now many overhead lines carry 400kV. This means that the width of the 'safe' corridors on either side of the lines are inadequate. Furthermore, those who live along these corridors are not told when the power companies upgrade the load. At the very least an adequate *cordon sanitaire* system forming safe corridors along all overhead and underground cables should be a legally enforced planning policy. An equally strong planning control is needed to protect those in close proximity to TV, radio and mobile phone transmission masts.

In the first major NRPB review since 1994, the Advisory Group on Non-Ionising Radiation (AGNIR) published its report 'ELF, EMFs and the Risk of Cancer' on 6 March 2001.[8] The team was led by Professor Sir Richard Doll and included Sir Walter Bodmer, Director-General of the Imperial Cancer Research Campaign, and Dr Michael Clark and Professor Colin Blakemore of the NRPB.

Professor Blakemore was quoted as saying that the report shows 'evidence that there is a slightly elevated risk of cancer near to power lines'. For the first time, the NRPB has publicly acknowledged that there is a link between high-voltage cables and cancer, and that EMF levels above 0.4 microTeslas increases the risk of childhood leukaemia. However, Professor Doll still insisted that there was no laboratory evidence.

Professor Doll, an eminent epidemiologist, discovered the link between smoking and lung cancer in the 1960s. He relied on the 'circumstantial' evidence of anecdotal and epidemiological evidence, but it took almost another forty years for the case to be scientifically proved. In contrast to this, through the 1960s and 1970s, Sir Richard and others convinced the government and the public that asbestos was safe. In 1965, writing about the asbestos products manufacturer Turner and Newall, Sir Richard suggested that it was likely that the specific occupational hazards to life had been completely eliminated. As late as 1982 he criticised the government for bringing in stricter controls of asbestos, and suggested that asbestosis and other asbestos-related diseases were no longer a significant risk to workers. Recall the figures in Chapter 1, which indicate that deaths from asbestos diseases will continue to rise and may not peak until about 2020 when fatalities may reach 10,000 a year.

The view that generated EMFs can be linked to serious health hazards had been steadfastly dismissed by the NRPB and yet, both the independent research scientists and affected members of the general public are convinced that the long-term anecdotal and strong epidemiological evidence has been overwhelming.[9]

Radio frequency transmission masts

Certain medical treatments, microwave ovens and heating for industrial processing of materials use high-power radio frequency radiation (RFR). Medium-power RFR is used for air traffic control guidance systems, civil and military radar, satellite broadcasting and telephone communications systems including cellular mobile telephones.

The demand for radio frequency power began in the 1920s with the birth of public service broadcasting; it increased after 1950 and now, in 2002, frequencies in the radio spectrum are almost unavailable. The demand for allocations in the higher frequencies in the VHF, FM and RADAR (microwave) bands used for cellular telephone communications systems has proliferated to the extent that governments have resorted to auctioning licences. Recent bids for licences in the US for the mobile phone band produced revenues in the order of $20 billion[10] and a figure of £22 billion was achieved in the UK in 2000.

For several years the Americans have used a multipoint microwave distribution system (MMDS) for transmitting TV signals. Conventional TV signals are transmitted around 800MHz but an MMDS operates at a frequency between 2.5 and 2.685GHz, which is close to a microwave oven band of 2.45GHz. The advantages of MMDS is that it can penetrate mist and cloud to improve reception and carry many different channels. Eire was the first in Europe to install an MMDS system and no doubt many more will follow.

Radiation from an MMDS transmission mast emits an omnidirectional beam and radiates in a below-horizon plane, whereas conventional microwave systems throw a fairly narrow beam in line of sight to the next receiver mast.[11]

There were over a quarter of a million TV signal and microwave telephone transmission towers in the US at the turn of the last decade. At the same time, in Britain the only operators were the four main TV channels, British Telecom and the Ministry of Defence plus a few others. By the late 1990s, the mobile phone radio band in the UK was virtually full, with 28,000 existing licences, resulting in the rapidly increasing demand for transmission mast sites. Broadcasting towers carrying radio frequency and microwave transmissions continue to sprout up everywhere and these, together with the proliferation of mobile phone satellite stations orbiting the sky to give total global coverage, means that wherever we choose to live – even on the most remote desert island – we are enveloped in an electromagnetic smog of invisible waves. (This may be of great comfort to those people who would take their mobile phone with them on a desert island holiday to ensure they are always 'connected'.)

In 2001, the Vatican Radio transmitters near Anguillara Sabazia, north of Rome, were under threat of having their electricity supply cut off over a dispute involving radiation hazards linked to leukaemia clusters in the vicinity, which were six times the national average. Recorded FM transmissions, said to be above three times Italy's current guidelines, were expected to lead to plans to reduce the output.[12]

The all-pervading smog is not just affecting humans. The phenomenon of whales beaching themselves may well be due to electromagnetic interference, and the secretary of the New Ross and District Pigeon Club in Ireland blames radiowaves emitted from mobile phone masts and satellite television networks for so many racing birds not returning to base. A pigeon's homing instinct depends on its natural ability to navigate by the Sun and the Earth's magnetic fields as well as by sight. Geomagnetic storms can also upset a pigeon's biological compass, but the incidence of birds failing to return home is increasing.[13]

So does this incessant smog cause us harm? Radio and microwave frequencies can pass through buildings and all other obstacles including our flesh, blood, organs and brain. It may be that most people are unaffected by radiowaves but the Environmental Health Criteria 137 published by the World Health Organization (WHO) in 1993 warned that radio frequency radiation for transmitters can have a similar hazardous effect as living under power lines.

The WHO report says: 'There is increasing concern about the possibility that radio frequency exposure may play a role in the causation of promotion of cancer, specifically of the blood-forming organs or in the central nervous system. Similar uncertainties surround possible effects on reproduction, such as increased rates of spontaneous abortion and of congenital malformations. At frequencies below a few hundred kilohertz, the electrical stimulation of excitable membranes of nerves and muscle cells is a well established phenomenon.'[14]

Very few studies have been carried out in the UK, however in other countries – the US and Sweden in particular – research work on the possible health hazard effects of electrical power lines indicates that prolonged exposure to those living near high-voltage transmission pylons, radio and TV transmitters, electrical sub-stations and transformers have a greater incidence of cancer and other health problems such as food allergies and electrical hypersensitivity. The WHO report suggests that there are hotspots where a cluster of radio frequency transmitters occurs and the strength of field is concentrated by overlapping beams. As the brain functions by extremely weak electrical currents, an electromagnetic field frequency could trigger a spontaneous reaction such as an epileptic fit.

Independent science and medical researchers have investigated the potential health hazards caused by civilian radio and TV transmitters and Ministry of Defence communications systems. As early as 1930 the USSR recognised the dangers of microwaves and the effects on the body of extremely low-frequency radiation. Ironically, it was the effect of microwave 'bombardment' by the Soviets on the American Embassy in Moscow that led to a significant change of attitude in the US. Whether the extensive microwave radiation beamed at the US building was used only for surveillance or was intended to disable the embassy personnel, the overall effect on the staff, discovered by US defence scientists, was a chronic malaise, and subsequent blood tests indicated that 43 per cent of the staff were classified as having experienced high-risk mutagenic exposure. The Americans were also using microwave radiation to spy on Soviet embassies, and eventually the CIA and KGB negotiated an agreement to reduce their respective levels of bombardment. Unfortunately it was too late for the Ambassador Walter Stoessel: his resignation and premature death was due to a rare blood disorder. Significantly, his two predecessors also died of cancer.

Results of the British Ministry of Defence research on radio frequencies and microwaves are being kept secret; however, US studies of civilian exposure to radar beams indicate that in the case of one particular residential building, which was in line of sight between two radar stations, there was a cancer death rate six times above a normal control group. Ann Silk, opthalamist and Fellow of the Royal Society of Medicine (see also pages 47, 64, 91 and 122), was part of a Forestry Commission Study in 1993 to investigate the 85 sites in the UK where oak trees were dying from the top down even though they had healthy root systems. All the sites were within a few kilometres from high-power multi-use radio and microwave transmission masts.[15]

Two studies carried out in Latvia in the vicinity of a pulsed radio station at Skrunda showed that of 966 children aged between 9 and 18 years, motor function, memory and attention were significantly worse in the exposed group. The children living in front of the station fared worst. A study made on brown Latvian cows near the radio station showed statistically significant differences in micronuclei levels in peripheral erythrocytes (red blood cells) in the exposed and controlled groups.[16] UK government funded studies in the mid-1990s found no evidence of carcinogenic hazard from exposure to electromagnetic fields but this does not accord with other, more independent, scientific and medical research such as the work of Dr Bruce Hocking who found that the mortality rate for children with leukaemia was more than doubled if they lived within 4 kilometres of a TV mast in Sydney.[17] Also, Dr Mark Payne, a specialist in environmental medicine, reported on his investigation of a significant cluster of leukaemia and lymphoma cases close to the most powerful mast in the UK, the Sutton Coldfield TV and radio transmitter in the Midlands. He also found a cluster of mental illness in the vicinity of the mast and referred to Dr Robert Becker's book *Cross Currents* in which Becker showed that mental illness can be associated with fluctuating magnetic fields. At the time the safety level used for power density radiation from such transmitters in both the UK and US was 10 milliwatts per square centimetre, whereas the Russian level was 10 microwatts per square centimetre (that is, 10 times lower).[18]

Further research by Dr Henry Lai and Dr N. P. Singh of Bioelectro Magnetics Research Laboratory, University of Washington, Seattle, has shown that exposure to radio frequency radiation can affect the nervous system: the effects include changes in neural tissue, neural chemistry, brainwave functions and behaviour patterns. Experiments on rats showed RFR caused DNA damage.[19]

It may be difficult to believe that scientists at the Microwave Research Centre in Marlborough, New Hampshire, began experimenting with a microwave 'home heating system which warms people by exciting the body's water molecules, thus raising body temperature'. The system used a standard 800-watt transmitter sending micro-waves into a room through a hole in one of the walls, which virtually turned the room into a very low-powered microwave oven![20]

Despite the mounting weight of scientific, epidemiological and medical evidence that exposure – especially prolonged exposure – to radio frequency and microwave radiation emitted from transmission masts can seriously affect biological systems, many US government and official agencies are publicly in favour, encourage and sometimes fund the growth in telecommunications systems and the erection of masts. The UK government issued Town Planning guidelines (PPG8A) allowing cellular phone companies to erect masts and antenna almost anywhere,[21] and the Scottish Office offered public money to help Cellnet and Vodaphone build 250 more aerial towers in the Highlands.[22]

Since then there has been a significant u-turn. In July 2001 new regulations came into force in Scotland requiring Town Planning consent for all ground-based masts, with limits also placed on the number and height of masts on buildings. Generally, masts will not be permitted in Conservation or National Heritage areas. South of the border in England, organised opponents to the indiscriminate siting of masts who have won landmark cases have based their objections on the serious harm a mast would cause to the visual amenity in the neighbourhood as well as the possible effects on the health of the residents.[23]

As early as 1994 the British Association of Metropolitan Authorities (AMA) and the Association of District Councils (ADC) met to discuss their concerns about the possi-ble links between electromagnetic fields and cancer, and how this should be taken into consideration when dealing with Town Planning applications. Their request for the government to issue guidelines to all local authorities on how to handle such applications involving equipment or installations generating electromagnetic fields was dismissed by the Department of the Environment on the grounds that evidence suggesting possible links with cancer or other health problems were inconclusive and therefore it would be premature to issue formal guidance.[24] Similarly, in 1996 the US government Telecommunications Act, signed by Congress, limited the power of state and local governments to control the siting of masts and similar wireless services. The Act stated: 'The National interest requires wireless services to be established with minimal delay in US communities and the power of local groups to control or refuse installations must be restricted'. This virtually deprived the public of the right to protect itself from potential health hazards.[25] If the emissions from a transmission mast were subjected to the same tests and scrutiny applied to a new drug product by a pharmaceutical company, their siting and transmission output would have been under stricter controls. Even with the more stringent regulations controlling the intro-duction of new drugs we still suffered the tragic circumstances of thalidomide, and second-generation children continue to suffer the long-term effects.

The telecommunications industry operates on the belief system that the emissions from cellular phone masts and pylons are completely harmless. Mobile phone companies have already erected 20,000 masts in the UK and another 100,000 are planned, which will subject hundreds of thousands of people, including young children, to near-constant low-level radiation. Recognising that informed public opinion is profoundly concerned about the potential health hazards and the protection of the environment, the companies have targeted school premises because most schools desperately need funds – the prospect of a substantial annual income for allowing a mast to be erected on the premises is a tempting offer and difficult to resist. More than 500 schools in the UK have so far been paid up to £10,000 each to allow mobile phone companies to build transmission masts on the school premises.[26] In the small town of Merton, Wisconsin, the school board accepted a 'very generous offer', but the parents, local community and local planning commission rejected the scheme and eventually defeated the erection of two cellular towers. A similar confrontation concerned a school in Ingatestone, a small town in Essex, where Orange proposed to erect a mast on the primary school premises. Parents and the local council battled against the scheme and after a year the Essex Education Authority was persuaded to ban all transmission masts on all school premises. In July 1999, parents threatened to remove children from a London junior school amid health fears over a 10-metre (32-feet) mobile phone mast erected at the school, again by Orange, which pays the school £6,000 a year. It was erected in 1996, at a time when little was known about the potential health risks. In November 1999, the parents of the schoolchildren celebrated winning their case to have the mast removed.[27]

Such local acts of public defiance are in direct contravention of the UK government's prohibition on all planning authorities from rejecting any radiating installations on the grounds of a potential health hazard. Dr Gerard Hyland of the Department of Physics at the University of Warwick suggests that evidence has shown that masts could affect the brain, may cause cancers and should not be erected anywhere near schools. Brain activity in children is changing until about the age of 12, and there is therefore a risk of interfering with that development.[28] Dr Hyland has also suggested that cordless phones may pose an even greater risk than mobiles because of the frequency and nature of their use.[29]

The subject became such a controversial issue in the US that President Clinton decreed that masts would be sited on Federal buildings instead of being located on school property. New Zealand and Australia followed suit but extended the ban on schools to include childcare centres, nursing homes, hospitals and residences and to ensure no mast be erected within 500 metres (1,650 feet) of these buildings. Other regulations controlled the monitoring of radiation emissions with annual checks being carried out. However, following the UK example, governments of other countries do not give their local planning authorities and community groups the support to enable the public to exercise caution and avoidance. Nevertheless, more enlightened local councils have found other means of interpreting their bylaws and Town Planning acts to successfully oppose the erection of transmission towers and keep them sited away from vulnerable buildings.

Tenacious and vigorous campaigning by those who are profoundly concerned about the potential health hazards and protection of the environment do have their voices heard but, almost without doubt, most individuals will be a mobile phone user, thus adding to the public's seemingly insatiable demand for more and more masts to be erected.

Advancing technology in the future may create many other microwave-operated gadgets which in turn will again increase the demand for electricity and more power transmission lines, resulting in even denser electromagnetic smog and the proliferation of 'hotspot' locations. Eventually the confrontation and conflicts of interest will have to be resolved. In the meantime, the ubiquitous use of the mobile phone continues to have a profound effect on our life, lifestyle, social mores and health. (For the evidence relating to mobile phones, see Chapter 5, 'The cybernetic age'.)

Daily exposure hazards

The general public at large does not tend to read about the likely health hazards of electromagnetic fields in scientific journals and papers; instead we glean snippets of information from the sporadic TV programme or newspaper article that rarely give an in-depth analysis of current research. Hardly ever are we advised how to avoid unnecessary exposure and, as most TV programmes have to give a 'balanced' view, we are left with no clear guidance. The government and the medical authorities show little or no concern for the possible health risks and, like architects and engineers, few doctors have any knowledge or interest in the subject. In the meantime, while the independent scientists and researchers continue their battle with their opponents who act for the electricity producers and manufacturers, the public is left in a state of unawareness, uncertainty and confusion.

Susceptibility and sensitivity to electromagnetic fields varies: some people can be exposed to high levels without feeling any adverse effect in the same manner as some people can be heavy smokers all their life and live to be 90 years old. However, an increasing number of people are suffering an electromagnetic sensitivity (EMS) so acutely that their lives are blighted by it.

The October 1998 issue of the women's magazine *Red* ran an article reporting the plight of two British EMS patients. The first case concerned a woman living in the north of England who was so sensitive that there were some rooms in her house she could not enter; neither could she use electrical equipment, listen to music or watch TV, otherwise her face went into a spasm and she often passed out temporarily or went blind. Even if she used the telephone it caused a painful reaction. Another woman, living close to London, cannot wear jewellery or metal zips. When she is so fatigued and cannot sleep, she uses a cable with a plug and single earth pin at one end and the bare wire at the other, tied in a loop around her fingers; she plugs the cable into a wall socket to relieve a severe attack.[30] The symptoms vary from severe skin reactions to headaches, dizziness, fatigue and internal organ disorders which, in extreme cases can progress to blackouts, fits and almost complete disablement and inability to lead a 'normal' life. Patients with mercury or other metal-based dental amalgam fillings have also been prone to develop hypersensitivity.

By a process of elimination, an American surgeon from Texas, Dr William Rae, discovered his own allergic and neurological symptoms were caused by the electromagnetic fields from the array of equipment and medical apparatus found in modern operating theatres. He soon realised there were many fellow sufferers of EMS who were not being taken seriously or treated because their physicians were either sceptical or ignorant of the condition and totally unprepared to deal with the problem. This encouraged him to start up his own environmental health centre in Dallas.[31]

Although there may be no outward or immediately apparent symptoms, the effects of EMS can still be life threatening. A study by Brigitta Floderus at the World Life Institute, Stockholm, Sweden, shows that people who in their work environment are exposed to strong EM fields run the risk of developing breast, testicular and skin cancer. This was significant in that as a result of EMF exposure these cancers had not previously figured as prominently as other cancers such as leukaemia and brain tumours. The studies, carried out between 1971 and 1984, showed the highest exposure group were train drivers and sewing-machine operators. The middle group included secretaries and architects and the lowest group included drivers and hospital workers.[32]

Telephone and power-line workers, electricians and power station workers – all those whose occupations expose them to electromagnetic radiation – have six times the expected rate of male breast cancer. The incidence was tripled for radio and communications workers. A study by epidemiologists at the Fred Hutchinson Cancer Research Centre in Seattle was based on 227 cases of male breast cancer over three years. Men who are under 30 years of age when first exposed run an even higher risk.[33] Studies carried out at Johns Hopkins University show similar results of increased risk of male breast cancer among New York workers exposed to switch gear. Also, at the Fred Hutchinson Cancer Research Centre, in June 1990 Paul Demers and Dr David Thomas found a statistically significant six-fold increase in breast cancer among telephone-line men, electricians and electrical power workers.[34] Similar studies of an increase in breast cancer among New York central office telephone technicians were reported in *The Lancet*,[35] and studies of Norwegian workers exposed to electromagnetic fields at work found a two-fold increase in the development of breast cancer.[36] The same magazine published another American study by Dr Dana Loomis of the University of North Carolina, reporting the US Department of Energy findings that female electrical workers had a 40 per cent increased mortality from breast cancer than women in non-electrical occupations.[37]

In 1990, the Boeing Corporation of Seattle, Washington, agreed an out-of-court settlement of $500,000 with a Mr Robert Strom over his claim that he had developed leukaemia as a result of exposure at work to electromagnetic pulse (EMP) radiation. The settlement also provided for a medical programme for the 700 Boeing employees on EMP testing since the 1960s. Strom worked inside a shielded room where EMP pulsers were fired hundreds of times a day to test the effects on the electrical and electronic equipment used in missiles. In 1985, aged 45, Strom was diagnosed as having chronic myelogenous leukaemia. It became known, during the case, that as early as 1979 Boeing had circulated a memo stating that there were indications that EMP radiation disturbs the whole chemical balance of the body. After the case Robert Strom and his wife used some of the settlement money to set up a foundation to disseminate electromagnetic field hazards information through schools, unions and other organisations.[38]

A leaflet on EMF exposure at work, published in 1995 by the Harvard Centre for Risk Analysis, reported that the evidence for the link with cancer is overwhelming and that the US alone was spending $25–30 million annually on research. A University of Southern California research programme in 1996 showed growing evidence that exposure to EMFs may be linked to Alzheimer's disease and indicated that the incidence is sharply higher among workers exposed to EMFs who have up to five times the normal risk of contracting the disease. The greatest risk was found among people who operated sewing machines and tools. Alzheimer's disease afflicts as many as 4 million Americans and causes about 100,000 deaths a year. Although researchers have linked at least two different genes to the disease, it is clear that environmental factors also play a major role.[39]

Canadian researcher Dr David Savitz presented his results of the examination of data on 140,000 employees of five electric utilities and found that 5 to 20 years of electromagnetic field exposure doubled the risk of developing the neuro-degenerative disorder amyotrophic lateral sclerosis (ALS), and that over 20 years' work exposure trebled the risk of developing the disease.[40] One group of people who are constantly at risk are those who are in the military services and the weapons research establishments. Ironically, in 1993, just as the NRPB in the UK raised its permitted microwave levels, two US military research bases reduced their permitted levels of radio frequency exposure because they acknowledged the published evidence for the harmful effects of high-frequency radiation on biological systems.[41]

The Royal Signals regiment based in Malvern recorded an incidence of brain tumours over six times the national average. An abstract from *The Science of the Total Environment* (1996) included the findings of Stanislaw Szmigielski on cancer morbidity in the whole population of military career personnel in Poland from 1971 to 1985. Subjects exposed in their work to radio frequencies and microwaves were found to have a death rate from malignancies of the haemato-lymphate and other cancers seven times higher than the usual risk rate.[42] (Radar screen operators may be particularly at risk. Second World War anecdotes spoke of Royal Navy personnel queuing up to sit on the large radar screens to irradiate their testicles before taking shore leave!)

Consensus records in Sweden showed a link between occupational and residential exposure to magnetic fields generated by power cables. Leukaemia and central nervous system tumour cases were identified from a population living within 300 metres (980 feet) of overhead transmission lines. The Institute of Environmental Medicine, Karolinska Institute of Stockholm, concluded that the results of the studies provided strong support for the association of magnetic field exposure and high-risk leukaemia at work and in the home.[43]

Perhaps the case most publicised in the British national press and on TV began in August 1993 when the Studholme family launched the first lawsuit against the local electricity company for damages on account of the levels of EMFs in their son's bedroom, alleging that these contributed to his death. Simon Studholme, aged 14, became anaemic and collapsed at school in 1990 just 21 months after the family moved into their new home in Bolton, Lancashire. He was diagnosed as suffering from acute lymphoblastic leukaemia and died two years later. Simon had spent some 6,000 hours in his bedroom where there was a high concentration of EMFs generated by the combination of the household electricity supply meter and alarm system located on the other side of the wall near his bedhead and two underground cables and a sub-station next door to the detached house. The strength of the magnetic field was observed to be more than 10 times the level which American and Swedish studies had linked to an increased risk of cancer, and over 17 times the usual average background levels. The Studholmes also sought damages for the epilepsy their 12-year-old daughter had begun to suffer about a year after they moved into the new house. Their other son also started showing signs of hyperactivity and skin rashes. Interestingly, the daughter's fits used to start at first around 2pm on Sunday afternoons, coinciding with peak electricity demands for Sunday lunch cooking, though later the fits occurred more frequently.[44]

The Studholmes were granted legal aid but by 1997, partly due to fatigue and the long drawn-out processes of the legal system, time limits and lack of funds, they had to abandon the action. Had they been successful the result would have had extraordinary implications for all the electricity supply companies throughout Britain which would have faced similar claims from thousands of homes, schools, offices and hospitals located in the vicinity of sub-stations, overhead and underground high-tension cables.

The health risk debate

Public apathy is a blessing to all politicians, public utility companies and the other authorities that seem to be in control of our lives. Informed opinion suggests that electromagnetic pollution may prove to be a far greater danger to life on Earth than chemical pollution to the soil, sea and air. Therefore, the bland reassurances from government departments and power producers need to be challenged, and those who create the built environment should practise procedures to avoid, reduce or eliminate the exposure risks.

While we may not be able to rely on the government and its agencies, such as the NRPB, or the electricity supply companies to take a lead in bringing public awareness of the likely health hazards, the elected councillors of many local authorities are far more conscious of the public's concern regarding electromagnetic fields and have made representations to the government to provide some practical guidelines. In 1998, in response to such requests, the Department of the Environment, Transport and the Regions (DETR) and the Department of Health jointly issued a circular to local planning authorities entitled 'Consultation Exercise: Land use, planning and electromagnetic fields'. This was intended to give advice on land use, planning and development such as overhead power lines and telecommunications base stations giving rise to the growing concerns about the possible hazards of EMFs. The document was accompanied by a pre-publication copy of a report by the WHO. Comments on both documents were requested by February 1999 but there was no indication as to when the final work would be published. The documents did not state that the two authors of the WHO report were Philip Chadwick and Zenon Sienkiewicz, who are members of the NRPB. It is not surprising therefore that the circular gives the NRPB's views on exposure risks, which the organisation considers to be either small or non-existent. This view does not reflect extensive international studies such as the American National Institute of Environmental Health Sciences (NIEHS) report classifying power frequency fields as 'possible human carcinogens'. The NRPB bias was well-expressed in paragraph 17, which stated:

> If local authorities are considering adopting policies which would have the effect of introducing any *cordon sanitaire* around telecommunications or electricity supply equipment (such as masts or overhead powerlines), or which otherwise seek to restrict such development, they should have regard to operators' responsibilities under health and safety legislation and the lack of convincing evidence of a causal link between exposure to EMFs and cancer.[45]

This negative statement ignored the overwhelming evidence from so many studies and research groups around the world, but one redeeming passage did offer a small glimmer of light. Referring to the 'material considerations' to be taken into account when a local authority is assessing a planning application, it stated: 'The courts have held that any genuine public perception of danger is a valid planning consideration, although the weight to be given to this will be a matter for the body determining the application, taking into account the particular facts of the case.'[46] However, this one promising passage does not counterbalance the most extraordinary misleading statements and lack of impartiality.

Such negative attitudes will do nothing to help the control of the proliferation of pylons and masts but simply add credence to the electricity industry's staunch refusal to accept any association between electromagnetic fields and health hazards such as cancer, clinical depression, headaches, suicide and particularly the effect on unborn babies and children. This in turn encourages architects and engineers to dismiss the likelihood of any potential health hazards – other than severe electric shock or as a source of a fire. Without regard to the effect magnetic and electric field levels may have on the occupants, high-power cables are run under buildings and in-house mains cables and sub-station transformers are installed allowing no safe distances from critical, occupied areas. In particular, protective shielding from magnetic fields is rarely considered except where the client may point out that the electronic business equipment may be subjected to interference. People are never considered.

From time to time, newspapers and TV programmes have helped to heighten awareness of the potential hazards, yet the public's interest and enthusiasm tends to be short-lived. However, a Channel 4 'Dispatches' programme in 1996 did make an impact on the electricity producers. After the broadcast a leading electrical supply industry magazine, *Electrical Review*, ran an 'opinion' column which concluded:

> In the meantime, it seems that we should be taking some precautions to minimise the risk – if one exists. For instance, it seems folly to build more new homes under or near power lines. In fact, after the recent TV CH4 *Dispatches* programme, it is doubtful whether any property developer will attempt projects of this type because the resulting homes will be almost impossible to sell, no matter how attractively they are priced. It would also seem prudent for power companies with lines running through housing estates to re-route or underground them. But, despite the possible PR value of this course of action, the companies will doubtless argue against it, both on the grounds of

cost and because it would be tantamount to admitting that their lines could affect the health of the residents below. One certainty is that, no matter how much the electricity industry would like it, this subject is not going to go away.[47]

The *Financial Times* ran a front page story on 11 October 1996 reporting that eight of Britain's leading electricity companies were planning to create an £8 million fund to fight claims that electromagnetic fields generated by high-tension power lines are hazardous to health. Wills Corron, an insurance advisor, said in a confidential report: 'A priority of the electricity industry must be to prevent legal precedent being established. This will require the strenuous defence of any claims and the associated costs are likely to be high'.[48]

While a growing number of independent scientists and environmentalists continue to challenge what they consider to be the lax and rather cavalier attitude of the NRPB, the National Grid company and British Nuclear Fuels, some British insurance companies, notably the Norwich Union, are getting tough in their risk assessments of public liability policies with electricity distributors. Some policies already restrict their exposure to pollution claims to exclude electric and magnetic fields from their liability policies. Other companies await further evidence of the link between electromagnetic fields and disease, but at the Lloyds of London Conference in 1998 insurance underwriters heard evidence from Dr Theodore Litivitz, Professor Emeritus of Physics at the Catholic University of America, who said he was convinced that electromagnetic fields cause the biological effects consistent with results from other scientists, and that EMFs played a role in promoting tumours and cancer.[49]

The Swiss Reinsurance Company of Zurich published a 37-page report in 1997 on the insurance and litigation implications of the possible health hazards associated with EMFs. The report focused on the essential issues and recommended that solutions should be sought, 'not before the courts or in the research laboratories but in the socio-political controversy of how to deal with risks'. The report concludes:

> As a consequence the EMF problem cannot be delegated to individual groups or institutions: that would be like leaving the formulation of a contract to just one of the parties. Dealing with phantom risks is a task for all of society, a task which in the final analysis will go so far as to require further developments of the democratic decision-making process and the partial reordering of society itself. It is not acceptable to force risks on individual human beings; neither is it in the interest of the general public to dispense with technological opportunity because of the possibility that individuals might suffer harm. What is required, therefore, is a general consensus on how much risk individuals may reasonably be expected to accept. Two consequences can be drawn from this: first, every citizen should be prepared to bear part of the collective burden of risk. Secondly, society must show its solidarity with victims by helping them to deal at least with the financial loss involved. Yet people in modern industrial societies are neither willing to participate in collective risks – they will tolerate their share at best – nor do they consider themselves under any obligation to help those who have suffered harm. As a logical consequence they demand compensation.[50]

In September 1998, a Swiss Senior Risk Management Officer, Mr C. Brauner, continued the debate at the Bristol University Conference. His view was that natural science and medicine still cannot finally confirm whether EMFs are hazardous, and that the only reliable answer at the moment is 'perhaps'. The relationships between EMFs and immune deficiency diseases such as cancer and Alzheimer's are complex, and current research methods are not developed sufficiently to mount an incontrovertible case. But when the escalating weight of public opinion is added to the improving scientific studies and research that continues in many countries, especially Britain, the US, Europe, Scandinavia and Japan, the perception of the health risk will hold sway and it will be the general public's opinion that will affect the outcome in a court of law. Our values, laws, customs and conventions that condition human interaction will be the final arbiter rather than the scientists or insurers.[51]

If the conflict continues to escalate, and claims are awarded, this could trigger the collapse of the insurance industry, which would have far-reaching and disastrous consequences affecting the basic structure of society. It is therefore imperative that the two opposing forces come to an acceptance that 'maybe' EMFs could be a health risk and therefore we, the general public, need not get alarmed but should be warned and encouraged to exercise 'prudent avoidance'. At the same time, national and local government authorities and power companies should limit development in the vicinity of power lines. This may well bring about a reaction affecting the values of property under, over or near transmission lines, but the cost of voluntarily paying out some reasonable compensation could well be offset by the high costs of litigation defence.

Unfortunately, prudent avoidance is not an adopted policy in Britain. The first problem is that the NRPB's acceptable levels of exposure are far higher, which allows the electrical industry to operate within guidelines that are less stringent than the threshold levels of safety set by other European countries such as Germany and Sweden. The second problem is fear: National Grid takes the position that if it ever adopted the stance of prudent avoidance by restricting the development or habitation of any building within, say, a 100-metre (330-feet) wide corridor along the length of a power line – overhead or underground – it would immediately cause panic to all those who already occupy property within those limits. (A similar argument was set up by mobile phone manufacturers who suppressed the sales of phones claiming to reduce the effects of radiation from the aerials.) The generating companies fear that exercising such prudent avoidance would be tantamount to an admission that power lines are a possible health hazard and open the floodgates for claims of compensation.

So far, the array of PR consultants and lawyers backed by sceptical scientists hired by generating companies have successfully repelled the evidence produced by the independent biologists, epidemiologists, physicists and environmentalists who are aligned against the view held by the establishment that electromagnetic fields are not proven to be hazardous. However, the more pragmatic view expressed by some insurance companies and property mortgage lenders indicates that the risks are very real and that despite the huge sums of money being spent on research and the conflicting opinions of the science experts, it will be the perception of society that will ultimately sway the balance.

National Grid and the NRPB have expressed the view that it is unlikely there would be massive claims similar to those related to asbestos and smoking, but insurers believe that a successful test case is inevitable in the foreseeable future.

Guardian Insurance of London reviewed its standards of risk assessment of public liability insurance with several power companies, including Eastern Electricity and Norweb, which led to premiums being increased because of likely future liabilities. Other insurance companies which already restrict their exposure to pollution liability claims will exclude electric and magnetic fields from their liability policies. As early as 1995 an article in the *Daily Mail* (25 September 1995) reported that major lenders were either refusing house mortgages on properties next to overhead power lines or insisting that the price be reduced. Some building societies tell their surveyors to not even bother valuing a house located under high-tension cables. Public awareness is increasing and soon, as in other countries, it may become obligatory for a house to be surveyed for electric and magnetic field levels. Property blight and the threat of legal action against surveyors and architects for professional negligence will bring a commercial realism to the debate. Other practical business considerations may well accelerate a change in attitude.

The Royal Institution of Chartered Surveyors (RICS) issued a 'Red Book' practice guidance statement recommending appropriate wording for surveyors to include in their structural reports to avoid leaving themselves vulnerable to professional negligence litigation. The guidance states that where the property is near high-voltage electrical supply apparatus (power lines, sub-stations) the surveyor should note in the report: 'There is a high voltage electrical supply apparatus within close proximity of the property. Public perception that higher than normal electromagnetic fields may affect health is likely to affect marketability and future value. Consideration should be given to further investigation prior to exchange of contracts'.[52] This statement, published in 1996, was subsequently amended in the 1997 revision section PSA 3.7 High Voltage Electrical Supply Apparatus as follows:

> There is high-voltage electrical supply equipment close to the property. The possible effects of electromagnetic fields have been the subject of media coverage, but the National Radiological Protection Board (NRPB), an independent body with responsibility for advising on electromagnetic fields, has concluded that, 'there is no clear evidence of adverse health effects at the levels of electromagnetic fields to which people are normally exposed'. Public perception may, however, affect marketability and future value of the property. If required, technical information can be obtained from the NRPB or the local electricity company.[53]

If the would-be purchaser of a house received a structural report containing such a paragraph and then contacted the local electricity supply company it is likely that he or she will be offered a test by one of the inspectors, followed up with a letter giving reassurances and quote words to the effect that 'statistical and biological research published in July 1997 and at the end of the year added support to the view that there was not a connection between low frequency magnetic fields and health. This research also led to the cessation of the impending legal action in the UK'. (This is a reference to the Studholme case referred to on pages 96–97.)

However, if the would-be purchaser checked other scientific sources he or she would find abundant evidence to contradict such claims by the electricity supply company. The purchaser would also find some mortgage companies unwilling to lend on the property unless the valuation was downgraded. With the exception of Scandinavia and perhaps a handful of other countries, at the moment no-one can rely on their respective government to recognise the possibility that the overwhelming evidence produced by independent scientists throughout the world clearly indicates a link between electromagnetic fields and some of the 'diseases of civilisation'.

References

1. 'Sweden officially recognises EMF–cancer link based on new studies (*Epidemiology* 1997, 8: 25–30)', *Electromagnetic News*, vol. 3, nos 5–6, December 1992, pp. 1 and 2.
2. 'Higher Leukaemia in Taiwanese adults living near power lines', *Electromagnetic Hazard & Therapy*, vol. 8, no. 2, 1997, p. 7.
3. Gowan, D. and Girdlestone, R. (1996) *Safe as Houses*, Bath: Gateway Books.
4. Collings, J. (1991) *Life Forces*, London: New English Library, pp. 197–98.
5. 'Hong Kong powerline operation continues', *Powerwatch Network Newsletter*, Issue 3, July 1995, p. 2.
6. 'Australian Senate EMF inquiry', *Powerwatch Network Newsletter*, Issue 6, January 1996, p. 4.
7. 'REVOLT and the Yorkshire powerline saga', *Powerwatch Network Newsleter*, Issue 4, September 1995, pp. 3–4.
8. NRPB, *The Advisory Group on Non-Ionising Radiation* (AGNIR), vol. 12, no. 1, March 2001.
9. Walker, Martin J. (2001) 'The Great Outdoors', *The Ecologist*, vol. 31, no. 5, 5 June, p. 28.
10. Dominic Rush and Claire Oldfield, *The Sunday Times*, 'Business Focus' (p. 5), 16 Apil 2000.
11. 'Concern grows over Irish microwave TV system', *Electronics News*, vol. 1, no. 5, October 1990, p. 6.
12. 'Vatican Radio to receive transmissions', *Electromagnetic Hazard & Therapy*, vol. 11, nos 2–4, 2001, p. 11.
13. Nuala Haughey, 'Pigeon fanciers put blame on mobile phones as birds lose their bearings', *The Irish Times*, 21 June 1997.
14. *Environmental Health Criteria* 137, World Health Organization (WHO) 1993.
15. Ann Silk, 'EMFs and tree growth', *Powerwatch Network Newsletter*, Issue 3, July 1995, p. 1.
16. 'RF/MW studies show significant effects from Latvian radar', *Electromagnetic Hazard & Therapy*, vol. 7, nos 3–4, 1996–97, pp. 10–11.
17. 'Leukamias and TV and radio station masts', *Powerwatch Network Newsletter*, Issue 12, January 1997, p. 4.
18. 'Letter to the Editor from Dr Mark Payne, "Cancer cluster near Sutton Coldfield transmitter"', *Electronics News*, vol. 3, no. 2, April 1992, p. 6.
19. Cherry Norton and Richard Woods, *The Sunday Times*, 'Focus' (p. 10), 20 December 1998.
20. 'Microwaving your home', *Powerwatch Network Newsletter*, Issue 12, January 1997, p. 4. (Reported in 18 December issue of *New Scientist*.)
21. Government Town Planning Guidance Note PPG 8A.
22. *Powerwatch Network Newsletter*, 7 March 1996. 'Celular Phones', p.2.
23. 'Mast controls', *The Magazine of the Institution of Planning Supervisors*, 'News File', vol. 4, issue 4, August 2001, p. 4.
24. 'Councils, cancer, planning and electromagnetism', *The Architects Journal*, 17 November 1994, p. 18.
25. USA EMR Alliance – Spring 1996, reported by *Powerwatch Network Newsletter*, Issue 9, 1996, p. 3.
26. Peter Gruner, 'Primary school parents threaten boycott over mobile phone mast', *Evening Standard*, 7 July 1999, p. 22.
27. 'Orange masts re-sited or rejected after health protests by residents', *Electromagnetic Hazard & Therapy*, vol. 9, nos 1–2, 1998 p. 5.

28. Peter Gruner, 'Primary school parents threaten boycott over mobile phone mast', *Evening Standard*, 7 July 1999, p. 22.
29. Steve Farrar, 'Cordless phones are as big a radiation threat to brain as mobiles', *The Sunday Times*, 4 July 1999.
30. *Red Magazine*, October 1998. Published monthly by Emap Elan on behalf of Hachette-Emap Magazines Ltd, London.
31. Becker, R. (1990) *Cross Currents*, Los Angeles: Tarcher.
32. 'EMF diary by Leif Sodergren, FEB, Sweden', *Powerwatch Network Newsletter*, Issue 7, March 1996, p. 3.
33. *Electromagnetic News*, vol. 1, no. 4, 1990, p. 1.
34. Rob Edwards, 'Electric jobs "carry higher cancer risk", *The Guardian*, February 1996.
35. 'Electromagnetic field exposure and male breast cancer', letter to *The Lancet* from Genevieve Mantanoski, Patrick N. Breysse and Elizabeth A. Eliot from the Department of Epidemiology, Johns Hopkins University, School of Hygiene and Public Health, Baltimore, Maryland, *The Lancet*, vol. 337, 23 March 1991, p. 737.
36. 'Excess breast cancer in EMF workers found in third study', *Electromagnetic News*, vol. 2, no. 1, February 1991, pp. 1 and 2.
37. 'US study finds breast cancer risk in female electrical workers', *Electromagnetic and VDU News*, vol. 4, nos 3–4, July 1993, pp. 1 and 3.
38. '$500,000 paid to settle EMP–Leukemia claim by Boeing', *Electromagnetic News*, vol. 1, no. 5, September 1990, pp. 1 and 7.
39. 'Alzheimer's Disease Source' (*Los Angeles Times* 18/12/96), *Powerwatch Network Newsletter*, Issue 12, January 1997, p. 2.
40. 'Lou Gehrig's Disease (ALS)', *Powerwatch Network Newsletter*, Issue 14, June 1997, p. 3.
41. 'US military cut levels', *Magnetic and VDU News*, July/December 1993, p. 6. Reporting from *Microwave News*, September/October 1993.
42. Szmigielski, S. (1996) 'Career morbidity in subjects occupationally exposed to high frequency (radio frequency and microwave) electromagnetic radiation', *The Science of the Total Environment*, vol. 180, 1996, pp. 9–17.
43. 'Leukaemia and powerlines report by M. Feychting, U. Henriksson and B. Floderus', *Powerwatch Network Newsletter*, Issue 14, June 1997, p. 3.
44. 'First UK child cancer case against local power company', *Electromagnetic and VDU News*, vol. 4, nos 3–4, December 1993.
45. DETR and Department of Health Circular, 'Consultation Exercise: Land use, planning and electromagnetic fields', 1998.
46. 'Draft document on land use planning involving EMFs invites comments', *Electromagnetic Hazard & Therapy*, vol. 9, no. 4, 1998, pp. 1–2.
47. 'Fieldinig the health issue', in the opinion column, *Electrical Review*, vol. 229, no. 5, 5–18 March 1996, p. 18.
48. 'Power groups plan fighting fund', *Powerwatch Network Newsletter*, Issue 11, November 1996, p. 4.
49. 'Lloyds underwriters assess EMF threat', *Electromagnetic Hazard & Therapy*, vol. 9, nos 1–2, 1998, p. 6.
50. 'Swiss Re, Electromagnetic Smog – A Phantom Risk', published by Swiss Reinsurance Co Zurich, 1996, p. 35.
51. Ibid., 'Summary', p. 17.
52. RICS Red Book Practice Statements, 1996 edition.
53. RICS Red Book Practice Statements, Appendix 3 (6/97 revised), p. 4.

Suggested further reading

Brodeur, P. (1989) *Currents of Death*, New York: Simon & Schuster.
Coghill, R. (1990) *Electro-Pollution*, Northants: Thorsons.
Phillips, A. (1997) *Living with Electricity*, Cambridge: Powerwatch.

5.
The cybernetic age

Cybernetics: the science of communication and automatic control systems in both machines and living things.[1]

The information technology (IT) whiz kids, systems gurus and magicians are a latter-day 'priesthood' who have become indispensable to every business organisation and government department. They are the twenty-first-century witch doctors who can eradicate cybernetic viruses and bugs.

Mobile phones

Conservative estimates in 2000 indicated that in the UK at least 27 million people (46 per cent of the population) were regular mobile phone users – 3 million handsets were bought in 1999 alone.[2] Worldwide there were 200 million users in 1999 and by 2006 the global figure could reach one billion. As the number of microwave transmission masts abound so the electromagnetic smog we live in becomes denser and multiplies the number of dangerous 'hotspot' locations in almost every country in the world.

At a local level the use of mobile phones in public places such as trains, buses, restaurants, theatres and concert halls has become a social nuisance. What used to be a peaceful journey by train when we could read, write or sleep has now become a stressful and disruptive 'office' due to the incessant ringing of telephones. The intrusive noise of bells ringing and people speaking in unusually loud voices (as if they were talking from the cockpit of a helicopter) has now reached such unacceptable levels that in response to the mass of complaints at least one rail company has fitted carriage windows with a special film to block out telephone transmissions. Theatres and concert halls have to make special announcements to ensure the audience has switched off their phones. Despite the increasing bans in many restaurants, pubs and other public places, London Transport (LT) proudly announced in August 1998 that it was installing a new communications network making it possible – in about four years' time – to use mobile phones on the Tube! A spokesperson for LT was unsure about how commuters would react to the news that the underground train system will no longer be a telecommunications 'black hole'. If the complaints of the commuters on the overground train services are taken as a guide, LT may be spending a lot of money for nothing.

Airline passengers are told they must not use their mobile phones – or any other electronic equipment such as laptop computers and games – to avoid interference with the plane's radio and guidance systems. There have been many cases of mobile phones endangering flying safety by interfering with the onboard electronic systems. Mobile phones switched on, but not in use, have caused air-conditioning systems to be shut down and interference with instrument, landing, and navigation equipment. Laws in Germany and the US ban the use of mobile phones in aircraft and yet the majority of companies ignore the potential dangers and leave the problem to air crews to struggle with stubborn, arrogant passengers who are obsessed with their toys.[3] A businessman who refused to switch off his mobile phone on a 737 British Airways flight from Madrid to Manchester was jailed for 12 months in 1999 for endangering the aircraft. Other reports have linked mobile phone emissions to malfunctions in incubators, respirators, pacemakers, hearing aids and electric wheelchairs. There are even warnings about the likelihood of mobile phones causing an explosion if used when filling the car with petrol.

Another social hazard has been the increase in road accidents directly attributable to drivers losing concentration and control of their vehicle while using a mobile phone. Dr Barry Grimaldi, a general medical practitioner in London's Harley Street area, includes the following information in his 'Practice Information' pamphlet:

> The use of cellular phones continues to bug some people and be the lifeblood of others. A pair of recent studies has lent some weight to the notion that we should probably watch out where we use them. In Toronto, a study of automobile accidents revealed that 24% of drivers involved in accidents had used a cellular telephone during the ten minute interval before the accident. This increase in risk, of about four times, was similar to the hazard of driving whilst drunk.[4]

Despite warnings and penalties, attempts to outlaw the use of phones while the vehicle is moving have, so far, proved to be ineffective. Meanwhile, the Institute of Physiotherapists has identified another form of repetitive strain injury called 'Telephonitis', otherwise known as 'mobile phone shoulder droop', which can render the arm powerless. Hands-free equipment has been on the market for some time but it is rare to see these devices being used.

Eminent scientist Colin Blakemore, Professor of Physiology at Oxford University and a member of the non-ionising radiation advisory committee of the NRPB, said he had restricted his use of the mobile phone to calls not exceeding two minutes and for a total of no more than ten minutes a day since experiencing short-term memory loss and other effects. He warned that the now strong evidence of adverse effects on 'cognitive function, memory and attention' could have serious implications for those using a mobile phone while driving. Other scientists including Professor Jim Penman, head of engineering at Aberdeen University, Professor David Howard, head of electronics at York University, Professor Ross Adey (see Chapter 3) and Dr Kjell-

Hansson Mild of the National Institute of Working Life in Umea, Sweden, have also publicly expressed their deep concerns. Having studied the research papers, all now curtail the use of their mobile phones to a maximum of ten minutes a day.[5]

Dr Roger Coghill also believes it is extremely hazardous to use a phone for longer than a 20-minute period. After the 1998 World Cup final was lost by the Brazilians it was discovered that their 21-year-old star Ronaldo – voted the best footballer in the World but who played so poorly in the match – had suffered an epileptic fit the night before, immediately after making a 3-hour mobile phone call to his girlfriend. This was well published in the Brazilian national newspapers and may have helped to explain why France won 3–0! Further damning evidence of mobile phone health risks including epilepsy was reported by Dr Gerard Hyland, senior lecturer at the Department of Physics, Warwick University. Light flashing at a certain frequency can induce epilepsy. Mobile phones similarly flash at 217 times a second but although this cannot be seen by the human eye it will have a similar effect as flashing visual light.[6]

At the Mayo Clinic in Minnesota a study of patients with implanted cardiac pacemakers showed that with cellular phone use 20 per cent had changes in their pacemaker activity. The effect was most marked for the new GSM digital phones. As these phones become increasingly powerful we might see some of our older brethren walking around with signs saying – 'Caution: No cellular phone use near me!'. In the meantime the message is that pacemaker users should stick to analogue phones and whatever they do, keep them away from the breast pocket!

At a personal level the majority of phone users will consider the convenience factor to far outweigh any likely health hazard, especially as the mobile phone operators and manufacturers give bland assurances that there is no risk. This is precisely what most people want to hear despite the continually mounting scientific evidence to the contrary. Over the past 10 years or more, international scientific and medical researchers have expressed their deep concern and strong warnings have been published, establishing that as much as 80 per cent of the transmitted energy is absorbed into the side of the adult head next to the mobile phone ear port. Smaller heads, such as those of a child or small adult, can absorb even more radiated energy penetrating deeper into the brain (90 per cent of the radiation comes from the antenna and 5 per cent from the ear piece). Research also shows that after a few minutes' exposure to mobile phone type radiation a 5 per cent active cancer can be transformed into a 95 per cent active cancer. Statistics indicate that about 10 per cent of Europeans suffer adverse health effects, which is significantly higher than Americans and may be due to the reduced level of energy transmitted by analogue phone systems.

The long-awaited, hugely expensive Stewart Report – the report of the Independent Expert Group on Mobile Phones (IEGMP), chaired by Sir William Stewart – published in May 2000, has left the public, employers, and particularly parents of young children in a confused state of mind. The report states that it cannot be said with certainty that the use of mobile phones or transmitter masts are a health hazard *but* a precautionary approach is needed. At the same time it advocates parents to restrict children from 'non-essential' use, and calls for the Town Planning laws to be tightened to control the development of masts to prevent beams from falling on school buildings and playgrounds. The report adds that the mobile phone industry should not target young people in their advertising campaigns, and points out that a child's nervous system, brain and skull have not fully developed until puberty and, therefore, the evidence of weak radiation emissions may increase the dangers to health.[7] Research from Om Gandhi, Professor of Electrical Engineering at Utah University, has shown that young children using mobile phones absorb in their brain up to 50 per cent more radiation than adults. Due to the size and thickness of a child's skull, radiation penetrates halfway through the brain of a five-year-old; this falls to about 30 per cent for a ten year old.[8] Estimates are continually being revised upwards but well over half of young people – 7–16-year-olds – own a mobile phone.

The Stewart Report's only positive advice is that further research is needed and that the subject be reviewed again in three years' time. In the meantime, it has recommended that the government send out a leaflet to every household to acquaint everyone with the mobile phone health issue.

Interestingly, the Report recommends that the UK should adopt the 1998 International Commission on Non-Ionising Radiation Protection (ICNIRP) guidelines that were incorporated in a European Council Recommendation in 1999 and agreed in principle by all the EU countries. In Germany, for example, the ICNIRP guidelines have been put on the statute book. It also recommends a form of health warning be labelled on each phone stating the specific absorption rates of energy being emitted, and that claims for the degree of shielding by various proprietary devices such as hands-free equipment should be regulated. Motorists should be banned from using both handheld and hands-free phones while driving because their level of concentration is lowered, the cause of a significant rise in road accidents.

The Report does strongly recommend an approach that respects consumer choice and gives the public independent, expert information. In particular, it criticises the UK's National Radiological Protection Board's (NRPB's) approach to issues of public concern, and advises that it should take a proactive rather than a reactive stance and respond in a more sensitive and informative manner. It also suggests that the NRPB takes into account more broadly-based, well-considered expert advice, including anecdotal evidence and non-peer-reviewed data. This indeed is a vindication of all those independent scientists whose research on mobile phones, transmission masts and electricity pylons has been summarily dismissed by the NRPB.

Since the benign Stewart Report came out in May 2000, the *Journal of Epidemiology* has published further research into mobile phone hazards. A German team, led by Dr Andreas Stang from the University of Essen, investigated a threefold increase in eye cancer among regular phone users. The disease, uveal melanoma, develops tumours in the iris and base of the retina. It is known that the watery contents of the eye can assist radiation absorption.[9] The Royal Society of Canada has also cooperated with the Eye Institute of Canada to carry out similar studies.

Sir William Stewart will continue to produce a further report on the Department of Health's research programme on mobile phone health issues including epidemiology and dosimetry.[10]

A more wide-ranging study is ongoing in Sweden at the Orebro University, by Professor Lennart Hardell. It is believed the research will show positive links between tumours and mobile phones, but whether the newer digital handsets will have similar effects to analogue phones will not be known until 2005 as tumours take several years to develop.[11]

In 1998, a magistrate's court in the UK gave Dr Coghill (see above) leave to bring a criminal action against The Telephone Shop UK Ltd, a retail distributor of Orange and Motorola mobile phones. His action claimed that the distributors failed to comply with the Consumer Protection Act 1987 by not affixing labels to all handsets giving warning of possible health risks if used for prolonged conversations.[12] In the US, a major lawsuit was also due to a full hearing in 1998 brought against Motorola by the trustees of Dr Dean Rittmann, a physician who died of a brain tumour, which his estate alleged was caused by years of cellular phone use.[13] According to the professional journals there are many other employees taking legal action against their employers for incapacity or inability to work due to memory loss, headaches and lack of concentration caused by the use of mobile phones demanded by their job. British entrepreneur Richard Branson instructed the staff at his Virgin Group to fit protective ear pieces to their mobile phones after a close friend, banker Michael von Clemm, who was a heavy mobile phone user, died of a brain tumour.[14]

One frequent mobile phone user since the early 1990s, Leslie Wilson of London, began to suffer headaches, migraine, pains in his head and ear, a numbness and redness of the skin and tingling sensations where the phone was held against his head. In 1993 Wilson took out a patent and in April 1996 the MicroShield mobile phone carrying case was launched in the UK. The case has protective shielding and a retractable aerial that slides up the phone's antenna and is claimed to absorb up to 90 per cent of the radio frequency radiation. MicroShield says its device cannot make a mobile phone safe. This can be compared to a tobacco company offering low-tar cigarettes: the health risk may be reduced but the inherent hazards remain. Within months of the launch, MicroShield had sold over 100,000 protective cases: its main customers were multinational organisations which were fearful of future litigation by their employees who were obliged to use mobile phones to carry out their jobs. The company has received calls and letters from over 1,500 private individuals who wished to purchase a case to relieve their headaches and other symptoms. It is believed ear-pieces or hands-free devices can reduce the effects of radiation to the head but if the actual phone is carried in a pocket or on a belt the effects of radiation are transferred to another part of the body.[15]

Mobile phones emit microwave radiation whenever a call is made. The electromagnetic signals are similar to those used for cooking in a microwave. However, the lower-intensity microwave radiation from a mobile phone affects the way message-carrying chemicals operate within the brain and inside nerve cells. These key chemicals have electrical charges that can be influenced by radiation. As the brain is made up of fluid membrane it can readily absorb microwave radiation and this can cause the tissue to heat up and be affected by changing the potassium and calcium ions. Radiation can also weaken the barrier that prevents harmful chemicals from entering the brain from the bloodstream.[16]

An independent study by Bo Borstell *et al.* at the IMTEC laboratory in Malmo,

Sweden, claimed that the major danger from mobile phones may not be radiation but seepage from the hazardous chemicals that leach out of the headset and become absorbed by the skin, causing headaches, dizziness and allergies. The researchers claimed to have proof that the source is the manufacturing processes of liquids and the casings from phenol plastic. Even the circuit cards may be implicated.[17]

In 1997, at the 'Mobile Phones – Is There a Health Risk?' second annual conference in Brussels (attended by the major mobile telephone manufacturers and a number of government and local government delegates though not open to the general public), eminent research scientists Dr Lai and Dr Singh of Washington University, Seattle, detailed the results of their research showing that repeated exposure to radio frequency radiation can have a cumulative adverse effect on the nervous system. Dr Lai also linked mobile phones with the slow onset of Alzheimer's and Parkinson's diseases.[18]

Inevitably there are conflicting and often confusing scientific views expressed by those, on the one hand, who discount any evidence that mobile phone use can cause health problems and, on the other hand, the views of independent scientists such as Dr Lai and Dr Singh. Dr Lai's research on rats (see Chapter 4), showed changes in the permeability of brain cell membranes to potassium ions during exposure to mobile phone radiation. The disruption of movement of the ions, vital to brain function, could account for the temporary memory lapses.[19]

Studies at the Bristol Royal Infirmary, sponsored by the Department of Health, offered the first objective evidence that mobile phones may alter memory and interfere with concentration and spatial awareness. Here, scientists found that the emitted radiation can affect the mobile phone user's short-term ability to perform simple mental tasks.[20] Similar findings were reported by Dr Coghill following experiments in which white blood cells, or lymphocytes, were taken from a donor and exposed to different electric fields: only a third of the cells exposed to microwave radiation from a mobile phone were still functioning after three hours. The immune system is partially controlled by the body's natural electromagnetic fields (EMFs) and mobile phone microwaves can interfere with the ability of the immune system to function properly.[21] An earlier study in 1996 by Dr John Holt, who was a director of the Institute of Radiotherapy and Oncology of Western Australia, discovered that cancer has specific increased conductivity and other electrical parameters compared to normal tissue, and in certain patients cancer resonated and fluoresced at the frequency of microwaves.[22]

A major breakthrough came on 20 June 1998 when the respected medical journal *The Lancet* published a report by Dr S. Braune and colleagues from Freiburg University Neurology Clinic in Germany on their study of 10 volunteers aged between 26 and 36 years. Each had a mobile phone attached to the right side of the head where usually a telephone would be held. The phones were switched on by remote control at varying intervals but without sound so that the volunteers would not know when they were being exposed to the electromagnetic fields. The recorded increase in blood pressure when the phones were switched on was sufficient to have had an adverse effect on people with high blood pressure leading to the conclusion that the increase resulted from constriction of the arteries caused by radio frequency electromagnetic fields. It was noted that the researchers did not examine the possible effect on those in the vicinity of mobile phone users.[23]

An article in the London *Evening Standard* (13 July 1998), entitled 'Do mobile phones fry your brains or just eggs?', reported the studies carried out in France at the Montpelier University on the effect of mobile phone radiation on newly laid eggs. The researchers had found that after 21 days there were considerably more dead chicks among those subjected to the active phones than in the control group.[24] Three days later the *Daily Mail* and the *Evening Standard* both carried reports by the British Defence Establishment Research Agency (DERA), funded by the Ministry of Defence, and the Department of Health. These studies found that mobile phone signals disrupt parts of the brain in charge of memory and hearing.[25] Two other separate studies reported that mobile phone use could cause a rise in blood pressure and may be harmful to pregnant women. Over the years mobile phones have been linked with brain tumours, cancer, headaches and tiredness, and Dr Rick Hall, Project Director of the DERA, said that although there was no evidence of long-term damage – how could there be since mobile phones have only been in use for a relatively short time? – he admitted that the report was the first real evidence that radiowaves do have an effect on the brain. The report also referred to a 1997 US study that found that rats exposed to 45 minutes of microwave radiation (similar to the levels emitted by mobile phones) lost their ability to learn simple tasks. What damages a rat brain will usually damage a human brain.[26]

In January 1999, the World Health Organization (WHO) announced a new series of studies in Australia, Canada, France, Italy, Israel and three Scandinavian countries to research the mobile phone's link with brain tumours. The head of the International Agency for Cancer Research (IACR) reported that the feasibility study would cover several thousand people aged between 25 and 50 years. It was noted that over a 10-year period, since 1982, the frequency of brain tumours in Australia had risen inexplicably in every 100,000 people from 6.4 men and 4.0 women to 9.6 men and 6.5 women.[27]

In an attempt to alleviate public concern, the phone companies changed their literature to indicate that mobile phones operate on radio frequencies and not radiation microwaves, but in 1998 ICNIRP issued new guidelines defining microwaves as being between 300MHz and 300GHz. The cellular phone operators use 900MHz, which does indeed fall within the microwave band. Another argument used by phone companies to defend their position suggests that any discussion on the biological impact of electromagnetic fields is highly charged with the general public's emotion, anxiety and bad feelings generated by sensational and evocative reports in the media.

Every year, mainly either in Europe, the US or Scandinavia, there are conventions and seminars to provide a forum for the latest scientific research to be aired in public. The usual format allows the independent scientists to present their latest research papers, followed by the opposing scientists (representing the electrical power-line companies or mobile phone manufacturing industries) who proceed to refute and dismiss the independent studies. The confrontation is then joined by more scientific evidence presented on behalf of a government watchdog such as the UK National Radiological Protection Board (NRPB), the US Federal Communications Commission (FCC), or some other agency responsible for setting the standards limiting exposure to electromagnetic radiation further adding to the obfuscation.

In December 1999 the Department of Health published the Government's response to a House of Commons Select Committee's September 1999 report on mobile phones. It accepted the guidelines advised by the NRPB and supported its view that '*there is no scientific basis for exposure limits for radio frequency radiation to be reduced to those levels proposed by the ICNIRP* [International Commission on Non-Ionising Radiation Protection]. However, the report did recommend that the industry and the NRPB explore ways to design mobile phones to limit personal exposure to radiation but, in effect, it endorsed the view that as there had been no recognised or new evidence by the scientific community, there was no need to change the guidelines.[28]

Unfortunately, the British government spokesperson was not acquainted with the overwhelming abundance of good research evidence from scientific institutions such as the US National Institutes of Health, whose research concluded that the electromagnetic fields from electrical appliances, including mobile phones, are indeed a possible human carcinogen.

The European Council issues directives to member states setting out the regulations and legal standards of product liability. For example, in the case of visual display screen equipment (see below), the minimum health and safety requirements state that employers shall ensure all workstations comply with certain standards, including that 'all radiation with the exception of the visible part of the electromagnetic spectrum shall be reduced to negligible levels from the point of view of the protection of workers' safety and health'.[29] On the other hand, the directive dealing with radio and telecommunications terminal equipment and electrical compatibility concerns the prevention of radio interference but says nothing about injury to people. The directive on safety at work for pregnant women or those who have recently given birth or are breast feeding requires the employer to make special risk assessments but again offers no guidance on electromagnetic radiation limits. Any amended proposal on exposure to electromagnetic fields and the risks to workers would impose an obligation on employers to assess, measure and reduce exposure levels set out in the directive to ensure adequate protection, information and training. Unfortunately the directive does not cover the possible carcinogenic effects due to electric or magnetic fields for which, it states, there is no scientific evidence establishing a causal relationship providing a basis for risk assessment. However, the earlier Electrical Equipment Directive of 1973 requires a manufacturer of equipment – such as mobile phones – to ensure 'that temperatures, arcs or radiation which could cause damage are not produced'.[30]

A mobile phone producer may be under the impression that if the product complies with the standards set by current scientific and technical knowledge this will be sufficient defence. But the legal position appears to be that the producer must be aware of the most *advanced* level of research being carried out and to the extent that available research is not relevant, must independently arrange the necessary research, whatever the cost, and use the results of such research in the design of the product to ensure users will have a high level of safety. Under the UK Consumer Protection Act

1987, just because a producer complies with the current standards this will not necessarily provide a defence against claims for civil liability in the event of a defect.[31] The American FCC was challenged in court by the labour union, Communications Workers of America (CWA) and the Ad Hoc Association (AHA) – a public interest organisation of concerned citizens – on the grounds that the FCC and other Federal health and safety agencies should be held accountable for failure to issue radio frequency radiation rules for wireless phone carriers which fully protect public health, safety and welfare.[32]

While researching for his action against a mobile phone shop for not labelling the phones with a health warning, Dr Coghill (see above) discovered seven applications for patents by leading mobile phone manufacturers (including Ericsson, Alcatel and Hitachi) to produce new phone components designed to reduce health risks. One application for a special type of antenna stated that the purpose of the device was to prevent injury to the health of the user. Other patents referred to the reduction of health risks and maintaining safe distances between the user's body and radiating systems. Some of these patent applications date back to 1993![33]

Since then, in June 2001, *The Times* published an article confirming that in the early 1990s the 'Big Three' – Nokia, Ericsson and Motorola – were patenting new devices to reduce the risk of brain tumours due to continuous exposure to radio frequency radiation. The patents may be used in evidence in a series of lawsuits against the phone companies, including Vodaphone. While the law firms on both sides of the Atlantic are gearing themselves up to deal with a substantial number of pending claims, the manufacturers will rely on what they believe to be a lack of available scientific evidence linking mobile phone use and negative health effects.[34]

How can the general public have confidence in the manufacturer's publicity and reassurances that mobile phones do not pose a health risk when, privately, they have acknowledged the hazards? Interestingly, the relatively new regulations on both health and safety and consumer protection can hold the individual directors of a producer company personally liable for claims, and while there are insurance policies covering the corporate structure this does not necessarily absolve the managing executives and personnel. Representatives of law firms and insurance companies have no doubt that inevitably, and sooner rather than later, the civil action for damages against the mobile phone producers by users claiming the phones caused tumours, damage to their immune systems and memory loss, will be in the order of billions of pounds.

In view of the mounting evidence, when the mobile phone producers have to acknowledge that there is a serious health risk they may come to rue the day they did not credit the general public with common-sense by giving reasonable warnings that holding a phone close to the head for long periods may cause harm and affect the function of the brain. Of course this would not stop people using their phones, no more than a health warning on a cigarette packet has stopped people from smoking, but at least the exposure might be minimised and young children severely restricted from anything other than very short duration calls or preferably not at all. This is even more difficult now since mobile phones became a status symbol among 10-year-old children or even younger. Discerning parents may have been able to exercise some control but high street shops and supermarkets sell mobile phones operated by a phone card system, allowing anyone, including children, to buy a handset without having to sign a contract.

This development was followed by a new range of mobile phone devices for insertion into teddy bears or other soft toys so that babies as young as three years old can talk to their parents. Other manufacturers were producing a small box to hang around the baby's neck so that wherever the parents may be in the world they could communicate with their offspring at any time of the day or night. While child psychologists have expressed extreme misgivings about such parenting at a distance – voice communication without the physical presence of a smile or a hug – the scientists who have researched mobile phone radiation emissions are far more concerned about the long-term damage to the developing brain of a young child.

Another leap into the unknown health risks of the future began in September 1998 when Iradium launched 66 satellites into orbit to provide a global network linked to ground-based transmitters to enable everywhere on the planet to be reached by new mobile phone handsets for phone calls, pagers, faxes, email and the Internet. Even laptop computers will have cell phones built in as standard. The industry predicts that in no time at all our domestic appliances – washing machines, cookers, etc. – will have cell phone microprocessors for instant communication with the users, and soon the skies will be teaming with even more satellites planned to rival the Iradium system. This will be matched by the next generation of terrestrial mobile phone licences to transform the handset into a computer allowing transmission of data and video images to make shopping, banking and TV viewing via mobile phone a commonplace reality.

Worldwide, the mobile phone industry is a huge business and is likely to continue to expand. So far it seems that very little money is being directed towards health and safety research but substantial sums are being spent on lawyers, scientists and PR companies to counter the growing likelihood of claims for compensation based on independent scientific evidence.

Computers

Current estimates indicate that there are more than 6 million computer operators in the UK, 40 million in the US and a further 40 million in the rest of Europe, totalling in excess of 100 million people using computer screens on a regular and frequent basis. The numbers increase daily and take no account of the millions of men, women, teenagers and children who spend many hours a day at a personal computer (PC) in their private home, such as the freelance writers, journalists, graphic designers, typists, students, children at school and those addicted to computer games.

As early as the 1980s it became evident that people using PCs and word processors were suffering a range of health problems such as eye strain, dizziness, dry throats, running eyes, skin allergies, skeletal and muscular disorders and repetitive strain injury (RSI). The use of computers both at work and in the home has increased many hundred times over and this may account for the strange anomaly that so many indoor workers were getting skin cancer. Is it that the magnetic fields inhibit cancer-fighting melatonin in the body, or could it be due to the shortwave ultraviolet (UV) light from fluorescent tubes plus the radiation from the screen of the visual display unit (VDU – or visual display terminal (VDT) in the US)?

Electromagnetic sensitivity is experienced by many VDU users in the form of extremely painful forms of dermatitis, which can develop into sensitivities to other electrical equipment and sunlight. The question of whether VDU screen use can be the cause of miscarriages and foetal deformities has been hotly debated for many years. However, in 1997 studies by Professor Madeleine Bastide at the University of Montpelier in France on the effects of continuous exposure of embryos and young chickens to electromagnetic fields emitted from both TVs and VDUs, revealed significant increased foetal loss (47–68 per cent) and depressed levels of immune, adrenal and pineal functions. Her findings indicated that continuous exposure adversely affects embryos and young chickens.[35]

In 1998 Ann Silk (see also pages 47, 64, 91 and 122) published her studies over the past 10 years on the effect of electromagnetic emissions from VDUs on eye function. Silk quoted other international authorities, including the WHO, and concluded that VDU radiation exposure can seriously affect the retina and iris, and the use of contact lenses can exacerbate the condition.[36]

When the alarm bells started ringing in the early 1990s, the European Commission was prompted to issue a directive to its member states to introduce regulations designed to minimise and control the health hazards associated with the use of VDU screens and keyboards. Principally the Swedish authorities were responsible for reducing the levels of magnetic and electrostatic radiation emitted by VDU equipment and the later computer screens conform to these more stringent standards, though several millions of older-type screens are still in use, especially in private homes. The new European regulations issued in the UK in 1994 by the Health and Safety Executive apply only to employees and not to the self-employed and private users who are unlikely to be aware of the potential dangers. Nor do they apply to the most vulnerable: the children and young persons using computers at school or at home, including the kindergartens for three- to five-year-olds. More than seven years later it appears there are a considerable number of employers and designers who are still unaware of the legislation or, indeed, the penalties imposed for non-compliance.

The European Council issues directives to member states setting out the regulations and legal standards of product liability. For example, in the case of visual display screen equipment, employers should ensure that all workstations comply with certain standards and that all radiation with the exception of the visible part of the electromagnetic spectrum shall be reduced to negligible levels from the point of view of the protection of workers' 'safety and health'.[37] The directive dealing with radio and telecommunications terminal equipment and electrical compatibility concerns the prevention of radio interference but says nothing about injury to people. The directive on safety at work for pregnant women or those who have recently given birth or are breast feeding requires the employer to make special risk assessments but again offers no guidance on electromagnetic radiation limits.

Most of the electromagnetic radiation from computers is emitted from the back and sides of the screen, rather than directly towards the face of the operator: therefore a person sitting up to a couple of metres behind someone else's screen can receive the same exposure dosage as the operator sitting close to the front of the screen. The new regulations have alerted architects to take greater care over planning workstations; eliminating glare from windows and overhead lighting; choosing the chairs and desks for their ergonomic qualities rather than appearance and to ensure that the workplace environment will maintain a healthy atmosphere rather than add to the risks. The regulations also demand that all employee VDU users are given regular free eye-tests and spectacles, and are properly trained on taking frequent breaks away from the screen and adopting good sitting postures to minimise the risks.

Before the advent of computers and word processors the business world relied on the typewriter, invented in 1867 by the US arms manufacturer Remington, and developed for commercial use in 1874. The basic design used worldwide by secretaries, copy typists, writers, journalists and so on did not alter until the 1960s when, for the next 25 years or so, the electric typewriter became standard office equipment. All standard mechanical or electrical typewriters required the typist to use considerable body activity and energy to press down the keys, push over the carriage, wind on the paper and so on. By contrast, the only physical effort needed to operate the electronic PC is concentrated into the hands and fingers. Typists moved and exercised their body whereas computer operators sit staring, zombie-like, at the screen in an immobile posture except for the fingertips pressing the keys. During the late 1980s, government agencies and health and safety research groups in Scandinavia, Europe and the US began to take notice of the growing reports of health hazards linked to office staff operating PCs.

The physical effort concentrated solely on the hands and fingers operating the keyboard can develop a deterioration of the nerve ends resulting in tingling sensations, numbness and chronic pain known as repetitive strain injury (RSI). The symptoms are not readily reversible. For several years employers and certain medical quarters believed RSI disability was a figment of the imagination of susceptible hypochondriacs until it became accepted, after much campaigning by those who had suffered, that thousands of people worldwide were afflicted by this chronically disabling and painful condition. RSI campaigners hailed a 1999 High Court award of a record £100,000 to a woman who damaged her thumb typing: she was medically retired in 1994 and since then her injuries had left her unable to be employed. It is likely the award will open the floodgates for massive claims for compensation by other RSI sufferers.[38]

A judgement against the Midland bank (now Hong Kong Shanghai Banking Corporation – HSBC) awarding £60,000 to five former women employees who developed RSI was upheld by the Court of Appeal. The staff at the bank's processing centre in Surrey, England, were required to input computer data at high speeds and were sacked if they did not maintain the production levels. They developed neck, arm and hand pains from working the keyboard under such stressful, demanding conditions. The bank's defence was that the pain was 'psychogenetic' and not physical.[39]

Children as young as seven years of age are suffering RSI due to the increased use of computers at school and the obsessive playing of computer games at home. A charity, set up to teach children how to prevent upper-limb disorders, found that in some classes of 11-year-olds, a significant number were experiencing the first symptoms of RSI normally associated with office workers. The Trades Union Congress (TUC) estimated in 1997 that five million working days were lost every year due to RSI.[40]

Although we are now in the twenty-first century, many doctors still refuse to recognise RSI as a medical condition. The American National Institute of Occupational Safety and Health believes the problem has increased over the last decade from 18 per cent of all workplace illnesses, to 56 per cent. Research suggests that computer users have a higher level of triphenylphosphate in their blood than non-users.[41]

Cramped working space, undersized desktops, rigid, non-adjustable chairs and sitting in a contorted posture are the causes of aching backs, stiff necks and shoulders that come under the general heading of upper limb, musculo-skeletal disorders. The choice of office desks and chairs by the architect, interior designer, office manager's secretary or, perhaps, the Chairman's wife, has most likely been based on style, aesthetic appearance and cost rather than good ergonomic principles. And the aches and pains due to unavoidably bad posture has resulted in unnecessary absenteeism and medical treatment.

Another problem associated with posture for computer operators has concerned eyesight acuity. Younger people tend to have 20:20 vision enabling them to readily adjust their focus, but those who are either near- or long-sighted need corrective spectacles. An operator's head is usually about 60 to 80 centimetres (2 to 2.8 inches) away from the screen, which is neither in range of their close reading nor their long-distance lenses. To overcome this focal length 'blind' zone, the operator must either crouch over the keys to get near to the screen, or stretch out the arms to reach the keys in order to see from a distance. It appears that none of these symptoms were usually suffered by people operating a typewriter.

During the 1970s and 1980s there was a tendency to artificially light offices to a very high level of brightness. Generally this suited the staff working on paper, but computer operators need much lower lighting levels to see the images on the screen more easily, bearing in mind the clarity of the actual image is dependent on the quality of the software and the adjustability of the brightness on the screen. Prevailing interior lighting conditions such as the strength of daylight glare from unshaded windows, reflections from shiny desk-top surfaces, dark contrasting colours and high artificial lighting levels all contribute to visually disturbing and confusing factors that cause eye strain, headaches and stress.

The environmental conditions of the workplace are another health concern. Not all air-conditioning and ventilation systems can cope with the heat load generated by the mass of electronic equipment now in use in business organisations. Higher temperatures, lower humidity, dust accumulation, negative ion depletion and static electricity generated from the screens increases the incidence of skin allergies and fatigue. Women tend to suffer skin complaints more than men, partly because more often they are sedentary in the work they do, generally expose more skin and wear synthetic tights and underwear. Studies also show that operators working on a daily basis for long periods without regular breaks are most prone to suffer a range of the various symptoms mentioned above.

Although the Visual Display Screen Equipment regulations have been in force in the UK since 1992, there are many employers (perhaps even the majority) who are either unaware of their legal obligations or choose to take no action. Since 1993 enforcement has been lax, even though a number of notices demanding improvement and compliance have been issued. Despite the publicity in the early days of 1993 and the general improvement in awareness of health and safety matters in 2000, the Health and Safety Executive information office was still receiving an average of 50 telephone calls a day from businesses enquiring what they should do to implement the regulations. Non-compliance can carry a maximum fine of £5,000 in a magistrate's court and £20,000 in a crown court. Rather than prosecution through the courts, the authorities have relied more on the issue of formal notices demanding improvement and compliance. The lack of enforcement has tended to shift the burden to employees who have suffered either acute or chronic disabilities to take legal proceedings against their wayward employers.

The cybernetic age at the end of the twentieth century is the latest milestone marking the evolution in physics that began in the nineteenth century when we discovered how to harness and generate electromagnetic energy. Our personal comfort, convenience and leisure time has been transformed beyond imagination over the past hundred years but, as ever, there is a downside to counterbalance the benefits in the harm and health risks that arise from our indiscriminate use of the wondrous new 'toys' we play with.

References

1. The Reader's Digest (1996) *Oxford Complete Word Finder*, London: The Reader's Digest Ass Ltd.
2. Dominic Rush and Claire Oldfield, 'Bidding for the five licences to run the next generation of mobile phones has topped £20 billion – with more to come', *The Sunday Times*, 16 April 2000.
3. Maurice Weaver, 'Jail for passenger who did not switch off phone', *The Daily Telegraph*, 22 July 1999, p. 5.
4. Dr Barry Grimaldi Practice Information updated (p. 8).
5. Maurice Chittenden, 'Top scientists give up "risky" mobile phones', *The Sunday Times*, 5. 'News' (p. 12), 28 February 1999.
6. 'Now mobile phones are linked to epilepsy', *Metro*, 27 May 1999, p. 7.
7. The Stewart Report – The Independent Expert Group on Mobile Phones (IEGMP), NRPB, Oxon, May 2000.
8. *IEEE Transactions on Electromagnetic Compatibility* 1999, 41: 234–45. Reported in *Electromagnetic Hazard & Therapy*, vol. 10, nos 3–4, 2000, p. 6.
9. Jonathan Leake, 'Scientists link eye cancer to mobile phones, *The Sunday Times*, November 2000, p. 30.
10. 'Department of Health invites proposals for £7m mobile phone research programme', *Electromagnetic Hazard & Therapy*, vol. 11, nos 2–4, 2001, p. 3. (Details www.doh.gov.uk/mobilephones/research)
11. Rachael Ellis, 'Mobile phones double risk of tumours', *The Mail on Sunday*, 17 June 2001.
12. Roger Coghill, Coghill Laboratories, Ker Menez, Pontypool, Gwent, Wales.
13. 'Law suit against Motorola given go-ahead permission', *Electromagnetic Hazard & Therapy*, vol. 8, no. 1, 1997, p. 4.
14. Cherry Norton and Richard Woods, 'Companies insist mobile phones are safe. Users suspect they

cause ill health. New scientists say the industry is downplaying evidence of the risks', *The Sunday Times*, 20 December 1998.

15. 'Mobile phones and user symptoms', paper presented by John Simpson at 'Mobile Phones: Is There a Health Risk' symposium, London, October 2001.

16. Cherry Norton and Steve Farrar, 'Top scientists give up "risky" mobile phones', *The Sunday Times*, 28 Feburary 1999, p. 12.

17. 'Chemical seepage worries Swedes', *The Magazine of the Institution of Planning Supervisors,* vol. 3, no. 3, June 2000, p. 3.

18. Dr Lai Singh, 'Mobile Phones – Is There a Health Risk?' Conference, Brussels, Belgium, 16–17 September 1997.

19. Lai, H. and Singh, N. P. (1996) 'Single' and double-strand DNA breaks in rat brain cells after acute exposure to radiofrequency electromagnetic radiation', *Int J Radiat. Biol*, vol. 5, 1996, pp. 513–21.

20. Johnathan Leake, 'Mobile phones "slow" the brain in new tests', *The Sunday Times*, 'News' (p. 7), 20 September 1998.

21. Nic Fleming and Michael Hanlon, 'Research prompts radiation scare', *The Express*, 15 October 1998.

22. Dr John A. G. Holt, 'Important non-thermal biological effects may have been demonstrated which could account for the development of brain tumours, asthma and lowering of male fertility', *Power-watch Technical Supplement*, no. 2, May 1996, pp. 2–3.

23. Dr S. Braune *et al.*,'Use of mobile phones raises blood pressure', *The Lancet* press release, 20 June 1998.

24. Chris Partridge, 'Do mobile phones fry your brains or just eggs?', *Evening Standard*, 13 July 1998, p. 60.

25. James Clark and David Derbyshire, 'Mobile phones in new health warning', *The Daily Mail*, 16 July 1998, pp. 1–2.

26. Jonathan Leake, 'Mobile phones "slow" the brain in new tests', *The Sunday Times*, 20 September 1998.

27. David Fletcher, 'Study into cancer link to mobile phone use', *The Daily Telegraph*, 7 January 1998.

28. The Scientific Advisory System: mobile phones and health: the Government's response to the report of the House of Commons Science and Technology Committee on the scientific advisory system: mobile phones and health/Department of Health CM: 4551, London: Stationery Office, 1999, ISBN 0 10 1455127.

29. Health & Safety (Display Screen Equipment) Regulations 1992, Guidance on Regulations Crown Copyright 1992, p. 38.

30. Electrical Equipment Directive 73/23, 19 February 1973 (OJL 77/29).

31. Paper by Philip Bentley QC at the Mobile Phone Conference, London, 14–15 October 1998. Case C – 300/95 Commission, United Kingdom (1997) ECR 1 – 2649.

32. 'American Ad Hoc Association appeal challenges FCC RF radiation rules', *Electromagnetic Hazard & Therapy*, vol. 9, nos 1–2, 1998, p. 6.

33. Sophie Goodchild, 'Mobiles are health risk, say makers'*, Independent on Sunday* , 25 October 1998.

34. Nic Fleming, Jan Cobain and Nigel Hawkes, 'Phone firms aware of risks in 1993', *The Times*, 11 June 2001.

35. 'VDU radiation increases death rate and reduces immune function in chicks', *Electromagnetic Hazard & Therapy*, vol. 8, no.2, 1997, pp. 8 and 9.

36. Ann Silk, 'RF study must include all environmental sources', *Electromagnetic Hazard & Therapy*, vol. 9, no. 4, 1998, pp. 6 and 7.

37. Health & Safety (Display Screen Equipment) Regulations 1992, Guidance on Regulations Crown Copyright 1992.

38. Joel Wolchover, 'At last, a degree for the upwardly mobile', *Evening Standard*, 28 May 1999, p. 25.

39. BBC Ceefax, 22 July 1999.

40. Joel Wolchover, 'Children log on to RSI threat', *Evening Standard*, 10 November 1997.

41. Martin J. Walker, 'The great outdoors', *The Ecologist*, vol. 31, no. 5, 5 June 2001, p. 25.

6.
Prudent avoidance

Electromagnetic pollution and smog will not diminish: instead the global demand for generated electricity will increase daily to meet our expanding lifestyles and to power the proliferation of new business equipment such as very small aperture terminals (VSATs), mobile phones, satellite broadcasting channels, radio stations, radar dishes, defence systems and, of course, the latest household gadgets we cannot possibly do without.

Through the media, we are becoming more aware that certain electromagnetic fields (EMFs) can be, or most likely are a health hazard. As long as we appear to be happy and contented and the health hazards or the death rate are kept within reasonable limits, governments and businesses are not inclined to take positive action by introducing controlling legislation. It is therefore a matter for each of us to make our own assessment of the situation and act accordingly. Possible personal damage limitation can be exercised by practising prudent avoidance – an American concept given its name by Professor Granger Morgan of Carnegie Mellon University:

Prudent   = actions that can be secured at reasonable cost
Avoidance = keeping out of harmful fields

Prudent avoidance, or the 'precautionary principle', is enshrined in the Treaty of Maastricht signed by all the European Union member states, and requires society to take prudent action when there is sufficient scientific evidence (but not necessarily absolute proof) that inaction could lead to harm and where action can be justified on reasonable judgements of cost-effectiveness.

The principle of prudent avoidance has been officially adopted in Sweden by the five regulating bodies controlling electromagnetic field exposure – the National Electrical Safety Board, Radiation Protection Institute, National Board of Health and Welfare, National Institute for Working Life and the National Board of Housing. The policy was endorsed in a document entitled, *Magnetic Fields and Cancer – A Criteria Document,* published in 1995. If measures generally reducing exposure can be taken at reasonable expense and with reasonable consequences in all other respects, an effort should be made to reduce fields radically deviating from what could be deemed 'normal' in the environment concerned. Where new electrical installations and buildings are concerned, efforts should be made at the planning stage to design and position them in such a way that exposure is limited. The overriding purpose of the precautionary principle is, eventually, to minimise exposure to magnetic fields in our surroundings, so as to reduce the risk of injury to human beings.[1]

While the science may not yet be in place to produce conclusive evidence, we must bear in mind the case of the health hazards associated with smoking. Government and legal action was taking place at least 10 years before there emerged final, conclusive, scientific evidence, and the dangers of passive smoking are still being tested. The health hazards of smoking were based, originally, on the balance of probabilities. It is suggested that the concept of prudent avoidance, based on the balance of probabilities, should be adopted by everyone – politicians, electricity companies, property developers, professional architects and engineers and, of course, ourselves, the general public. We have now passed through the phase of believing that the magical, life-enhancing benefits of electricity have no downside effects and growing public concern should demand that the policy of prudent avoidance be officially adopted.

What can we do to help ourselves?

Power lines and masts

In 1990, pioneer researcher Dr Robert Becker (see Chapter 4, page 91) proposed to a US Congress committee that all transmission lines, sub-stations and distribution lines be required to produce a maximum of 100 nanoteslas (nT) in any adjacent dwelling, school or public building, and all existing installations be reduced accordingly by the year 2000.[2] Subsequently, Dr Ross Adey (see Chapter 3, page 77) chaired a committee of the National Council on Radiation and Measurements (NCRM), which included a range of members of scientific and medical organisations. The draft report, in 1995, recommended that for new building projects:

1. New daycare centres, schools and playgrounds should not be built where ambient 60Hz magnetic fields exceed 200nT.
2. New housing should not be built below or in such close proximity to high-voltage lines so that ambient fields exceed 200nT for more than two hours daily.
3. New lines should not produce fields exceeding 200nT in existing houses.
4. New office and industrial environments should be planned with the aim of reducing exposures to a 200nT level over a range from a few Hz to 3,000Hz.

The proposals included adopting a policy to progressively reduce exposures in existing buildings to a level 'As Low As Reasonably Achievable' (ALARA).[3] In the UK, neither the NRPB nor the electricity power companies have adopted these precautionary guidelines and the government has continued to decline support to those local authorities who want to limit new development near existing lines.

If you intend to buy a house near either high-tension overhead or underground cables, an electricity sub-station or in the 'shadow' of radio frequency or microwave transmission masts or radar stations, the best recommendation is *don't*! If you already live in such a property you can invite the local electricity company to take readings of the EMFs and keep those for future record purposes. One day, they may prove to be important. Invite an independent expert to test the EMFs and take note of the various support groups which may be able to help you, bearing in mind it depends on how far away you are from the power lines: as the distance from the cables increases so the hazard is reduced. The rule of thumb method for safe distances from high-tension cables is to halve the voltage and call it metres – that is, a safe corridor to a 400kV cable is 200 metres (about 700 feet) and for a 132kV cable is 66 metres (240 feet). But beware: generating companies can upgrade the loadings at any time, which means that buildings just outside the 'safe' corridor carrying a low voltage may well fall within the risk range when the loading is increased. Some pylons are carrying super-charged voltages greater than 400kV.

If you are concerned, check with the local medical services to see whether there are others experiencing health problems; make a comparison of the price of houses in the vicinity, which might indicate a lower valuation because of the proximity of the power lines or sub-station; contact mortgage and insurance companies about any modification to their rates due to likely EMF hazards, and if so keep up a constant campaign for compensation. Selling the property to another family will not solve the fundamental problem.

If new cables, a sub-station, or a transmission mast are about to be installed anywhere in the vicinity of your house, farm, local school or hospital, take action: there are many groups such as REVOLT and other environmental organisations, and support will always be offered by campaign magazines like *Powerwatch News*, *Electromagnetic Hazard & Therapy* and *Microwave News*.[4] Plague your local authority and make sure your voice and concerns are heard. Governments and establishment bodies depend on the general lethargic quiescence of the population to allow them to do most of the things they want to do without too much serious opposition.

Electrical wiring

Any live cable or wiring circuit connected to the electricity supply main will generate an electrical field radiating outwards around the cable. The lead to any appliance plugged into the socket will generate an electrical field even if the appliance is switched off. A magnetic field will only be present when the current flows through the wires and, like the electrical field, it radiates outward. In both cases, the strength of the field diminishes as the distance increases. High levels of magnetic fields can be found in the home, workplace or even in a property that may be located far away from a power line or sub-station. The source may be due to underground cables, power surges, 'spikes' and 'looping' from the incoming main cable or the lack of proper earth bonding (known as 'grounding' in the US). Battery chargers and transformers for mobile phones, laptop computers, children's games, fish tanks, ionisers, electric toothbrushes, low-voltage lamps and dimmer switches are sources of magnetic fields. Electromagnetic fields from sewing machines and power tools can be hazardous if the equipment is used for long periods.

British ophthalmologist and researcher Ann Silk (see pages 47, 64, 91 and 114), may have discovered one of the likely causes of breast cancer in women. Her research suggested that the wires used in underwired bras could act as re-radiating antennas. Natural resonances occur over a wide range from low Hertz to about 3GHz, covering mobile phones, visual display units (VDU)s and microwave ovens. Such bras could resonantly amplify radiation in this range and attract the energy to the breast. A Spanish company, Intima Cherry, has launched a range of underwear made from Nega-Stat, a material it claims cancels out EMFs![5]

Changing patterns of employment and ever-expanding computerised technology have brought personal computers (PCs), printers, fax machines, photocopiers and other electrical gadgets and equipment into the home. The home use of battery-operated laptop computers can give off very high electric fields when run directly from mains adaptors (for more on computers, see Chapter 5; and see below for more on prudent avoidance regarding the use of computers).

Throughout our life we spend at least seven hours asleep in the bedroom where our head stays relatively still and in the same position on the pillow. During this period our extremely low electrical brainwave activity is busy releasing hormone secretions to restore and bolster our immune system. (The night-time secretion of melatonin is a known suppressor of cancer cells.) When we are asleep the body naturally heals itself and revitalises the depleted energy. Electromagnetic fields can set up interference patterns to disturb our brainwave activity during this most vulnerable time of the 24-hour cycle. If you sleep fitfully, suffer from insomnia, wake up tired or with headaches and tight muscles this may be the first indication that the electromagnetic smog is taking effect. Most electrical equipment will increase the positive ionisation of the air in a room, which can drain our energy and vitality.

Some bedrooms heated by electrical night storage heaters are charged up at night; the hot water immersion heater or the electric mains meter may be housed on the landing outside the bedroom but close to the bedhead; on the bedside table there may be an electrically operated clock, a radio, a lamp and perhaps, for the older generation, a 'teasmaid' machine for automatically making early-morning tea. Also clustered around the bedhead there may be light switches, power points and switch controls for an electric blanket. Stereo equipment and a TV set may be close by and, in a child's bedroom there may be a computer and electronic toys and games being recharged overnight.

Any appliance or piece of equipment should be turned off at the power point when not in use and, in particular, electric blankets should be unplugged from the wall socket. To avoid the inconvenience of switching on and off, demand switches can be installed at the meter to break the flow of current to any appliance until it is switched on. This is an especially important precaution to take for the circuits serving the bedrooms. (Unfortunately, you may have to make extensive enquiries before you will find a qualified electrician who knows anything about demand switches.)

Call in a specialist electrician to check the electrical intake has been properly bonded (earthed, or grounded) to water or gas pipes and ensure the neutral terminal on all plugs to electrical appliances is properly connected.

In the bedroom, avoid exposure by moving electrical equipment as far away as possible – at least one metre (3 feet) from the bed. Avoid metal-framed beds and electrically heated water beds, and always unplug electric blankets at the mains because even when turned off completely the wires will act as an antenna to attract weak magnetic field geopathic stress. Epidemiological studies show a higher rate of miscarriages occur among couples exposed to the type of magnetic field generated by electric blankets and water beds.

In the nursery, a battery-operated baby alarm is virtually free of electromagnetic fields but a mains-operated alarm should be sited at least one metre (3 feet) away from the baby's head. If the parent's listening receiver is a portable device it will generate radio frequency radiation towards the monitor located near the cot. Higher than normal fields have been reported in cases of sudden infant death syndrome (SIDS), commonly known as 'cot death'.

In the kitchen, avoid standing near dishwashers, washing machines, electric cookers or any other electrical gadget or appliance, especially the microwave oven, while they are operating. Microwaves cause the food to heat up by vibrating the food molecules at very high speed. If the oven is not properly shielded or it 'leaks' – as the older types tend to do – the microwave energy will agitate and heat up the molecules of anything in range, including the cook! Follow the manufacturer's instructions and leave the cooked food to stand for a few minutes to allow the molecules to restabilise, otherwise you will be eating 'agitated' food.

The microwave oven is an example of how we rush into using the latest technology without assessing the downside, always looking at the features that will save us time, money or improve everyday conveniences. According to the watchdog magazine *What Doctors Don't Tell You*, there is now strong evidence that microwave ovens could prove to be a source of cancer. Parents are also being warned that the nutrients in children's food cooked in microwave ovens could be destroyed by the microwave radiation process. The report warns that the heating of milk in the microwave decreases the level of anti-infective properties. Convenience food packaged for microwave cooking, which has additives to artificially produce the colours and flavours, can release a number of susceptor chemicals.[6]

Computers

If you are an employee, check that your employer has an ongoing policy to implement the VDU regulations. This will become apparent if you are provided with training and are invited to have your eyes tested for the purposes of VDU work. Also check if records are being kept of environmental conditions of the work-space. Your workstation should conform to minimum standards of desk and chair size and adjustability. In the UK a copy of the VDU regulations and other details can be obtained from your local Health and Safety Executive office.

Whether you are an employee or a private person working from home, there are ways to avoid the potential health risks:

- Check your PC conforms to the Swedish Mark II or the newer TCO99 standards of low radiation emission safety levels. Whatever the level of radiation, it is known that the person sitting behind the computer will be exposed to a greater degree of radiation than the operator sitting in front of the screen. If necessary use an anti-static filter over the screen.
- Buy the best quality, high-resolution software for visual clarity and definition.
- Install PC equipment on a desk top large enough to allow the screen to be as far away as possible to comfortably suit your reading of the text. Maintain as great a distance as possible between the screen and the keyboard to keep the hands and fingers close to the body and far away from the radiation of the VDU.
- Position the PC to avoid strong reflections or glare affecting the visual clarity of the text.
- Do not sit closer than one metre (3 feet) to the back of someone else's PC where the radiation is stronger than at the front of the screen. Magnetic fields travel through walls, therefore check the next-door office where a PC may be located close to your sitting position.
- Do not sit in a cramped-up position. Maintain a good, upright posture using a chair with adjustable height, backrest and seat.
- If you use or need spectacles check that you can clearly see the characters on the screen from a comfortable distance without hunching your shoulders or bending close. Ensure the lenses are calibrated to a focal length to suit the distance of your eyes from the screen.
- Keep general lighting levels as low as is comfortable. The lighting in the room should be a little darker than the brightness of the screen.
- Keep clutter off work-tops and put all papers and files away when not in use to reduce accumulation of dust.
- Keep the floor spaces free of trailing wires, files and boxes to avoid unnecessary trip hazards.
- Turn off PC screens when not in use to reduce static electricity and radiation as well as conserve energy. An aquarium, vase of flowers, a fountain or a bowl of water will help maintain humidity levels and reduce static.
- Keep the room as cool and well-ventilated as comfort will allow.
- Avoid spending long hours at the screen; take frequent breaks, at least 10 minutes every hour. Go to another room or do something to exercise and stretch the body. Look out of the window or find some other visually enjoyable, contrasting scene or painting to rest the eyes.
- Spend as little time as possible at the PC.

Finally, if you are a parent and intend handing down your old PC to a child, check that it is not the type emitting high radiation levels and that the software is of a good visual standard. Most importantly, strictly limit the time your child spends in front of the screen.

In the household 'office', follow the recommendations for VDU screen operators and create a healthy, well-ventilated environment. Severely restrict the periods young people spend at their computers and train them in good practice and ergonomics. In any case, the time spent on the PC for homework, surfing or computer game playing should be restricted and interspersed with long breaks. Photocopiers and printers are not only a source of high magnetic fields; the printing process can also give off gases requiring good ventilation, and toner must be handled with care.

Personal shielding devices

There are many products ranging from a simple crystal necklace to elaborate pendants and wrist bands made of precious stones, copper spirals, gold, silver and magnets, that the inventors claim will protect the wearer against electromagnetic stress and loss of vitality. (Since ancient times, amulets, talismans and jewellery have been worn to bring good fortune, ward off evil spirits and shield us from disease.) All stones, minerals and metals have unique characteristics of colour, vibration and frequency, which can interact with the body at an extremely subtle microcosmic level in the same manner as the Sun, Moon and planets interact with life on Earth.

Quartz crystals are used as computer microchips and in the making of electric oscillators because their regular, geometric shape is determined by the structure of atoms, ions and molecules arranged in an ordered, repeating pattern. They also have piezoelectric qualities: strike a crystal and the energy force of the blow will transform into an electrical spark; squeeze a crystal and a few electrons will be released until the pressure is eased when it will reabsorb electrons from the atmosphere. These properties of quartz crystal have been used throughout the ages, much as they are today, for healing, rebalancing energy flow and absorbing negative thought patterns. Cleopatra is said to have worn a lodestone magnet on her forehead and, according to ancient teachings, the jewels embedded in crowns and coronets were chosen for their specific properties to enhance the spiritual and psychic powers of a royal personage or high priest.

Modern amulets are sold as 'bio-electric shields' with such brand names as the 'Q-Link' and 'Spiral of Tranquillity'. Anecdotal evidence from the many thousands of satisfied customers, backed up by people like Cherie Blair, Hillary Clinton and other celebrities who wear the products for protection against harmful radiation and stress, suggests some benefit may be gained. The inventor of the 'Q-Link', Dr William Tiller, Professor Emeritus at Stanford University in California, says the pendant has a microprocessor which interacts with the body of the wearer by rebalancing the stress caused by chaotic particles activated by electromagnetic fields. Dr Tiller believes that the technology used in 'Q-Link' is working in a new realm of physics but such claims generally tend to be dismissed by scientists who rely on reductionist investigation.[7]

A note of warning: Whether these personal devices have any effective shielding qualities remains to be seen. Wearing one cannot do any harm but the danger and concern is that pendants and jewellery of this type may give the wearer a false sense of invulnerability to the hazards of electromagnetic fields at the expense of not properly exercising prudent avoidance. Even when you may feel adequately protected, the common-sense approach must be to follow the guidelines and avoid the hazards whenever and wherever possible.

Commercial shielding

Modern commercial shielding against electromagnetic interference (EMI) and radio frequency interference (RFI) has evolved from its early beginnings when it was discovered that medical staff and researchers needed protection from exposure to lethal X-rays. The worldwide development of electronic communications, computer systems and particularly the latest guided weapons of war has expanded the shielding business to include protection for commercial and industrial buildings, research establishments, military facilities and ships as well as hospitals. Even civilian ships need their navigation systems and radar to be shielded.

As electromagnetic 'noise' increases in volume, so the demand for EMI shielding will increase. Some buildings housing military and other research centres and certain commercial organisations have been completely shielded, but more often the protected zones are confined to the areas where sensitive equipment has been installed. The shielding is designed to absorb or reflect the unwanted electromagnetic signals. Security companies now offer to clad complete buildings or provide compartments within a building to effectively shield the sensitive electronic equipment from external electromagnetic radiation interference. In certain locations the cost of providing shielding could be so high as to render a development project unprofitable or, if the building is built without protection it could be rendered unusable or even unsaleable.

Increasingly, the number of companies located close to airports, railways, radio frequency transmitting stations and overhead grid lines are suffering serious slow-down, error, or even total breakdown of their computer equipment due to EMI. The source of the problems can be nearby electrical motors, electric trains, transformers as well as the main cabling within the building itself setting up stray magnetic fields. Even radar equipment on sea-going vessels can affect computer equipment in offices located near river estuaries where, in certain areas, the problem is reaching epidemic proportions.

Magnetic field shielding is more difficult and more expensive to achieve than electric field protection. Shielding can never completely eliminate all unwanted electromagnetic signals entering or leaving a protected area but the strength of the interference can be reduced to an acceptable level without affecting vulnerable equipment. Steel and copper sheeting, copper mesh, aluminium-faced plaster board, metal tiles and impregnated fabrics such as Mu-metal can be used to line the walls, floor and ceiling of the area to be protected, though gaps in window or door seals will allow radio frequencies to pass through. In extreme radiation cases such as X-ray emissions, protective screens are made of sheet lead bonded to plywood panels. New products on the UK market for general building use include electroconductive concrete, tiles and bricks manufactured by Manta Ltd. In the US AntiMag is a magnetic shielding, and E-Stop paint is claimed to block electric fields from house wiring and other sources (when the paint has dried it needs the film to be attached to a wire for earthing).

Architects and engineers specialising in hospitals, military and research facilities or buildings such as the broadcasting centres and airports are used to dealing with EMI; however, the majority of property developers and their professional advisers appear to be unaware of the hazards. Until more recent times, relatively few architects had encountered the problems of electromagnetic pollution where the operation of their client's business machines and equipment had been seriously affected. However, when new building projects are discovered to be susceptible to environmental 'noise' and a shielded enclosure is needed to protect part or the whole of the building, the inevitable substantial costs can have serious financial consequences affecting the viability of the project and are likely to lead to expensive litigation and negligence claims.

The building bylaws in Germany and other European countries address the potential hazards of electromagnetic fields, whereas in the UK, architects, engineers and surveyors have paid little or no attention to the likely sources of electromagnetic interference when carrying out surveys and due diligence investigations. When evaluating a prospective building site or existing property, however, local Town Planning authorities are now demanding electromagnetic field surveys to be carried out before planning consent will be granted.

Shielding is becoming a regular necessity to protect electronic equipment against the electromagnetic and radio frequency interference of the polluting 'noise' in the environment. But if such interference can affect the electrical impulses of a machine, what effect might it have on the minute, supremely sensitive electrical pulses of a human brain – or indeed any other living organism? The paradox is that, largely, the allopathic medical establishment remains silent on the subject of the potential hazards and yet the effects of a wide range of extremely weak and very strong electromagnetic fields are well known and extensively used as diagnostic tools in a variety of curative treatments.

The healing power of electricity and magnetism

Electrical current and magnet therapies have been used in ancient cultures for thousands of years. There is evidence that Megalithic stone circles and dolmens – low structures with a stone slab roof – were built to harness the Earth's magnetic currents to create a healing refuge. Electric rays (or torpedo fish) found mainly in the shallow warm waters of temperate regions have been used for centuries to relieve pain and treat ailments: the tingling sensation felt when paddling in a pond filled with electric eels had a curative effect and in Roman times was a well-known treatment for arthritis and gout.

A recent archaeological excavation in Mesopotamia discovered a first-century pottery jar with a copper tube and iron rod through the middle. This early 'battery' (when acid – even a crushed grape – is added to any two dissimilar metals in contact it will produce a voltage) was found with other artefacts in the house of someone who must have been a magician: traditionally, magicians were also doctors. The battery could have been used for electroplating gold and silver but, more likely, it was used to relieve pain.

Lodestone or magnetite – a black, magnetic iron ore – was the basic component of the magnetic compass, invented by the Chinese about 300 BC and used in Feng Shui practice to harmoniously align dwellings with the magnetic currents on the Earth's surface. The beneficial, healing properties of lodestone were well known in ancient Egypt, India, Greece and the Middle East.

Throughout history the therapeutic value of magnets has been known and widely used except by Western medical practitioners. The German physician Franz Mesmer (1734–1815), who linked the life force with magnetism, used magnets strapped to the body of his patients to cure various ailments. His fellow doctors ostracised him as a charlatan for his magnet therapy and his views on the benefits of hypnotism – 'to mesmerise' and 'mesmerism' were disparaging words coined from his name by his detractors. Modern medical science has since proved that very weak electromagnetic fields can have a profound and beneficial effect on living organisms. Recent research in Scandinavia, Europe and America has shown that weak magnetic field magnets can produce pulsed or alternating waveforms to resonate with the similar wave patterns naturally generated in the body. (This might explain how some people have 'healing powers' by laying on hands.) Blood and water are excellent conductors of energy: a magnetic field will affect the behaviour of iron in red blood cells, and electrically charged ions in the blood will be deflected by the pole of a magnetic field: this, in essence, is how a pulsed electromagnetic field stimulates and accelerates the healing process.

Magnetic healing is now becoming a widely expanding business in the West and apparently American vets spend more than \$4 million a year on magnet therapy for the treatment of horses and other animals.[8]

Magnets can be used in a range of products: in mattresses, pillows, seats and even inner soles for shoes. The Queen Elizabeth Hospital in Birmingham found that electromagnetism increases blood flow and repairs damaged cells. Other research in Europe shows that magnets reduce limescale build-up in water pipes, and that magnetised water will tend to improve crop yields. Controlled electromagnetic therapies have shown they can accelerate bone repair, improve tissues, induce sleep, suppress pain, cure certain diseases and successfully treat drug and alcohol addiction. The development of such techniques may even prove to be the medicine of the future, offering a viable alternative in certain fields to allopathic drugs and intrusive surgery.

The Chinese have used magnets in acupuncture therapy for centuries. It is a leap of faith by Western science to come to terms with the concept that the thousands of acupuncture points cannot be seen on the structural features in the body tissue and – perhaps even more bizarre – invisible meridians or 'veins' of energy correspond to lines of electromagnetic oscillations connecting each point to a remote organ or function in the body. When stimulated at these points, the electrical resistance of the skin shows a precise decrease. A needle inserted in an acupuncture point will generate some extremely weak electrical potential and the body is capable of registering such minute electrical sensitivity. The effect is to revitalise the iron molecule found in each of the red blood cells, or haemoglobin, in the body. Similarly a magnet will stimulate oxygenation to reactivate the energy levels.

The life force – known as *Ond, Prana* or *Ch'i* – (see Chapter 7 'Masters of Geomancy', page 146) – circulates through the meridians creating the biorhythms affected by the external electromagnetic field environment, which include the naturally occurring gravitational forces and cosmic radiation activity in outer space. The acupuncture needle releases accumulated toxins and restores the body's natural electrochemical balance. Our metabolism and biorhythms can be regulated and restored by synchronising pulses from the Schumann Waves (see Chapter 3, page 62).[9]

State-of-the-art infrared and photon counter instruments can measure the electromagnetic fields emitted from our cells and organs. Our body acts like a radio transmitter, both sending out and receiving information through our bioelectrical system. An electrical change in the body predates any biological or anatomical change. The extremely low electromagnetic frequencies vary according to the parts of the body and the different types of disease.

Diagnostic instruments have been developed to register the wavelength patterns that vary according to our moods and state of health. Techniques used by modern electromagnetic medicine, called bioresonance therapy (BRT), resulted in the development of the Biocom machine, which registers the extremely faint body frequencies and decodes the signals to identify any pathological disorders. The device then applies the body's beneficial frequencies to cancel out the disturbed pathological signals. In 1997 there were about 4,000 Biocom machines being used worldwide, and results indicate the technique can treat a variety of ailments including allergies, degenerative diseases and pain.[10]

Other microcurrent-based therapies are now being used in both medical and beauty treatments. In essence, a normal, healthy cell acts like a battery producing an extremely weak voltage, which can be stimulated by the microcurrent treatment to strengthen and rejuvenate the body's organs, skin tissue and circulation. A technique known as plasma-kinetic technology uses radio frequency energy to dissolve prostrate tissue to avoid major intrusive surgery. It can also be used to treat sports injuries and disorders of the uterus.[11]

Since the 1950s, low-energy, time-varying magnetic fields have been used by osteopaths, chiropractors, physiotherapists and even some of the more orthodox allopathic practitioners to accelerate the healing of broken bones; to stimulate blood flow, to reduce pain and increase relaxation. The development of other low-energy pulsed electromagnetic field (PEMF) therapies indicates that a number of disorders and diseases outside the musculo-skeletal sphere may successfully respond to the appropriate strength of PEMFs. Bone mass once lost through osteoporosis led to early NASA experiments to prevent similar bone loss in astronauts due to weightlessness. It appears that well-controlled PEMF therapies have proved to be considerably cheaper than intrusive surgery and with a reduced risk of side-effects.

The latest machine and diagnostic techniques developed by medical science may have a far greater biological impact than the relatively benign therapies mentioned above. Computerised axial tomography (CAT, or CT) scans create a three-dimensional image by taking X-rays from all around the body: ultrasound produces a three-dimensional image by bouncing soundwaves off organs and is frequently used to look at a baby in the womb. Magnetic resonance imaging (MRI) scanners are used to detect diseases such as cancer by comparing the different magnetic properties of tissues in the body. This now commonly used diagnostic tool subjects the patient to very high intensity fields that momentarily change the arrangement of the structure of the cells of the tissue before an image can be recorded. However, there must be deep concern about the risks to cells and the autonomic nervous system induced by subjecting the body to such powerful frequencies. No doubt early diagnosis enhances preventive medicine techniques but the side-effects may far outweigh the benefits.

We know the ailing body will respond positively to extremely weak electromagnetic fields, and electric shock treatment has been an established – but controversial – treatment for psychiatric patients. However, this high-powered electroconvulsive therapy (ECT) can be so intrusive and often destructive that it now has many detractors. Psychiatric patients who have unnecessarily suffered brain damage through ECT have sued health authorities, and ECT may yet prove to be as hazardous as the early, indiscriminate use of X-rays.

Medical science recognises the often harmful effects of electromagnetic fields and yet, almost without exception, in our modern temples of healing every bed in a hospital ward has a battery of electronic equipment and devices with power and lighting points, TV, radio and alarm controls – all of which are located immediately behind the patient's head! If the medical electronic gadgetry were placed at least as far away as the foot of the bed, the general healing process may be improved and possibly accelerated. The bed itself, usually made of steel, also tends to amplify the electromagnetic smog. Even greater improvement would be seen if patients were to sleep on wood-framed beds and the electrical equipment kept on portable trolleys and brought to the bedside only when absolutely necessary.

Undoubtedly, the body can respond positively to weak electric and magnetic fields, but uncontrolled, needless exposure will be detrimental. In the light of modern developments and techniques in medical science, it is astonishing to find so much resistance on the part of the medical profession, electricity-generating companies, producers of mobile phones and other electrical equipment to accept that electromagnetic fields can and do affect our resistance to disease, mutate our genes or bend our mind. If we have any doubt we should remind ourselves of the new lethal and non-lethal microwave weapons that are already in use today.

The nineteenth- and twentieth-century pioneers of generated electricity were the latter-day alchemists who created their version of an elixir of life and an unprecedented form of 'magic' that has transformed our everyday lives. However, this has also wreaked inestimable damage to both the ecology of the planet and our own health and well-being. As we saw in the earlier chapters of this book, our often-blind fascination with high technology and the use of untested synthetic materials and techniques has also been a major source of illness at home and at work.

References

1. 'Low-frequency electrical and magnetic fields – the precautionary principle for national authorities: guidance for decision makers', *Magnetic Fields and Cancer – A Criteria Document*, Sweden, October 1995.
2. *EM Fields Information Booklet No. 1*, published by EM Fields in conjunction with Powerwatch UK and Scientists for Global Responsibility, pp. 22, 23, and 45.
3. Professor M. J. O'Carrol, 'Electromagnetic fields in the home – a statistician's view', *Powerwatch Network News*, Issue 5, November 1995, p. 4.
4. *Powerwatch Network News, Electromagnetic Hazard & Therapy* can be found on www.powerwatch.org.uk

and www.em-hazard-therapy.com. *Microwave News* (bi-weekly), PO Box 1799, Grand Central Station, New York, 10.1.63.

5. 'Are bras a risk?', *Electromagnetic VDU News*, vol. 6, nos 1–2, 1995, p. 4.
6. Ian Fletcher, 'Microwave ovens can cause cancer, new report claims', *Evening Standard*, 9 March 2000.
7. Catherine Bassindale, 'Headache? Try pendant power', *Evening Standard*, 8 August 2000, p. 28.
8. Sean O'Neill, 'Magnetic footwear helps lame horse return to ring', *The Daily Telegraph*, 19 January 1999, p. 10.
9. Smith, Dr C. and Best, S. (1989) *Electromagnetic Man*, London: J. M. Dent.
10. 'Bioresonance offers effective therapy for variety of ailments', *Electromagnetic Hazard & Therapy*, vol. 8, no. 2, 1977, p. 10.
11. Roger Dobson, 'Radio waves melt prostate trouble away', *The Sunday Times*, 11 April 1999.

Suggested further reading

Bentham, P. (1996) *VDU Terminal Sickness*, London: Jon Carpenter Publishing.
Coghill, R. (1992) *ElectroHealing*, Northants: Thorsons.

Part II
Perennial Wisdom

7.
Lessons from the past

Alternative technology

The development of modern technology has changed virtually every aspect of our daily lives. In the field of medicine alone it has brought us the most extraordinary advances in healthcare. High technology is magical, seductive and cannot be condemned out of hand but how often do we bother to consider alternative solutions that may be equally effective and much less harmful to the environment, ourselves and future generations?

For several years the Building Research Establishment (BRE), Royal Institute of British Architects (RIBA) and other organisations have produced a mass of technical data on low-tech methods and systems that can minimise global warming, acid rain, ozone layer depletion as well as reducing the overall demand for generated electricity. In addition to solar panels, wind and wave power, there is a relatively new and available technology called *photovoltaics,* which is a system of silicone semiconductors formed in wall facing panels that react to sunlight and can produce up to 50 per cent of a building's energy consumption. Regrettably, apart from a small number of recent government and owner-occupier buildings, the building industry and property developers appear to have little inclination to implement energy-saving devices and techniques.

The question is why should we expect our architects and engineers to become more innovative and spend time and effort researching low-energy, non-hazardous, non-polluting solutions when an easy, high-technology answer is immediately available? Instead of believing that modern science and technology are the only way forward there may be lessons to be learned from nature and the traditional master builders whose low-technology, benign, passive systems were ecologically sustainable and health hazard free. We need look no further than Japan – ironically the twentieth-century's hub of high technology – to discover two fine examples of ancient low-technology building.

Ancient technologies

One of the most elegant, aesthetically pleasing, low-tech, hazard-free, non-electronic almost totally maintenance-free intruder alarm security systems, the 'Nightingale floor' was installed about a thousand years ago. It is still in working order and can be found in a palace in Kyoto, the former capital city of Japan (AD 794–1192). The magnificent palaces and temples in Kyoto were built of timber with translucent screens separating the inner apartments and state rooms from the wide corridor around the perimeter of the building. The corridor flooring is made of wide planks of timber set on joists with each plank fixed by nails hooked on to other 'nails' in the joists underneath the boarding. The nails have been 'tuned' so that when a person walks across the floor the slight spring in the boarding causes the nails to rub together to make the dulcet, soothing sound of a nightingale bird singing. Those asleep in the apartments will be gently but positively alerted by anyone crossing the floor.

The structural 'earthquake proof' design of a new 37-storey high office building for Mitsubishi has been based on a technology also devised around a thousand years ago. When the industrial city of Kobe was shattered by an earthquake in 1995, over 6,000 people died and swathes of the city were devastated. However, the ancient, fragile looking pagoda remained standing in the midst of the ruins. Nara, Japan's first capital city, has many historical monuments, including a six-storey high pagoda built in the eighth century AD. It too withstood a massive earthquake in the fifteenth century and thousands of other quakes since. There are some 500 ancient pagodas in Japan and only two have collapsed due to earthquakes.

The pagoda is a wooden tower built as a shrine to house relics of Buddha, and only the priests are allowed to enter the inner sanctum areas. Most are five storeys high although others are considerably taller. None of the storeys are rigidly fixed to each other; the large overhanging eaves are heavily weighed down with roof tiles that act like a balancing pole used by a tightrope walker. Inside, a central column of solid timber runs from top to bottom, and is not attached to the floors. When the floors start to shake from side to side in an earthquake, the timber column acts like a buffer to absorb the violent vibration. The new Mitsubishi office building has been designed with a non-structural central column of 'soft' steel independent of the main structure of the building, which will 'cushion' earthquake vibrations at each floor level. This has yet to be tested in an actual earthquake but simulators indicate that the building will not collapse.[1]

Other low-technology lessons to be learned from nature and the traditional builders of the past can show us how to thrive even in extreme climatic conditions. In tropical regions, termite ant nests are built of huge mounds of earth. The temperature inside the maze of tunnels is maintained at a constant level by a complex system of ductways and passages aligned on a north–south axis to ventilate the nest. The Innuit people of the Arctic regions of North America and Greenland use ice and snow to build their dome-shaped igloo dwellings: vents in the dome, along with their own body heat modifies the extremely cold conditions to generate a habitable environment. Other Arctic inhabitants construct semi-subterranean earth shelters or cover their skin tents with snow. The architectural form and materials of the African mud hut evolved a roof shape with openings for light and air to maintain good interior conditions.

Natural ventilation

A development of the mud hut can be seen in Ad Diriyah, the old capital of Saudi Arabia, where two- and three-storey high houses built of thick, sun-baked mud with small shuttered openings and a wooden front door provided comfortable living conditions. Nearby, in the Arab Emirates, also one of the most hot, dry desert regions of the world, the traditional, vernacular houses were built with tall wind towers to catch the slightest zephyr breeze from any direction. Air is drawn down the vent shafts into the rooms around the inner courtyard keeping the whole building cool, aired and protected from the heat and sand of the desert. This form of low technology not only made a dwelling habitable, it also created the unique architectural feature of the towers. Apart from a few notable exceptions hardly any of the old houses have survived the building boom of the past few decades. Now, almost the entire population of Dubai lives either in air-conditioned blocks of apartments or newly built houses with protruding air-conditioning boxes stuck out through the walls or windows, while inside, the rooms rattle with the noisy motors.

An example of a traditional technology developed over centuries to meet the social needs of the people who live in rural areas of Upper Egypt is an all-in-one water cooling and purification system using large, unglazed ceramic jars called *maziara*. Water from the Nile, unfit for drinking, is stored in the porous *maziara*. The water that seeps through the jar is collected in bowls and is pure enough to meet drinking water standards. Evaporation occurs as the water passes through the porous jars, and in effect absorbs the heat of the day. Air passing over the jars becomes cooled and the difference in temperature outside and inside the house means that the cool air circulates like a sophisticated air-conditioning system.[2]

In the 1970s the author was commissioned to study a number of likely sites and existing buildings for an international American bank looking for new premises to expand its operations in Cairo. High on the list of preferred options was a palace built in 1913 for Kaiser Wilhelm II (Kaiser Bill), though due to the start of the First World War he never occupied the completed building. A detailed dimensional survey revealed a modular coordinated geometry associated more with ancient buildings of the past. Equally impressive were the light, cool and pleasantly comfortable interior rooms. There was no inner courtyard, no air-conditioning or artificial ventilation and yet a gentle breeze continually flowed through the building even though the July midday temperature outside was extremely high and the surrounding streets were hot, dusty and airless. The architects may have learned something from the termites!

These traditional technologies were developed using the local climate and materials to their best advantage. What is appropriate for the Arctic or desert regions will not be suitable for temperate Western conditions but lessons about the most advantageous orientation of a building have been part of the teachings of master builders from the earliest times.

The twentieth-century high technology that has had the greatest influence on architectural design has been the development of mechanical air-conditioning. It has also had a serious – even disastrous – impact on both global warming and the depletion of natural resources, and is the source of various forms of health hazard. Mechanical air-conditioning has presented architects and their clients with a technology to create an internal microclimate that insulates the occupants from the external environment, however inhospitable and extreme the conditions may be. Technology has allowed us to build virtually any type of building of any shape, size or volume anywhere in the world. Unless there is some major catastrophe in the foreseeable future it is unlikely there will be any meaningful reduction in the demand for bigger and taller buildings to suit commercial interests and an ever-expanding population. There is no shortage of technical ingenuity to develop large high-rise buildings, however escalating running costs, scarcity of fossil fuels and a worldwide insistence on the reduction of polluting gas emissions will demand that alternative technologies be employed. (It is accepted that there will be a few buildings designed for specific purposes that could function only with some form of mechanical air-conditioning system.) However, more recently developed ecologically sustainable alternative technologies are now readily available and in use.

Windpower technology has existed for thousands of years in the Middle East. Now, Western engineers are studying wind patterns over different sizes and heights of modern office blocks to establish the feasibility of future buildings to capture sufficient wind through a system of roof-top funnels and turbines to produce sufficient air changes which would be equivalent to good air-conditioning practice. In certain locations, it may well be that enough power could be harnessed to generate an electrical supply to supplement the lighting consumption of the average office or factory building. Japanese and European companies are looking at prototype designs to assess whether the technology can be marketed commercially: particular interest has been shown in Germany where there is significant concern about 'green' issues. The impetus to use such wind power will not come from architects (who generally have to do their client's bidding), nor from the clients who follow the advice of estate agents (whose judgement is based on current market trends): the need to find low-cost, energy-saving solutions will arise in the near future from socio-political pressures to impose heavy taxes on the consumption of fossil fuels, for example the Climate Change Levy imposed by the British government in April 2001. The demand for alternative solutions may also stem from the business community who will not be able to afford to occupy high-energy-consuming modern buildings.

A working party was set up in 1992 by Brian Moss, president of the UK Chartered Institution of Building Services Engineers (CIBSE), to explore the design and application of naturally ventilated buildings to challenge the concept that large high-rise, deep-floor planned buildings such as concert and assembly halls, offices, hospitals and schools had to be mechanically air-conditioned.[3] Since then, notable British architects have pioneered the way forward to 'greener', naturally ventilated buildings. Lord Norman Foster's Commerzbank headquarters in Frankfurt, which is Europe's tallest building, uses gardens at each of the 58 storeys as part of the natural ventilation system. Foster's Reichstag building in Berlin uses the same ventilation principles including photovoltaic panels on the roof to generate electricity. Sir Michael Hopkins' Parliament building in Westminster, Lord Richard Rogers' design for the new Welsh Assembly building in Cardiff and many other less prominent non-commercial, owner-occupied buildings such as university halls and theatres have been commissioned to be naturally ventilated and as ecologically sustainable as current technology will allow. American architect William McConnel has also designed several naturally ventilated high-rise buildings and, no doubt, the trend will soon gather momentum in other countries.

Lesser-known ecologically minded 'green' British architects have encountered strong resistance to natural ventilation technology from their property developer clients and the conservative estate agents' advisors who are reluctant to use anything except conventional air-conditioning systems in their speculative office buildings. The few architects who have been successful believe their persuasive ecological arguments based on the reduction of greenhouse gases and continuing low energy for the life of the building have held little sway compared to the evidence of improved staff productivity and enthusiasm. The experiences of Commerzbank and other owner-occupier business organisations clearly show that, compared to when in mechanically ventilated buildings, staff feel more invigorated, enjoy the sense of breathing in fresh air and generally do not suffer the usual high absenteeism and health problems encountered in sealed environments. Natural ventilation technology will change the architectural appearance of the next generation of buildings when chimney stacks and funnels will feature on rooftops and become a significant and challenging design expression, somewhat reminiscent of the tall wind towers of the houses in Dubai, except the function will be to draw the air up and out rather than down and into the interior.

The considerable advantages and benefits of natural ventilation for the building owner, the occupants and the population at large include reduced capital costs as there is no mechanical plant to install; the operating costs are minimal; there is zero ecological damage and the occupants have greater personal control over their environment with greater user flexibility. In most air-conditioned buildings, all the bulky ductwork, mechanical equipment and pipework located above the ceiling are concealed with suspended ceiling tiles, whereas in a naturally ventilated building using the same envelope of structure the suspended ceiling height can be raised to give the space a greater sense of light and airiness because there are no ducts or equipment to conceal. A survey carried out by the CIBSE showed that 89 per cent of the people interviewed preferred natural ventilation with the ability to have some control over their immediate workstation environment. The perception was that the sometimes higher temperatures could be tolerated provided there was a sense of even the slightest air movement.[4]

To design a naturally ventilated high-rise building with deep floor plans the architect and engineer must first address the low technological requirements to create the interior 'chimney stack' effect to control the air movement throughout the building. This means the architect will have to return to certain fundamental principles of traditional building technology that have been practised for millennia. Design factors hitherto discarded and ignored will have to be relearned, understood and implemented. For example, orientating a building to suit prevailing wind directions and compass bearings related to the Sun; designing projections on the façades to shield solar gain, traffic noise and creating the thermal mass of the structure to regulate fluctuations in temperature. All these will have a strategic impact on the methods and techniques taught in the schools of architecture and engineering.

Finding the ideal site

Writing 2,000 years ago about two of the fundamental principles of architecture – propriety and economy – in his *The Ten Books on Architecture* Vitruvius said:

> Propriety will be due to natural causes if, for example, in the case of all sacred precincts we select very healthy neighbourhoods with suitable springs of water... For when their diseased bodies are transferred from an unhealthy spot, and treated with waters from health giving springs, they will more speedily grow well... There will be natural propriety in using an eastern light for bedrooms and libraries, a western light in winter for baths and winter apartments, and a northern light for picture galleries and other places in which a steady light is needed... Economy denotes the proper management of materials and of site, as well as a thrifty balancing of costs and common sense in the construction of works. This will be observed if, in the first place, the architect does not demand things which cannot be found or made ready without great expense.[5]

In other words, the selection of a site appropriate for its qualities and the use of the building, correct orientation and conservation of natural resources and matters of ecology should be the responsibility of the architect. Today, architects for a building in, say, London, are likely to specify materials that have to be transported from various countries in Europe or even further afield rather than adapting a design to suit materials and equipment that may be more readily available in the locality, or at least within the shores of the UK.

The work of Vitruvius will be discussed more fully later, but at this point it is sufficient to say that in the major work mentioned above he stated that the architect/engineer must carefully study and understand the consequences of the patterns and features of climate, geography, topography, prevailing winds and orientation of the locality before finally choosing the site of a building or city. This included the observation of the local flora and fauna, not only to take note of their habits and temperament associated with the four elements – earth, air, fire and water – but also to have high regard for the 'methods of old times' (that is, before 2,000 years ago!). Vitruvius cites one 'old times' method for testing the water and the farming quality of the soil of a prospective city site: one or two native animals feeding off the land were killed, the entrails picked over, and from an examination of the heart, kidneys, liver and pancreas the healthiness and qualities of the soil of the site could be 'divined' or dowsed. (Picking over entrails sounds like witchcraft, but in fact it makes common-sense.)

Vitruvius' primer guide on the criteria for determining the suitability of a site for a city states:

First comes the choice of a very healthy site. Such a site will be high, neither misty nor frosty, and in a climate neither hot nor cold, but temperate; further, without marshes in the neighbourhood. For when the morning breezes blow toward the town at sunrise, if they bring with them mists from marshes and, mingled with the mist, the poisonous breath of the creatures of the marshes to be wafted into the bodies of the inhabitants, they will make the site unhealthy... These variations in heat and the subsequent cooling off are harmful to the people living on such sites.[6] [An example of the European version of Feng Shui!].

He goes on to say that the layout and pattern of streets should be designed according to the quality and direction of the winds, as the effect of cold and wet winds can be reduced by observing the prevailing climatic conditions. He then lists the many diseases that are hard to cure in unhealthy neighbourhoods because the inhospitable wind directions have not been addressed by the design of the layout of the streets.

Vitruvius cites the unfortunate case of a town called Old Salpia, built in a poor, unhealthy location:

Year after year there was sickness, until finally the suffering inhabitants came with a public petition to Marcus Hosilius and got him to agree to seek and find them a proper place to which to remove their city. Without delay he made the most skilful investigation, and at once purchased an estate near the sea in a healthy place, and asked the senate and Roman people for permission to remove the town. He constructed the walls and laid out the house lots, granting one to each citizen for a mere trifle. This done, he cut an opening from a lake into the sea and thus made of the lake a harbour for the town. The result is that now the people of Salpia live on a healthy site and at a distance of only four miles from the old town.[7]

A refreshing commentary on those in authority who listened to the people, took notice and then did something about it.

Every site possesses its own unique qualities determined by climate, topography, flora and fauna, the composition of the topsoil layer, the strata of rock formation below, the subterranean minerals and water as well as the local effect of terrestrial and cosmic forces, such as magnetism and other radiation, which can vary in magnitude within a few metres. For example the Physic Gardens of Chelsea and Henry VIII's manor house close by were established in that particular location because the site was found to be a healthy microclimate especially suitable for plant life. The decision was not based upon market forces or site availability.

'Feeling' the earth energies, sensing the sounds, tasting and smelling the natural landscape of a site, observing the essence of the locality and the indigenous people and wildlife, and using the intuitive as well as the conscious mind should be standard practice when choosing a site. How often, in our Western culture does the planner, architect or engineer visit the prospective site to study its harmony, balance and healthiness? Sometimes even the orientation and aspect of a site will be disregarded leaving only the physical dimensions to be checked against an ordnance survey map of the area to ensure the locations and boundaries are correct. Government departments and their town planners who select the sites for our new towns and housing estates appear to pay scant attention to the natural qualities and healthiness of the location. Leaving aside the subterranean strata, earth magnetism and the lesser-known natural properties of the land, little attention is given to the actual environmental conditions that can be seen, smelled, touched, tasted and heard. In the twentieth century we became over-dependent upon the science of modern engineering technology to provide intercity infrastructure such as transport systems for food and goods and a network of pipes, cables, and conduits to supply power, water and sewerage disposal. Is that all we need to create a healthy, spiritually uplifting quality of life? If architects and doctors were able to communicate with each other in a common language, there could be a breakthrough in their understanding of how to avoid the worsening health hazards in the built environment.

Megalithic legacy

A dependency on the bounty bestowed by nature and its rhythms leads to a deep sense of respect, reverence and sacredness of the Earth and heavens. The Sacred Earth tradition of the indigenous North American Navaho goes back to a Megalithic stone age belief system in which the Earth was mother, the sky was father, and thunder their mating call, with their marriage producing the fertility and abundance of the soil. The 'death' of the Sun in the evening and its 'rebirth' the next morning was a metaphor for the cycle of rebirth and transformation. Mountains, rocks, rivers and trees were imbued with a life-force, power and moods that personified either the female or male form of energy. The feminine principle represented fluidity, darkness, cool colours, receptivity and intuition; the masculine represented solidity, brightness, warm colours and rationality, and in different cultures they were symbolised by Mother and Father; Moon and Sun; Yin and Yang; Shakti and Shiva; Sirius and Osiris.

The Neolithic stone age marked the beginning of the period when we made the significant change from being nomadic hunter-gatherers to farmers tied to the land. Stable isotope analysis of eating habits indicate that this changeover to forming settled agricultural communities with animal domestication took place over a relatively short period of about 200 years. Survival, life, fertility, death and immortality have always been the fundamental issues of human beings but the powerful forces of nature – wind and water – could either destroy or nurture the crops and grazing pastures. To live in harmony with the environment it became imperative to devise some means to measure time, predict the changing patterns of the Sun, Moon, planets and the seemingly eternally fixed position of the stars, and to track the grand cyclical nature of the cosmic forces affecting the seasons and climate.

The heavenly bodies exert energies, vibrations, magnetic, gravitational and other forces that vary according to their movements and relative positions to the Earth. The interference patterns set up by their juxtapositioning at any given moment create positive and negative reactions in all living matter which, like DNA, can enable predictions to be made about a likely course of action or event. Accurate astrological predictions are dependent upon knowing precisely the position and movement of the bodies at any given time. Megalithic and other earth cultures built massive structures, such as Stonehenge, for astrological purposes to predict the most advantageous time for sowing and harvesting their crops. The North American Indians lay seeds in a particular alignment with the magnetic north to maximise the nutritional value and size of the crop. In *Secrets of the Soil*, Maria Thun, a farm researcher for the German government, gives data on the effect of plant growth related to planetary oppositions, times and conjunctions. Nodes (where orbits intersect), occultations (when a body passes in front of another) and outright eclipses (obscurity) are unfavourable for sowing and planting work, and it was found that on node days there is a statistically significant rise in traffic accidents.[8] (The effects of the phases of the Moon on cattle breeding was established by Rudolf Steiner: 'If bull is taken to cow on a node day either the cow remains barren or the calf is born with undesirable characteristics.') Ancient farming practices indicate they were well aware of the best times to reap and sow, which are still well understood in many parts of the world by non-industrialised farmers.

In 1967, retired Scottish Professor of Engineering, Alexander Thom, published the controversial results of his meticulous surveys of the many Megalithic sites in Britain.[9] Although the shape of many of the stone circles, including Stonehenge, had become disturbed and somewhat dilapidated, Thom found that the stones had been set with great precision and the ground plans were based on the accurate geometrics and elaborations of the circle, ellipse and Pythagorean triangles to produce highly complex astrological alignments, later confirmed by the astrophysicist Professor Fred Hoyle. A standard unit of measurement, the 'megalithic yard', also established by Professor Thom, has been shown to be the same basic length of rod used to build the Pyramids, also built to extraordinary geometric and astronomic precision.

The findings of Dr Gerald Hawkins, author of *Stonehenge Decoded*, published at about the same time, concluded that the Aubrey Holes[10] at Stonehenge formed a perfect eclipse, marking the 56-year lunar cycle.[11] This too was confirmed by Hoyle. The 56 timber posts of the colonnade represent the number necessary to trace the Moon's 28-day cycle related to the weather patterns, seasons and tides. Noting the time of day was relatively simple by observing the lengthening of the shadows cast by the Sun: but to build a calendric 'instrument' in the Stone Age to reconcile the 13 lunar, 28-day months, the 14-day waxing and waning cycle, the 7 days of the week, the 4 seasons, the 365 days of the Sun's return as well as marking the solstice and equinox times and planetary movement, was a highly complex and sophisticated piece of geometry. (Excavated Stone Age bones dated about 30000 BC were found to have ordered patterns marking a number system of counting corresponding to the 13 lunar cycles.)

To have acquired the knowledge to build Stonehenge and other stone circles to such extraordinary precision and to such purpose must have been the result of patient observation and meticulous sightings over an extremely long time-scale. Modern computer modelling programmes such as Skyglobe and Redshift display the changing night-sky patterns of the constellations going back over thousands of years, enabling today's researchers to understand the depth of ingenuity and brainpower of our ancestors who masterminded the design and construction of Stone Age structures. If Stonehenge is as advanced as many researchers believe, it predates, by several hundred years, the orthodox view that sophisticated astronomy began with the Babylonians about 2000 BC.

Astrologer Alan Butler believes that the Megalithic peoples fully understood that the Earth was a sphere, and had the knowledge to accurately calculate its circumference based on Professor Thom's megalithic yard, which appears to have been in existence as early as 3500 BC. In his book *The Bronze Age Computer Disc*, Butler sets out how he cracked the secret hidden in the markings on the Phaistos disc discovered about a hundred years ago in the Minoan palace of Phaistos in Crete. The disc, dated about 2000 BC, has 31 divisions of spiral designs on the face comprising 123 symbols composed of 37 pictograms, and the obverse side has 119 symbols of the same 37 pictograms. Butler concluded after many years of study that this is a computerised calendar based on the Minoan system of using a 366° circle which allowed them to reconcile the measurement of time and distance.[12] He also verifies the hypothesis put forward by French researcher Xavier Guichard in the 1930s that the Megalithic people had devised a series of lines of latitude and longitude, much like those used on our present-day maps, which were similar to Alfred Watkins' ley-lines to produce a form of 'compass' for navigation.[13]

Our modern-day history books tell us that the sixteenth-century Renaissance astronomers Copernicus and Galileo were the first to pronounce that the Earth moved around the Sun, and the Greek Eratosthenes (276–194 BC) was the first to calculate the Earth's circumference (he has since been proved to have been accurate to within a thousand kilometres). And yet the Megalithic people could not have developed their sophisticated science of astronomy unless they knew the Earth was round and that the solar system was heliocentric and not geocentric. It is also clear that the ancient people who built the thousands of stone buildings, including Stonehenge and the Egyptian pyramids and temples, most certainly understood the geometry of the Pythagorean triangles and the Golden Section (see Chapter 9, page 191) at least some two thousand years before Pythagoras was born. The ancient Greeks treated these geometric constructions as 'sacred' – closely guarded secrets of esoteric wisdom.

Robin Heath's views expressed in his book Sun, Moon and Stonehenge,[14] are well supported by an earlier work, published in 1982, entitled *Time Stands Still*, a brilliant and beautifully illustrated book on Neolithic culture by the architect and philosopher Professor Keith Critchlow.[15] Critchlow shows photographs of Neolithic granite stones, about the size of a small melon, carved to form a series of the regular mathematical symmetries known as the twelve Platonic Solids, such as the tetrahedron, the icosahedron and dodecahedron (see Chapter 9, page 199). These precise geometric stone objects were believed to have been used as a teaching tool and clearly establish that three-dimensional mathematics was indeed known at least a thousand years or more before Pythagoras or Plato were born. Professor Critchlow came across the stones in a museum in Scotland where they were displayed as being an ancient form of cannon ball! The only other place where he had seen anything remotely similar was among the Egyptian antiquities in the British Museum. Critchlow says:

> Here we have the hardest stone found in Scotland being chosen to create beautiful mathematical symmetries for no apparent utilitarian use! It is just this latter aspect of the objects that has baffled archaeologists to date. However, their very existence demonstrates a degree of mathematical awareness which the old school of archaeology still remains reluctant to concede to Neolithic peoples. We believe they can demonstrably be taken to reinforce Thom's calculations and proposals which were so tardily received by the majority of the archaeological fraternity. The study of the heavens is, after all a spherical activity, needing an understanding of spherical coordinates. If the Neolithic inhabitants of Scotland had constructed Maes Howe[16] before the pyramids were built by the Ancient Egyptians why could they not be studying the laws of three-dimensional coordinates? Is it not more than a coincidence that Plato as well as Ptolemy, Kepler and al-Kindi[17] attributed cosmic significance to these figures?[18]

A popular concept assumes that the Megalithic peoples living in Britain and mainland Europe were static, landbound, simple, and relatively primitive people who were eventually 'civilised' by a steady drift westwards of Middle Eastern culture where 'civilisation' began. However, as we have seen, Neolithic monuments – standing stones and circles – are to be found beyond the shores of Europe, across the Middle East and as far afield as Asia. Somewhat surprisingly to many establishment historians and archaeologists, a 12-metre (38-feet) diameter stone circle was uncovered in Miami, Florida, in January 1999. Local archaeologists likened the carved stones to a miniature Stonehenge and preliminary investigations confirmed that its elliptical shape had positive celestial alignments. Mathematical calculations related to the other post holes found outside the main circle were sufficient evidence that the structure was an astronomical observatory, calendar or almanac. The general opinion was that the circle was built about 2,000 to 3,000 years ago by the Maya when the civilisation spread northwards from Central America.

The popular belief that American history began with the arrival of the Europeans ignores archaeological evidence that 10,000 years ago the prehistoric indigenous peoples were a highly cultured Neolithic society. Recent studies carried out in Brazil by biologist Walter Neves, from the Laboratory of Human Evolution at São Paulo University, show that the excavations of about 600 skulls are more than 12,000 years old and their bone structure and teeth are completely different from the indigenous Amazonian Indians.[19] Other dwellings and tools found in Monte Verde, Chile, in 1997 date back at least 12,500 years and the features of the skulls confirm the view that these people had immigrated from Asia and Siberia, across the frozen-over Bering Straits to occupy both North and South America.[20]

Undoubtedly, the Megalithic peoples were formidable travellers. Other discoveries of prehistoric mummies at several sites in the Tarim Basin in Western China have been dated between 3,000 and 4,000 years old. Elizabeth Wayland Barber's book *The Mummies of Urumchi* found in the same grave one mummy of a man 6ft 6ins tall and three women, one being 6ft tall with plaid fabrics used by the prehistoric Celts of Central Europe. More remarkable were their European, Caucasian features of light brown, reddish or blond hair, round eyes and long, thin noses. The graves also contained bundles of Ephedra twigs, which produces the effect of cannabis or opium found in Neanderthal graves 50,000 years old.[21]

Reputed to be 8,000 years old, the Hindu Vedas –(Sanskrit meaning 'divine knowledge') are probably the best known record of ancient wisdom based on the oral spiritual teachings of India. The Vedas comprise four main sections, one of which – the Rig Veda – refers to an even earlier period and speaks of a knowledge of astronomy and time cycles that suggests a period, at some time in prehistory, when an advanced civilisation was brought to an abrupt end by some cataclysmic event. Many cultures, spread wide over the planet, have a story of a great flood and a myth of creation as part of their folklore. Is this a mythology embedded in the collective unconsciousness of the human psyche or has it any factual substance? Whether or not an earlier 'Golden Age' existed before the Ice Age began will no doubt continue to be argued and researched but there remain a number of mysteries yet to be solved: Stonehenge, the great pyramids of Egypt, South America and thousands of other archaeological Megalithic stone relics were built with such awe-inspiring accuracy, precision and knowledge of mathematics, geometry and astronomy, and yet seemingly there is no 'history' of such intellectual development taking place.

Masters of geomancy

Throughout the ages, healers/priests and master builders have been acutely aware of the Earth's magnetic fields, global grid patterns and geopathic stress zones. The subterranean strata, water streams, natural features of the landscape, flora and fauna, prevailing winds and orientation were investigated and addressed to ensure the location and design of a building – whether it be a humble dwelling, majestic palace or temple of worship – would create the most harmonious influences for the health and prosperity of the occupants. Early cultures had a profound understanding of the characteristics and moods of nature and in many parts of the world they developed their own codified set of rules and guidelines to create environmental conditions in tune with nature and cosmic forces. Known today by the name of *geomancy*, these rules set out the most auspicious and beneficial location and orientation of a building. They gave directions on the best orientation for ventilation, the thickness of walls, the safest soil for foundations, the healthiest layout of the dwelling and the methods to prevent ill health from the bitter cold winds from the North. These 'laws' can be thought of as a highly sophisticated set of building codes, similar to our modern-day building by-laws and public health regulations, except that they go far beyond the merely practical, physical aspects of creating a healthy building in addressing the whole range of subtle energy fields that affect us mentally and spiritually. The codes also included comprehensive instructions for the correct siting of ancestral graves and the orientation of the body to ensure a safe passage to the next life – a spiritual practice corresponding to the religious philosophy and burial ceremonies of many ancient peoples.

The mainstream tradition of the North European Megalithic priesthood was passed on to the Egyptians and culminated in the esoteric schools of Greece and Rome, continuing through the Celtic tradition to the present day. The teachings were the basis of the fundamental principles of the location, design and construction of the magnificent architecture of the Egyptian, Greek, Roman and Gothic periods including the great buildings of Islam in the Middle East and India. Whatever the style, period or function, these ancient principles integrating and cooperating with natural energies and cosmic order are still more or less covertly practised in many parts of the world.

Vestiges of the Western European tradition survived Christianity's oppression and suppression of Celtic paganism and although there appears to have been no one comprehensive codified system, such as the forms of geomancy found in China and India, there is an abundance of writings from Pythagoras and Plato to Vitruvius and on through to the present day that are available for all those who are interested to study and practice. The little-known Celtic geomantic tradition has been researched and well documented by Nigel Pennick in his book, *Earth Harmony*.[22]

Comparable Eastern systems are known in China as *Feng Shui*, *Dai Ly* in Vietnam, and *Yattana* in Burma, and in India *Vastu Shastra* (*Vastu* = house, *Shastra* = science or technology, that is, the science of building a house).[23] While the ancient Celtic tradition and Vastu Shastra are thought to predate Feng Shui, all are based on the same tenets but neither are so well known or publicised as the Chinese system.

India has a long history steeped in the science of physics, chemistry, astronomy/ astrology and symbolism. The foundation of Vastu Shastra was the ancient Hindu texts on life force known as *Prana*, or channels of energy. The *vital prana* comprising a network of 72,000 subtle channels, flows through the main power centres, called *chakras* – wheels or whirlpools of light – and their quality and efficiency determine a person's health. The free flow of prana, or breath of life, through the landscape and the interior is affected by the location, orientation, siting and layout of a building. A damaging effect may be caused by disturbing the natural tellegro-geognostic energy lines in the terrain, as this too can influence the direction and flow of prana. In the Celtic language the life force is known as *Ond*, the Japanese call it *Ki* and in Chinese it is *Ch'i* or *Qi* (pronounced 'chee'). The sum total of earth energies, cosmic radiation, the heavenly bodies, air, water, human emotions and activity, and the whole of the natural world is a life force carried on the wind (*Feng*) and contained by water (*Shui*). In the West we find this same principle in the biblical account of the Creation in Genesis: 'The Spirit [also 'breath' or 'wind'] of God moved upon the face of the waters'.

The principles of Feng Shui

The masters of the art and science of esoteric teachings were the highly trained initiates of the healer/priesthood. In our Western culture they were known as *Locator*

Civitatis, the Celts knew them as *Wizards* or *Shamans*. In China they were *Dragon Masters* – the high-priests of Feng Shui.

Agriculture, architecture, interior design, landscape and medicine were all encompassed within the Feng Shui (pronounced 'Fung Soy' in Cantonese, or 'Feung Shoy' in Mandarin; an acceptable Anglicised pronunciation is 'Fung Shway' but never 'Feng Shooee'!) tradition, which also acknowledges the underground earth energy fields and positive streams. A fourteenth-century text, devoted to the dowsing of geopathic stress, mentions the various associated diseases. The Dragon Master would identify the 'acupuncture' points in the ground and use something – a stake or standing stone – to act like a needle to neutralise the hazard.[24]

The principles of Feng Shui have remained virtually unchanged for about 4,000 years. It has continued to flourish in China, Hong Kong, Taiwan, Japan and many other parts of Asia, and now, in a simplified form, it has spread to the US, Europe and Australasia. When Mao-Tse Tung's communist regime took over China in 1949 it was actively discouraged as an old-fashioned superstition but was still covertly practised on the mainland and continues to be part of the culture and way of life.

Originally, Feng Shui was a closely guarded (sacred) discipline used to ensure the good health, wealth and power of the Chinese Imperial dynasties. The keepers of this knowledge were the Dragon Masters who were highly respected scientists and astrologers charged with sustaining the good fortune of the royal court. The principles of Feng Shui were applied even to the planning of towns such as the great cities of Beijing, Hanoi, Seoul and Hong Kong. The Dragon Masters had a profound depth of understanding of the *Yin* (feminine) and *Yang* (masculine) relationships necessary to create harmony with nature and within the family household or business organisation.

As the *Ch'i* flows through the human body along invisible veins called meridians linking the power centres (chakras), so the Earth's *Ch'i* flows through the 'veins' of energy in the soil and rock formations known as 'Dragon Lines'. (Our pagan Western ancestors called them Dragon or Serpent pathways.) In Chinese mythology, the dragon is a superior, all-powerful animal: the dragon's cosmic breath – *Shen Ch'i* – and its tail have vitalising qualities. The characteristic shape of the tail is sought after in the landscape to imbue the building with the powerful energy, and where you find the dragon, that other mythical creature, the tiger, will be present. The 'killing breath' or *Sha Ch'i* – the negative lines of energy – are a harmful source of disturbance and disease. The inauspicious *Sha* can accumulate in stagnant water, in poorly drained soil or can be carried on sharp, cold winds; it can travel along straight lines such as canals, railway lines, overhead power or telephone lines including along a direct path leading to a house.

The task of the Dragon Master is to identify these subtle forces and to deflect, disperse and neutralise the *Sha Ch'i* to allow the positive *Shen* force to flow and interact with the occupants to bring them goodness, health and prosperity. To do so, the Dragon Master needs a deep insight and awareness of the uniqueness of the nature, spirit and *soul* of a given location or building by dowsing, feeling, seeing, listening, smelling and tasting everything about the subtle energies of the place and its environment, whether the building is a house, office, hospital, school, bridge, tunnel or a new town. The vibrant energy centre or nucleus (known in Western tradition as the *Anima Loci,* or the soul of a place) is identified as the heart or spiritual focal point of the property.

So is all this mumbo-jumbo or plain common sense? Can there be some fundamental, rational basis for these apparently superstitious or arbitrary codes and design principles? Why should the Chinese favour the colour red to bring good fortune? Colour is a sensation produced when light of different wavelengths falls on the human eye. At a subliminal level we respond to these vibrational variations. Each colour affects our subtle power centres (chakras) – for example, red will increase our vitality and energy levels to take positive action, which creates the circumstances where good fortune can arise. The colour of soil is determined by mineral content. White and yellow soils are rich in calcium, potassium, manganese and magnesium, which tend to have natural pest control properties. They also have good load-bearing capabilities and the likelihood of waterlogging and settlement are low risk factors. Black soils contain certain minerals and crystals that tend to swell, produce poor bearing capacity, have low insulation qualities to the cosmic solar energy and magnetic flux lines. Blue-black soils are acidic and generally unhealthy. Of course these properties of soil and sub-strata may be applicable only to China. Vastu Shastra gives a different set of colours for the Indian soils and in other countries the colour indicating varying properties and characteristics would change again, therefore those practising Feng Shui must beware of applying the 'rules' too rigidly even though the general principles may be valid. On a more mundane note Feng Shui masters are careful to plan the 'correct' hanging side of a door leading into a room. Similarly, most Western houses built before the advent of central heating had their doors hung so that as it was opened it shielded a cold draft from entering directly into the room; it also prevented the open fire from belching out smoke. It is all a matter of good common sense.

The flow of fresh air through a building will reduce negative ion depletion (see page 34) inducing a sense of vitality; an aquarium, fountain or bowl of flowers will maintain a healthy humidity level, reduce static electricity and breathe a feeling of movement and life. Morning sunlight streaming through a window, the enjoyment of beneficial energy flows, a clean, uncluttered environment free from dust-collecting papers and other paraphernalia avoids vermin and bugs; the orderly, conscious placement of a few chosen objects in a room can be a constant reminder of the orderliness of the natural world about us. When we become aware of our interaction with nature and the rhythms of life it heightens our vitality and is conducive to a positive, uncluttered state of mind which, at a subtle level, affects our thought processes and feelings of optimism. This may account for those who have been 'treated' by the Dragon Master's work who later experience life-changing turning points in their health, prosperity and relationships. Undoubtedly, a clean, orderly house, properly arranged, orientated to give good natural light and air with harmonious colours will create a stress-reduced environment in the same manner that plants thrive or fail depending upon the quality of the soil and the climatic conditions – wind, water, sunlight and the changing seasons.

Before British architect Lord Norman Foster's design for the Hong Kong Shanghai Bank's new headquarters in Hong Kong was presented to the board of directors, the scheme had to be vetted and approved by the bank's Dragon Master who made a number of changes to the plans to avoid inauspicious design features. The architects had to amend their proposals accordingly. Ironically, at the time the building was the most technically advanced and electronically controlled in the world, yet aspects of the overall design concept had to be changed to conform to principles laid down 4,000 years ago!

Sceptics may consider Feng Shui as the whimsical indulgence of a gullible building owner, but it should be borne in mind that when Hong Kong was a British Protectorate operating under British Law, the Feng Shui rights of a property were legally safeguarded and applied in much the same way as the British Right to Light Act or the protective American Air Rights. If, for example, a newly constructed building or electricity pylon adversely interfered with the Feng Shui of an existing building, the owner could sue for damages and compensation was awarded by the courts.

Feng Shui in the West

While Feng Shui has flourished for centuries in Asia, it has only gained prominence in the West since the 1990s and now, in the US, UK, Europe and Australia, it is not only common parlance but often on the boardroom agenda. Newly emerging Western practitioners are well sought after by house owners, stall holders, taxi drivers, restaurateurs, small business operators and multinational corporations in the hope that by design, placement of objects and making the appropriate 'corrections' they will attract beneficial influences and bring health, prosperity and harmony into their daily life at home and at work. Some Western businesses have used Feng Shui in the hope that it will give them an edge over the competition; some have a more caring and hospitable attitude towards their staff and will use any innovation to improve working conditions; others feel obliged to address Feng Shui out of deference to their Asian clients. Undoubtedly a good working environment in a climate of well-being and good will engenders a sense of success and may encourage employees to remain loyal to the corporation. Those who have braved ridicule from certain quarters and openly declared their use of Feng Shui include British Airways, BUPA, Orange, Virgin Airlines and Virgin Megastores, the Bank of England, the Hong Kong Shanghai Bank Corporation, Marks & Spencer and many others in Britain and the US. Other companies have gone further by adopting the Asian practice of *Tai Ch*'i exercises for their staff.

The credibility major Western business corporations have given Feng Shui has added to the general popularity generated by celebrity users such as members of the Royal family, actors, film stars and pop musicians, as well as extensive media exposure and a plethora of books, magazines and seminars. This fashionable surge of interest has spawned many spurious self-styled 'Dragon Masters', many of whom have set themselves up as experts after attending a weekend workshop or reading a couple of books. Such amateurism can offer inappropriate and unhelpful advice through lack of experience, depth of knowledge or a too rigid interpretation of the 'rules', which in many instances may be inappropriate to Western conditions.

To become a Dragon Master one must be prepared to devote several years of continuous study under the tutelage of expert teachers. Architects in Vietnam must take extensive training courses before becoming proficient in the understanding of the fundamentals, but in the West our demand for the quick-fix and easy-to-do package has encouraged a high degree of charlatanism and misunderstanding of Feng Shui's depth of wisdom. Nevertheless, the growing popularity of dowsing and the ever-increasing interest can make a significant contribution to the general awareness of our immediate surroundings, of nature and the subtle energy forces that affect our psyche, health and well-being.

There are, of course, a number of well-established professionals who have under-gone expert training. Some Western architects are already well versed in Feng Shui and use the principles as a matter of design discipline; others have been instructed by their clients to accept a Dragon Master's input as part of the design process. While rigid adherence to Feng Shui can be frustrating and, in many ways, inappropriate for Western application, addressing these issues of orderliness and design discipline can produce a moderating influence and depth of awareness that may result in a superior and more creative solution. Modern architects who lack the training, experience or interest in the arrangement of furniture, colours, doors and positions could well benefit from the discipline of being more consciously aware of the overall orientation of a building and how it relates to the spirit and uniqueness of the natural environ-ment. It is better to work to some form of guidelines than to have no underlying design principles at all.

Generations of healers/priests, geomancers and master builders – the forebears of the professional architect – taught and practised the accumulated wisdom found in our own rich Western European heritage of geomancy, metaphysics, mystical teach-ings and literature. Today these more esoteric aspects of design are no longer an integral part of the curriculum in our schools of architecture. Indeed, there is not even mention of them. As a consequence modern architects have little or no under-standing or practical use for the fundamental principles that created not only the great sacred buildings such as Stonehenge, the great pyramids, cathedrals, mosques and temples but were also extended into secular architecture. These fundamental princi-ples of design are common to any period or style of architecture.

In contrast to the architectural profession's disregard for these basic teachings, the general public's interest in geomancy and ancient wisdom has generated the popu-larity of Feng Shui in the West and, on balance, it would seem far better to be served by an imported Eastern tradition than be devoid of any environmental or holistic awareness whatsoever. In the meantime, our architects, engineers and town planners not only ignore our own cultural wisdom but continue to design and build dehuma-nised houses, schools, offices and hospitals, many of which are known to be the root cause of illnesses.

Holistic medicine

In the first century BC, Vitruvius wrote that 'an architect should have a knowledge of the study of medicine on account of the question of climate, air, the healthiness and unhealthiness of sites and the use of different waters. For without these considerations, the healthiness of a dwelling cannot be assured'.[25]

Does the architect of the twenty-first century require a similar understanding of medicine? It is likely most architects would answer a resounding 'No'. They would argue that the Public Health Acts and strict building codes will ensure modern buildings are soundly built, wind- and weather-tight, well ventilated or air-conditioned and vermin controlled. Therefore, a clean, healthy environment is guaranteed. As for water, fuel supplies and sewerage disposal, underground service pipes are normally readily available for connection to the building. What else is there a need to know? Doctors might tend to agree on the basis that modern medicine is so highly specialised, compartmentalised, technically advanced and drug/surgery orientated that even medical practitioners themselves find it difficult to understand what some of their colleagues are doing or talking about. But apparently such plausible arguments do not answer the underlying question: why, despite advanced technology and the mass of available data do the new towns, estates and buildings of the latter half of the twentieth century often prove to be a source of personal sickness and social dysfunction?

Throughout history, the development of architecture and medicine have run a parallel course: the healer/priest/master builder of ancient times was the original root source from which both professions derived and, until the more recent past, both professions maintained close affinities with each other, giving rise to the old joke: 'What is the difference between a doctor and an architect?'. Answer: 'Doctors bury their mistakes; architects can only prescribe a covering of creepers!'.

However, the similarities continue even today. Both professions require a five-year full-time training course plus two years' practical experience before final qualification; both can be classified as an art and science; both claim their primary concerns are the health, welfare, comfort and well-being of humanity, and both, perhaps justifiably, will complain that they are overburdened with bureaucracy, matters of law and administration. Architecture and medicine have become highly dependent on advanced technology and electronics, and both have brought into use techniques, synthetic materials and certain 'wonder' drugs before their impact on human beings has been fully tested and assessed. Nowadays, however, perhaps the greatest similarity between the two professions is that neither demonstrates an understanding of the holistic nature of human beings and the fundamental interaction of the body's subtle energy systems and life forces with the natural environment.

Since the industrial revolution our obsession with materialism and insistence on scientific 'proof' has led to the modern-day concept of what constitutes 'reality' or 'the real world'. What we now perceive as reality would be more accurately defined as the *actuality* of the material world of matter whereas reality implies a *quality of being*, or one person's underlying interpretation and experiences of both the external and inner worlds, which will not necessarily be the same for everyone else. There is a physical, material actuality but in the metaphysical, occult (hidden) realms there are infinite realities. 'In my Father's house there are many mansions' elegantly expresses St John's mystical view of the multi-levelled realities. Concepts of black holes, a multi-dimensional universe, the vastness and number of galaxies, non-linear time and infinity can be as incomprehensible and meaningless as notions of purgatory, heaven and the divine realm of the eternal soul. Where the nature of reality is concerned, our dilemma was summed up by Einstein in *The Evolution of Physics*:

> Physical concepts are free creations of the human mind, and are not, however it may seem, uniquely determined by the external world. In our endeavour to understand reality we are somewhat like a man trying to understand the mechanism of a closed watch. He sees the face and the moving hands, even hears it ticking, but he has no way of opening the case. If he is ingenious he may form some picture of a mechanism which could be responsible for all the things he observes, but he may never be quite sure his picture is the only one which could explain his observations. He will never be able to compare his picture with the real mechanism and he can not even imagine the possibility or the meaning of such a comparison.[26]

Subtle bodies

Though not equipped with our present-day scientific technology, the teachings of the healers/priests show that somehow they knew about unseen realities: they understood about the power centres in the human body and could harness these energy fields. Biologist Dr Rupert Sheldrake calls this unseen life force that surrounds all living and inert matter the 'morphogenetic field'. In his book *A New Science of Life* he states: 'A rough analogy is provided by the "lines of force" in the magnetic field around a magnet; these spatial structures are revealed when particles capable of being magnetised, such as iron filings, are introduced into the vicinity. Nevertheless, the magnetic field can be considered to exist even when the iron filings are absent; likewise, the morphogenetic field...exists as a spatial structure'.[27]

A technique of photography developed about 30 years ago by a Russian couple, the Kirlians, produces an image of high-frequency waves making the energy field (or aura) graphically visible. They called this the 'bioplasma body' and likened it to the glowing Northern Lights of the Aurora Borealis phenomenon. A 'Kirlian photograph' is a freeze frame of radiating energy lines flowing from, say, a person's hand or a plant leaf showing a marked difference between healthy leaves and seeds to those which are decaying or have been irradiated.

A more recent invention by another Russian, Professor Dr Konstantin Korotkov, is an electrical instrument – called a GDV – which is attached to a personal computer and processes and prints a 'photograph' of the electrical field producing a visible gas discharge around the object to reveal a range of diagnostic information such as diet, drugs and environmental factors. It is also claimed that the energy fields technique can show the way a person has died – whether by shock, trauma, suicide or natural circumstances.[28]

The ancient concept of the physical body being enveloped in a spectrum of subtle energy fields has been the foundation of spiritual teachings throughout the world. Statues, paintings and drawings of the saints and other luminaries of Christianity, Buddhism, Sufism and Hinduism are depicted with the whole body or just the head shrouded in an aura or halo of shimmering energy – the light of a divine person. We lesser mortals also have a sheath of subtle energy fields, albeit not so bright and clear as those mystics who are fully realised beings. In keeping with the ancient dictum 'as above, so below', a human being is not just skin, bone, muscles and organs; nor is the planet Earth just a mass of physical material. At a macrocosmic level, the extremity of the Earth's gross or solid body is the crust of soil and rock we stand on. Surrounding this physical matter is the atmosphere, the stratosphere, the ozone layer, the Van Allen Belt and so on, which are the 'subtle bodies' of the Earth. Together, the Earth's gross body and subtle body form an integral, unified holistic system that is essential to sustain life.

At the microcosmic level, the extremity of the gross or material body of a human being is our skin. This is enveloped in a spectrum of energy fields called the etheric, auric and astral subtle bodies. The etheric body, extending a few centimetres from the skin, is a protective sheath that can be felt by sensitive hands as a soft balloon or cushion. When a person (or animal or plant) is in a state of disease the sheath feels jagged or broken, allowing the body's life force to 'drain' away. Beyond the etheric body is an aura or halo of colour like a rainbow. The varying 'pulses' and bands of colour will give a clear indication of a person's physical and psychological state. Beyond the aura is the astral body, which is where our thought patterns reside. All living organisms are a holistic, integrated combination of the gross and subtle bodies.

The chakras

Sanskrit – 'the language of the gods' – is the sacred language of the Hindu religion founded about 5,000 years ago. It has highly differentiated terminology to describe extraordinary states of consciousness, mental and spiritual processes and subtle body physiology for which there are no known equivalents in the languages of the West. *Chakra* (meaning wheel or circle) is the Sanskrit word for the power centres located in the physical body in the areas of the genitals, abdomen, solar plexus, heart, throat, brow and crown of the head. Each of the seven main chakras has a specific number of points or 'petals', and one's health, state of mind and metabolism are registered by the rate the wheels are spinning. Meridians or invisible veins carry the life force or energy through the body – the same as blood flows through our physical veins – interlinking the whole chakra system. (Chinese acupuncture needles are inserted into meridians to release blocked energy.) These chakras can be sensed but are invisible to the conscious eye.

The Eastern traditions of yoga, meditation and other mystical practices are intended to gradually open the chakra energy centres to release the extraordinary potential power in the body and facilitate the blending of the right and left hemispheres of the brain, leading ultimately to spiritual transcendence. In Western terms, C. G. Jung called this state of being 'individuation' – the attainment of becoming a fully realised person. Is there a 'science' underlying these ancient traditions based on the subtle energies of the body?

Dr Serena Roney-Dougal's thesis on parapsychology, *Where Science and Magic Meet,* published in 1991, speculates that while the ancients did not have the knowledge of modern medical science, there is a strong correspondence between the endocrine glands and the Hindu chakra system. Roney-Dougal suggested that the natural secretions of the glands correlate to intangible expressions of sexuality, earthiness, instinctual feelings, love, creativity and spirituality. The two lower chakras – the root or base, located at the genitals and abdomen – correspond to the unconscious, instinctual mind. The function of the third chakra – the solar plexus – controlled by the adrenal glands, is related to 'gut feelings' and 'butterflies' in the stomach when stress levels – the fight or flight reaction – release adrenaline. The fourth chakra centred around the heart secretes prolactin, the hormone of love, the breast and parenting. The thyroid gland in the throat chakra secretes thyroxin, which relates to creativity and the power of speech: an overactive thyroid can increase sexual drive and controls our heartbeat, mind activity and metabolic rate. The pineal gland, known as 'the seat of the soul', is centred close to the sixth brow chakra, sometimes referred to as our 'sixth sense' or 'third eye' – our intuitive sense, psychic awareness and innate knowingness. The culmination of spiritual initiations is the opening up of the seventh or crown chakra to experience the 'flowering of ten thousand petals' when we enter the realms of divine mysticism.[29]

According to Hindu teachings each chakra has a specific colour coding (which varies slightly in certain traditions). The sequence is the root chakra as red; the abdomen, orange; the solar plexus, yellow or gold; the heart, green; the throat, blue; the brow, indigo; and the crown, violet. Each chakra is stimulated by its corresponding colour. For example, red fires up energy and excites the root or sex chakra: it is no coincidence that cities have 'red light' districts. The earthy colour orange stimulates our instincts, impulsive feelings and our connection with the natural world. Yellow demands reason, logic and intellectual application: a yellow room or clinical ward will be extremely disturbing to mentally unstable patients such as schizophrenics. Green or rose pink are associated with harmony, balance and the heart: a green-coloured boardroom would encourage consensus and agreement, but the board members may find they are spending too much time weighing and considering rather than taking positive decisions. Blue, lapis and turquoise – the colours of healing, creativity and speech – are linked with the throat chakra. Indigo blue is the colour of the 'third eye' – intuition and psychic experiences. Purple or violet, the colour of the crown chakra, are associated with royalty, spirituality and the 'higher self'. If the main entrance and corridors of a hospital are painted with shades of violet the feeling of low self-esteem often experienced by those suffering an illness may be dispelled. The strength or tonal value of the colour varies the degree and quality of influence: for example, a subtle, pale 'pastel' shade will be less pervasive and imperative than a solid primary colour. These colour codings may highlight why we prefer or respond to certain colour combinations and explain how light and colour can be an effective healing treatment.

Ancient medical traditions

Paradoxically, the 3,000-year-old Ayurvedic medicine derived from ancient Vedic philosophy based on rebalancing the chakras, meditation, yoga and massage, is not only still practised extensively in India but is now one of several 'alternative' treatments gathering popularity in the West. Ayurveda (meaning 'knowledge of life') is a logical method of treating the root cause (rather than the symptoms) through diet, detoxification and prescribing the necessary lifestyle changes to return the body to wholeness. It is based on the principle of connecting the physical constitution with the mind, body and spirit, as well as with the environment and the movements of the planets. Universities and Ayurvedic hospitals in India provide the six-year basic training. In the UK the growing popularity of Ayurveda has encouraged the Thames Valley University to run a degree course by the Ayurvedic Company of Great Britain.[30]

Tibetan medicine established 2,500 years ago is also practised today and run from the headquarters of the exiled Tibetan Medical and Astrological Institute now based in Dharamsala, North India, where the herbal and precious metal medicines are made and students receive their seven years' training. The Tibetan laws of medicine are based on the premise that all disease is the result of an inhibited soul life. The art/science of the healer is to release the soul so that its life force can flow through the organism of the body. Understanding the patient's thought patterns and desires will guide the healer to know where, in the etheric body, the healing energy should be directed. The students must have knowledge of Tibetan linguistics, grammar and poetry to study their science of healing based on the Buddhist philosophy of the three poisons – desire, hatred and delusion – and the five basic types of personality or constitution related to the five elements: air, fire, water, earth and ether. The four levels of treatment range from changing poor diet to correcting improper behaviour, to prescribing medicine and finally 'surgery', which consists of massage, bloodletting, gold needle therapy and heat treatment. Again, the fundamental doctrine is to treat the cause of the disease or illness and not the symptoms.[31]

Buddhist teachings on the arising of suffering state that 'Before treating a sick man it is essential to discover the cause of the ailment. The efficacy of the treatment depends on the removal of the cause'. This lies square with the view of Socrates (469–399 BC) that 'When a physician is asked for advice his first question should be: if you are seeking health, are you willing to avoid the cause of illness in the future?'. Only then should an attempt be made to heal the person.

The ancient Greeks also believed health could be restored by appropriate diet, hydrotherapy, massage, exercise and good environmental conditions promoted by fresh air, light and a close interaction with nature. Aesculapias, the mythological Greek god of medicine, son of Apollo and Coronis, was taught by the centaur Chiron, a master of wisdom and knowledge of medicine. The healing temples at Epidaurus and on the island of Kos in the Aegean were dedicated to Aesculapias where the sick came to sleep in the belief that the god had the power to cure them through dreams. The Asklepeon sect established a school of medicine on the island of Kos where Hippocrates (460–377 BC), a contemporary of Socrates, studied and later broke away to develop his own methods which influenced medical science until the eighteenth century when modern orthodox allopathic medicine began.

This coincided with another significant change when medical practice became separated from botany. Ancient treatments based on herbs and plants that had been evolved and used successfully for a few thousand years – and still found in medical text books until the beginning of the twentieth century – were being superseded by a new science of chemical technology that, 200 years ago, was the forerunner of modern synthetic pharmaceuticals. (It is interesting to note that the 'old-fashioned' herbal medicines are now being widely researched in Europe and the US as pharmaceutical companies are rediscovering that the unique natural properties found in common herbs and plants are far more effective in the treatment of many of today's diseases, such as cancers, AIDS and diabetes, than artificially manufactured compounds.)[32]

Allopathic medicine

Allopathy is the use of drugs, surgery or other means to induce a reaction in the body that will counteract the symptoms of a disease. By contrast, homeopathy developed by Samuel Hahnemann of Leipzig in 1796, is the system of treating illness using infinitesimally small doses of a drug that in larger quantities would cause the symptoms in a healthy person. Homeopathy is based on resonance – the principle of 'like cures like', expressed in the Latin adage *similia similibus curantur* – whereas allopathy is based on the principle of counteraction or polarity (fighting disease with opposing forces). Thus began the allopathic concept of treating the symptom rather than attempting to heal the underlying cause of the illness. Modern medicine seems to focus more on dealing with illness rather than creating health. The concept of preventive medicine could be learned from the Chinese doctors who were paid only while their patients stayed well!

Attitudes to illness and disease underwent a further change in the eighteenth and nineteenth centuries when hospitals became institutionalised and supported by philanthropists. A hospital is supposed to be a healing temple; a place to restore vitality and the spirit; an environment to facilitate the patient's own self-healing; to engage nature's healing powers and to make us 'whole'. The word 'hospital' derives from the French word meaning hospitality – kindness in welcoming strangers or guests – a hospice or a shelter for travellers, usually kept by a monastic religious order where the body and spirit could be revived. The Hospitallers was a religious order of Knighthood: the Order of the Hospital of St John of Jerusalem provided a refuge for the pilgrims to Jerusalem in the eleventh century and it served as a military hospital during the Crusades.

Florence Nightingale (1820–1910), the British reformer of hospitals and founder of the nursing profession, led a party of nurses to work in the military hospitals of the Crimean War. She set about transforming the appalling conditions where men were dying of disease rather than wounds, and prescribed a calm atmosphere, good airy spaces, views of nature and the natural world to bring about a return to health. (A standard therapy prescribed by the ancient Greeks!) Rudolf Steiner, the early twentieth-century mystic and educationalist, prescribed similar holistic curative processes including colourful art to create healing places that appeal to the senses and serve the soul, to enhance the therapeutic environment and to provide privacy and dignity as well as offering current medical technology where appropriate. Such holistic concepts were followed through later in 1978 when Angie Thieriot founded the Planetree movement in San Francisco and again in 1985 by Erik Asmussen's Vidar Kliniken hospital in Sweden (mentioned earlier) using colour, space and outdoor elements of plants, trees, hills and water – incidentally, all reminiscent of good Feng Shui principles – to provide an environment to facilitate the patient's own self-healing process.

A major milestone in allopathic orthodoxy in 1840 was when gasses were used as an anaesthetic. Suddenly, for the first time a diseased part of the body (the symptom) could be cut out and the patient sewn up again with an increased chance of survival. Soon, medicine became entirely dependent on radical surgery and chemical drugs to cure the physical effect of illness, which only encouraged medical practitioners to focus even more on eradicating the symptom and disregarding the cause.

Attempting to cure the symptom rather than the cause of the illness has been likened to a faulty deep-freeze: when the warning light begins to flash indicating that something is wrong you would not expect the maintenance engineer to arrive and do nothing more than simply unscrew the lamp to effect a complete repair. The red light is only the symptom – the effect – indicating that something is wrong with the inner workings of the machine. However, while contemporary allopathic medical practice principally focuses on the body and little or no attention or time is devoted to understanding the inner 'workings' of the patient, there is a growing public demand for healing practices to treat the full spectrum of the whole person. At the same time the increasing resistance to the use of traumatising drugs and surgery has led to a grass roots reaction to allopathic orthodoxy, and a demand for 'complementary' treatments and changes to standard medical practice are already taking place.

Although a small minority of Western allopathic trained practitioners are beginning to introduce a more holistic approach to medicine, they can run the risk of being struck off for unprofessional conduct as the medical establishment considers such methods to be quackery. Nevertheless, in response to the public's resistance to the dehumanised methods of current medical practice, some practitioners are making serious studies of dietary remedies, meditation, colour and sound therapies and etheric body healing. These and other so-called 'fringe', non-orthodox but effective ancient treatments are not only less intrusive, they recognise that we are multidimensional, intelligent, holistic – mind, body and spirit organisms.

At a British Medical Association (BMA) conference in London in June 2000, it was accepted that general medical practitioners may now use acupuncture as an approved treatment. However, these observations in no way detract from the often miraculous advances in modern allopathic treatments such as keyhole surgery, organ transplants and so on.

The healing power of illness

The ancient healers/priests understood and used the power of the patient's subconscious mind – the psyche – to generate the flow of natural life energy forces to restore wellness. Illness was interpreted as a message from the gods: a blessed communication to the sufferer or patient, encoded in signs and symbols which, when decoded, gave a clear guidance on what action needed to be taken. In other words, illness is a warning – even a demand – that something in our life must change. In a sense it serves a similar purpose to a dream, which can be read as a message from the psyche pointing out the path to follow to achieve fulfilment and wellness. A dream, like an illness, may also be a warning, it may dispel false illusion, or be a vital directive couched in symbolism and coded signals. Such metaphoric language can be complex and confusing to the uninitiated but the healers/priests provided the interpretation: they translated the codes into the direction needed to return to 'wholeness' – a symmetry of mind, spirit and body. Traditional healing developed through their knowledge and understanding of the root causes of illness.

This ancient approach to understanding is expounded in *The Healing Power of Illness* by Dr Rudiger Dahlke and German psychologist Thorwald Dethlefsen, who runs a private clinic in Munich. In the Foreword the authors state that:

> This is an uncomfortable book, in that it deprives people of illness as an alibi for their unresolved problems. We propose to show that the patient is not the innocent victim of some quirk of nature, but actually the author of his or her own sickness. Thus, we shall not be addressing ourselves to environmental pollution, the ills of civilisation, unhealthy living or similar familiar scapegoats: instead we propose to bring the metaphysical aspect of illness to the fore. From this viewpoint symptoms are seen to be bodily expressions of psychological conflicts, able through their symbolism to reveal the patient's current problems.[33]

Illness demands a change of lifestyle and much of the suffering of illness could be avoided if only we listened to the 'quiet inner voice' – the message from the gods. Every emotion and trauma experienced will register itself somewhere in the body and sooner or later it will manifest as an illness, disease or accident. While plants, herbs and other natural medicines were used to accelerate the healing process, it was the characteristic of the illness and where it was located in the body that enabled the healer to help the patient to understand for him- or herself the important message and to accept the changes necessary to effect a recovery.

As an example of how this works in reality we can turn to the lower torso where the body fluids are located. To the healer/priest the primary cause of an illness centred in this area would be interpreted as some form of emotional stress. (Symbolically water is associated with the calms and storms of mood and feelings.) A bladder condition urging the person to frequently urinate with little or no urine actually being passed can be an expression of an inability to let go, even though the pressures, the substances and associated psychological themes involved have outlived their usefulness and now represent only so much excess waste.

Heart disease results in the death of millions of people in the Western world, yet very few people are born with a diseased or malfunctioning heart. Medical science has developed the most wondrous, multiple bypass surgery and, with a seemingly magical wave of a wand, a patient can be fitted with a completely new plumbing system of pipes and valves. Despite the wizardry, if the patient does not make radical changes in his or her life to improve diet, take regular exercise and avoid situations causing emotional stress then he or she will die prematurely of heart failure.

Everyone has cancer cells in their body so what is it that triggers the cells to develop a cancerous growth? Organic pathogens such as asbestos fibres can cause diseases and electromagnetic radiation from power lines and electronic equipment may weaken the immune system, but it is the characteristics of the disease and where it manifests itself in the body that appear to be related to the psychological make-up of the individual.

Our emotions and thoughts as well as everything we ingest – medicine, smoke, air, food and drink – will alter the chemistry of our blood. The Sybil Syndrome was named after a schizophrenic woman who had 16 distinct personalities. Tests showed that as each personality took control of her mind, so the changes in her blood chemistry produced a different profile related to each of her sub-personality characteristics, which even expressed different tones of voice registering distinctive vibrational frequencies. This suggests that consciousness, thought patterns, chanting, meditation, prayer and the whole range of moods from rage to laughter to love will induce a chemical change in the blood. These emotional changes affecting our endocrine gland secretions of hormones give credibility to the esoteric teachings that affirmations and positive thinking can bring about significant life changes. The corollary is that negative thought patterns will induce negative results: if we think the worst will happen or we keep telling ourselves that we are stupid, unworthy or poor in spirit then such negative self-talk creates a self-fulfilling prophecy that is likely to induce depression, low self-esteem and illness.

It is not surprising that the medical and scientific establishment largely rejects these views on the anatomy of illness because, if it were true that personality could trigger a mechanism for the body to accept a virus, create a biological malfunction or even set up the conditions for an accident to occur, then current medical practice of prescribing drugs could, to some extent, become obsolete. However, there is now a greater acceptance that illnesses and some accidents can have psychosomatic (*psycho* = mind, *soma* = body) origins because every thought and action begins in the unconscious, instinctual mental plane of the mind that largely controls our own unique personal experience and recognition of the world about us.

Some doctors advise their patients to practise visualising the chakras or repeat a mantra to clear the mind while in a state of meditation. This form of self-healing prescribed in the ancient Indian and Tibetan texts has become a daily ritual for many Westerners who enjoy the benefits of deep relaxation: it is an energising process that calms the mind, improves concentration, boosts creativity and relieves the stress and strain of everyday life. Child psychologist David Fontana, based at the University of Cardiff in Wales, has co-authored a book, *Teaching Meditation to Children,* to encourage young people to practise the technique. He is convinced meditation will help to overcome some of today's childhood and teenage over-burdening illnesses and emotional problems due to our materialistic and highly competitive modern world. [34]

The 3,000-year-old practice of using leeches for curative purposes, which had come to be considered an archaic, punitive form of medical treatment, has now been resurrected at the cutting edge of medicine. More than a hundred hospitals in the UK now make regular use of leeches in the treatment of people who have had limbs, fingers and toes reattached after accidents. Blood in the arteries and tiny veins congeals and blocks the circulation between the body and severed parts but leeches can prevent this by means of an anti-coagulant in their saliva. At the headquarters of Biopharm UK in Swansea, Wales, set up 10 years ago by American physician Dr Roy Sawyer, about 30,000 leeches are bred per year and now exported to many countries. [35]

The Chinese use of magnets and needles for acupuncture therapy dates back to 2500 BC and has become an accepted treatment in the medical establishment. The Air Travel Advisory Bureau (ATAB) suggest that children aged 5 to 15 years old who are prone to travel/motion sickness use knitted elasticated wrist bands called 'seabands' that have a plastic button that presses against the spot on the wrist known as the acupuncture 'Nei-Kuan' point. [36] Another ancient remedy was revived in the 1920s when magnetised water was used to condition water for livestock and crop irrigation to produce a bacteriological and fungicidal effect that increased yields, shelf-life and resulted in a reduction in disease.

Medicine and architecture

The wondrous achievements of modern medical science cannot be disputed, but the tide is turning against the establishment's almost sole dependency on machines, high technology and drugs. There is a feeling that allopathic medicine can be bad for your health! However, an awareness of the holistic nature of human beings and how all external phenomena can profoundly impinge upon the psyche and energy fields has yet to trickle down into the mainstream of the teaching and practice of architecture. This is partly because we unwittingly collude with our professionals to create the medical care and architecture we collectively demand. Hospitals are a fine example to indicate the parallel trends in medicine and architectural design.

A British TV programme featured the Kangaroo Project, so named after the marsupials that carry their young in a stomach pouch. Hospitals in Colombia, South America, had run out of Perspex life-support capsules used for premature babies where they are incubated for several weeks in a warm, protected, comfortable, hygienic environment until they are strong enough to live a normal existence. As a last resort to overcome the desperate shortage of capsules, the mothers were given their naked, premature babies to hold next to their breast. Together, wrapped in a blanket, mother and child spent much of the day and night in kangaroo fashion. Subsequently, a London hospital discarded the use of orthodox Perspex capsules in favour of the kangaroo technique when it discovered that not only was the survival rate at least as good, if not better, than using Perspex capsules but the physical bonding of mother and child accelerated lactation – the flow of natural nourishment. The programme concluded that a baby's sterile isolation in a Perspex capsule was detrimental to its development and recovery. 'Perspex boxes', 'sensory deprivation', 'isolation', 'infrequent human contact', 'artificial ventilation', 'unnatural environment' – are these phrases reminiscent of some of our contemporary buildings?

Frank Lloyd Wright's view was that 'hospital patients should never be imbued with the idea that they are sick.... . Health should be constantly before their eyes'.[37] A hospital should not be a production line to 'cure' illness; it should be a sanctuary for renewal and the restoration of vitality; a temple for healing the spirit as well as the body. Of course a hospital must be a functional, hygienic place where modern medical technology and nursing staff can operate efficiently but the healing process is also the patient's responsibility. A meditation room, access to gardens and nature and the patient's ability to have a degree of control over temperature, lighting levels, noise, air and privacy would facilitate a sense of renewal, regeneration and reactivate the flow of energies. This is borne out in an abstract from a paper entitled 'View from a window may influence recovery from surgery', which stated:

> Records on recovery after cholecystectomy of patients in a suburban Pennsylvania hospital between 1972 and 1981 were examined to determine whether assignment to a room with a window view of a natural setting might have restorative influences. Twenty-three surgical patients assigned to rooms with windows looking out on a natural scene had shorter postoperative hospital stays, received fewer negative evaluative comments in nurses' notes, took fewer potent analgesics, and had slightly lower scores for minor post-surgical complications than twenty-three matched patients in similar rooms with windows facing a brick building wall.[38]

New hospitals – described by Professor Keith Critchlow as 'body workshops'[39]– are designed to house high-technology machinery, equipment and mainly to facilitate the efficiency of the medical staff. They look more like space-age laboratories and do little to alleviate the anxiety and stress felt by people going into hospital for treatment.

The President and Chief Executive officer of the American Centre for Health Design, Wayne Ruga, has organised the annual series of symposia on healthcare design since 1988. The 1995 meeting held in San Diego was attended by 1,500 architects, designers, physicians, nurses and health-care decision-makers and 'almost everything about health facilities design was based on function or medical technology. There was very little concern with the quality of the patient's experience'.[40] This suggests architects appear to have little or no interest or awareness of the potential health hazards created by their buildings nor do they consider the mind, spirit and psyche as being relevant. Design is focused on producing high-tech, sanitised buildings to satisfy the material, physical functions and bodily uses. This twentieth-century one-dimensional view was expressed by the Swiss architect Le Corbusier when he stated that 'a house is a machine to live in' – a phrase that typifies the ethos of the architectural profession and the current Western view of human beings and the natural world.

The architecture of every period in history is like an open book: a precise chronicle recording the social conditions, prevailing culture, philosophy, political and spiritual structure that reflects the life and times of the people. The form, appearance and performance of the buildings of our modern era will change only as our values and attitudes change. We cannot wait in hope for government intervention, bureaucratic regulations or professional rigour to design and build healthy environments and respect the holistic essence of human nature: instead we have to be prepared to make our own investigations, be vigilant and demand action.

It is said that all professionals are only as good as their clients will allow or demand them to be. This suggests that a good building is the product of a good architect *and* a good client. In effect, everybody is a 'second generation' or 'surrogate' client because, day by day we, the 'ordinary people', occupy and use a wide range of different buildings and have to suffer whatever inherent defects there may be. For the sake of our own health and well-being we too need to become 'good clients'.

The preceding chapters are intended to provide information that will allow us to become good clients so that we can accelerate the necessary process of change and facilitate the long-overdue improvements to the built environment. In the next chapter we shall examine the proposal that the present crisis in the architectural profession is an opportunity for architects to review their current status in terms of the ancient traditions of what it means to be an architect.

References

1. BBC 'Tomorrow's World', 22 July 1998.
2. *The Ecologist*, vol. 12, January 1982, p. 2. Editorial by Hildygard Nicholas.
3. *Natural Ventilation in Non-Domestic Buildings*, Application Manual AM10 1997, The Chartered Institution of Building Services Engineers (CIBSE) UK, 'User Preferences', p. 2.
4. Ibid.
5. Vitruvius (1960) *The Ten Books on Architecture*, Book 1, Chapter 11, Paragraph 788, New York: Dover Publications.
6. Ibid., Book 1, Chapter IV, Paragraphs 1 and 2.
7. Ibid., Book 1, Chapter V, Paragraph 12.
8. Tompkins, Bird (1992) *Secrets of the Soil*, London: Arkana.
9. Thom, A. (1967) *Megalithic Sites in Britain*, Oxford: Oxford University Press.
10. The Aubrey Holes were discovered by John Aubrey (1626–97), an author, playwright and amateur archaeologist. They comprise an outer ring of 56 pits forming holes for timber posts. Some of the holes are marked with white discs in the grass.
11. Hawkins, G. (1965) *Stonehenge Decoded*, New York: Doubleday.
12. Butler, A. (1998) *The Bronze Age Computer Disc*, Berkshire: Foulsham & Co.
13. Watkins, A. (1970) *The Old Straight Track*, London: Garnstone Press.
14. Heath, R. (1998) *Sun, Moon and Stonehenge*, Cardigan, Wales: Bluestone Press.
15. Critchlow, K. (1982) *Time Stands Still*, New York: St Martin's Press.
16. A conical domed structure.
17. Al-Kindi, latinised to Alkindus, was born around 805 in Kufah. An Islamic philosopher of pure Arab descent, he wrote a treatise on the Platonic Solids called *On the Reasons why the Ancients ascribed the Five Figures to the Elements*.
18. Critchlow, op. cit., p. 148.

19. Christian Lamb, 'Amazonian Indians 'were not the first Brazilians'', *The Sunday Telegraph*, 16 May 1999, p. 31.
20. Ibid.
21. Barber, E. W. (1999) *The Mummies of Urumchi*, New York: Norton & Co.
22. Pennick, N. (1997) *Earth Harmony*, Berkshire: Capall Bann Publishing.
23. Sahasrabudhe, N. H. and Mahatme, R. D. (1998) *Secrets of Vastushastra*, New Delhi: Sterling Publishers.
24. Richard Creightmore, 'Feng Shui', *The Journal of the British Society of Dowsers*, vol. 39, no. 268, June 2000, pp. 12–16.
25. Vitruvius, op. cit., Book 1, Chapter I, Paragraph 10.
26. Einstein, Albert and Infield, I. (1938) 'The rise of the mechanical view', *The Evolution of Physics*, Cambridge, Cambridge University Press.
27. Sheldrake, R. (1983) *A New Science of Life*, London: Granada, p. 77.
28. Jackie Sievey, 'Russian GDV instrument', *Region 14 Newsletter*, The National Federation of Spiritual Healers, summer 1999.
29. Roney-Dougal, S. (1991) *Where Science and Magic Meet*, Dorset: Element Books.
30. The Ayurvedic Medical Association, Garrat Lane, London SW7.
31. Sither Bradley, Tamdin (2000) *An Introduction to Tibetan Medicine*, London: Harper Collins.
32. Roger Dobson, 'Healing groovy', *The Sunday Times*, 'Style' magazine, 9 May 1999.
33. Dethlefsen, T. and Dahlke, R. (1992) 'Foreword', *The Healing Power of Illness*, Dorset: Element Books.
34. Fontana, D. (1998) *Teaching Meditation to Children*, Dorset: Element Books.
35. Christopher Middleton, 'Suck it and see', *The Sunday Times*, 'Style' magazine, 28 March 1999, p. 35.
36. Passenger Safety Fact File leaflet issued by the Air Travel Advisory Bureau.
37. Quoted in *The New England Journal of Medicine*, 14 September 1995, Scale Page 738, Healing by Design.
38. Ulrich Rogers, 'View through a window may influence recovery from surgery,' *The American Association for the Advancement of Science*, vol. 224, 27 April 1984, p. 420.
39. Critchlow, Keith and Allen, Jon (1995) *The Whole Question of Health*, London: The Prince of Wales's Institute of Architecture.
40. David O. Weber, 'Life enhancing design', *The Healthcare Forum Journal* (undated), p. 3.

Suggested further reading

Ardalan, N. and Bakhtiar, L. (1979) *The Sense of Unity*, Illinois: University of Chicago Press.
Bamford, C. (ed.) (1994) *Rediscovering Sacred Science*, Edinburgh: Lindisfarne Press & Floris Books.
Brennan, B. (1988) *Hands of Light*, New York: Bantam Books.
Davidson, J. (1988) *Subtle Energy*, Essex: CW Daniel.
Graves, T. (1980) *Dowsing & Archæology*, Northants: Turnstone Books.
Grof, S. (1984) *Ancient Wisdom & Modern Science*, New York: State University of New York.
Hall, A. (1997) *Water, Electricity & Health*, Gloucestershire: Hawthorn Press.
Hapgood, C. (1996) *Maps of the Ancient Sea Kings*, Illinois: Adventures Unlimited Press.
Lau, K. (1996) *Feng Shui for Today*, New York: Tengu Books.
Lip, E. (1995) *Feng Shui for the Home*, Singapore: Times Books International.
Michell, J. (1983) *The View over Atlantis*, London: Thames & Hudson.
Strachan, G. (1998) *Jesus the Master Builder*, Edinburgh: Floris Books.

8.
The crisis/opportunity

Master builders

It may come as a surprise that what has been covered so far about the built environment and what will be covered in this chapter regarding the fundamental principles of architecture and design generally is neither taught in the schools of architecture nor understood by the majority of practising architects. At the moment no-one is acting in the traditional role of the master architect. Instead it is left to chance whether a building will be spiritually uplifting and conducive to health and well-being or whether it will be disturbing, inherently sick and detrimental to all those in occupation.

According to Professor Keith Critchlow, a master, teacher and practitioner of the sacred arts and sciences of architecture:

> Architecture is the constructed environment about us which has been created from appropriate means into forms which reflect the nature of the Universe and Humanity's relation to it.[1]

And he has defined architecture thus:

ARCH:	Relates to first principles; the archetypal, in the sense of being in the realm of the infinite or divine.
TECT:	Concerns technical skills, craftsmanship and knowledge based on experience.
URE:	Refers to the earthiness of the physical world of matter and materiality.[2]

The word 'architect' means 'master builder' – one who masterminds the complete design concept, construction and cost of a building; one who has studied the art and science of architecture and its fundamental principles; a philosopher who has a wisdom and spiritual insight into the nature of humanity and the natural world about us. The master builder conceives and determines the 'soul' of a building as well as controlling the total design of the setting, the exterior, the interior design, decoration and furnishing and their related costs and buildability that will satisfy its function, purpose and needs. A master builder also understands the 'systematic arrangement of knowledge'. As will be shown later, the Roman architect Vitruvius sets out what the architect needs to study and understand to become a master builder. (Architecture as practised today did not become a separate professional discipline until about 200 years ago.)

The architects/master builders of, say, Stonehenge, the Egyptian pyramids and temples or the Gothic cathedrals, conceived the purpose, function and etheric (or 'sacred') geometry of their buildings and then directed the master masons who carried out the building works. Even the great architects of the Renaissance from the fifteenth century onwards were not trained to be professional architects. For example, Brunelleschi (1377–1446), the founder of Renaissance architecture, was trained as a goldsmith and took up architecture later in life after studying Roman remains and Roman building techniques. Alberti (1404–72) was a scholar, author, musician, mathematician and athlete who had a profound understanding of the arts, and he too studied the ancient Roman builders and their principles of design. He treated architecture as an intellectual discipline and a social act requiring skills in painting and mathematics. He was the first to 'design at a distance'. Leonardo da Vinci (1452–1519) was a painter, sculptor, inventor, engineer, biologist, botanist and geologist who designed buildings but had no training to be an architect, and Palladio (1508–80) trained to be a stonemason before becoming one of the great architects of the period.

Similarly, in England Inigo Jones (1573–1652) – a contemporary of Shakespeare – was a painter, festival designer, masque maker, antiquarian and military engineer. Although he was educated as an Elizabethan he brought the Palladian-style Renaissance architecture to Britain and created some of the finest buildings of the period. Sir Christopher Wren (1632–1723), physicist, astronomer, mathematician and founder of the Royal Society regarded architecture as a hobby. He introduced the Baroque style to England, and in addition to St Paul's Cathedral he built 51 churches, 36 company halls and the Greenwich hospital, and was probably England's most successful baroque architect. Sir John Vanbrugh (1664–1726), another famous architect, was also a soldier, playwright and theatrical designer. [3]

Although all the great master builders throughout history were not trained in the same way as the modern professional architects of today, in order to become what the French term a *maître d'oeuvre* – literally, 'master of the work' – they acquired a profound understanding of the fundamental principles of 'divine harmony' through a study of the sacred teachings of ancient perennial wisdom that are quintessential to the concept of any building, whether ecclesiastical or secular and whatever the style or period. A master builder is one who has the intellectual and visionary qualities, including leadership and authority, to mastermind and manifest an aesthetically cohesive, unified – that is, holistic – healthy, life-enhancing building fit for human habitation. The vast majority of our professional architects do not measure up to these essential requirements.

Several factors have contributed to the decline of twentieth-century architects and architecture, the prime factor being that Western schools of architecture do not teach humanistic philosophy and the fundamental principles of design. This has left practitioners floundering, without understanding how to deal with the extraordinary advancement in building technology. This in turn has created a new spectrum of specialists and experts who have brought their separate disciplines to contribute to the 'design team'. Again, due to this lack of essential basic training and understanding, the architects themselves have allowed their role as *maître d'oeuvre* to be eroded to the level where, more often than not, they have become little more than a person who 'draws up plans' and designs appropriate façades, much like a cosmetic artist or theatrical costumier creates whatever dramatic effect may be desired.

Why are modern architects so preoccupied with superficial façadism? We live inside, work inside, play inside and spend the vast majority of our lives *inside* buildings. Surely, the layout, volumes, proportions and design features of the interior spaces should be the architect's main focus of attention. And yet more often than not, when architects present their designs for a new building they show plans, sections and external elevations, sometimes accompanied by a model or artist's impression to illustrate the massing and materials of the façade. Rarely will there be any views of the interior spaces. How can the exterior of a building be detached from what goes on inside?

The exterior is a shell that should express the use, purpose and design of the interiors in the same manner that our facial expressions, body language, words and deeds are an external reflection of our psychospiritual inner being. It is not surprising that the vacuum left by architects has been filled by the interior design specialists. In effect, this new breed of professional has, to a large extent, become far more prominent and important than the architect because he or she has taken control over that part of the building which has the greater impact on our day-to-day lives – the interior elements. As will be shown, this is just one of the several spheres of work and services the architect has allowed others to take over.

Currently there are some 30,000 members of the Royal Institute of British Architects (RIBA) in the UK, about 100,000 American architects who are members of various bodies such as the American Institute of Architects (AIA), and several thousand more architects working in Scandinavia and Western Europe. Taking a broad view of modern buildings, it would not be unreasonable to assume that the great majority of architects produce a competent wind- and weather-tight skin to envelope the required accommodation to house the items of plant, machinery and other demands imposed by the technical experts. The latest technology provides the ability to build virtually any shape and size to enclose whatever the function or purpose of the building may be. Almost anything and everything can now be achieved, but there are no constraints or guidelines as to the architectural design treatment of what is now, essentially, a box constructed of glass, concrete, steel and plastics.

At the beginning of the twentieth century the greatest influence on Western art and architecture was the Bauhaus School of Design founded in Weimar, Germany, in 1919. Traditional subjects and aesthetic standards were abandoned to give rise to an entirely geometric form, embracing all the arts, that in architecture might be called 'functionalism'. During the past forty or fifty years we have seen an abundance of architectural fads and fashions that have dressed up façades in 'brutalism', 'heroic modernism', 'postmodernism' and 'Edwardianism' in an attempt to create something 'new' but without any ideological foundation to underpin the changing 'styles'. Have all these fashions largely come about because architects do not know what to do next to dress up their 'boxes' in some unusual, fancy clothes to resemble a bygone style which may be nothing more than a faddish search for treatments to appease a nostalgic dream of the past? Such applied gimmicks are a desperate, sterile attempt to create an acceptable pastiche of a neoclassical, Georgian or Victorian design in the hope it will distract our innate perception of what is 'good' or 'bad' architecture. Ignorance of the fundamental and 'sacred' principles has been fostered by aesthetic deviousness and the general public's apathetic acceptance of what is second best. (Hiding ignorance can be a very busy, lucrative business.) It is also an expression of society's fascination with materialism and 'what's new?' rather than a deeper comprehension of non-materialistic values. As has been shown earlier, it would appear that we are not even greatly concerned whether or not our buildings provide a healthy environment.

Of the most recent architectural '-isms', perhaps 'eco-techism' has the possibility of creating a somewhat 'new' architecture: for a building to function efficiently using natural ventilation, low-energy technology and be ecologically sustainable the design must incorporate chimney vent stacks, passive solar or wind power. Also the exterior protection from solar gain with projections, 'shelves' or other design techniques must be developed as an integral part of the overall basic concept. In other words, true eco-techism cannot be bolted on to a building at some later stage. Whatever the style there are deeper dimensions to architecture than providing a well-functioning protective skin.

The significant difference between all the changing styles before the mid-nineteenth century and the '-isms' that have emerged since is that prior to the mid-twentieth century the education of an architect was founded on the ancient wisdom and esoteric teachings of Plato, Vitruvius and others. Metaphysics and anthropometric understanding were considered as intrinsic to architectural design as the material needs, function and requirements of a building.

The gradual decline of architecture accelerated towards the end of the nineteenth century with the harnessing of electrical power and the commercial use of oil and its byproducts, from which developed a rapid advancement in technology affecting every aspect of daily life, especially in the construction, equipment and furnishing of buildings. Non-traditional materials, new machines and building industry techniques led to an equally rapid growth in the demand for taller, larger, high-performance buildings which in turn led to a necessary proliferation in the rules and regulations to control design and construction. The architect became overburdened with keeping up with the volume of building by-laws and the latest materials and electronic devices. These pressures encouraged the use of many new, untried, untested products and systems without a comprehensive evaluation of their effect on the health and well-being of the building operatives and those who would ultimately occupy the building. The architect became preoccupied with the physical construction of the building rather than the essential design concept. This trend was exacerbated in Britain by the introduction of the 1947 Town and Country Planning Acts giving local authorities powerful legislation to control building development, which encouraged property developer clients to select the architects most likely to squeeze the greatest volume of building out of the site rather than commission those with a reputation for their more humanistic qualities as master builders.

Parallel with the increasing complexities of planning laws and building code regulations, as well as the demand for high-performance technology, has been the tendency on the part of clients, and the public at large, to become more litigious. This is yet another necessary distraction to engage the architect's attention in order to protect him- or herself from claims of negligence rather than expend energy on the fundamental principles of design.

Dealing with the mundane matters of law and administration are burdens an architect has always had to bear, but now many of the architect's traditional services have been taken over by allied professions. Even with this additional specialised technical expertise and support provided by separate professional disciplines, the architect has still not rediscovered or recreated the role of being the master builder. Modern buildings are now 'put together' like a Legoland set by a team of experts who have been trained to give professional advice within their relatively narrow field of operation, and, of course, all these specialists who are part of the 'professional team' undoubtedly make significant and highly technical contributions to the building project. Now everyone in the team – including the architect – is trained to give tactical support to each other, but today it seems no-one has been trained to mastermind the grand strategy that transforms a building worthy of the name of architecture. This point can be illustrated by looking at the current composition and responsibilities of the professional team for a typical building project:

- The architect used to be the leader of the team with direct contact with the client: now, with the exception of minor projects, the leader is the *project manager* through whom all communications and instructions are passed.
- The architect used to have control of the building estimates and budgets: now this work is the sole responsibility of the *cost control manager* or *quantity surveyor*.
- The architect used to determine the structural elements and foundations: now this is in the entire domain of the *structural engineer*.
- The architect used to design the internal environmental ventilation, lighting, heating and cooling conditions: now this is the specialised work of the *electrical* and *mechanical engineers*.
- The architect used to have the free choice of specifying materials and the method of construction: now every decision is under the scrutiny of a health and safety expert called a *planning supervisor* (who incidentally neither plans nor supervises but deals with every aspect of health and safety in the design and construction of the building).
- The architect used to design every detail of the interior features and furnishings: now this has been taken over by the *interior designer*. And if the client is a Feng Shui enthusiast the whole concept may also be subject to the deliberations of the *Dragon Master*.
- The architect used to design the orientation, siting, landscape, the overall volume, shape, size and external appearance of the building: now, all these significant elements of the architectural concept are subject to the scrutiny and often arbitrary

dictates of a committee of lay members of the local authority and/or the *town planning officers* or *civic design officers* who may have a degree in sociology or economics but generally have no expertise in architectural design.

- In the case of speculative commercial projects such as offices and shopping centres, it is not unusual for the developer to first consult the *real estate advisors* and *marketing agents* who may determine the shape and size of the floors, the location and treatment of the main entrance, the layout and materials for the toilets and the 'style' of the building *before* the architect has put pen to paper, and sometimes, even before the architect has been appointed.

- The architect used to supervise and control the programme and construction of the work on-site: this is now undertaken by the *project manager* or *construction supervisor*.

- The architect used to be concerned with creating environments and buildings that would provide a sense of security and discourage the opportunities for crime: now, under the Crime & Disorder Act 1998, Town Planning application procedures should include consultations on crime prevention measures recommended by the *architectural liaison officer*.

In addition to the above, the professional team may also include *acoustic engineers, lighting designers, IT experts, landscape architects, toxic materials specialists* and *environmental specialists*. Furthermore, according to RIBA, during the past decade 40 per cent of the major new building works in the UK were being carried out under a 'design and build' contract. This means in effect that the professional team, including the architect, is appointed by the main contractor who acts as the 'client' and the whole of the design, specification and construction of the building is under the total direction and control of the *builder*. Often, the architect is engaged to create a 'design concept' only and is not allowed to have direct contact with the building owner or developer client.

So why have architects relinquished their position and authority? All the allied professionals – engineers, quantity surveyors, interior designers, project managers and building contractors – are trained to be tactical, technical advisers but they cannot operate or take action until the architect draws a line! Cynics might point out that it is not surprising that other professionals have filled the voids left by the architects because they are notoriously weak on financial constraint; rarely punctual on the delivery of drawings and information; lax on practical engineering; slack on site inspection and supervision; indulgent in using the latest material or construction technique before rigorous health and safety tests have been carried out; and vague or indifferent on interior design matters. Clients might also complain that architects are too compliant with the demands imposed by town planning officers and other bureaucrats. Of course, not all architects can be accused of possessing some or all of these negative qualities and it is most likely that such deficiencies have been levelled against architects for thousands of years, ever since people first engaged the services of someone to advise them on how to build a building for their own requirements.

The problem with this 'corporate' system of building is that every member of the professional team, including the architect, is levelled down to being a tactical advisor who provides a technical service as part of the overall supply chain input of information necessary to build a building. When 'architecture' is synonymous with eye-catching materialism there is no need for a master builder or a *maître d'oeuvre*. In any case, under the present system, no-one has been educated in the specialised, philosophical, intellectual and spiritual as well as the practical aspects of architecture that would equip a person to fulfil the role to design a life-enhancing, healthy and spiritually uplifting building. In other words, the master builder, the person who determines the 'soul' of the building, has no role to play in the 'design team' of today. Put another way, at the moment the architect is in the orchestra pit, playing a particular instrument sitting alongside all the other specialist individual musicians. But who is the composer of the music, and who is supposed to be conducting the orchestra? A composer has the inspiration: one who knows how to create the desired emotional effect to be expressed through the spirit of the music. Accordingly, the composer sets the key, arranges the notes and rhythms to create the symphony. In the same manner, the 'keys' of architectural composition are the harmonic ratios, proportions and order of number and geometry set by the architect and based on the natural laws that govern the world about us.

An architect needs to study and have knowledge of many subjects, much as the composer of a symphony needs to be well versed in the potential and limitation of all the musical instruments to be used for the composition, but it is not essential to be an expert player in each section of the orchestra. Neither should the conductor sit in among the players while conducting the music, otherwise each musician could be interpreting the music in his or her own way and own time. Who, then, is the composer/conductor of our architectural compositions? Who is the master builder? It certainly is not the project manager, quantity surveyor, structural engineer nor the building contractor. However, now that the architect is supported by so many technically well-equipped specialists – like gifted musicians in the pit – he or she has the opportunity to expend more time, energy and ingenuity on the essential elements of design to create a healthy environment that can nourish and uplift our spirits, provided he or she is educated and trained in the appropriate subjects.

Unfortunately, the gathering momentum of a new altruistic *Zeitgeist* could be retarded because it is likely that none of the mainstream schools of art and architecture currently has the tutors who possess the understanding and knowledge of the appropriate teachings of perennial wisdom.

According to Professor Keith Critchlow:

> The fundamental axiom of perennial wisdom is that there is an inner determination for all appearances and outward forms. For example, not only are there layers of meaning to each of the scriptures in human, worldly, moral and philosophical dimensions but there is also an inner interpretation of the science of mathematics – the latter being a cosmological expression of the archetypal ideas on which our world depends – a hidden numerical and geometrical basis of the manifest universe. Therefore, art and architecture should not be speculative but an integration of the metaphysical laws.[4]

To discover how anyone who aspires or professes to be an architect can be raised to the status of master builder one need look no further than the teachings of Vitruvius and other masters of wisdom such as Plato, Pythagoras and the ancient mystery schools.

All masterpiece works of art and architecture have underlying principles controlling order and discipline which are as pertinent and applicable to a modern 'glass box' as they were to the temple of Minerva, Chartres Cathedral or a Palladian villa. These apparently arcane or 'sacred' qualities do not happen by coincidence: all great works possess inner qualities that may appear to be mysterious, but the architects/master builders have been taught throughout history and must be taught again. If all our new buildings, including small houses and factories, embodied these basic design principles, an authentic architecture and architectural 'style' would organically evolve to express our nuclear/electronic age. If the architects of today understood and practised these principles their buildings would confidently express modern design, materials and technology without being cloaked in spurious, period costume. Such architectural gimmicks would be unnecessary because the unadorned, underlying geometry and harmonics would satisfy the soul.

Art colleges used to teach drawing skills to be practised daily in order that pupils become proficient pencil artists – a basic requirement to be able to competently draw a nude, plant or still life. A glance at the prolific sketch books and early works of surrealistic painter Picasso demonstrates his mastery of 'representational' art that was the foundation of his later paintings. Today, schools of architecture are turning out graduates who do not have the ability (nor inclination) to draw manually with a pen or pencil – everything is done on computer. The schools also used to teach the history of art and architecture as a way of understanding the present as a continuum of the past; students had to study the grammar of architecture and the classical orders of Vitruvius, and measure and draw at least one period building, or part of it, as an in depth exercise to get into the mind of a master architect.

Certainly when the author was a student half a century ago, and no doubt even earlier, the schools of architecture were not teaching anything about earth energies, the multi-dimensions and subtle bodies of living organisms and how our energy field is influenced by, interacts and responds intelligently with, the immediate environment. On location visits we were not encouraged to feel, hear, smell or 'taste' the site. No mention was made of electromagnetic fields (EMFs); colour and sound were not discussed and while ecological and environmental matters were perhaps not such pressing issues as they are today, the architect's responsibilities to address these subjects were not considered to be worthy of our attention. We were left ignorant of the natural sciences, natural phenomena, philosophy, the scale of man, the fundamental principles and the esoteric aspects of the 'laws' of the cosmos.

If, as student architects, we had learned about the 'laws' that transcend architectural periods, style, ornament and decoration, and taught how to design according to those arithmetic and geometric disciplines, no doubt we would have considered our freedom of expression and creativity to have been stultified without appreciating that the whole of the universe – that vast array and variety of design, shape, colour and texture in the natural world – is determined by the laws of number and geometry. We had pretensions to become master architects but graduated without any idea about the architectural language of symbolism and metaphor, or how to translate from abstract, unmanifested number and geometry into concrete manifestation.

Vitruvius

We know that the natural world turns in cycles: it is therefore not surprising to discover that our present situation is, more or less, a repeat pattern of the circumstances that occurred at about the time of the millennium 2,000 years ago. In the first century BC, Roman architect and engineer Marcus Vitruvius Pollio, known simply as Vitruvius, witnessed a decline in the quality of architecture which he attributed to architects being distracted by peripheral indulgences and their lack of education in the sacred arts, sciences and the fundamental principles of design. Vitruvius was keenly aware of the decline in the quality of buildings and the poor choice of sites. He also knew there was little point in trying to get architects and their tutors who were preoccupied with non-essential details to respect the sacred fundamental principles handed down from the healer/priest 'builders' and masters of ancient wisdom. (Distracting the eye with trivial excess or spurious historical references was and remains the trickery of most inferior art and architecture.)

Although the practical, day-by-day business of building is about budgets, fees, legalities, materials, construction techniques and functional space, the essence of architectural design must be based upon the natural laws or canon of the universe. Everything we need to know about the teaching and practice of architecture can be found in Vitruvius' book, *The Ten Books on Architecture*, which has been recognised as one of the great classical works of antiquity and perhaps the Western world's most important book on the subject. The book is, in fact, one single volume divided into ten sections, each setting out the subjects an architect should study. They cover aspects of the design of houses, temples and cities; the classical orders; finding water; the proportions of the human body to be reflected in the design of buildings; and even the design of war machines and fortifications. Much of the work may now only be of historic interest, such as the Vitruvian method of using musical scales to design and 'tune' his weapons of war, or his techniques to amplify sound in a theatre by varying the amounts of water in bronze urns. But an esoteric knowledge of geometry, the harmonic ratios of music, the movement of heavenly bodies, the measure of man and the fundamental principles of architecture are as important today to the planning and design of buildings and cities of the twenty-first century as they were 2,000 years ago and beyond.

The *Ten Books on Architecture* was lost for about 1,500 years until the sixteenth century when Italian Daniele Barbaro translated the work into *Vitruvii de Architectura Libri Decem*. It became the bible for all great Renaissance architects, painters and scholars such as Michelangelo, Leonardo da Vinci, Palladio and others, who in turn influenced Western art and culture for the next 400 years. Until the last few decades of the twentieth century, the *Vitruvii de Architectura Libri Decem* had been obligatory study – especially the classical orders – for all student architects. Now there may be only a very few schools of art and architecture – if any at all – where, even out of historic interest, Vitruvius is included in the curriculum. Tutors may feel modern architecture owes no allegiance to history, but, more likely, the work is dismissed out of hand because they do not understand the import of what is being said.

Although the book is about architecture, significantly it was addressed directly to Augustus Caesar, the Emperor of Rome, advising him – in effect warning him – about the necessary standards of education and training he should look for in architects before commissioning any of them to carry out the extensive programme of new buildings and cities he was about to commence, having recently returned from his successful campaigns abroad. With due deference and humility, Vitruvius advised Caesar what the Emperor and grand patron should know about the education of architects and the philosophy, science and art of architecture. Throughout the book Vitruvius constantly refers to the Emperor to remind the reader that it is the knowledge of the client – the one who commissions the building – rather than the architect alone who has the power to influence and effect the necessary changes to improve the quality of the architecture and enrich the quality of life for the citizens of Rome.

In a most forthright manner Vitruvius told the Emperor that if he wanted excellence he had to become a well-informed patron – or client – who would understand the prerequisite qualities to be found in a good architect:

…The architect should be equipped with knowledge of many branches of study and varied kinds of learning, for it is by his judgement that all work done by the other arts is put to test. This knowledge is the child of practice and theory…

He ought, therefore, to be both naturally gifted and amenable to instruction…let him be educated, skilful with the pencil, instructed in geometry, know much about history, have followed the philosophers with attention, understood music, have some knowledge of medicine, know the opinions of the jurists, and be acquainted with astronomy and the theory of the heavens.[5]

Vitruvius acknowledges that architects cannot be expected to become expert practitioners in every field but should nevertheless have a good working knowledge and understanding of these subjects.

Of course, taken at face value, some of these subjects are taught in our schools of architecture today. For example, architects have to learn something about geometry, physics and arithmetic to enable them to draw their buildings and to make sure they are structurally sound. As for legal matters, our architects could justifiably argue that they have to learn too much contract and planning law, as well as spending much time and effort avoiding litigation. The history of architecture is usually taught in the early student years but the subject, regrettably, is generally downgraded to one of anachronistic and minor importance. It could be argued that medicine is now so specialised that all an architect needs is a competent knowledge of the Public Health Acts and the Health and Safety Regulations that control the design and construction of buildings. However, it has already been shown that the architect of today most certainly needs a far greater understanding and knowledge of medicine than merely a familiarity with the public health codes. An understanding of legal matters is a requirement for any practitioner, whatever the chosen profession, and without a basic education and skill in arithmetic and geometry it is unlikely anyone would choose to be an architect. So, why should a modern architect need a greater working understanding of medicine, music, astronomy and philosophy as well as the more obvious subjects of arithmetic, physics, geometry, law and history?

If we look a little deeper we are given some insight when Vitruvius tells Caesar that all these subjects have a 'common bond and union of intercourse with one another',[6] which reaches beyond the mere practicalities. In other words he is saying that all these apparently diverse and disparate subjects have a covert, arcane linkage, which together forms the curriculum necessary for the complete education of an architect. For example, when speaking about arithmetic and geometry he is referring to their symbolic (or sacred) language and the architect should understand music so that he or she may have a knowledge of canonical and mathematical theory. In other words, the essence of music is about keys and the harmonic ratios that embody numerical proportions, geometry and physics on an esoteric plane far beyond a simple appreciation of tuneful melodies. Also, music and astronomy have a common ground based on the relationship between the geometric patterns followed by the movement of heavenly bodies and the harmonic proportional ratios in the musical scale.

An architect who has understood this ancient wisdom will have the skills to create a building that has the power to heal and nourish our spirits and to eternally remind us of our roots and our common bond with all that is in the universe. Vitruvius goes on to say that:

> ...men have no right to profess themselves architects hastily, without having climbed from boyhood the steps of these studies and thus, nursed by the knowledge of many arts and sciences, having reached the heights of the holy ground of architecture.

> ...Those, therefore, who from tender years receive instruction in the various forms of learning recognise the same stamp on all the arts, and an intercourse between all studies, and so they more readily comprehend them all.

> ...architects who have aimed at acquiring manual skill without scholarship have never been able to reach a position of authority to correspond to their pains, while those who rely only upon theories and scholarship are obviously hunting the shadow, not the substance.

> ...He ought, therefore, to be both naturally gifted and amenable to instruction.[7]

Vitruvius had been initiated into the profound philosophical teachings of an ancient mystery school which was most likely the Dionysian Sect, founded over a thousand years before he was born. (See Chapter 11 for more on mystery schools.) The Dionysians, adepts of Bacchus, originated with Hermes Trismegistus (meaning 'thrice graced' – not to be confused with Hermes the Greek messenger god) in ancient Egypt. They were the custodians of the secret and sacred knowledge of architectonics and were the master builders who built the temples at Thebes and

Karnak, the temple of Diana at Ephesus and all the great public buildings, monuments and places of worship throughout Central Europe, Asia and India. All can be traced back to the teachings and practises of the Dionysians, who produced buildings that were in harmonic resonance with the structure of the universe; the dimensions and geometry within the architecture were a reflection of the laws governing the cosmos.

The supreme master builder of the Dionysian school was Hiram Abiff, architect, craftsman, goldsmith and decorator, who was commanded to build the Temple of Solomon. Many legends surrounding his life and murder in 1570 BC Care the subject of Christopher Knight and Robert Lomas' book *The Hiram Key*, which traces the stories from ancient Egypt through Christianity to present-day Freemasonry.[8] The thread of Dionysian influence can be traced from the mason's marks and symbols that can be seen cut into the stone in the chambers of the Pyramids of Gizeh, the underground walls of Jerusalem, Herculaneum and Pompeii, the Roman walls, Greek temples, buildings and monuments of Islam, India, Mexico, Peru and Asia Minor through to buildings and ruins in England, Scotland and Europe. The resemblance between these marks suggests that all the master builders belonged to the sects that were direct genealogical descendants from the same Dionysian school as Vitruvius.

We may have some further insight into Vitruvius' Dionysian connections and his relatively humble and studious lifestyle when we read between the lines of the following extract:

> I am very much obliged and infinitely grateful to my parents...for having taken care that I should be taught an art, and that of a sort which cannot be brought to perfection without learning and a liberal education in all branches of instruction. Thanks...(to) my parents and the instruction given by my teachers, I obtained a wide range of knowledge, and by the pleasure which I take in literary and artistic subjects, and in the writing of treatise, I have acquired intellectual possessions whose chief fruits are these thoughts: that superfluity is useless, and that not to feel the want of anything is true riches. There may be some people, however, who deem all this of no consequence, and think that the wise are those who have plenty of money. Hence it is that very many, in pursuit of that end, take upon themselves impudent assurance, and attain notoriety and wealth at the same time.
>
> But for my part, Caesar,...(I) have gone on the principle that slender means and a good reputation are preferable to wealth and disrepute...(but) my hope is that, with the publication of these books, I shall become known even to posterity...the ancients used to entrust their work in the first place to architects of good family, and next inquired whether they had been properly educated, believing that one ought to trust in the honour of a gentleman rather than in the assurance of impudence. And the architects themselves would teach none but their own sons or kinsmen and trained them to be good men, who could be trusted without hesitation in matters of such importance.
>
> But when I see that this grand art is boldly professed by the uneducated and the unskilful, and by men who, far from being acquainted with architecture, have no

knowledge even of the carpenter's trade, I can find nothing but praise for those householders who, in the confidence of learning, are emboldened to build for themselves. Their judgment is that, if they must trust to inexperienced persons, it is more becoming to them to use up a good round sum at their own pleasure than at that of a stranger.

Nobody, therefore, attempts to practise any other art in his own home – as, for instance, the shoemaker's, or the fuller's or any other of the easier kinds – but only architecture, and this is because the professionals do not possess the genuine art but term themselves architects falsely. For these reasons I have thought proper to compose most carefully a complete treatise on architecture and its principles, believing that it will be no unacceptable gift to all the world.[9]

Vitruvius believed that all buildings, whatever their class or purpose, including time-pieces and machinery, should be built with due deference to durability and convenience with appropriate arrangements and orientation. They should be beautiful, pleasing, in good taste, and so that all its parts are in due proportion according to the principles of symmetry.

The fundamental principles of architecture

According to Daniele Barbaro's sixteenth-century translation of Vitruvius, the fundamental principles of architecture are *ordinatio* (order), *dispositio* (arrangement), *eurythmic* (eurythmy), *symmetria* (symmetry), *decor* (propriety) and *distributio* (economy).[10] The old Italian meaning of the words remains largely the same in modern English. Wittkower, quoting the work of Daniele Barbaro, claims that:

Every work of art must be like a very beautiful verse, which runs along according to the best consonances one followed by the other, until they come to the well ordered end. The proportions of the human body are consonant and harmonious like the chords of a guitar. Of singers it is expected that their voices should be in tune, and the same applies to the parts in architecture. This beautiful manner in music as well as in architecture is called harmony, mother of grace and of delight. The beauty of order is symmetry as eurythmy is the beauty of disposition.

It is not enough to order the measurements singly one after the other, but it is necessary that those measurements be related to each other, that is to say that there must be some *proportion* between them. Thus, where there is proportion there can be nothing superfluous. And as nature's instinct is the ruler of natural proportion, so the rule of art is master of artificial proportion. From this it results that proportion belongs to form and not to matter, and where there are no parts there cannot be proportion. For proportion originates from composite parts and their relationship to each other: and, as has been shown, there must be at least two terms in each relation.[11]

Barbaro referred to proportion as the secret of art. In other words one needs to search below the surface in order to rediscover the truth in things.

Order concerns the measure of each element and parts of the building. The whole of nature, from the macrocosmic movement and dimensions of the heavenly bodies to the microcosm of all life on Earth, including subatomic structures, all are *ordered* according to proportional relationships found in number, geometry and music. Where these universal ratios correspond there will be goodness, beauty and truth, which do not have to be supported by decorative embellishments. (Decor or decoration concerns *elegance.*)

Arrangement is putting things in their right places with an *elegance* generated from the plan, elevation and perspective. According to Frank Lloyd Wright, before an architect picks up a pencil, in his or her mind's eye, he or she should be able to walk through every part of the design of the building. In other words, before rushing to a sketch pad or computer an architect should meditate on the client's brief – visualisation, or giving one's intuition a free reign, enables the design to evolve and flow without the physical constraints of committing ideas to paper or screen. Many of us abort creativity by rushing prematurely into the easier-to-manage technical areas of processing the *how* and the *when* – the getting from A to B – rather than focusing on the inner strategy of the *concept* that evolves from intuitive development. Architectural 'arrangement' is like musical composition: first the composer selects the key of a symphony and then 'designs' all the multiple variations of notes, chords, melody and timing consistent with harmonic ratios within the discipline of that specific musical key.

Traditional Japanese architecture is consistent with the teachings of Vitruvius. The elegant, serene simplicity of Japanese buildings integrates the inside and outside with a clarity of expression which is especially admired and appreciated by Western architects of the modern school. Room sizes are determined by the size of the tatami woven rush mat. Each mat measures just under 1 metre × 2 metres (3 feet x 6 feet) which is the harmonic proportion 1:2. As every room size is designed according to the module of a tatami, all interior spaces from the smallest to the largest are based on the harmonic proportions of 1:2 or 2:3 or 3:4 and so on, rising along the musical scales and ratios. The walls of Shoji rice paper and wood screens are also designed in accordance with the proportions of the mats and the geometric ratios of the 'golden section' (see Chapter 9). However diverse the interior spaces and façades may be, the architecture expresses a harmonious, unified whole.

Eurythmy, said Vitruvius is 'beauty and fitness in the adjustments of the members…when all the elements of a work are of a height suited to their breadth and to their length…'.[12] In other words, everything expresses a proportional correspondence which *remains in key.* Rudolf Steiner used the word 'eurythmics' to describe his system of teaching music and dance through the body's physical response to rhythm. Eurythmy – a word seldom, if ever used in today's vocabulary of art and architecture – implies a graceful, harmonious rhythm of structural order and movement.

Symmetry is the proportional agreement between the parts and the whole. Without symmetry and proportion, said Vitruvius 'there can be no principles in the design…if there is no precise relation between its members, as in the case of a well shaped man'.[13] Therefore, symmetry is the correlation between the various elements of the design of the whole building. He then described the symmetrical harmony found in nature between the forearm, foot, palm, finger and all the other parts of the human body and the precise proportional relationship of the parts to the whole. He described the proportions of a 'well shaped man' with the navel as the centre point to generate the geometry of the square and the circle. Centuries later, Leonardo da Vinci and other Renaissance architects and artists illustrated these master key measurements and proportions which set the canon for their great creative works of art and architecture.

Master builders from the ancient Egyptians onwards have understood symmetry as defined by Vitruvius, but in our present-day schools of architecture the term 'symmetry' is now used to mean an equal number of identically shaped architectural features arranged on either side of a centre line. Where an architectural composition comprises unequal shapes, volumes and features with no axis or centre line, this is defined in current terms (incorrectly) as 'asymmetrical'. Modern student architects and practitioners tend to favour so-called asymmetrical designs to eliminate any hint of a classical centre line, which is considered to be anathema to the modern movement and may account for the misconception of the word.

The Collins English Dictionary's modern definition of 'symmetry' – 'similarity, correspondence or balance among systems or parts of a system…beauty or harmony of form based on a proportionate arrangement of parts' – falls in line with Vitruvius' view. Expressed as a mathematical equation, $X + Y = Z$ is a symmetrical equation in which X, Y and Z are all *different* values but remain *in proportion*. The dictionary's definition of asymmetric is 'misproportioned' and in musical terms consists of any odd number of beats to a bar divided into uneven combinations. Where there is no order, correspondence or relationship to a key, the music or architectural design will be unfulfilling and displeasing.

Without an appreciation of aesthetics, mathematics and music the fundamental principles of proportion, ratios and dynamic symmetry may be somewhat difficult to grasp. But if we look at the history of architecture, there are abundant examples of buildings – classical temples, Gothic cathedrals, Renaissance palaces – which are not composed about a centre line. In our own time the mobile sculptures of surrealist Joan Miro illustrate symmetry in modern art – the sails and wires are all varied in shape and length but move in perfect balance and harmony around a fulcrum point in dynamic equilibrium.

Propriety, according to Vitruvius, concerns fitness for purpose, appropriateness of style and the nature of the site so that all buildings, including utilitarian structures, be durable, convenient and designed according to the principles of symmetry and to the scale of human beings. He also believed architects should be concerned with every aspect of life including matters of security and public morals.

Vitruvius' example concerns the planning of the walls of a city with that ring of effective simplicity that, once said, seems to be so obvious: the fortification towers must project beyond the wall so that an enemy would be exposed to the fire of missiles on his open flank; the approach road to the city gates should be steep and curved from right to left so that the right side of the assailants would be left unprotected by their shields; the walls should be wide enough to allow armed men to pass one another at the top; the towers should not be more than a bow shot apart and they should be either round or polygonal because square towers are more easily shattered.

Excluding the new threats of global terrorism, compared to the past, the incidence of murder and kidnapping may be relatively low but the rates of burglary, theft, mugging, vandalism, antisocial behaviour and the fear of crime can severely restrict our freedom and impair the quality of life to the extent that the city dweller might well feel as besieged, threatened and vulnerable as the city dwellers of a bygone age who had to repulse an invading army. Two thousand years ago, if the city's walls and fortifications had been poorly designed, the defenders could have suffered high casualties or even failed to beat off the attacker. The quality of design and attention to human scale detail might have been a more acute matter of life or death than it is today but despite extensive research directions and government legislation during the past decade, few modern architects and planners appear to be aware of the correlation between design and the incidence of crime. We no longer have to build fortifications to repel barbarian hordes, however we can improve security by designing environments to protect ourselves against urban crime.

More recently, the sudden impact of global terrorism has demanded a comprehensive review of the design and construction of major buildings. But perhaps because the increase in crime and the fear of crime has permeated more insidiously into the life of the community over the past decades, it has not attracted the attention of architects and planners, and this is the Boiled Frog Syndrome at work!.

Despite the initiatives of government legislation given below, the current situation can be summed up by the following quote from the introduction to a book published in 2002 entitled *Planning for Crime Prevention,* by Associate Professor Richard Schneider of the University of Florida and Professor Ted Kitchen of Sheffield Hallam University in England:

> If planning and other related professional activities concerned with the quality of the environment are to substantiate claims about being 'for people', then it seems to us that one of the most basic requirements is that they should address themselves to the concerns of those people in relation to their environments and not just to the concerns and interests of the professionals themselves. And yet, with some clear exceptions, we would assert that the relationships between planning activities, crime prevention and the design of the built environment have not registered as major concerns of planners and indeed typically do not feature very highly on planning education curricula.[14]

As early as 1961, with the publication of Jane Jacobs' book *The Life and Death of Great American Cities,*[15] and other major research programmes and practices, the concept of crime prevention through environmental design (CPTED) became established. During the 1970s and 1980s the movement was developed by police officers and a few architects and planners, and finally came to prominence in 1996 when the first international CPTED conference was held in Calgary in Canada. Its mission statement was 'to create safer environments and improve the quality of life through the use of CPTED principles and strategies'.[16]

The International CPTED Association (ICA) now has over 300 members in 30 countries worldwide. The ICA Chapter in the UK, known as the Design Out Crime Association (DOCA), was established in 1999. The principles are embodied in the police initiative known as Secured by Design (SBD), which aims to design out factors conducive to crime and disorder at the early planning stage when development plans are submitted to the local authorities for approval. In theory, all applications could/should be vetted and commented upon by the local architectural liaison officer who is usually a police officer with a background in crime prevention. (SBD principles have now been incorporated into the building codes in Holland and other European countries may soon follow suit.)

Perhaps one example of successful SBD principles was reported in October 1999 by Rachel Armitage of the Applied Criminology Group at the University of Huddersfield on the evaluation of the refurbishment of existing public-sector housing schemes throughout the West Yorkshire area. The work to the external and internal parts of the buildings incorporated changes based on CPTED concepts and a before-and-after analysis showed that on two of the schemes the crime rates per dwelling had reduced by 66.6 per cent on one and by 50 per cent on the other.[17] Not all SBD schemes can claim to match these spectacular percentage reductions but there are many similar examples that show encouraging results. Even so, it is only in the past two or three years that security has featured in the training of architects, dealing with design related to the community and crime and environmental design principles to reduce the risks.

It should also be mentioned that the proponents of SBD do not claim that this set of rules can be applied to any given situation. In fact, some of the features such as 'target hardening' and the closing off of likely escape routes is contrary to the American New Urbanist approach favoured by others, though the similarities far outweigh the differences. (Contrary to expectations, a comparison of similar types of individual crime rates, excluding murder and the use of firearms, shows that in the US the rates have been steadily falling whereas in the UK there has been a continual long-term rise.)

Until the Crime & Disorder Act 1998, there was no imperative for architects, local government officers and elected members to implement the concept of CPTED. Section 17 of the Act states:

17-(1) Without prejudice to any other obligation imposed on it, it shall be the duty of each authority to which this section applies to exercise its various functions with due regard to the likely effect of the exercise of those functions on, and the need to do all that it reasonably can to prevent crime, and disorder in its area.[18]

This places an obligation and a duty of care on all local authorities to implement a strategy for tackling crime and disorder which extends to a whole range of services and activities beyond Town Planning matters alone. This includes the maintenance and management of properties, bearing in mind the lack of funds to carry out services does not excuse a local authority from its statutory duties. It should also be borne in mind that creating a physical environment that is non-conducive to crime is only half the story. The sustained and appropriate maintenance and management of the environment and buildings is an equally significant factor in the prevention of crime: the rapid removal of graffiti and repair of vandalism, eliminating the signs of social disorder, enforcing eviction of antisocial tenants and controlling noisy neighbours are all covered by the Crime & Disorder Act 1998. And now, under the Human Rights Act 2000, everyone has a right to liberty and security, respect for private and family life and protection of property. This gives us, the 'ordinary citizens', the powers to not be at the mercy of an indolent, uncaring local authority which does not provide adequate education, housing and crime prevention facilities and services.

To return to Vitruvius, apart from his views on crime and security, he also instructed architects on how the location of certain buildings could affect public morals: 'we have to treat the choice of sites for temples, the forum and other public places with a view to convenience and utility'.[19] He recommended the temples for Jupiter and Juno be located on the highest point in the city; Mercury should be in the forum; Apollo and Father Bacchus near the theatre; and Mars at the training ground. In particular, the temple of Venus should be outside the city walls 'in order that the young men and married women may not become habituated in the city to the temptation incident to the worship of Venus'.[20] Vitruvius continued that the shrines for Vulcan and Ceres should also be sited outside the city walls to reduce the risk of fires used in religious rites. The reasoning is elementary and yet such basic thinking seems to elude some of our present-day planners and designers who, all too often, site buildings on land known to be inadequate or unsuitable for their purposes. Today, our potential problems are less to do with fire and more to do with health hazards, industrial pollution, traffic and aircraft noise, security and the safety of the users of the buildings.

Vitruvius described 'fitness for purpose' as '...principles [that]...derive from the truth of Nature' and ornament and decoration as 'a language' which has its own rules of syntax and grammatical arrangements.[21] The architect should choose carefully which language will be used in the building and to ensure that the 'grammatical' rules are not broken. (Despite this, architects such as Wren broke the classical rules but only a master can do so with such great effect). Propriety is brought to our attention to encourage architects to be disciplined and respect the canon or laws of nature. After all, nature operates within the five limitations of earth, air, fire, water and ether and yet creates an infinite variety of form.

Finally, propriety relates to the nature of the site, its healthiness and fitness for human habitation as well as the environmental conditions and the correct orientation of a building for daylight, views and prevailing winds. Vitruvius described how a stick or gnomon, set in the ground to create a sun shadow, was the centre or focal point of the first circle drawn on the ground. The precise North–South, East–West crossings could be determined by the shadow and the 'Vesica' arcs generated from the circle to establish accurate right angles, triangles and all the other fundamental geometry of the building.

Interestingly, much of what Vitruvius had to say about the more practical aspects of propriety and the natural conditions to be addressed when planning a new town or designing the arrangement, layout and siting of a new building is not only reminiscent of the guidelines set out in Feng Shui and Vastu Shastra, it has also become most pertinent and relevant to today's 'eco-tech' architects who must learn again the skills of the 'old ways' of yesterday's master builders. The successful design of naturally ventilated, ecologically sustainable, environmentally friendly buildings depends on the skills of understanding appropriate orientation, wind directions, solar heat gain, daylighting and overshadowing.

Economy, said Vitruvius, denotes the proper management of materials and the site, as well as a thrifty balancing of cost and common sense in the construction of works. He advocated the careful conservation of resources, the selection of materials readily to hand in the locality and the design of buildings fit for their purpose. The issues of economy and ecology are, again, even more pertinent to us today than 2,000 years ago!

Caesar was also urged to introduce laws to curb the financially extravagant and wayward architect. Vitruvius reminded Caesar that in the Greek city of Ephesus there was an ancient ancestral law whereby an architect's estimate of the cost of the building was handed to a magistrate; the architect's own property was then pledged as security until the work was done. If no more than a quarter of the estimate had to be added to the final cost it was subsidised by the treasury and no penalty inflicted, but when more than a quarter was exceeded the architect paid. He concluded:

> Would to God that this were also a law of the Roman people, not merely for public, but also for private buildings. For the ignorant would no longer run riot with impunity, but men who are well qualified by an exact scientific training would unquestionably adopt the profession of architecture. Gentlemen would not be misled into limitless and prodigal expenditure, and the architects themselves could be forced, by fear of the penalty, to be more careful in calculating and stating the limit of expense.[22]

Although the practical, day-to-day business of building is about budgets, fees, legalities, materials, construction, techniques and functional space, the essence of the design of architecture must be based upon the natural laws of the universe. These laws or canon are known as sacred laws. (Sacred – as opposed to profane or mundane values – bears no relation to the word 'religion'.) In effect, *The Ten Books on Architecture* is a partially covert treatise on the perennial tenets of the sacred arts and the elementary, fundamental principles of design. Vitruvius sets out a complete curriculum of the training and work essential for the practising architect: to become a master builder, an architect had to study and practise the full spectrum of the arts, sciences, matters of health, security, morality and spiritual development, as well as building construction and engineering.

If we are to get the architecture we need and want, the twenty-first-century schools of architecture will have to be prepared to teach a curriculum based on these principles.

References

1. KAIROS Essay No. 2, Architecture – A Return to Sacred Principles', 1984, by Peter David Gilbert and Keith Critchlow.
2. Ibid.
3. *The Macmillan Encyclopædia* (1984), London: Macmillan.
4. From a Kairos lecture given by Professor Keith Critchlow.
5. Vitruvius (1960) *The Ten Books on Architecture*, Book I, Chapter I 'The Education of an Architect', Paragraphs 1 and 3, New York: Dover Publications
6. Ibid., Paragraphs 10 and 12.
7. Ibid., Paragraphs 2, 3, 10 and 11.
8. Knight, C. and Lomas, R. (1996) *The Hiram Key*, London: Century.
9. Vitruvius op. cit., Book VI, Paragraphs 4, 5, 6 and 7.
10. Vitruvius op. cit., Book I, Chapter II, Paragraph 1.
11. Wittkower, R. (1971) 'The problem of harmonic proportion in architecture', in *Architectural Principles in the Age of Humanism*, New York: W. W. Norton & Co, pp. 138–9.
12. Vitruvius op. cit., Book I, Chapter II, Paragraph 3.
13. Vitruvius op. cit., Book III, Chapter I, Paragraph 1.
14. Schneider, R. and Kitchen, T. (2002) 'Introduction', *Planning for Crime Prevention*, London: Routledge, p. xix.
15. Jacob, Jane (1961) *The Life and Death of American Cities*, New York: Vintage Books.
16. Designing Out Crime Association (DOCA), PO Box 355, Staines, TW18 4WX.
17. Armitage, R. (1999) *An Evaluation of Secured by Design Housing Schemes Throughout the West Yorkshire Area*, The Applied Criminology Group, The University of Huddersfield, October 1999, p. 66.
18. Crime & Disorder Act 1998, Chapter 37.
19. Vitruvius op. cit., Book I, Chapter VII, Paragraph 1.
20. Ibid.
21. Vitruvius op. cit., Book IV, Chapter III, Paragraph 6.
22. Vitruvius op. cit., Book X, Introduction, Paragraph 2.

Suggested further reading

Clarke, R.V.G. and Mayhew, P. (1980) *Designing Out Crime*, Her Majesty's Stationery Office.
Crowe, T.D. (1991) *Crime Prevention through Environmental Design*, Massachusetts: Butterworth-Heinemann.

9.
The divine harmony

We have cracked the cosmic code. We, who are animated stardust, have a glimpse of the rules on which the universe runs. How we have become linked into this cosmic dimension is a mystery. Yet the linkage cannot be denied.[1]

Human beings have forever tried to explain how the world began, explore the secrets of life and discover the underlying order that binds the cosmos into one unified whole. From their meticulous, systematic, long-term observation of the physical world from the vast movement of the heavens to the minutest detail of plant growth and the human body, the ancients evolved the 'idea' that everything in the universe operates according to a divine plan of ordered patterns of numbers, harmonic ratios, rhythms and geometric proportions. This theory of correspondences is based on the axiom or law of Hermes Trismegistus: the macrocosmic realm of the universe is reflected in the microcosmic realm of man and nature on Earth – 'As above, so below'.

The seven liberal arts

The esoteric wisdom relating to the divine harmony was divulged only orally to the initiates of the mystery schools until Plato set out the fundamental principles in his *Timaeus*.[2] For the first time the sacred teachings he called the 'seven liberal arts' were committed to the written word. Plato was criticised for not following the oral tradition of *Dogma Agrapha* (unwritten doctrines) but defended the work as written commentaries for guidance purposes only. In his *Seventh Letter* he responded to his critics thus:

> The publicising of these secrets I do not deem a boon for men, excepting for those initiates who are able to discover them with no more than a given hint. For the others it would produce a stupid derision or else a self-glorification in a mistaken idea that they have eaten wisdom in spoonfuls.[3]

The Seven Liberal Arts were divided into the *Trivium* (3) and the *Quadrivium* (4), the two numbers representing the trinity of heaven with the four-foldness or cube of earth.

The Trivium

The art and science of the Trivium were *grammar, rhetoric* and *logic* (or dialectic). All three are related to the proper use of language:

Grammar	is the exact choice of words or construction of phrase to unambiguously convey a precise meaning to express in noble language innermost thoughts, ideals and ideas and the personification of GOODNESS.
Rhetoric	is the quality of communicating in beautiful and convincing language, style, analysis and presentation to personify BEAUTY.
Logic	is the organisation of language in search of the truth by means of the power of deduction and reasoned debate without the egotistical desire to win an argument. It is making the full use of intellectual facilities to discover TRUTH.

As Plato said: 'If we are not able to hunt the Good with one idea only, with three we may catch our prey: beauty, symmetry, truth are the three'.[4] Undoubtedly we hunger and search for goodness, beauty and truth because instinctively we know that whatever we manifest should reflect the qualities of our natural state of being and our individual uniqueness should not separate us from the wholeness of nature and the universe.

Gematria – a Hebrew word derived from the Greek *geometria* (geometry) – is the architecture of language, where words are related to their sense to number, and numbers to geometry. Whether a text or a building, if there is an underlying 'sacred' geometry the form will contain more than meets the eye and will express an essence which is eternal and infinite. It was considered by the ancients to be a 'science' to reveal the deeper mysteries of God and the esoteric dimensions of space, music, astrology and architecture.

The early languages of Egypt, India, Greece and the Hebraic tradition used the letters of their alphabets as an arithmetical expression of numbers, such as the Roman numeral system of letters, that is, $III = 3, V = 5, X = 10, XX = 20$ and so on. It can be seen that arithmetical calculations and all expressions of numbers using letters of the alphabet can produce intelligible words. Therefore, words could be spelt in such a manner that it would help a young initiate to memorise the sacred teachings by a mathematical formula corresponding to a succession of letters that added up to numerical values. For example, the names of gods and goddesses correlated to specific numbers that had a significance which created a sacred language: each letter, word and sentence had mystical values where the principles of number, sound and form (geometry) were associated with each letter of the alphabet, and when linked together, generated extended dimensions and meaning. According to Socrates: 'the knowledge of names is a great part of knowledge'. Gematria was used to compose the Hebraic scriptures, Christian texts of the New Testament and the cryptic codes of Plato, the Gnostics, the Alchemists and Kabbalists.

One of the few living masters of the sacred arts, Professor Keith Critchlow, discovered that both the Koran and the original texts of the Bible and Kabbalah have the number 19 as the key to the texts.[5] All names, words and phrases were 'designed' to produce the number 19, which has many mystical and astrological associations such as the 19-year period for the Sun and Moon to return to the same relative position. Unfortunately, the gematriatic integrity and the more profound hidden meanings of the scriptures are lost when the texts are translated into another language. Gematria is not only the exchange of letters for their numerical equivalents but it also expresses a method of determining, by an analysis of its measurements, the mystical (sacred) purpose for which a building or other object was constructed. F. Bligh Bond, an architect, and Dr T. S. Lea, vicar of St Austell, produced a small book entitled *Gematria: A Preliminary Investigation of The Cabala*, first published in 1917 and republished through Rilko (Research Into Lost Knowledge Organisation) in 1977. The authors wrote on geometric truth that:

> Mere words of natural significance fail to interpret spiritual ideas unless a figurative meaning be added to them. By type and symbol alone can the essence of truth be conveyed. In myth and parable the poet, prophet and religious teacher in all time present to us the realisations of the spiritual sense. And not in the imagery of words alone, but in architecture, and its allied arts, some of the most sublime of human conceptions have been conveyed.[6]

The Quadrivium

The Quadrivium was preparatory to the highest art and science of philosophy – meaning 'love of wisdom', from the Greek *philo* (love) and *sophia* (wisdom). Its four components – arithmetic, geometry, harmonics (music) and cosmology – were an intrinsic entity that could not be taught separately any more than we can separate body from soul or spirit. However, with the dawn of the 'Age of Enlightenment' it was decreed that the soul was not appropriate for rational study. Since then mathematics and geometry have also been taught as individual sciences, leading to the modern compartmentalisation of today's disciplines and the breaking up of the integrity of the traditional teachings.

The Quadrivium has greatly influenced Western art and architecture as well as Western thought. All its four components express certain universal truths that transcend language (in any language there can be no argument that $2 + 2 = 4$) and are fundamental to understanding the nature of existence: they are sacred languages of symbolism.

Arithmetic   is pure number known as the 'Queen of the Sciences'. Plato's arithmetic is the key to magnitude, proportion and the mystery of the universal order. Addition, subtraction, multiplication and

Geometry
division were based on the Abacus until the thirteenth century when Roman numerals were replaced by Indo-Arabic symbols and the introduction to the concepts of algebra, decimals and zero.

is number in form or space and the harmony and rhythm of angles and the philosophy of organisation. Geometry literally means 'measure of the Earth' (stereometry is the measure of volume). Using only a straight-edge and compass, the plane, solid and spatial geometry of Pythagoras and Euclid can be produced as a philosophical discipline to discover profound meanings as well as having a practical purpose in building and engineering.

Music
is number in time governed by the laws of harmonic ratios such as those expressed in the rhythm and movement of the celestial bodies. (The discordance and cacophony of some of our contemporary music are indicative of our conflicts with nature and the environment).

Cosmology
is number in time and space expressing the interrelationship between man (the microcosm) and the universe (the macrocosm). While Plato's cosmology was based on the geocentric view of Ptolemy and Arab astronomy (rather than the heliocentric view of Copernicus, Kepler and Galileo), the philosophic concept remained constant and reflected the awesomeness of unknown power.

The mystical language of numbers

Everything in the universe, from subatomic structures to the vast galaxies, is arranged according to certain repeated patterns of number and geometry. From the movement of the planets, to the growth of a plant, the shape of a shell and the bones in our body, all natural phenomena conform to the laws of proportion determined by those patterns of numbers. Ancient masters of wisdom used number, geometry and music as symbolic languages to reveal the sacred meaning of the mysteries of life and to understand the divine, sublime intelligence controlling and unifying the entire cosmos. These masters were the healers/priests, the master builders and mystics who understood and integrated the divine harmony of the universe with science, religion and medicine into one philosophic system embracing and reconciling the exoteric (earthly), mesoteric (occult/psychological) and esoteric (mystical/spiritual) worlds. This philosophic system was the foundation of the ancient teachings of the mystery schools (see Chapter 10). As an abstract language of symbols, number was a means to understand the universe and bring the initiates of the mystery schools closer to their spiritual goal of understanding the underlying Divine Intelligence. As St Augustine said: 'Numbers are thoughts of God... The Divine Wisdom is reflected in the numbers impressed on all things... [and] the construction of the physical and moral world alike is based on eternal numbers'.[7]

It could be said that the true 'mystery' of numbers is the symbolic source and link between heaven and Earth: between the unmanifest and the manifest. Those who understand the abstract significance of number and geometry are able to translate this profound knowledge into physical form in such a manner that, in the case of a building, its resonance with a universal harmony will be sensed by those who enter. The mere application of the laws alone by the simple reproduction of symbolic numbers and geometry, without understanding their esoteric meaning will result in a barren, soul-less building.

The mesoteric symbolism of numbers, which transcends our current understanding of the arithmetic of addition, subtraction, multiplication and division, can be summarised as follows:

ONE is the unity of all things; sameness; the beginning of creation; God and the Divine Spirit.

TWO is duality; separation into masculine and feminine; Adam and Eve.

THREE is the trinity; the reconciliation; the return to wholeness; the dynamic symmetry of mind, body and spirit.

FOUR is the manifested, material world of matter; the four elements of fire, earth, air and water.

FIVE is the product of 2 (the first prime even number, which represents the female principle) and 3 (the first odd prime number, which represents the male principle). Five symbolised humanity, love harmony and health. The five-pointed star – the pentacle – is the sigil of man.

TEN – the Decad – represented the whole of creation. The early Greek philosophers defined the number of nature (the cosmos) as the *Decad*. They also expressed the enigma of the creation with the riddle 'ten is complete at four', which can be interpreted as meaning that the cosmic creative process has four stages – expressed symbolically through the numbers 1 (unity), 2 (duality), 3 (trinity or reconciliation), and 4 (the manifested world) – which together add up to the whole of creation (that is, 10). It can therefore be said that 10 (the cosmos) completes itself at 4 (the manifestation of the material world), as demonstrated in the mathematical formula $(1 + 2 + 3 + 4 = 10)$. This formula was expressed geometrically as the *Tetractys* (see Figure 9.1).

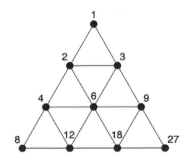

Figure 9.1   The Tetractys

Certain sequences of numbers, called 'Magic Squares' (see Figure 9.2) were used to express other esoteric teachings. These mathematical metaphors added up to the ancient concept that there is unity in all existence – everything tangible, everything we can sense and even our thought patterns. Numbers also express a metaphoric correlation similar to the two and three dimensions of geometry:

The *point* is the seed of creation (called the *bindu* in Hindu Tantra).
The *circle* also represents God, the heavens, eternity and the unknowable.
The *line* or *diameter* represents duality or separation.
The *triangle* represents the trinity, the reconciliation, the return to wholeness.
The *square* or *cube* represents the manifested, material world.
The *pentagram* represents man.
The *hexagram* represents the masculine and feminine; the Seal of Solomon; the Star of David and, in Hindu Tantric theology, divine harmony.
The *heptad,* a seven-pointed star in a circle, represents a mystical figure of the Moon cycles, the seven colours and the seven days of the week. (It is not possible to divide a circle into seven equal parts, either mathematically or geometrically.)
The *octagram* represents the energies or vibrations connecting heaven and Earth.
The *enneagram* is the nine-sided figure representing completion.

The secrets of the natural world are hidden behind the enigma of irrational numbers. A rational number, say 24, is a complete integer that can be reconciled as a whole number. However, an irrational number is one that can never be reconciled into a complete whole number. For example, if the side of a square is unit 1, the diagonal is 2 (the square root of 2) which is 1.4142... and so on to infinity. This

8	1	6
3	5	7
4	9	2

16	2	3	13
5	11	10	8
9	7	6	12
4	14	15	1

13	25	7	19	1
17	4	11	23	10
21	8	20	2	14
5	12	24	6	18
9	16	3	15	22

Figure 9.2 Examples of magic squares

number can be run on a computer but will never end as a reconciled decimal place whole number. Similarly, a circle of diameter unit 1 will have a circumference of 3.14159... to infinity. This number is known as $Pi(\pi)$. Whatever the diameter of a circle may be, the circumference is always the diameter multiplied by 3.14159 (π). Therefore, the numerical proportion of Pi is constant. Numerically we cannot know precisely the area of a circle nor accurately know the diagonal length of a square, but they can be demonstrated with precision by geometry using a straight edge and a pair of compasses.

The Fibonacci Series and the Golden Section

A thirteenth-century Italian mathematician, Leonardo of Pisa (known simply as Fibonacci), first formulated a remarkable sequence of numbers. Each number in the series is the sum of the two previous numbers: 0, 1, 1, 2, 3, 5, 8, 13, 21, 34 *ad infinitum*. When any number in the series is divided by the previous number – for example, 13 divided by 8 – it equals approximately 1.62; when a number is divided by the following number – say, 8 divided by 13 – it equals approximately 0.62. These numbers 1.62 and 0.62 are approximately the same throughout the series to infinity. They are known as irrational numbers and the invariable proportions are repeated in the fundamental patterns of growth found in living organisms and mineral structures.

The left- and right-hand spirals of a daisy flower are arranged in a Fibonacci series of 21 clockwise and 34 counter-clockwise spirals; a pineapple has a pattern of 8 spirals in one direction and 13 in another. Typically, leaves grow around the stem of a plant in a similar proportional relationship. This is known as 'gnomonic expansion' – that is, growth expressed as number in a succession of increments through time. The growth of a tree, a ram's horns, the spiral inside a nautilus shell, sunflowers, elephant trunks, the umbilical cord, the shape of the inner ear – all follow the same proportional number sequence as the bones of the middle finger, to the palm, to the arm to the whole body of a human being. The movement and orbits of the planets and galaxies also conform to these same harmonic patterns.

Keith Foster, writing in the *Journal of the British Society of Dowsers*, refers to Lawrence Edwards' book *The Vortex of Life: Nature's Patterns in Space and Time*, in which Edwards suggests there are little understood universal laws (or canon) that guide the growth of all living organisms, including our organs, plant life, and embryos into pre-determined patterns.[8] These 'pathcurve' forms are mathematical constructs inherent in all living things. In the nineteenth century, Felix Klein and Sophus Lie were the first to discover the forms or shapes that all living things must follow as they grow. Pathcurve forms result from two interlocking vortices flowing up from the Earth and down from the cosmos. Electron energy spiralling up from the Earth's surface is created into an anti-clockwise spin by the negatively charged magnetic field. Energy from the Sun is positively charged with a clockwise spin. These two counter-balanced but opposing forces take the movement line of least resistance which creates a flow to evolve the beautiful dynamic forms and curves of nature and the natural growth patterns of flower buds, pine cones, sea urchins, eggs, and the shape of the heart.[9]

The mysterious series of numbers and proportions called the Fibonacci Series was known to the ancients as the 'Divine Proportion', the 'Golden Section', or sometimes the 'Sacred Cut'. The Golden Section, described by Plato as the key to all physics, is not the product of an abstract mathematical 'idea' but a principle of the laws of equilibrium, balance and harmonies that correspond to a natural order. The formula can be found in art, architecture, poetry and music. Whether or not we are either consciously or unconsciously attracted to such shapes and patterns because the human body and living organisms follow the same divine laws of proportion, undoubtedly the psyche senses the relationships, resonances and correspondences which may account for our perceptions of aesthetics and beauty. In other words, harmony is synonymous with beauty and goodness: when we recognise the good, and sense the subtle harmonic ratios in nature, these are recognised as being present in our soul. A contemporary and friend of Leonardo da Vinci, Luca Pacioli suggested that divine proportion was one of the two 'jewels' of geometry known as the Golden Section.

The Golden Section is the only geometric formula that will allow gnomonic growth patterns to either increase or decrease the surface or volume without changing the basic shape of the spiral or proportions (see Figure 9.3). In other words it always remains similar to itself. The proportional cut of a line or the ratio of length to width of a Golden Section rectangle, which the ancient masters kept secret, divulging the arcane system only to their initiates, can only be produced accurately by geometric means.

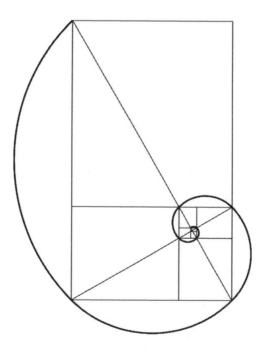

Figure 9.3   A spiral based on a $\sqrt{3}$ rectangle

The Golden Section is the division of a line into two, such that the shorter piece is to the longer piece as the longer is to the whole line. A line *AC* is cut at *B* so that *BC* is to *AB* as *AB* is to *AC.* The golden rectangle is where one side is a measurement of a unit one and the other side is a unit measurement of 1.618 (see Figure 9.4).

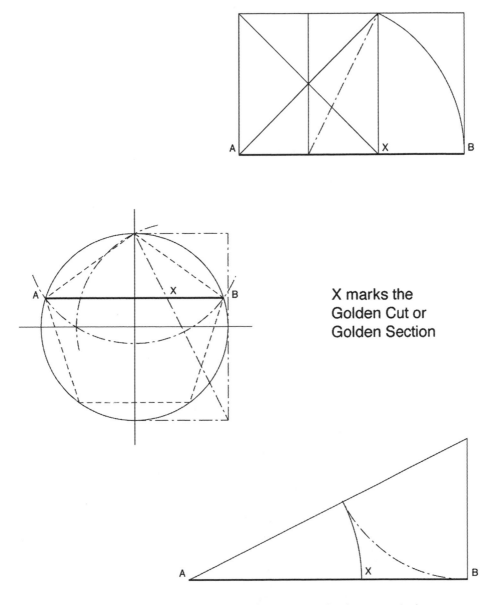

X marks the
Golden Cut or
Golden Section

Figure 9.4   The Golden Section (three methods of construction)

The Greeks symbolised this golden proportion as Φ (*Phi*). It has many unique qualities in terms of number, algebra and geometry:

$$\frac{1}{\Phi} = 0.618$$

$$\Phi = \frac{\sqrt{5} + 1}{2} = 1.618$$

$$\Phi = \frac{\sqrt{5} + 3}{2} = 2.618$$

$$\Phi = \frac{\sqrt{5} + 5}{2} = 3.618$$

The geometric method to produce Φ or the Golden Cut is generated from the pentagram – the five-sided figure – which is the basis of the square root of 5. Each of the triangles in the pentagonal star have two equal sides that relate to the third side as 8 does to 5 (approximately) in the Golden Section (that is, 1.618 related to 1). These reciprocal relationships create a square root of five Golden Section rectangle.

The metaphysical geometry of *Phi* is evident in the proportions of the ideal human body. If the full height $= 1$, then from feet to navel $= 1/\Phi$ and from navel to head $= 1/\Phi$. The sex organs divide the body exactly in two. At birth, the navel divides the child in half but on maturity the navel moves to the point of the *Phi* division. The height of the face equals the vertical distance between the middle of the body and the navel. The top of the head and the navel equals the distance from the tip of the medium finger to the floor. The proportion of *Phi* is found in the three bones of the middle finger. Leonardo Da Vinci's drawing of a man was based upon Vitruvius' concept of the ideal (average) human body expressing the laws of proportion and commensurable ratios.

Masterpiece works by Leonardo Da Vinci, Michelangelo, Alberti and Palladio, and Bartok's *Sonata for 2 pianos and percussion* are but a few examples where the Fibonacci Series will be found. Even the cyclical movement in the stock markets conforms to similar patterns, and sociologists have detected Fibonacci ratios linked to unconscious behaviour and certain social and sporting activities. Calendar 'good' or 'bad' days seem to coincide with the same ratio patterns. The modern piano keyboard has five black keys arranged in a 3:2 ratio, the octave is the eighth key making the thirteen notes of the completed chromatic scale which links to the Fibonacci number series of the Golden Section and *Phi* (see Figure 9.5). The European 'A' format sized paper introduced to Britain in the 1970s also conforms to the geometry of the Golden Section, that is, the long side of the fomat is identical in length to the short side of the A3 size and so on. Thus from the largest size of Al all the other sizes are proportionally the same. As early as 1790 the 'A' format was in use in France and possibly because of practical economies, it gradually became accepted throughout Europe.

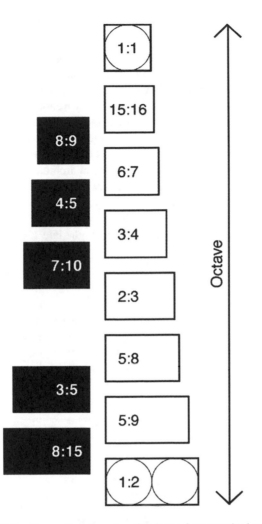

Figure 9.5   Proportional rectangles based on musical notes

As we have seen, proportion means that the several parts or elements of the composition or form will have a corresponding relationship with all the other parts and will relate to the whole building to complete a design interrelatedness and an inherent beauty. Socrates believed that beauty was the harmony of all numbers, so that nothing can be taken away, added or changed. Alberti believed beauty in an individual building depended on three qualities – number, proportion and location (disposition and arrangement) – which unite to form a well-adjusted whole and bear a relationship to the human body. He also believed that beauty is something that is proper, innate and diffused throughout the whole, while ornament is something added and fastened on, rather than proper and innate. In other words, harmony does not result from personal fancy but from objective reasoning.

Rudolf Wittkower, writing on 'Architectural Principles' said:

> The conviction that architecture is a science, and that each part of a building, inside as well as outside, has to be integrated into one and the other same system of mathematical ratios, may be called the basic axiom of Renaissance architects [or any other architect worthy of the name]. We have already seen that the architect is by no means free to apply to a building a system of ratios of his own choosing, that the ratios have to comply with conceptions of a higher order and that a building should mirror the proportions of the human body: demand which became universally accepted on Vitruvius' authority. A man is the image of God and the proportions of his body are produced by divine will, so the proportions in architecture have to embrace and express the cosmic order. But what are the laws of this cosmic order, what are the mathematical ratios that determine the harmony in macrocosm and microcosm? They had been revealed by Pythagoras and Plato, whose ideas in the field had always remained alive but gained new prominence from the late 15th century onwards.[10]

Squaring the circle

The ancient masters faced an enigmatic challenge to find a geometric as well as a metaphysical answer to the paradox or 'mystery' of 'squaring the circle'. There is a geometry to produce a square which has the same area as a circle and, likewise, a geometry to produce a square which has the same length of perimeter as the circumference of a circle, but both can never be reconciled (see Figure 9.6).

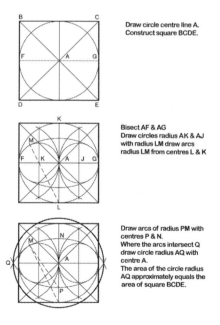

Figure 9.6 Squaring the circle of approximately equal areas.

However, the master builders of the Great Pyramids of Cheops achieved this by building the height of the vertical half section and, taken as a radius, this produces a circle with a circumference equal to the perimeter measure of the square base (see Figure 9.7). In symbolic language, the square (or cube) represents the four elements – earth, air, fire, water – the four squareness of the physical world; the circle (or dome) represents the heavens – the subtle divine world of the spirit and eternity. Spiritual teachings and religious traditions were concerned with uniting the material world – the human body and existence – with the unseen world to create a relationship with the soul and God. This expressed the uniting of heaven and Earth and personified the quest of a human being to achieve a dynamic balance between body and soul.

Squaring the circle can be a complex process in architectural terms: how to achieve the transition from, say, the cubic body of a mosque to the hemispheric circle of the dome? Whether the building is the Pantheon in Rome, the Hagia Sophia in Istanbul, the Taj Mahal, St Paul's Cathedral or the White House, the constructional system usually employed was to build out from the square or rectangle plan shape a series of corbels in the form of octagonals to resolve the plan into a circle. Incidentally, Sir Christopher Wren built St Paul's Cathedral with three domes: the outer dome shape for external appearance, and the inner dome, immediately above the 'whispering gallery' to create a more aesthetically pleasing effect from the Nave. Between the two is a brick cone-shaped dome that holds everything together. At the base of the

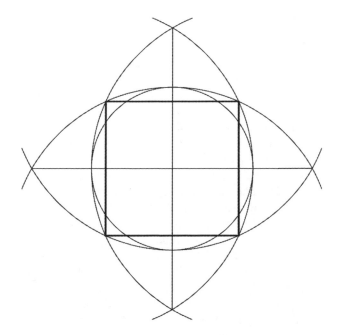

Figure 9.7   Squaring the circle. The Vesica Piscis generates a square and circle of approximately equal perimeters

domes, around the perimeter, are heavy chains to restrain the force of the outward thrust of the structure.

According to Greek Sophist Protagoras (485–15 BC): 'Man is the measure of all things'. The same theme was expressed by Vitruvius in his *Book III*, on temples, where he states that the proportions of the ideal human should be reflected in the proportions of buildings. He describes how the figure of a well-built man with extended hands and feet fits exactly into the geometry of a square and a circle – that is, the relationship of man to the physical Earth (the square) and the spiritual heavens (the circle).[11] The circle is also found in abundance in nature – the dome of the sky, the orbits of planets, the Sun and Moon, the shape of a daisy flower, the nests of birds and the Earth itself.

Our present-day understanding and appreciation of the mentality, ingenuity and profound wisdom of the ancient master builders to represent our human microcosmic correspondences with the cosmos is indebted to R. A. Schwaller de Lubicz, a French Egyptologist and archaeologist who in 1949 published the results of fifteen years of meticulous research into the Eighteenth Dynasty Temple of Luxor.[12] Over a long intensive period of many years he painstakingly measured every part of the entire building to prove that the plan of the temple was based on the principles of the proportions of the human body to symbolise the Egyptian Pharaoh who represented the divinity and perfection of man. From the carvings of the bas-reliefs lining the walls to the overall layout and plan of the temple, the geometry of the Golden Rectangle has been used throughout. Schwaller de Lubicz summarised the principles as follows:

> The sages have always endeavoured to hand down to posterity the revelation of the spirit disguised in the form of the words and parables of the sacred texts. These texts are syntheses of Knowledge whose basis is always the same, though adapted to the times and to the state of consciousness of a people or peoples. The means adopted for transmitting this teaching are manifold, comprising legends, tales, and customs, as well as monuments, statues and temples. Thus, up to the end of the Middle Ages, the Christian tradition assigned specific attributes are a veritable scripture revealing what cannot be said in plain words. Temples – whether Hindu, Egyptian, Jewish, Christian, or Moslem – are always conceived according to a canon that respects certain elements which explain the teaching. Esotericism should not be understood as a rebus or a secret writing, but rather as the 'spirit of the letter' – that is to say, *that which cannot be transcribed clearly*, not because there is any desire to conceal it, but because of the 'cerebral' intellect's inaptitude for comprehending it. Each (person) will see in the parable or in the architecture of the true temple, what he can see: utility, aesthetics, myth and legend, philosophical principle, or vision of material and spiritual genesis. It appears quite distinctly that the secret pharaonic teaching was based on the vital functions for which the (human) organs are the living symbols. There can no longer be any doubt of the Ancients' knowledge with regard to what might be called 'spiritual metabolism', from the assimilation of nourishment to the liberation of the Energy – or Spirit – manifested in the intellectual faculties and the powers of Consciousness.[13]

Arcane geometry

Plato said that no-one could understand his philosophy without knowing geometry, since geometry contained the fundamental secrets of all ancient science. The geometry he referred to was a symbolic language expressing profound 'sacred' meanings: through number and geometry we can experience both internal and external time and space and by studying the measure of the Earth, man could understand the heavens – 'As above, so below'. In his *Timaeus* Plato related the Golden Section and the five regular polygons, known as the 'Platonic Solids' to the basic elements of earth, air, fire, water and ether, which also have correspondences to be found in atomic structures, natural growth patterns and the orbits of heavenly bodies:

The *tetrahedron* represented fire.
The *octahedron* represented air.
The *cube* represented earth.
The *icosohedron* represented water.
The *dodecahedron* represented the cosmos.[14]

A regular solid has equal sides, equal regular faces, equal angles and is contained within a sphere. The five Platonic Solids are the only polygons falling within these parameters. Each solid has an affinity, interrelationship and three-dimensional compatibility with the others.

Studies of the integration of all the Platonic Solids has produced a sphere combining the Dodecahedron with the Icosohedron. Where the node points coincide, when transposed on to a globe of the world, they closely coincide with some of the significant religious or sacred places on Earth such as Jerusalem, Lhasa, Rome and several others.

The three-dimensional geometry of the solid rectangle (a right-angled parallele-piped) is defined by the three faces producing ratios of proportions governing the volume, surfaces and lines. These solid rectangles are of particular importance to architects, furniture makers and indeed any designer working in three dimensions. Some of the most celebrated examples of the art and architecture of antiquity are based on dynamic rectangle solids derived from the Golden Section, the double cube and other properties generated from the five Platonic regular solids and the circle or sphere. It is believed the eye reduces complex patterns to simple rectangular shapes such as the circle, square, triangle, pentagram and hexagram in order to understand and comprehend the object and appreciate its aesthetic qualities.

Before Plato, Pythagoras revealed the mystery of the right-angled triangle. Known as the Sacred Triangle, it is expressed in the theorem 'the square on the hypotenuse is equal to the sum of the squares on the other two sides'. It is the only triangle with an arithmetic progression of the sides 3, 4 and 5, and is the simplest one to create by using a rope knotted at 3, 4 and 5 intervals. Plato described the equilateral triangle as being the most beautiful, and the isosceles triangle – having two equal sides – as the 'sublime' triangle (see Figure 9.8).

Regular rectangles fall into two categories: one group is *static*, the other *dynamic*. Static rectangles have arithmetic rational number fractions such as 1/2, 2/3, 3/3, 3/4,

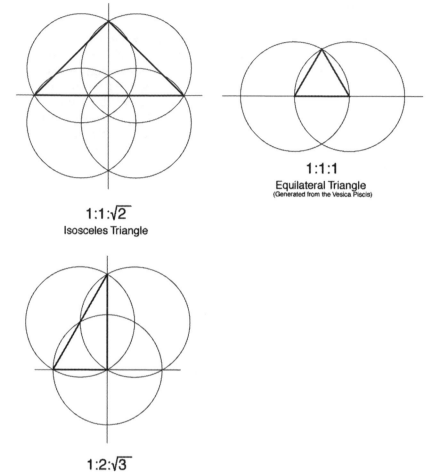

$1:1:\sqrt{2}$
Isosceles Triangle

1:1:1
Equilateral Triangle
(Generated from the Vesica Piscis)

$1:2:\sqrt{3}$
Right Angle Triangle

Figure 9.8   The Pythagorean triangles

whereas the dynamic rectangles have geometric fractions that are irrational numbers such as 2, 3, 5 (see Figure 9.9). Only the dynamic rectangles can produce subdivisions that automatically fall into proportional or harmonic relationships with the whole. These harmonic divisions produce dynamic symmetry such as the two-dimensional form of a golden rectangle where the parts always relate to the whole.

The Vesica (also known as the *Vesica Piscis,* meaning 'fish bladder') is a geometric figure formed by the intersection of two equal-diameter circles where the centre of one is located on the perimeter of the other (see Figure 9.10). The proportional relationship between lines *AB* and *CD* in the ratio of 26:15 was a symbol of the hidden

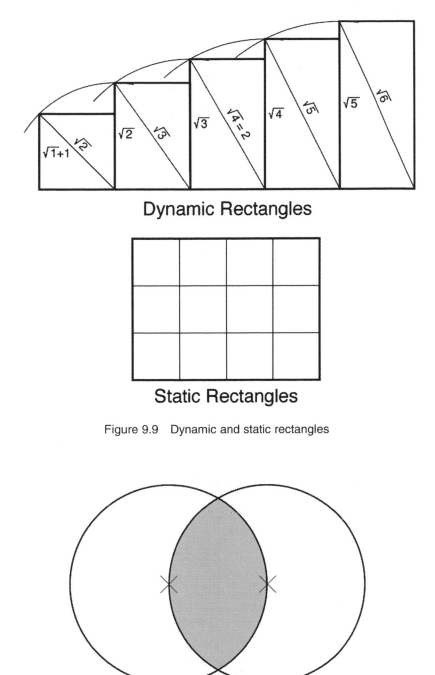

Dynamic Rectangles

Static Rectangles

Figure 9.9   Dynamic and static rectangles

Figure 9.10   The Vesica Piscis is constructed by two circles of equal radius with the centre of one circle on the circumference of the other circle. The shaded area is an orifice or 'Vessel of the Fish'

canon of nature. This length-to-width proportion generates the physical forms of the irrational geometry of the Golden Section, the basic polygrams, regular polygons and the three essential triangles.

Symbolically, the Vesica Piscis represents the genitals of Mother Earth and the creation of life. In the Hindu tradition, the Vesica was the symbol of the *Yoni* – the womb of the universe. Christianity adopted the Vesica Piscis to represent the Virgin and the female aspect of Christ and the 'wound'. (The zodiacal sign of Pisces, the two fishes, became the symbol of the Age of Christianity.) Also the length and width proportions of the Vesica coincide with the four circles of Mercury's orbit producing a diagram resembling the symbol of Christ. It was also the geometric foundation for the siting, orientation and the setting out of the metaphysical master plan of some of the great temples and cathedrals such as Chartres (see Figure 9.11) and other architectural masterpieces of the past.

Vitruvius described the method of placing a stick in the ground to establish the orientation of the building and setting out the angles by a method using the Vesica from which the geometry and proportion of the entire building was generated. The ratio of the plan shape of the Great Pyramid to the length of the side is in the same

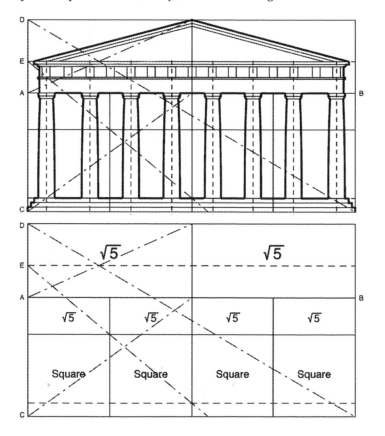

Figure 9.11   The Parthenon – harmonic analysis

proportion as the Vesica (see Figure 9.12). If modern architects used the same geometric foundation for the siting, orientation and the setting out of the metaphysical master plan, and allowed the proportions and placements of the building to derive from the 'seed' instead of using arithmetical calculations, this would achieve, at least in some measure, a coordination expressing a wholeness and to resonate with human beings.

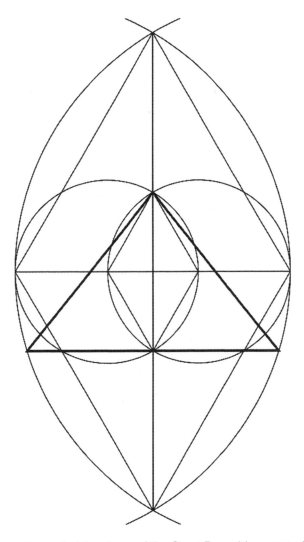

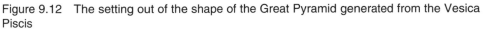

Figure 9.12   The setting out of the shape of the Great Pyramid generated from the Vesica Piscis

The music of the spheres

The term 'music of the spheres' – coined by Pythagoras in the sixth century BC – describes how the movement patterns of the heavenly bodies follow the same harmonic ratios found in musical progressions. His discovery of the correspondences between abstract numbers, music and harmonic theories led him to pronounce that 'Number *is* music and music *is* number'. The effect of music on mind and body led Pythagoras to call it 'musical medicine'. Much later, in the eighteenth century, Johann Titus and Johann Bode identified a relationship between the Sun and the distances and orbital patterns of the known planets, indicating that they corresponded to a chain of octaves known as 'Bodes Law'. Gaps in the chain eventually led modern astronomy to discover other planets and planetoids that also conform to the same patterns of harmonic and pitch frequencies predicted by Pythagoras:

> The key to harmonic ratios is hidden in the Pythagorean Tetractys or pyramid of dots [see Figure 9.1]. The tetractys is made up of the first four numbers – 1, 2, 3, and 4 – which, in their proportions, reveal the intervals of the octave, the diapente and diatessaron. To Pythagoras music was one of the dependencies of the divine science of mathematics, and its harmonies were inflexibly controlled by mathematical proportions...[he]...applied his newly found law of harmonic intervals to all phenomena in Nature...[including]...the harmonic relationship of the planets, constellations, and the elements to each other.[15]

Robert Cowley, writing an appreciation of Barbara Hero's work in the *Rilko Journal*,[16] says the American mathematician, musician, artist and educationalist has focused her lifetime's work on the study of the Lambdoma generally attributed to Pythagoras (see Figure 9.13). The Lambdoma, based on *lamda*(the Greek letter Λ), shows correspondences with the Greek alphabet, musical intervals and rational numbers comprising whole numbers on one side and fractions on the other, showing

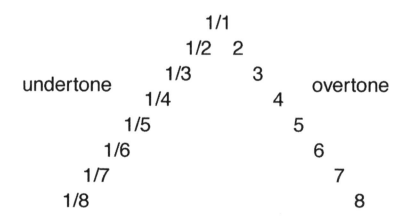

Figure 9.13   The Lambdoma

the relationship between overtones and undertones. (Overtones are harmonics based on the major chord and undertones on the minor chord.)

Barbara Hero believes the mathematics of the Lambdoma was known by the ancient Egyptians who used the proportions in the design of the pyramids. This sacred knowledge continued in the tradition of the mystery schools and was used in the Gothic Cathedrals and Cistercian Abbeys.[17]

Pythagoras defined three forms of music:

Musica Instrumentalis	the music of instruments that have the power to move us. (Pythagoras the healer, used *musica instrumentalis* as a remedy for every illness.)
Musica Humana	a music unheard but which continuously emanates from the human organism.
Musica Mundana	the music or harmonies of number and geometry made by the movement of the heavenly bodies (the Music of the Spheres).[18]

Plato used the same harmonic ratios that control the heavenly bodies to devise an ideal political society.[19] In his theory of music, Plato defined the numerical ratios between the frequencies of notes and wavelengths to produce naturally harmonious sounds within the context of an octave that can be translated into the geometry expressed in nature. The resultant proportions seen in architecture and heard in music are recognised at both the conscious and subconscious levels and significantly affect our state of mind and emotions.

Music is the expression of ratios. The harmonic relationships between notes are determined by mathematical principles – the pitch of a sound from a plucked string depends on the length of the string and the harmonious sounds that are given off the strings depends on the ratio of the string lengths – these ratios being composed of simple whole numbers.[20] The metaphysical system of the integration of whole numbers and harmonic ratios is expressed in the prime octave, the fifth and the fourth to produce the proportions of 2:1 (octave), 3:2 (fifth) and 4:3 (fourth).

These harmonic musical relationships are to be found in the great works of art and architecture, which accords with Alberti's view that music and geometry are fundamentally the same. Commenting on Pythagoras, Alberti said he reduced symmetry to symphony and harmony of sound to a kind of harmony in sight. In other words, music is geometry translated into sound (see Figure 9.14). A similar view was held by the eighteenth-century German poet, scholar, statesman and mystic Johann Goethe, who described geometry (that is, architecture) as 'frozen music'. When we hear the harmonies of music in a building the geometric harmonies are brought to our subconscious awareness. 'Sacred' geometric volumes and proportions that produce specific sound vibrations will set up varying reverberations within the thorax. Vocal prayers, the singing of hymns, the Buddhist chant of 'Om' or a mantra will resonate with the acoustic qualities of a building to enhance the spiritual experience. The chanting sound 'Om' is held to be a primal vibration: a reflection on Earth of a spiritual realm where the sound is inaudible. 'Om' is thought to be a vibration present in all substances and forms in creation expressing the essence of pure cosmic energy. Or, as

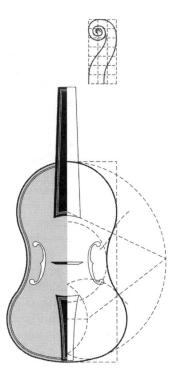

Figure 9.14   The sacred geometric principles of musical instruments

the Hindu mystic Ramakrishna said, 'the Universe is only God repeating his own name to himself'.

Students of the sacred Indian texts of the Rig Veda believe the Hindu mystics expressed the theory of the music of the spheres a few thousand years before Pythagoras. The sacred Hindu mantra 'Nada Brahma' means sound (*Nada*) and God or Creation (*Brahma*) – that is, 'The world is sound' – or, put another way, 'In the beginning was the word'. The Hindu tradition uses a *mantra* (a vocal vibration) in conjunction with a *yantra* (a sacred geometric composition) to produce a powerful, dynamic imagery of matter or physical form as condensed sound. A yantra is an archetypal geometric expression of cosmic unity based on the energies of the masculine and feminine principles symbolised in the Hindu tradition by their gods and goddesses.[21] (See Figure 9.15.)

Sanskrit, the classical literary language of the Hindu scriptures spoken in Northwest India since 1500 BC is still used today as a sacred language. The letters of the alphabet are based on number, geometry and sound, and each letter is a mathematically precise metaphor for occult mysticism. The vibration caused by the sound of the letter creates the actual pattern of the individual letter, and in that sense it is a pure and sacred alphabet. (Information technology scientists chose Sanskrit as the language to be used by computers designed to talk to each other because these inherent properties are not found in any other written script.)

Figure 9.15   The Sri Yantra is a sacred symbol of the Hindu tradition. Each triangle symbolises a god or goddess, representing the spectrum of the masculine and feminine principles that create the energy and power of the universe

Indian and Chinese music appears to be more concerned with the cause rather than the outer effect. The mathematics embodying the sacred, cosmic proportions present in their traditions uses music for spiritual transcendence and uplifts both the listener and musician to higher states of consciousness. Ravi Shanka, probably India's best known exponent of Indian music, plays different chords in the morning, afternoon and evening to help the soul progress to enlightenment throughout the day. The music does not concern itself with melodic, sentimental sounds created solely for entertainment or sheer sensuousness and physicality: it is music as a sacred metaphysical science. To the average Western musician or person interested in music, the numbers and ratios have no esoteric significance: for example Debussy's *La Mer* appeals to the physical, emotional and mental level but not to the spiritual or sacred. This distinction between the sensual and the spiritual is expressed clearly in the *Katha Upanishad*:

> The good is one thing; the sensuously pleasant is another. These two, differing in their ends, both prompt to action. Blessed are they that choose the good; they that choose the sensuously pleasant miss the goal. Both the good and the pleasant present themselves to men. The wise, having examined both, distinguish the one from the other. The wise prefer the good to the pleasant; the foolish, driven by fleshly desires, prefer the pleasant to the good. [22]

Modern science has rediscovered that traditional harmonic intervals and chords do indeed have unique qualities. For example, while making a list of the elements in ascending order of their atomic weights, John A. Newlands discovered that at every eighth element a distinct repetition of properties was revealed. This is now known in modern chemistry as the Law of Octaves. Swiss scientist and doctor Hans Jenny photographed smoke, fluids and powders he subjected to sounds and found that they created the same extraordinary, orderly shapes, patterns and arrangements to be seen in nature. He called this new science *Cymatics* – meaning 'wave'. The study of vibrations at every level in the cosmos – from the molecule to the solar system and beyond – suggests that some universal law of vibrational energy is operating through-out creation based on the laws of physics, numerological relationships, geometry and harmonic ratios present in living organisms. It has also been discovered that suba-tomic particles react to 'nodes of resonance' which are like interference patterns of various frequencies that vibrate about twenty octaves above or twenty octaves below our range of hearing. Vibration is the very essence of all natural phenomena: our electrical brainwave activity and all our senses are based on varying frequencies of vibration. Sound provides us with a sense of balance and by listening at the deepest, unconscious level we keep in tune with the Earth and the heavenly bodies tuning to their own rhythms and 'music'.

In the early nineteenth century Chladni discovered that when soundwaves were played on sand, syrup, iron filings, paste and other substances, they would change shape according to the pitch and resonance of the vibration frequency. Making vibrating waves visible shows patterns and the dimensions of change – like the organic concentric circles of tree rings and zebra stripes, hexagonal grids like honey-comb packing, wheel spokes like jelly fish and vanishing spirals. All these could be reproduced so that archetypal sound patterns reflected the actual life forms express-ing meaningful numerological, proportional and symmetrical qualities.

The early Chinese, Hindus, Egyptians and Greeks used singing and instrumental music in their temples of worship and theatres to complement poetry and drama. As mentioned earlier, Pythagoras also recognised the emotional and healing effect of music on the body and mind but also understood that music expressed in terms of the 'divine science' of number, geometry and proportional ratios reflected the coherence and inter-relatedness of the cosmos, nature and human beings. This occult interpreta-tion and understanding of musical proportions in art and architecture has been discarded since the seventeenth century when the decline in the mystical tradition created a breakdown between art, science and philosophy. Each went their separate ways and now music is established as an 'art' form exclusively for leisure and aesthetic enjoyment.

Tonal music – that is, music which is *in tune* with the universe – has been researched and found to be healing and to enhance the regeneration of body, mind and spirit of individuals and society as a whole. The cells of living tissue are responsive to the power of sound. Atonal music will produce the opposite, negative effect. When the body is undergoing stress and anxiety, or when subjected to an abnormally high volume of music, the heart beats rapidly, blood vessels constrict, pupils dilate, skin pales and stomach, intestines and oesophagus are seized in spasm due to the hormone epinephr-ine being shot into the bloodstream to counterbalance the cause of the stress. A three-year study showed that a person under constant pressure from the sound of 70 decibels will suffer from vascular constriction. Harmonic (sacred) music played at an acceptable volume can induce plants to grow, hens to lay more eggs and cows to give more milk. In one experiment rats were given a choice of two boxes. In one box the rats could listen to Bach; in the other they could listen to a rock band. The rats spent all the time in the Bach box. Russian and Canadian experiments on wheat seedlings showed those treated with quality sound grew three times as large as those left untreated.

When a sound or a building is discordant – meaning it does not conform to the laws of harmonic ratios – we will experience disturbance and displeasure. Hence the analogy of music and architectural proportions (symmetry and eurythmy). Therefore, if the master builders/architects understood and expressed the same source of harmonic ratios, patterns and proportions found in the grand architecture of the universe, their buildings would reflect the divine cosmic order and beauty. In other words, if the design and every part of the fabric of the building – whether a humble dwelling, palace, theatre or temple – recreates the same proportional principles, it will be uplifting, revitalising and satisfying to the soul. We will subliminally sense the subtle, vibrational resonances that unify and integrate us with nature and the world about us.

The patterns and rhythms of natural phenomena reflect the source of the unity of all things. This ancient holistic view of the universe was based on the premise that All is One and everything within it is interconnected: the Whole is not only mirrored in each of its parts, but each part contains within it a reflection of all the other parts – the principle of a modern hologram. The message from Vitruvius is that as the proportions of the body of man reflect a divine will, so the proportions of architecture should reflect the divine order of the cosmos. Luca Pacioli expressed the same view in *De Divina Proportione* that from the human body (the microcosm) derive all measures found in the universe (the macrocosmic) by which God reveals the sacred secrets.[23]

The fundamental axiom of this perennial wisdom is that there is an inner determination for all appearances and manifested forms. There are covert (sacred) layers of meaning expressed as mystical proportions unified by the mathematical sciences of number, geometry, music and cosmology which reflect the structure of the universe and all living organisms.

As above, so below

Life is governed by the daily cycles of the light of day and the dark of night. When the Megalithic peoples became farmers they needed to understand the changing seasons and when to plant, reap and sow, which evolved a knowledge of time and mathematics that enabled them to design massive astrological instruments to accurately predict the movement of the heavens. The 365-day yearly cycle, the 13 lunar months each with a 28-day period that divided into 4 equal periods of 7 were the only numbers needed to produce a circular 'calendar' to provide all the information required to understand the basic mathematics of the heavenly bodies. This knowledge was kept secret by the priests to maintain and boost their power and wealth. (The Egyptian word for priest meant 'star watcher'.)

In his *Book I*, on astronomy and astrology, Vitruvius describes the geometry for making a device for ascertaining the wind direction when planning a new city. He says:

employing mathematical theories and geometrical methods, discovered from the course of the Sun, the shadows cast by an equinoctial gnomon, and the inclination of the heaven that the circumference of the Earth is two hundred and fifty-two thousand stadia, that is, thirty-one million five hundred thousand paces, and observing that eighth part of this, occupied by a wind, is three million, nine hundred and thirty-seven thousand five hundred paces, they should not be surprised to find that a single wind, ranging over so wide afield, is subject to shifts this way and that, leading to a variety of breezes.[24]

Initiates of the sacred sciences would have recognised these precise measurements as coded numbers for planning a new city, designed according to a divine pattern to create an environment where human beings would feel at ease and integrated with the world. St John's 'New Jerusalem', Plato's 'Magnesia' and his 'Republic' were ideal political states, planned and governed according to esoteric principles based upon the laws or canon of proportion and the harmonic ratios of music, geometry and arithmetic. Even the maximum number of inhabitants and the acres of land occupied were determined according to the sacred sciences.

In *The Dimensions of Paradise*, John Michell describes how human beings have attempted to recreate a heavenly city on Earth to reflect cosmic patterns and order.[25-] Vitruvius' dimensions were expressed in ancient units of measurement that correspond with other known units of antiquity. The imperial measurement of yards, feet and inches evolved from earlier sacred measurements based on the dimensions and proportions found in the human body and the natural order. The Egyptian Royal *ell* or *cubit*, once deciphered, makes the dimensions of the Great Pyramid more readily understood and reconcilable, indicating that all ancient systems were based on the measure of the Earth, man and nature. The nineteenth-century British poet Percy Bysshe Shelley in *Prometheus Unbound* said: 'speech created thought which is the measure of the universe'. Over 2,000 years earlier the Greek philosopher, Heraclitus (535–475 BC), believed that the quest of wisdom was to understand the eternal dynamic principle that everything is always changing. In contrast, the modern metric system was imposed upon Europe at the time of the French revolution when the zealots of 'reason and logic' deliberately set out to find a measurement unlike any previously known system. Originally, the revolution also wanted to change the calendar to a 10-month year and a 20-hour day, which also defied any relationship with the natural phases of the Sun, Moon and nature. Fortunately this was resisted, but the Republic still imposed heavy penalties on those who did not conform to the new metric system of weights and measures. Apparently Napoleon lifted the severity of enforcement, but, despite violent reactions from the people, the metric system survived and spread to other parts of Europe, eventually penetrating the British Isles. The metric system is symptomatic of the decline in our understanding and relationship with nature and the universe.

Computer analysis of the design and alignments of ancient structures such as Stonehenge and the pyramids of Egypt has shown how advanced these cultures were in complex mathematics, geometry, divine proportions and their understanding of the movement of heavenly bodies. Their spiritual 'science' attributed human beings with the four-fold characteristics corresponding to the four elements – fire, earth, air, water – representing the spiritual, physical, intellectual and emotional realms of existence. Consistent with the series of numbers, harmonic progressions and geometry related to the phases of the Moon, Sun cycles and changing patterns in the sky, the ancients evolved a philosophy that integrated astrology/astronomy with religion that appears to have been a worldwide phenomenon expressed as the journey of the soul to a reincarnated afterlife in the constellation of stars – the transition from life on Earth to an eternal existence in heaven.

In addition to Bauval and Gilbert's *The Orion Mystery*,[26] Graham Hancock's *Fingerprints of the Gods* and *Heaven's Mirror*,[27] Greg Rigby's *On Earth as it is in Heaven*,[28] Robin Heath's *Sun, Moon and Stonehenge*,[29] others have set out their views that the prehistoric stone circles of Britain, the Sphinx and Pyramids of Giza, the pyramids of the Incas, the temples of Angkor Wat in Cambodia and the major cathedrals of France are not only linked by a common measurement related to the geometry and distances of the Earth and the planets, they also reflect the patterns of certain constellations in the sky, thereby replicating the macrocosmic realm of heaven on Earth. (Plutarch said that Eratosthenes, the famous Alexandrian astronomer, was the first man to calculate the circumference of the Earth in *c*.255 BC.) Furthermore, according to Hancock, the dimensions and geometry of the buildings are a set of codes that 'record' the astronomical data and this, in turn, relates to the date of 10500 BC when a series of cataclysmic disasters, including the 180° reversal of the Earth's magnetic pole, changed the face of the planet and destroyed a 'Golden Civilisation'.

The abovementioned authors produce compelling evidence that the Sphinx reflects the constellation of Leo, the Great Pyramids of Egypt reflect Orion, and the temple of Angkor Wat reflects the pattern of the constellation of Draco. Likewise, the mysterious Nazca lines and gigantic depictions of animals and birds on the plains of Peru may also be connected to the zodiacal symbols given to groupings of stars in the sky. The Nazca lines were formed in the desert and are thought to have been created as early as the first century BC. They remain a mystery but it is believed that the straight lines and other human figures of animals were designed for some astrological representation. It is difficult to imagine how the Nazca people could produce such wonderful art without being able to view it from the air!

Medieval astrology was also essentially a practical device by which church builders attempted to relate earth patterns to cosmic patterns to create their heaven on Earth. In *The Mysteries of Chartres Cathedral*, Louis Charpentier's analysis of the sacred geometry of the cathedral reveals a correspondence with the heavenly constellations. He also reveals how the seven stars of Ursa Major are mirrored by some of the major cathedrals and other ancient shrines in Northern France. Plotting the alignments of a certain number of twelfth- and thirteenth-century cathedrals bearing the name 'Notre Dame' in an anti-clockwise direction, from Chartres to Reims to Amiens to Bayeux to Evreux, there is a remarkable correspondence with the constellation of Virgo (the Virgin) as seen in the sky – that is, Gamma, L'Épi de la Vierge, Zeta, Epsilon respectively with smaller stars falling on the cathedrals of Evreux, Étampes, Laon and Paris. There is even a Notre Dame-de-l'Épine, which was built later and falls under the star L'Épi (see Figure 9.16).

Another example is the pattern of Benedictine abbeys of the Caux region replicating on Earth the form of the Great Bear above.[30]

The entire structure of the Islamic mosque is an expression of astrological symbolism. The cubic main body of the mosque metaphorically expressed the four-squareness, earthiness, and the four elements of the natural world and the illusion of the

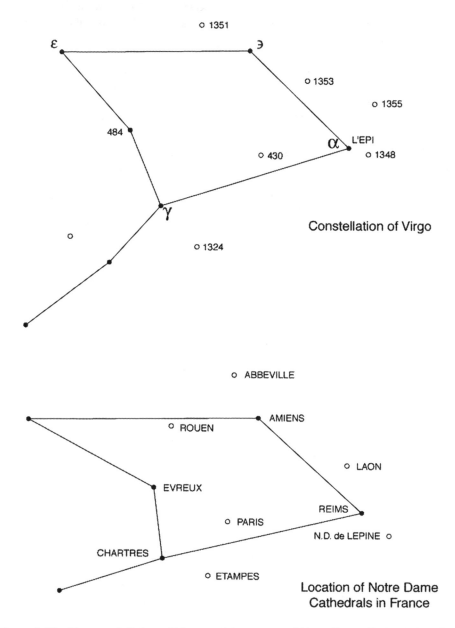

Figure 9.16   The constellation of Virgo and the pattern of Notre Dame Cathedrals in France

senses. The dome represents the heavens and the spiritual realms of eternal truths. A circular dome can be built over a square cube by a series of corbelling in the form of an octagon. In esoteric geometry, the octagon is said to be the transitional geometry uniting the realms of heaven and Earth. In Christian cathedrals octagonal-shaped fonts, octagonal floor patterns and plan form of a spire can usually be found.

The cosmic dance

Astronomy is the science of the celestial bodies of the universe. Astrology is the study of the motions and relative positions of the heavenly bodies in terms of their influence on living organisms and human activity. Astronomy and astrology were one and the same art and science until the fifteenth century when the separation began with the Polish scientist Copernicus (1473–1543) who formulated the modern heliocentric theory of the solar system (originally set out much earlier by the ancient Greeks). The paths became more divergent when Italian mathematician Galileo (1564–1642) and German physicist Kepler (1571–1630) supported Copernicus' ideas. Galileo's refracting telescope, and a generation later Newton's seventeenth-century invention for the measuring and positioning of the planets and stars, enabled the sky and the composition of the heavenly bodies to be investigated in detail to give birth to astronomy as a separate science.

The Chaldeans were the great astronomers/astrologers of the ancient world. Astrology passed on from Babylonia to Greece, India, China, the Middle East and eventually arrived in Europe via the Arabs in Spain. Vitruvius mentions the 'illustrious and most renowned Eleusinian school on the island of Kos'[31] where astrology was developed into a highly evolved art and science for the prediction of weather patterns and optimum periods for seed planting, as well as casting natal horoscopes and the study of natural phenomena. The movement of the heavenly bodies, the cyclical, geometric patterns of the 'wandering lights', their changing, radiating powers of influence on life on Earth became a metaphor to unify man, nature, religion and the cosmos.

Vitruvius refers to astrology as a 'natural philosophy'. He lists Thales, Anaxagoras, Pythagoras, Xenophanes and Democritus as men of great genius 'who have, in various ways investigated and left us the laws and the working of the laws by which nature governs it'. He defines the word 'universe' as:

> the general assemblage of all nature. It also means the heavens made up of the constellations and the courses of the stars...there is a broad circular belt composed of the twelve signs, whose stars, arranged in twelve equivalent divisions, represent each a shape which nature has depicted...they are all visible or invisible according to fixed times...(and they)...work and move in the opposite direction, with the laws and numerical relations under which they pass from sign to sign and how they complete their orbits.[32]

The twelve signs form the astrological zodiac marking the Earth's yearly orbit around the Sun. In turn, the Sun orbits the solar system in what is known as the *precession cycle*, or Great Year (sometimes called the Platonic Year by astrologers). The effect of precession is like the rotation of a spinning top around its axis: at first it is vertical but as the top slows down it begins to *precess* about its original position. This action causes the gradual westward motion of the equinoxes around the ecliptic or annual path of the Sun and the Earth's axis of rotation due mainly to the gravitational pull of the Sun and Moon on the 'bulge' at the equator. The axis precesses over a period of 25,920 years until returning to the original starting point, hence the progressive change or 'slippage' of the position of the point of the rising Sun when observed from Earth and the progressive change of the Earth's relative position to the constellations in the night sky. By contrast, the Moon orbits the Earth every 27 to 32 days: it takes 18 years and 7 months to complete its ecliptic cycle.

Ancient astrologers tracked sunrise position against the background constellation and discovered that it changes as the Earth progressively moves anti-clockwise in a grand orbit which, in astrological terms, means our planet passes from one of the twelve 'houses' or 'ages' to the next every 2,150 years. We have just transited from Pisces (the symbol and era of Christianity) to the present Age of Aquarius (the water bearer and replenisher of the Earth). The pre-Christian period of about 2,000 years before Christ was marked by the Age of Aries, the astrological sign of fire and intellect symbolised by the Ram and Mars; a period dominated by the Greek and Roman conquests and great works of art and philosophy. Taurus, the Bull, and the sign of beauty and solidarity personified the age of the Egyptian dynasties and Stonehenge in the period from about 4000 to 2000 BC. Before this, up to 6000 BC was the Age of Gemini, when ancient religions became established and forms of writing were developed in China and Egypt. Farming and fertility rites were well established in the previous Age of Cancer, a sign 'ruled' by the Moon and the culture of 'Mother Earth'. The precession to Leo takes us into the Stone Age period of about 10,000 BC. Leo the Lion also represented the Sun and this dated the period of the cave paintings and social communities of our early Megalithic ancestors.

Ancient monuments such as the pyramids at Giza and Stonehenge relate to the pattern of stars at the time they were being built. Now, with the benefit of the Sky Globe and Red Shift computerised system (see page XXX), at any one time researchers can study the changing constellations in the sky due to precession over thousands of years. This has led to a review of the traditional dating of the Sphinx, a solid rock carving of a lion now dated as far back as the Age of Leo, about 12,000 years ago. Evidence of erosion when Egypt was a heavy rainfall region lends credibility to this revised dating.

Traditionally, the horoscope (*horo* = hour or time) was an astrological chart for predicting the most auspicious timing of an event. A Hermetic law says that inherent in the beginning of something there is a blueprint for the unfolding of future events and the ultimate outcome. For example, if an apple seed – which contains the blueprint for the tree – is planted at the wrong time of the month, in the wrong month of the year and in the wrong place, the quality of the fruit will be impaired. Therefore, the auspiciousness of the timing when something is inaugurated is an essential factor affecting the outcome.

In the thirteenth century, a college specialising in the study of astrology was set up in Paris. The subject became standard in other European universities until the Age of Enlightenment about 300 years ago when the teaching of metaphysics, philosophy and astrology were no longer taught in the general syllabus. Since the seventeenth century, physicists and astronomers have tended to ignore astrology as being unworthy of study. However, until the 1600s the Royal Observatory in Greenwich was still an authority and source for preparing horoscopes for military leaders, businesspeople and people from all walks of life. Doctors would study a patient's astrological chart before prescribing treatment. Throughout the ages, wherever you were living – in Western Europe, the Americas, Middle East, India, China – if you were about to embark on some new course of action or enterprise, such as getting married or going to war, it was considered to be prudent to first consult the local astrologer to establish the most auspicious time.

Reference to the astrological signs of fire, earth, air and water is often to be found in Gothic cathedrals. These four elements are represented by a lion (Leo), a bull (Taurus), a man with a pitcher (Aquarius) and an eagle (Scorpio, the higher plane of the scorpion being the eagle). The Gospels of St Matthew, St Mark, St Luke and St John were written in the key of air, fire, earth and water. Presumably, modern orthodox Christianity rejects astrology as unacceptable to the Christian faith because of the popular association with fortune telling, however there are distinct astrological references to be found at Chartres Cathedral in the Madeleine of Vézelay, the Baptisteries in Florence, Bergamo and Parma, and on the fresco cycles of Salone of Padua and the Schiffanoia Palace in Ferrara. Even the oldest Jewish temple in Jerusalem has a floor mosaic depicting the 12 signs of the zodiac, each represented by a figure of a man yet not one of them circumcised!

Master historian of art and the occult, Fred Gettings, uncovered the secrets of the Florentine church San Miniato al Monte built in AD 1207. In his book *The Sacred Zodiac– the Hidden Art in Medieval Astrology,* he reveals how the thirteenth-century masons used the orientation of the church, the sunlight, lapidary inscriptions, art forms and secret methods of writing to embody one united creation of art, symbolism, philosophy, theology and architecture. The key to this magnificent arcane puzzle is the constellational zodiac on the floor of the nave.[33]

Religion and astrology are more overtly expressed in the Indian Hindu temples where shrines to planets feature with various deities such as the elephant-headed Ganesh – the god of astrology and good fortune. Although Eastern and Western astrology sprang from the same ancient source, the Indian Vedic system considered the moon sign more significant than the sun sign. (The East views the Sun to be a 'hostile' rather than a positive force or energy.)

The tradition – some may call it 'old wives' tale' – of planting crops according to the phases of the Moon has been practised for the past two decades by Nicholas Joly, the owner of a vineyard producing one of the most highly regarded and expensive white wines of France, the Coulée de Serrant. Joly discovered that the time of the new Moon, when everything is at a slower pulse, is the best period for fermentation. When the Moon, on the wane, causes least disturbance he bottles the wine. Other treatments to the vines are carried out when the Moon is full and on specific dates depending upon the whereabouts of the Moon within particular 'houses' of the zodiac. (If the Moon can cause billions of tons of tidal water to rise and fall twice a day it seems likely the huge oceans are not the only natural phenomenon affected.)

Mainstream astrology is being reintroduced into British universities in Manchester, Plymouth and London's Warburg Institute. Southampton has also formed a research group to investigate the effect of planetary movements on human behaviour. The group is particularly interested in the theory that at birth, a baby's pineal gland becomes sensitised to the electromagnetic forces emanating from the planets. Their scientific tests may throw some light on astrology's historical associations with archaeology, sociology and anthropology. The group will also analyse results from 12,000 people suffering mental illnesses that seem to have correlations with astrological predictions. In the United States, the Kepler College of Astrological Arts and Sciences in Seattle offers an academic BA degree course in Astrology.[34]

Astute businesspeople and politicians in the West are realising how market trends and social patterns of behaviour seem to frequently recur in cycles, and a powerful computer programme has been developed to analyse stock-market data linked to planetary movements. As with Feng Shui Dragon Masters, astrologers are now being used to a far greater extent than corporations and politicians are prepared to admit.

The original purpose and integrity of astrology has become grossly trivialised and debased to the level of superstitious fortune telling and predictions, such as when we are likely to meet 'a tall dark stranger'. With the misuse and misunderstanding of the power of the oracles we have lost our awareness of how life and the universe are dominated by rhythms and endless, repeating cycles. During the more recent past, physicists who have studied and recorded the daily variations of the Moon and the Sun's negative effect on the Earth's magnetic field have opened their minds to the view that the energy fields, vibrations and gravitational forces of the heavenly bodies do indeed exert an effect that varies according to their movements and relative positions in the solar system. In other words, their juxtaposition has a significant interaction with all living organisms. Astrophysicist Dr Percy Seymour proposed a model in which the reaction of the planets to the magnetic fields of the Moon, Sun and Earth impinges upon the pineal gland's super sensitivity to weak magnetic field changes. These may create positive or negative resonances and, like the DNA 'blue-print', enable predictions to be made about a likely course of action or event.[35]

As we saw in an earlier chapter, cosmic energy fields also set up the global grid patterns networking the Earth. The conventional image of the universe shows individual star systems separated by huge expanses of emptiness, but many scientists now believe that the emptiness is actually filled by a criss-crossing network of immensely strong gravitational forces that affect the stars and planets. Collapsed stars – black holes – thousands of light years away may be keeping our own solar system in place.[36]

Should the movement of the heavenly bodies be of any concern to the architect of the twenty-first century? At a practical level the correct orientation of a building, the prevailing winds, the daylight penetration and solar heat gain should be simple, elementary factors recognised and taken into account when designing a modern building. But if the orbital patterns of the planets and the Sun and Moon also influence our biological patterns, our waking, sleeping rhythms, our state of mind and every other form of living organism on Earth, our architects should certainly understand, be conscious of and address these dynamic forces of nature.

When we enter many of the surviving buildings of the past we may experience a sense of fulfilment, an inner pleasure – a certain wholeness – which in some measure, may be due to factors other than the geometry of the architecture. For example, the traditional materials used in older buildings naturally create a harmony with the environment; often the rooms are larger; decoration and ornament arrests the eye; the scale of the building may relate to human beings; the building may be sited over positive earth energy fields, and so on. Undoubtedly, all these factors influence our reaction in a pleasing and comfortable manner. However, most modern buildings do not appear to have these inherent factors. Is this because the architects have not designed according to the fundamental principles and not addressed other factors such as terrestrial and cosmic fields? If so, it is therefore not surprising that there is no feeling of comfort, pleasure, rapport or resonance.

References

1. Davies, Paul (1993) *The Mind of God*, London: Penguin Books.
2. Plato, *Timaeus and Critias* (1971), London: Penguin Books.
3. 'Plato's Seventh Letter', *Plato's Phaedrus and Letters*, trans. W. H. Hamilton, London: Penguin Classics.
4. Noted from a slide presentation by Keith Critchlow.
5. KAIROS Lecture by Professor Keith Critchlow.
6. Bligh Bond, F. and Lea, Dr T. S. (1997) 'On geometric truth Part II', *Germatria: A Preliminary Investigation of The Cabala*, London: Rilko, p. 95.
7. Ibid, 'Epigraph'.
8. Edwards, L. (1993) *The Vortex of Life: Nature's Patterns in Time and Space*, Edinburgh: Floris Books.
9. Foster, Keith (2000) 'Pathcurve vortex generators', *The Journal of the British Society of Dowsers*, vol. 39, no. 268 (June), pp. 5–8.
10. Wittkower, R. (1971) *Architectural Principles in the Age of Humanism*, New York: W. W. Norton & Co.
11. Vitruvius (1960) *The Ten Books on Architecture*, Book III, Chapter I, New York: Dover Publications.
12. Schwaller de Lubicz, R. A. (1977) *The Temple in Man*, trans. Robert and Deborah Lawlor, Vermont: Inner Traditions International.
13. Ibid., 'Summary of principles', pp. 46–47.
14. Plato *Timaeus and Critius* (1965), London: Penguin, p. 73.
15. Hall, Manly P. (1977) 'The Pythagorean Theory of Music and Colour', in *The Secret Teachings of All Ages*, Los Angeles: The Philosophical Research Society Inc, pp. LXXXI and LXXXII.
16. Robert Cowley, 'The Great Pyramid, Means and the Pythagorian Lambdoma', *Rilko Journal 57*, autumn/winter 2000, p. 20.
17. Hero, B. (1992) *Lambdoma Unveiled*, Maine: Strawberry Hill Farm Studies.
18. James, J. (1995) *The Music of the Spheres*, New York: Springer-Verlag.
19. Plato (1955) *The Republic*, trans. Sir Desmond Lee, London: Penguin.
20. Levin, M. H. (1994) *The Manual of Harmonics*, Michigan: Phanes Press.
21. Khanna, Madho (1997) *Yantra: the Tantric Symbol of Cosmic Unity*, London: Thames & Hudson.
22. *Katha Upanishad* (1949) 'The Upanishads', vol. 1, trans. Swami Nikhilananda, New York: Ramakrishna-Vivikananda Centre.
23. Pacioli, Luca (1509) *De Divina Proportione*, ed. Constantin Wintervberg 1889, reprinted 1974 in *Quellenschriften Fur Kunstgeschichte un Kunsttechnick des Mirtelalters und der Neozeit*, Hildesheim: Georg Olms Verlag.
24. Vitruvius op. cit., Book I, Chapter VI, Paragraph 9.

25. Michell, J. (1971) *The Dimensions of Paradise*, London: Thames & Hudson.
26. Bauval, R. and Gilbert, A. (1994) *The Orion Mystery*, London: Heinemann.
27. Hancock, G. (1995) *Fingerprints of the Gods*, London: Heinemann; Hancock, G. and Faiia, S. (1998) *Heaven's Mirror*, Harmondsworth: Penguin.
28. Rigby, G. (1996) *On Earth as it is in Heaven*, Guernsey: Rhaedus Publications.
29. Heath, R. (1998) *Sun, Moon and Stonehenge*, Wales: Bluestone Press.
30. Charpentier, L. (1972) *The Mysteries of Chartres Cathedral*, London: Rilko.
31. Vitruvius op. cit., Book IX, Chapter VI, Paragraphs 2 and 3.
32. Vitruvius op. cit., Book IX, Chapter I, Paragraph 2.
33. Gettings, F. (1989) *The Sacred Zodiac – The Hidden Art in Mediæval Astrology*, London: Arkana.
34. Senay Boztas, 'On another planet', *The Sunday Times*, 17 June 2001, p. 14.
35. Seymore, Percy (1992) *The Paranormal: Beyond Sensory Science*, London: Penguin.
36. Comet trails through the solar system in *Reed Cyclopaedia* (1820).

Suggested further reading

Azzam, K. and Critchlow, K. (1997) *The Arch in Islamic Architecture*, London: The Prince of Wales's Institute of Architecture.
Brunes, T. (1967) *The Secrets of Ancient Geometry*, Vols I and II, Copenhagen: Rhodos.
Burckhardt, T. (1977) *Mystical Astrology according to Ibn 'Arabi'*, Gloucestershire: Beshara Publications.
Cooper, J. C. (1982) *Symbolism The Universal Language*, Northants: The Aquarian Press.
Critchlow, K. (1976) *Islamic Patterns*, London: Thames & Hudson.
Critchlow, K. (1987) *Order in Space*, London: Thames & Hudson.
Critchlow, K. (1997) *Proportional Rectangles*, London: The Prince of Wales's Institute of Architecture.
Doczi, G. (1981) *The Power of Limits,* Boston: Shambhala.
Edwards, L. (1982) *The Field of Form*, Edinburgh: Floris Books.
Flegg, G. (1984) *Numbers*, Harmondsworth: Penguin.
Ghyka, M. (1997) *The Geometry of Art and Life*, New York: Dover.
Godwin, J. (1987) *Harmonies of Heaven and Earth*, London: Thames & Hudson.
Guthrie, K. S. (1987) *The Pythagorean Source Book & Library*, Michigan: Phanes Press.
Hambridge, J. (1967) *Elements of Dynamic Symmetry*, New York: Dover.
Hancox, J. (1992) *The Byrom Collection*, London: Jonathan Cape.
Hersey, G. L. (1980) *Pythagorean Palaces,* Ithaca: Cornell University Press.
Huntley, H. (1970) *The Divine Proportion*, New York: Dover.
I Ching, trans. Richard Wilhelm, Routledge & Kegan Paul, London, 1975
Ivins W. M. Jnr, (1964) *Art & Geometry*, New York: Dover.
James, J. (1995) *Music of the Spheres*, London: Abacus.
Javine, F. and Bunker, D. (1971) *Numerology and the Divine Triangle*, Pennsylvania: Para Research Inc.
Marchant, P. (1997) *Unity in Pattern*, London: The Prince of Wales's Institute of Architecture.
McClain, I. (1984) *The Myth of Invariance*, Maine: Nicolas-Hays Inc.
McClain, I. (1984) *The Pythagorean Plato*, Maine: Nicolas-Hayes Inc.
Michell, J. (1981) *Ancient Metrology*, Bristol: Pentacle Books.
Michell, J. and Rhone, C. (1991) *Twelve Tribe Nations*, London: Thames & Hudson.
Nasr, Seyyed (1993) *An Introduction to Islamic Cosmological Doctrines*, Albany: State University of New York Press.
Pennick, N. (1982) *The Mysteries of Kings College Chapel*, Northants: The Aquarian Press.
Pennick, N. (1994) *Sacred Geometry*, Berkshire: Capall Bann Publishing.
Raleigh, A. S. (1987) *Occult Geometry & Hermetic Science of Motion & Number*, California: De Vorss & Co.
Raleigh, H. S. (1991) *Occult Geometry*, California: DeVorss & Co.
Stirling, W. (1981) *The Canon*, Research into Lost Knowledge Organisation (Rilko).
Tame, D. (1984) *The Secret Power of Music*, New York: Destiny Books.

10.
Arcane tradition

What is sacred architecture?

What is meant by *sacred geometry* or *sacred architecture*? In the language of the perennial wisdom, 'sacred' means that whatever the overt expression of the building, music, painting or other graphic symbol may be, it also has a hidden, covert meaning that expresses the profound spiritual or philosophical concept that was the source of its inspiration.

Every sacred art is…founded on a science of forms…on the symbolism inherent in forms…a symbol is not merely a conventional sign. It manifests its archetype by virtue of a definite ontological law…according to the spiritual view of the world, the beauty of an object is nothing but the transparency of its existential envelopes; an art worthy of the name is beautiful because it is true. It is neither possible nor even useful that every artist or craftsman engaged in sacred art should be conscious of the Divine Law inherent in forms; he will know only certain aspects of it, or certain applications that arise within the limits of the rules of his craft; these rules will enable him to paint an icon, to fashion a sacred vessel or to practise calligraphy in a liturgically valid manner, without its being necessary for him to know the ultimate significance of the symbols he is working with. It is tradition that transmits the sacred models and the working rules, and thereby guarantees the spiritual validity of the forms. Tradition has within itself a secret force which is communicated to an entire civilisation and determines even arts and crafts the immediate objects of which include nothing particularly sacred. One of the most tenacious of typically modern prejudices is the one that sets itself up against the impersonal and objective rules of art, for fear that they should stifle creative genius. In reality no work exists that is traditional, and therefore 'bound' by changeless principles, which does not give sensible expression to a certain creative joy of the soul; whereas modern individualism has produced, apart from a few works of genius which are nevertheless spiritually barren, all the ugliness – the endless and despairing ugliness – of the forms which permeate the 'ordinary life' of our times.

One of the fundamental conditions of happiness is to know that everything that one does has a meaning in eternity; but who in these days can still conceive of a civilisation within which all vital manifestations would be developed 'in the likeness of Heaven'?[1]

In a sacred building, function and form are unified by the source stemming from the seed of inner meaning. For example, at a subconscious level the psyche is aware of the defining geometry of a building or a vase but only those who have been initiated into the metaphoric language will fully understand the underlying, symbolic meaning. The term 'sacred architecture' is therefore a quality that can apply to all building types and is not confined necessarily to buildings used for religious ceremony. In contrast, the term 'profane' – which stems from *pro*, meaning 'outside', and *fanum*, meaning 'temple' or 'sacred place' – denotes that which is not initiated into the inner mysteries.

When the master builders applied the secret mysteries of the symbolic system of number and geometry to generate the entire design of their buildings – the 'bones' of the building if you like – the building's 'soul' inherently expressed the laws of nature in tune to resonate with the actual bones or body and spirit of human beings. The cosmos, nature and all living organisms are 'built' on the same fundamental principles of sacred geometry. When we enter such buildings we feel connected in time and space.

The geometric analysis of, say, a Greek temple, a Gothic cathedral or a Palladian villa, or indeed any other great work of architecture, reveals a proportional relationship consistent throughout the building. As Rudolf Wittkower found, in considering the most remarkable architectural productions of all periods, 'Harmony, the essence of beauty, consists…(of)…the relationship of the parts to each other and to the whole, and, in fact, a single system of proportion permeates the façade, and the place and size of every single part and details is fixed and defined by it'.[2]

In a sacred building, the plans, sections and elevations are designed according to a fundamental geometric strategy and certain proportional ratios that determine the line and rhythm of structural columns, the height of rooms, the siting of windows and doors, the position of an altar or the reception counter in an entrance hall and so on. The proportions of a room or architectural concept affecting our mood or emotional attitudes is largely to do with the natural affinity with proportions and harmonic ratios of the human body. For example, where a room has been designed according to a selected dynamic harmonic ratio, and every part of that room – its architectural features and decoration – relate to that ratio (in the same way as a piece of music relates to a key), the subliminal mind registers the geometric proportions and these will resonate with the human body's own coordinating proportions.

Perhaps because Andrea Palladio's work of the sixteenth-century Renaissance has survived and his philosophy well illustrated in his book *I Quattro Libri dell' Architectura* (The Four Books of Architecture),[3] he is considered to be one of the great architects and most initiated of the period whose designs incorporated the divine harmonic proportions of antiquity. Each project would be assigned a proportional 'key', such as 1:2 (octave) or 3:2 (fifth) or 4:3 (fourth), depending on what 'mood' or 'spirit'

Palladio wished to invoke. Each architectural drawing would be inscribed with the 'key' – such as 3:2 – for that particular building design, including the landscape, setting, plans, sections, elevations and interior design, to ensure his assistants working on a specific project would be left in no doubt as to the proportional ratio basis of the whole concept. (Inigo Jones used the double cube as the key for the design of Wilton House, England.) The building was thus *tuned* according to the Pythagorean musical harmonic proportions (see Chapter 9). Palladio also recommended seven volumes for rooms that were most appropriate for the 'mood' or 'state of mind'. Each example described the method for designing the most harmonious length and width of the heights related to the plan of the room. Proportions – the equality of two ratios – or number sequences are progressions known as 'means'. The three ratios are:

Arithmetic	1, 2, 3, 4, 5, 6...
Geometric	1, 2, 4, 8, 16, 32...
Harmonic	1, 1/2, 1/3, 1/4, 1/5, 1/6

These ratios, or laws, are the foundation governing our perceptions of beauty, our experiences of delight and our sense of aesthetic pleasure. Subconsciously – intuitively – we tend to lean towards choices, preferences and patterns of behaviour conforming to the ratios repeated in organic growth formations.

The design, construction and tuning of musical instruments also follow the same Platonic and Vitruvian principles of sacred geometry and harmonic proportions based on the measurements in man and the whole of nature to create the sound resonating from the 'soul'. Each instrument should be aesthetically appealing as well as being geometrically and harmonically symmetrical; it must be acoustically tuned by correctly proportioning the length of strings to the sound box and generally every component would have a purpose and function, leaving nothing superfluous. It must also be ergonomically designed to fit the person playing the instrument. In other words the shape, form and design evolved from the purpose, function, use and *raison d'être* of the instrument to create a specific sound or 'key'.[4]

Perennial wisdom suggests that architects should plan their work according to the systems of proportion and harmonic ratios in the same manner as a music composer would plan a symphony. A key should be selected and every part of the composition would then relate harmonically and rhythmically according to the predetermined 'symmetry'. All the dimensions, volumes and areas, once predetermined by the 'key', would ensure that everything – the siting, the landscaping, the building, including its individual rooms and features – would be in proportional relationship to the whole and the whole would correspond to the metaphysical patterns found in man, nature and the cosmos. Harmonic proportions not only affect the acoustical properties of the room to create enjoyable sounds, they will also be a delight for our eyes and the psyche. The master builders understood the universal harmonies of music determined by the intervals and consonance of the scale, and translated these ratios into the geometry of their buildings to resonate with the harmonies of the natural world: hence Goethe's idea that architecture (geometry) is frozen music. However, the mere application of the sacred laws alone will not suffice without the inspiration of the architect. It needs that divine spark of genius within all of us to create a work of art.

Sacred resonance

Vitruvius also held the view that the microcosmic/macrocosmic correspondences, proportions and harmonic ratios expressed throughout the natural world should be the basis – the *key* – for determining the dimensions, shapes and volumes of a building. It follows that in such buildings the body and soul will experience uplifting, subtle, subliminal visual and acoustic resonances. Thus the study of music theory, scales and harmonic proportions (including architectural proportions) – that is, symmetry and eurythmy – was essential for any student architect. A knowledge of the consonance and disconsonance of sounds was the basis of architectural design in which the exterior *and* interior were harmonious in themselves as well as having a harmonious relationship with each other.

Vitruvius gives practical instructions on how to avoid acoustic interference in a theatre and carefully notes the science of the sound of the human voice: 'The ancient architects, following in the footsteps of nature, perfected the ascending rows of seats in theatres from their investigations of the ascending voice, and, by means of the canonical theory of mathematicians and that of the clearness and sweetness to the ears of the audience. For just as musical instruments are brought to perfection of clearness in the sound of their strings by means of bronze plates or horn, so the ancients devised methods of increasing the power of the voice in theatres through application of harmonics'.[5] He also describes the placing of bronze vessels in niches to amplify the sound, using mathematical principles to determine the volume of the vessels so that they were proportional to the size of the theatre. The vessels were arranged in accordance with harmonic laws and thus the voice from centre-stage could spread and strike the cavities of the different vessels to increase the clarity of the sound and 'make a harmonious note in the unison with itself'.[6] When touched, they produce with one another the notes of the fourth, the fifth, and so on up to the double octave. Vitruvius noted that if the theatre is large the height should be divided into four parts so that the horizontal niches are constructed to produce one for the enharmonic, the other for the chromatic, the third for the diatonic system and omitting sound vessels on the middle tier as no other note in the chromatic system forms a natural concord of sound. Using these same laws of music, he describes how siege machine catapults were primed by tuning the stretch of the strings 'to the proper pitch by musical sense of hearing'.[7]

An example of sacred music – the music 'of the soul' – created by the architectural manifestation of harmonic geometry can be heard in the Romanesque abbey in the village of Le Thoronet, which lies a few kilometres above St Tropez, north of the autoroute between Le Muy and Le Lac in the south of France. It was founded as a monastery in 1135 by the Cistercians and for a number of years has been occupied by a sect of nuns. The simple stone building, comprising a vaulted nave and a single window above the altar with a pair of niches on either side, is bereft of decoration, ornament or furniture except for rough wooden benches in the transepts. As one steps into the building there is a 'demand' for silence and however softly and silently one treads and moves there is a concern not to disturb the serenity. Before mass, without a sound, twenty or so nuns dressed in grey hooded habits glide into the nave and begin the most haunting, angelic chanting. The whole building resonates with harmonic overtones that can be felt vibrating through every fibre of the body.

Like a musical instrument, Thoronet was designed to create an extraordinary acoustical quality for the human voice. Apparently, from time to time, concerts are performed in the nave but it has been found that modern instruments produce a disturbing sound. Several years ago, Professor Keith Critchlow, the founder of educational charity Kairos, received permission to measure the building and discovered the geometry of the nave is in the ratio of 1:2 (the octave) and the golden proportion *Phi* (Φ) of the vaulted ceiling produces the 'heavenly choir' effect and the equal volume and quality of sound throughout. When writing of his experiences of Thoronet in *Parabola* magazine in 1994, another faculty member of Kairos, philosopher and author Professor Robert Lawlor, said:

> I don't know why the acoustics at this particular location in the nave reproduce the effects of a sphere. Perhaps it is a residual effect of the round vaulted arch. More speculatively, it may have been an intention of the great Masonic mystic geometer Achard, who was a close associate of St Bernard. In sacred geometry, the sphere – the circle – represents the perfect, unmanifested unity, while phi (Φ) the Golden Section represents the Creator's conscious power of self-division which, by rupturing unity, produces the universe. This unique proportion reproduces the perfection and glory of the original unity through oscillating geometric progressions, (which we may think of as evolution) in the manifested, divided Universe... Whether or not this particular acoustical effect is simply coincidence, it is certain that from the darkest times, sacred geometry has been able to express the mystic relationships between phi (Φ), the function of division, and pi (π) the function of the circle or unity.
>
> In choosing musical ratios as the basis for architectural proportions the Cistercian masons were in effect unifying the objective visual world and the emotionally experienced sensations of sound. This related their work to the tradition of acoustic temples in widely separate cultures and epochs, from India to ancient Egypt and Mesopotamia, to Greece and Celtic Britain.[8]

We have become a society dominated by the visual images of TV, the cinema, photographic pictures in every magazine and newspaper, virtual reality and computer technology. 'One picture is worth a thousand words' sums up our reliance on the eye for communication but often the visual images we are seeing may become distorted or inaccurate depending upon the quality of our eyesight and our conscious or subconscious reactions, whereas with hearing we can instantly recognise and precisely distinguish the most subtle variations of tone without necessarily becoming intellectually involved. The ear has three times as many nerve connections with the brain than has the eye with the brain. We depend on the ear for balance and spacial orientation. The ear is an organ of superb accuracy whereas often the eye can only approximate – 'the eye compares and estimates; the ear measures'. Undoubtedly, sound can have a far greater impact on our emotions and state of mind and when audible sound – music – follows the law of harmonic ratios, our perceptions resonate with delight and harmony. The relationship is described as the link between the outer measured form (arithmetic) and the inner harmonic ratios that are unified by the geometric principles governing everything in the universe.

The purpose of *sacred space* is to provide nutritive food, charging the body with the energy of universal harmonies. Without the knowledge, the precision of Pythagoras' geometry and the proportional scales of music, the temples and cathedrals of the past could not have produced ethereal, uplifting sounds such as at Thoronet.

The eye does not crave for decoration. The Romanesque churches had no ornament, but whether the observer is a worshipper or tourist, such buildings produce a serene calmness and a profound sense of mystery which emanates from the sacred geometry – the harmonic proportions appealing directly to psyche. Modern buildings do not need applied decoration or to be dressed up in some pastiche style. The psyche delights in pure form and line but for any design to be fulfilling and satisfying at a level beyond mere superficiality, a work of art must remind us of our bond with nature and the universe. We have an 'all-knowing' mind that registers these occult vibrations. The very existence of such energy fields can no longer be dismissed as the fanciful imaginings of the ancient mystics. Advanced modern science confirms the view that the 'vibrations' exist and the subliminal mind – the psyche – can see, hear, feel and resonate with these geometric patterns and harmonic ratios.

Chartres Cathedral

One of the finest examples of a sacred building in the West is Chartres Cathedral. My first introduction to the most intriguing, enigmatic expressions of the transcendental language of symbolism that has been embodied in the location, numbers, geometry, construction and the very fabric of the building, decoration and carvings was one of Professor Keith Critchlow's lectures on the Cathedral. Here there is no 'art for art's sake' – every form and element of Chartres had a practical significance as well as expressing a covert (sacred) teaching of the masters of esoteric mysticism of the Neo-Platonist School who inspired and created the Cathedral to reflect the divine universe. The building has a magnetic power to draw you into its presence. However often I go there, there is a need to return, knowing there will be yet another discovery to deepen the sense of the extraordinary insights and mystical knowledge that was manifested in such beautiful, material terms.

The provincial, self-contained town of Chartres lies in the great plain of Beauce, about 45 minutes or so by train from Paris. The cathedral stands in the centre of the town, on a slight mound: below is an ancient maze of caverns, a grotto and spring about 30 metres (100 feet) or so below the crypt. The rural countryside is littered with Megalithic stone circles, obelisks and dolmens. Centuries before the Christian era, Chartres was an important shrine for Celtic pilgrims and others who came from far afield in the East, making their extremely hazardous journeys to bathe in the positive earth energy fields, take the healing waters and spend time in the grotto in prayer and penance. In the ruins of the shrine, the Christians found an old Druidic statue carved in pear wood, blackened with age. It was christened the 'Holy Black Virgin' and dedicated to the church. A Romanesque basilica, built over the older ruins above the grotto, was destroyed by fire in the eleventh century and the building of the new church was also destroyed by fire. In 1194 the devoted people of the town decided they were going to put their heart, soul and energies into the awesome task of rebuilding, and it was they who quarried the stones, cut the timbers and carried out the hard manual work for the master masons and sculptors. The cathedral that now stands was consecrated in 1260 (the north tower is a sixteenth-century addition).

Chartres is one of several other Gothic cathedrals in the region dedicated to Notre Dame, and as mentioned earlier forms a pattern on the ground that mirrors the constellation of Venus – the Virgin – in the sky to symbolise a heavenly paradise, a 'City of Jerusalem' on Earth (see Figure 9.16). But why is Chartres not precisely orientated as other cathedrals on the four cardinal points; why are the West Front towers so different in height and design; why are there no scenes or sculptures of the crucifixion; why are there sculptures of pagan Greek philosophers; why has the pavement labyrinth been 'covered up' by the Church authorities; why, whatever the time of day – even at dusk – and whatever the weather, be it dull or sunny outside, is the Cathedral always bathed in an opalescent spectre of light?

Studies of some early cathedrals reveal that the basic alignment of the nave often coincides with a geodetic line along the central aisle and ends in a blind spring at the chancel steps, at right-angles to the transepts. The first of many anomalies is why Chartres does not follow the tradition of aligning the building on a precise North–South and East–West axis. The apparently arbitrary orientation of 46° 54' to the northeast was determined by the natural magnetic earth energy veins known as 'snake currents' or 'dragon lines' following the line of subterranean water from the grotto well. It was also important for the navel, or spiritual centre of the church to be located over the spring. Where the cathedrals nave and chancel, choir and chapels are 'bent' – that is, are out of precise, straight or right-angled alignment – this is due to the ingenuity of the master builders to conform to the subtle geodetic, subterranean patterns, known only to the hierarchy of priests who closely guarded their secrets. The intention was to ensure that where great monuments were built – as in the case of Chartres – they were sited over very ancient sacred shrines in precise alignment to avoid disturbance to the existing positive earth energies and radiating streams below. It is also believed that centres of spiritual teachings and mystery schools such as Stonehenge, the Great Pyramids, Newgrange in Ireland, Chartres Cathedral, and other significant buildings and monuments around the world are key markers or power points conforming to a vast global energy grid.

Chartres' location was already well established as an ancient sacred site with very positive earth energy fields. (It was the site of the chief training college of the Gallic Druids many years before the cathedral was built.)[9] The 'etheric foundation' of the Cathedral was established by a point precisely over the power centre of the land. This 'point' is like the Hindu *bindu* – the seed from which the whole building is generated and manifested. From a stick marking the 'bindu' point the geometry of the Vesica Piscis was drawn on the ground to establish the orientation and all other proportions and ratios from which the 'order' of the entire building came into being.

The sacred geometric keys and symbolic dedications were set by the 'clients', who were the mystic priesthood. They directed the master builders (architects) who had been initiated generation after generation into the secret knowledge that enabled them to translate the metaphysical master plan into a physical reality. It is likely the priests of the school of Chartres were Knights Templar Neo-Platonists who brought back to France the 'seven liberal arts' and the alchemical knowledge of the Middle East embracing a philosophy of matter, spirit and the soul that are generated by the divine laws of the cosmos. Undoubtedly, the large, prominent West front sculptures of Pythagoras, Euclid, Boethius and Ptolemy refer to the Greek source of the *quadrivium* of number, space, time and the movement of the heavens (see Chapter 9).

One authority on Chartres, Louis Charpentier, linked the identical numbers, geometry, measurements and proportions of Chartres to those governing the Great Pyramid and the King's Chamber. Erected several thousands of years apart, the two buildings used the same universal laws relating the dimensions to the measurements of the Earth as well as applying the science in different applications – that is, using the same basic keys. In his book *The Mysteries of Chartres Cathedral*, Charpentier says:

> As to this key or clue, one sees traces of it easily enough in history, even when what one is after looks like legend. To go no further back, it persists from the Pyramids to Moses, who wrote it on the Tablets of the Law; it passes from David to Solomon, his son, who was 'instructed in all the wisdom of the Egyptians (Kings) and used it for the building of his Temple'. The *Document de Damas* tells that the Saviour had knowledge of it. The Persian adepts seem not to have overlooked it after Jerusalem fell to Islam. The first Knights Templar handed it to the Cistercians, who drew from it the three initiatory *Notre Dame*. Then it was hidden once again and will so remain until the right time shall come, for the growth of civilisations follows a temporal rhythm, a pulsation of the great Seasons of the Eras. And we may note that there was a period of one Era between the Pyramids and Solomon's Temple, another between the Temple and Chartres.[10]

The clues for deciphering the geometric master scheme are found on the statues of Christ holding a sacred book which is a rectangle in the proportion of the Golden Section and St John holding a book in the proportion of 2:1. The master builders would not have used arithmetical calculations to determine measurements and scales: this was done by a compass and straight-edge to translate the proportions from a two-dimensional plan to a three-dimensional structure. When a mason needed to know the shape and size of stone he was about to cut, the master mason had to draw in the sand the basic key for the proportions of the block. The key ensured that every piece of stone would conform to the same proportions and ratios of the whole structure of the building.

Another authority, Titus Burckhardt, established that the governing pattern or genetic model is the pentagon governing the ground plan and the decagon from which the Golden Section is produced. The heights of the storeys are built to the same harmonic proportions thus:

The length of the intersection (of nave and transept) is equivalent to the height of the wall pillars (from the columns of the arcades to the start of the vault), and this is the same as the width of the nave (if measured, not from pillar-centre to pillar-centre, but between the columns) and the height of the vault in the aisles…from the total height of the nave (from the ground to the crown of the vault), the next smaller stretch of the 'golden section' is the height of the nave up to the beginning of the vault, then the above-mentioned height of the wall pillars (from the columns of the arcades to the beginning of the vault), then the height of the columns of the arcades themselves (from the plinth to the springing-stone of the arch), and finally the distance between the springing-stone and the lower cornice. To this harmonic cadence is linked, as in the groundplan, the simple proportion of two to one, emphasized by the upper cornice on the wall pillar.[11]

The harmonic wholeness of the Cathedral is not only aesthetically fulfilling – the eye subliminally senses the coordination – the body responds to the resonance of proportion and the ear can readily hear the ethereal acoustic qualities that are registered by the musical scale corresponding to the heights of the vaultings.

The two towers to the West front are, at first sight, somewhat puzzling: they are not identical, in fact they differ considerably from each other in design features, shape and height. Atop the northern spire is the sign of the Sun and the southern, lower tower is the sign of the Moon. Symbolically, the Sun represents Christ and the Moon the feminine principle – the Virgin Mary. These symbols not only direct us towards an understanding that the church has astrological significance but the relative heights also have a dimensional significance related to the geometry and lengths in the nave. As with most medieval church architecture, there are usually some references to the zodiac and the four gospels: for example the bull (Taurus), the fish (Pisces), the eagle (Scorpio) and a man (Aquarius) are carved on the lectern in the nave.

The West front façade bears another unusual resemblance to the Hindu chakra system. You will recall that the chakra wheels have a number of 'spokes', points or 'petals' (see Chapter 7). The root chakra has 4 petals; the abdomen has 6; the solar plexus has 10; the heart has 12, the throat has 16; the brow or third eye has 2 and the crown chakra has one representing the infinite. Professor Critchlow pointed out the architectural features on the West front as 4 pillars, 10 panes of glass between the mullions of the tall windows; 12 roundels and ovals of glass in the great circular window; 16 arches with inset figures above the window and 2 figures on either side of the Virgin.[12] It seems unlikely these correspondences are nothing more than coincidence.

The north entrance known as the Door of the Initiates – those seeking the alchemical holy grail of spiritual enlightenment – is marked by a statue of Melchisedek, holding the cup in his hand, together with other figures of Moses, Abraham and Samuel carrying tablets of the universal laws and a carving of the Arc with wheels. The south door is tall enough for a person to ride into the church on horseback – a recognised symbol of one who is an initiate such as the Knights Templar. Their creed, combining the tenets of Christianity and Neo-Platonism, did not accept that Christ was the man on the cross, hence the absence in the Cathedral of any sculptures depicting the crucifixion.

Each of the magnificent stained-glass windows, described by Ruskin as 'flaming jewels', tells a story from the Bible to remind the worshippers of the teachings of Christ. The light inside the Cathedral has an iridescent quality that 'glazes' the stone floor. Most of the original glass remains intact but where small panels have been replaced with modern pieces the light shining on the floor is dappled with tiny patches of blue, red or white. No-one has yet discovered the secret, said to have come from the alchemists of ancient Persia, of how the different coloured glasses produce this diffused, unworldly, opal 'haze' that stays a constant quality of light throughout the length of day from dawn to dusk.

While, miraculously, Chartres has survived many major wars and revolutions without serious damage, it did however suffer vandalism in the eighteenth century when one of the bishops knocked out some of the upper windows so that the congregation could see him more clearly!

If the great West window (the cosmic wheel of eternal spirit) at Chartres were folded down 90° on to the nave it would cover the same area as the labyrinth (the pathway or journey of the soul). The labyrinth (see Figure 10.1) is a white marble

Figure 10.1   The labyrinth pavement, Chartres Cathedral

pavement about 13.5 metres (42 feet) in diameter inset into the stone floor. Narrow black marble slips mark the path which is just 40 centimetres (16 inches) wide and about 266 metres (865 feet) long. The labyrinth is like a Hindu *mandala*: the centre resembles a six-petaled lotus or rose around a central core – it is a circle of the cosmos, embracing unity and oneness. Part of our inner ear is referred to as labyrinthine: sea-sickness – labyrinthitis – is due to an imbalance or disharmony.

A labyrinth is not a puzzle or test of ingenuity: it is a one-way uni-cursive path requiring no thinking or 'working out' how to get to the end – only meditation. The pavement at Chartres is located close to the West front entrance so that worshippers could traverse the 'pilgrims way' before approaching the altar. Various forms of labyrinth have been used as a spiritual tool for thousands of years. Labyrinths were built into the pavements of many cathedrals, at Sens, St Martin, St Omer, Poitiers, Toussaint, Auxerre, Reims; all but three, Bayeux, St Quentin and Chartres, were either defaced or removed as they were considered to be a relic of a pagan past! (If only they had understood how 'pagan' – that is, pre-Christian – were the fundamental principles of Gothic architecture.) On my previous visits to Chartres, the pavement labyrinth had been covered with chairs and as others before me had found, this seemed to be a taboo subject for the church authorities, not open for discussion or information. However, when my wife and I arrived at the Cathedral late one after-noon in 1998, to my pleasant surprise in one part of the nave there was an exhibition extolling the virtues and symbolism of the labyrinth.

Unfortunately very few people alive today have had the opportunity to experience walking the path at Chartres. Now that the church authorities have taken a more open view of the labyrinth and all that it symbolises, it is hoped that many others may be allowed to follow. Whatever one's religious or non-religious persuasion, Chartres is the organic manifestation of universal esoteric teachings that stretch back thousands of years. There is always something new to discover which, like an alchemical trans-mutation, has the power to transform.

Putting the sacred into practice

Thomas Sandby, Professor of Architecture at the Royal Academy of Arts in 1771, said of student architects that 'It is, above all things, necessary that the young student should, as early as possible, habituate himself to the story of the sublime and beautiful ...[and] the stupendous works of Nature'.[13]

Any building, however important or insignificant it may appear to be, will not be a work of architecture unless it has been designed according to coordinating principles where the plans, sections, elevations and all those parts within the building have one unifying geometric proportional system. Working within these disciplines the designer has the same infinite scope of artistic expression as a composer of a grand symphony, but every part of the composition will be *controlled* and within the frame-work of the *key*. A mundane choice of uncoordinated, unrelated dimensions, the arbitrary proportion and placing of windows or doors where the one has no harmonic relevance to the other will never produce a building that can be classified as a great work of architecture.

In his book Chartres and the Birth of the Gothic Cathedral, Titus Burckhardt comments:

> Nothing is as senseless as the opinion that compliance with a geometrical law might inhibit artistic creativity; were this so, one would have to regard the natural harmonies in music as inhibitory to the creation of melody...there is a correspondence between geometric proportions and musical intervals...the dependence on a specific set of proportions, derived from a regular polygon, finds its sonorous counterpart in the modal music of antiquity, the Middle Ages, and the present-day Orient...a keynote...confers a very specific 'mood' or quality on every melody deriving from it. Relying on the basic schema of the mode, the medieval musician could multiply his melodic patterns without ever 'losing the thread', just as the medieval architect, by remaining within the geometric order that he has chosen, could freely develop and change the individual elements of a building without any risk of losing the unity of the whole.[14]

The manifestation of a sacred building also requires the divine spark of genius and inspiration of the architect. This divine spark is within every human being, otherwise we could not recognise goodness, beauty and truth. Working to a basic geometry that is the key to generating the entire volumes and proportions of a building may appear to today's architects to be a severely restrictive, unnecessary discipline and out of keeping with the spirit of freedom of the modernism of the art and architecture of the twentieth and twenty-first centuries. But when the sacred sciences are taught again in the schools of architecture by masters who have a profound understanding of the 'mysteries', our architects will produce buildings that create and enhance a sense of wholeness and a return to unity with the environment. The mystery school teachings of number, geometry, harmonics, time, space, alchemy, medicine and the understanding of their 'common bond' are essential to our understanding of the sacredness in all things, and that we too are subject to the same universal laws that maintain creation. This was the purpose of the mystery schools.

References

1. Burckhardt, Titus (1997) 'Introduction', *Sacred Art in East and West*, Middlesex: Perennial Books, pp. 8–9.
2. Wittkower, R. (1971) 'Alberti's approach to antiquity in architecture', in *Architectural Principles: In the Age of Humanism*, New York: W. W. Norton & Co, p. 45.
3. Palladio, A. (1965) *The Four Books of Architecture*, New York: Dover Publications.
4. Coates, K. (1991) *Geometry, Proportion and the Art of Lutherie*, Oxford: Oxford University Press.
5. Vitruvius (1960) *The Ten Books of Architecture*, Book V, Chapter V, Paragraphs 1–8, New York: Dover Publications.
6. Vitruvius, op. cit., Book V, Chapter V, Paragraph 3.
7. Vitruvius, op. cit., Book X, Chapter XIII, Paragraph 2.
8. Robert Lawlor, 'Geometry at the service of prayer. Reflections on a cistercian mystic architecture',

Parabola Magazine, vol. 3, no. 1, 1994 (reprinted by kind permission Society for the Study of Myth and Tradition).

9. Sir Geoffrey Tory, 'Aspects of dowsing', *Journal of the British Society of Dowsers*, vol. 38, no. 260, June 1998, p. 69.
10. Charpentier, L. (1992) *The Mysteries of Chartres Cathedral*, London: Rilko, p. 188.
11. Burkhardt, T. (1995) *Chartres and the Birthplace of the Cathedral*, Ipswich: Golgonooza Press, pp. 97–98.
12. Lecture by Professor Keith Critchlow.
13. Text on display at the Sir John Soane Exhibition at the Royal Academy London, 11 September to 3 December 1999.
14. Burkhardt, T. (1995) *Chartres and the Birthplace of the Cathedral*, Ipswich: Golgonooza Press, p. 94.

Suggested further reading

Artress, L. (1996) *Walking a Sacred Path*, New York: Riverhead Books.
Green, M. (1988) *The Path through the Labyrinth*, Dorset: Element Books.
James, J. (1985) *The Master Masons of Chartres*, London: Routledge & Kegan Paul.
Querido, R. (1987) *The Golden Age of Chartres*, Edinburgh: Floris Books.
Meurant, R. C. (1989) *The Aesthetics of the Sacred*, Auckland: The Opoutere Press.
Schwaller de Lubicz, R. A. (1961) *Sacred Science*, Vermont: Inner Traditions International.
Whone, H. (1990) *Church, Monastery, Cathedral*, Dorset: Element Books.

A more detailed study of the sacred mysticism in number, geometry, music and architecture can be found in many books, pamphlets and through organisations and seminars. With a simple, inexpensive pair of compasses, a straight-edge, a pencil and paper, anyone can explore and experience for themselves the most profound mysteries and paradoxes of life through geometry. Workbooks such as *Sacred Geometry* by Robert Lawlor give an elementary, step-by-step exercise taking you into the meditational realms and repeating those same fascinating experiences of the sacred enjoyed by the ancient masters. See Lawlor, R. (1992) *Sacred Geometry*, London: Thames & Hudson.

11.
The perennial wisdom

When men lack a sense of awe, there will be disaster.[1]

We are born into the exoteric world of survival, economics, business, politics, disease, pollution, poverty and riches, life and death. We also have to come to terms with the relationships we have with others, with the planet Earth, the cosmos, creation, the infinite spirit or divine intelligence we may call 'God' and the relationship we have with ourselves. When we become aware that there is more to life and living than survival and gratification of the senses there is a need to discover the source of oneself – a desire to know both intellectually and spiritually, and to lift the veil of illusion and self-deception.

The phenomenon, fairly commonplace in Western society, called the 'mid-life crisis' manifests in various guises such as alcoholism, drug abuse, sudden illness, separation and divorce, or frustration, anger and resentment with the family, employers, or society in general. Underlying these outward forms of crisis is an inner crisis of a psycho/spiritual nature that triggers a need to seek fulfilment through the exploration of the mysteries of life. Sooner or later, in our quieter moments, we may come to ask ourselves three questions: 'Who am I?', 'Why am I here?' and 'What is my destiny?'. It takes courage to purposely seek the answers because, to do so, one must embark on an inner journey into the realms of the unconscious, the occult or mesoteric world and beyond to the esoteric world of mysticism.

At whatever age, to begin such a journey in the modern world is not easy as bona-fide teachers of the mesoteric and esoteric teachings have become rare. Religious or spiritual tuition has been all but eliminated from many state-run schools and there are no rituals or initiations for the young.

Initiation into wisdom

Initiation is intrinsic to human nature, however formalised, structured initiation processes are no longer practised in the 'civilised' West, and those remnants that do survive seem to have lost much of their original mystical purpose. In India the Parsees celebrate the Novjot for their children between the ages of 8 and 11 years: to survive childhood in India is sufficient in itself to warrant a party in any case, but the original underlying purpose was not simply to rejoice in achieving young adulthood. The Confirmation initiation of the Christian tradition deals with the young person's spiritual development; the Barmitzvah deals with the mind and the spirit but both religions have discarded a human being's holistic nature of spirit, mind and body.

According to Louis Charpentier initiation is not a degree of knowledge but a state (of grace).[2] Throughout history every culture has had its own form of mystery school teachings where both the young and adults are initiated into the secrets and ancient wisdom of the tribe or society. The so-called 'primitive' societies still found in Africa, Australia, Asia and North and South America all follow corresponding patterns of initiation. For example, the North American Indian culture, like most other Earth traditions, is based on a mystical philosophy of the soul's integration and being at-oneness with the cosmic forces and nature. The forests, rivers, rocks, mountains and sky personify invisible creatures; the Sun symbolises the spirit of goodness and their concepts. Their initiation rites are not dissimilar to the mystery school initiations of ancient Egypt. Through the rites of passage a neophyte can begin to comprehend the symbolism that is everywhere for us who have eyes to see and ears to hear. The Upanishads say 'it is impossible for us to learn elsewhere what we are incapable of learning within our bodies'. In other words, our body is a microcosmic model of the whole universe.[3]

Tribal elders – the Shaman and the healer-priests – who are the guardians and teachers of the mysteries of life have always been with us and even contemporary, Western elders or initiators into the sacred arts can still be found, though they maintain a low profile. Those neophytes who are determined to follow the path of esoteric initiation will do so by instinct and intuition, perhaps knowing that 'when the student is ready, the teacher will appear'. Whether we belong to a primitive tribe or are the product of a highly intellectual materialistic society, there is a need, buried deep in our psyche, which requires some form of initiation into the mysteries – the mysteries of becoming a man, becoming a woman, the mysteries of life and the sacred teachings. The basis of all initiation is transcendence, the graduation from one plane of existence to the next higher level. Initiates had to undergo rituals to experience confusion, disorientation and have 'reality' turned inside-out, much as the Zen masters use Koans and paradox to break down the time and space concepts of the five physical senses as a prelude to a transformation to a new level of consciousness and spiritual understanding.

Such psycho-spiritual transformation exists within the context of all orthodox traditions but often the underlying purpose is lost in dogma or a lack of understanding by those who profess to be teachers. The absence of sacred initiation practices leaves a gaping unhealed wound in the collective unconsciousness of our society.

An authority on mythology and religions, Mircea Eliade, said that: 'Every man wants to experience certain perilous situations, to confront exceptional ordeals to make his way into the other World – and he experiences all this on the level of his imaginative life by hearing or reading fairy tales'.[4] Perennial wisdom means eternal, enduring wisdom: like the seasons, sometimes it blossoms, at other times it lies dormant, but the seed is always with us. Vestiges of the classical mystery schools still exist in the West.

The mystery school tradition

From the most ancient peoples to the present day, secret schools of initiation into esoteric wisdom have flourished. The arts and sciences of master building, mathematics, geometry, medicine, law, music and philosophy and astrology/astronomy can be traced back through to the mystery school initiate philosophers and priests who, according to the Egyptian third-century AD theologian Origen, have a sublime and secret knowledge respecting the secret of God. The word 'mystery' is derived from the Greek *muo*, meaning 'to close the mouth'. The ancient word *mystes* is the probable root of the modern word 'mystic', meaning a seeker after truth, and to the Greeks 'Truth' meant the whole cosmic system. The mystery school teachings were therefore a codified system of wisdom that integrated the arts, sciences and spirituality with nature and the universe.

In every community and civilisation the mystics and sages were, and still are, deeply versed in the laws of nature and the universe: they believe that without having a fundamental understanding of the divine laws, we cannot live intelligently. The masters of the schools, the custodians who have passed down this sacred knowledge as it evolved from generation to generation, taught secret practices to those who had reached appropriate levels of ordered discipline. The teachings were profound, potent, powerful and remained almost entirely oral in order to protect the knowledge from being misunderstood or unscrupulously misused by the uninitiated. The purpose was not to conceal the truth of nature's secrets, nor to mystify, but for the initiate to fully understand man as a microcosmic symbol of the whole universe. Such written material that was produced was couched in covert, symbolic language that would only be significant and comprehensible to initiates.

The ancient mystics went to extraordinary lengths to ensure the sacred knowledge was preserved for future generations and would be protected from uninitiated superstition and vandalism. Mathematics, geometry, astrology, harmonic ratios and hieroglyphics were symbols used by the masters of the mystery schools to teach the sacred knowledge. These teachings were concealed within the orientation, dimensions and symbolism of volume, spaces and decoration of their buildings to encode the esoteric meanings of life, death and the universal laws.

A mystery school provided the map and compass bearings for those about to explore both the natural phenomena of the outer worlds and their own inner world of human nature and the psyche. The teachings recognised three principle levels of reality: the *exoteric*, physical realm of matter; the *mesoteric* realm of the mind and spirit; and the *esoteric* realm of divine mysticism. In essence, mystery school teachings were an initiation from the profane to the sacred realm, while the curricula of the great academics of the Hermetic, Pythagorean Western tradition and those of

India and China of the Eastern civilisations were fundamentally the same as the Shamanic tribal societies of, say, the Australian outback or jungles of South America: their purpose was to guide the neophyte along the heroic path of spiritual rites of initiation into the mysteries of our relationship with nature, the cosmos and a divine spirit that some people may call 'God', and to reawaken our soul through 'remembrance'.

Western mystery school teachings were in essence divided into the lesser (minor) mysteries and the greater (major) mysteries. The former concerns our experiences of the occult, or hidden mesoteric realms such as the illusion and unreality of life on Earth; our intuitive insights; our inspirations, instincts and unaccountable sensations; the power of healing, oracles and other psychic phenomena; all leading to self-development and self-knowledge. The greater mysteries are the mystical, ineffable, profound 'knowingness' of the spiritual and divine realms reached through a liberation of the soul. In the words of Herbert Whone, 'Wisdom is the transcending of personal knowledge – the true end of religion where the vision of Man has become one with God'.[5]

Esoteric teachings that elevated adepts to the realities of intellectual and spiritual mysticism were revealed only to a few highly attained initiates: the majority remained at the mesoteric level to live a virtuous and fulfilling life of integrity, in tune with the divine order and the principles of the law of nature. All the major religions and spiritual teachings appear to have been drawn from a universal, ancient source of philosophy, metaphysics, art and science that has sprung and continues to evolve from the masters of the mystery schools of the world who have dedicated their lives to the search for divine truths, the beauty of man and creation and to lead the uninitiated out of blind ignorance.

European mystery schools

Before the Roman conquest of Britain and France, the ancient Celtic priesthood known as Druidism had been well established. Their esoteric knowledge and Sun worship seems to have been derived from the Eleusinian mystery school teachings of Egypt and Greece, embracing a deep understanding of Kabbalah, astrology, natural theology, geometry and the physical sciences. The priests were also physicians who used magnetism and amulets for healing, as well as herbal medicines and crude surgical instruments. They also worshipped the nature spirits and believed in the immortality of the soul. Julius Caesar, who wrote about them, was very hostile to their practices and eventually the Romans wiped them out on mainland Europe and Britain by AD 61. Those who escaped to Ireland survived only until the Christian missionaries arrived. Vestiges of the Druid Brotherhood are still with us today when we can see them gather at Stonehenge for the equinox and solstices: otherwise they remain a covert society.

An early Christian sect established in Rome in the second century AD was known as the 'Gnostics'. *Gnosis*, or *Nous*, is a Greek word for 'knowledge' – meaning 'self-knowledge' or 'knowledge of the eternal through personal experiences' rather than blind faith – the religious person *believes*; the mystic *knows*. (On one of his rare appearances on television, C. G. Jung was asked 'Do you believe in God?'; he replied 'I don't believe, I *know*'.) Despite persecution from Rome, Gnosticism spread throughout Europe and as far afield as Persia, Iraq and China.

Humanism developed as the basis of the Renaissance in the fourteenth century that began in Italy after the rediscovery and translations of the ancient Greek and Roman writings such as Plato and Vitruvius, who were concerned with the structure and proportions of the human body, human achievement in the arts and sciences and our interrelationship with nature, the universe and God.

Despite the overt revival of classical esotericism expressed in the scholarship, art and architecture of the Renaissance up to the sixteenth century, opposition to Christian dogma survived covertly until a German Protestant brotherhood called the Society of the Rosicrucian Order openly published its manifesto, *Fama Fraternitatis,* in 1610. Rosicrucians believed the material arts and sciences were a reflection of divine wisdom and only by penetrating the inner secrets of nature could human beings achieve understanding and appreciate reality based on the eternal doctrine of Neo-Platonism and Hebrew and Hindu theology. Although the Order did not flourish in England, there were many notables such as Sir Christopher Wren who were adepts. During the eighteenth century, Rosicrucianism turned towards the New World: the American War of Independence represents the Rosicrucian political experiment to establish a national government based on the principles of divine and natural law. The concept of liberty, fraternity and that all people are created equal was inspired by Sir Francis Bacon's vision of his New Atlantis and the aspirations of secret societies. The symbolism contained in the Great Seal of the United States is a constant reminder of Rosicrucian occultism.

Another significant incident in the early history of America is recorded in a book by Allan Campbell, entitled *Our Flag*. It tells the uncanny story of the design of the flag in 1775 and an unnamed man who was well known to General George Washington and the philosopher Dr Benjamin Franklin, who was believed to have been a Rosicrucian initiate. Franklin and another mysterious figure, the Marquis de Lafayette, are the two who played an important role in the circumstances that led up to the thirteen American colonies becoming a free and independent nation.[6]

Virtually the last link in the chain of Western occult science after the Rosicrucians is the Brotherhood of Freemasonry. It was founded in the early 1700s by 'nobles and leading citizens' who combined to start a 'grand lodge' as an ethical branch of practical building. They too were influenced by Sir Francis Bacon's alchemical secret society and his belief in universal education and democracy. They were familiar with Plato's 'seven liberal arts' and other mystery school esoteric philosophies. Their doctrines, symbolism, the work of Hiram Abiff and the ancient Dionysian school of architecture had connections with the Knights Templar and the medieval masonic guilds.

Washington DC was planned on the symbolism of the Masonic five-pointed star motif and the star Sirius. All of the ceremonies linked to the building of the Washington Monument obelisk, from the laying of the cornerstone on 4 July 1848 to the final dedication ceremony on 21 February 1885, were chosen to coincide with the motions of Sirius. The Masonic ideal, symbolised by a glowing capstone on top of a pyramid, can be seen on the US one-dollar bill.[7]

The alchemists

The ancient discipline of alchemy is one of the golden threads woven into the fabric of mystery school teachings and perennial wisdom. The modern words, 'alchemy' and 'chemistry', came from the word *Khem*, being the name of the land of Egypt. The most revered alchemical formula is the Emerald Tablet of Hermes Trismegistus known as the *Tabula Smaragdina*. The old alchemists referred to the secret chemical writings as 'Hermetic' and the term is still used today to describe the sealing of glass by fusion.

Traditionally, the alchemists used three symbolic substances – salt (body), mercury (soul) and sulphur (spirit) – with a fourth mystical element called *azoth* being the limitless spirit of life – a life force akin to the Celtic *Ond*, the Chinese *Ch'i* or Indian *Prana*.

The alchemists were not trying to conjure something out of nothing but attempting to improve that which already exists. Did they actually transmute base metal into gold? It sounds impossible, but certain individuals and museum authorities claim to have possession of alchemically transformed gold objects. King Henry IV of England was sufficiently convinced to declare the 'multiplying of metals' to be a crime against the Crown. When William and Mary succeeded to the throne, they repealed the Act in 1689 but thereafter all alchemical transformations of metals had to be handed over to the Mint – straight into the Royal coffers! After this, understandably, they encouraged alchemy.

Although alchemy was driven underground, the ancient wisdom continued through the Templars (the Knights of Christ and of the Temple of Solomon) and found expression in the coded messages of the troubadours of Elizabethan England. Much of the works of Shakespeare and the actual paper and numbering of the written folios have been analysed to explore the hidden messages which would have been understood by adepts. Ben Jonson's *The Alchemist* (1610) was treated as a satire but it contains profound insights into the philosophy of alchemy.[8]

A reaction against the dogma and the new materialistic science drove British physician Robert Fludd (1574–1637) to take up the ideals of the Rosicrucians and defend the allegorical interpretations, astrology and alchemy. Sir Isaac Newton (1642–1727) was not only a great scientist, President of the Royal Society and Warden of the Mint, he was also an astrologer and Neo-Platonist, and wrote a million words on the philosophy of alchemy. He too was searching for the Holy Grail that would resolve the interaction between the cosmos – heavenly bodies – and the materiality on Earth.

Modern chemistry evolved from its early beginnings in ancient Egypt but it treats alchemy as a pseudo-science akin to magic and superstition without understanding the symbolic language. The chemical experiments now used to transform substances are not that different, except today we do not have a spiritual imperative.

Why are our present-day scientists incapable of duplicating the achievements of medieval alchemy, even though they meticulously follow every step – is it because the subtle element of alchemical philosophy gained through initiation is missing from the experiments? This analogy can be found in modern architecture: however much the principles of sacred geometry and harmonics are followed and incorporated into the design, unless the architect has an understanding of the philosophy and has experienced the step-by-step esoteric teachings, a building will be moribund and without that inner quality expressing goodness, beauty and truth. Instead it will be like a work produced by painting in numbered squares.

References

1. Lao Tzu, Tao Te Chung, 72 Wildwood House, Hampshire (1986).
2. Charpentier, L. (1992) *The Mysteries of Chartres Cathedral*, London: Rilko.
3. *Katha Upanishad* (1949) 'The Upanishads', vol. 1, trans. Swami Nikhilananda, New York: Ramakrishna-Vivikananda Centre.
4. Eliade, M. (1957) *Myths, Dream and Mysteries*, New York: Harpers & Row.
5. Whone, H. (1994) *The Hidden Fact of Music*, London: Gollancz.
6. Hall, Manly P. (1997) 'Fraternity of the Rosicrucians', *The Secret Teachings of All Ages*, Los Angeles: The Philosophical Research Society, p. CXLIII.
7. Ibid., 'Episodes from American history', p. CC.
8. Ibid., 'Alchemy and its exponents', p. CXLIX.

Suggested further reading

Baldock, J. (1997) *The Alternative Gospel*, Dorset: Element Books.
Burckhardt, T. (1986) *Alchemy*, Dorset: Element Books.
Case, D. F. (1985) *The True and Invisible Rosecrucian Order*, New York: Samuel Weiser.
Churton, T. (1987) *The Gnostics*, London: Weidenfeld & Nicolson.
Fabricius, J. (1989) *Alchemy*, Northants: The Aquarian Press.
Gilbert, A. and Cotterell, M. (1995) *The Mayan Prophecies*, Dorset: Element Books.
Godwin, J. (1979) *Kircher*, London: Thames & Hudson.
Godwin, J. (1979) *Robert Fludd*, London: Thames & Hudson.
Halevi, Zerben Shimon (1979) *The Way of Kabbalah*, London: Thames & Hudson.
Khanna, M. (1979) *Yantra*, London: Thames & Hudson.
Klossowski de Rola, S. (1973) *The Secret Art of Alchemy*, London: Thames & Hudson.
Scott, W. (1993) *Hermetica*, UK: Solos Press.
Steiner, R. (1999) *Architecture as a Synthesis of the Arts*, Dorset: Rudolf Steiner Press.
Taylor, T. (1980) *The Eleusinian & Bacchic Mysteries*, San Diego: Wizards Bookshelf.
Wood, Florence and Wood, Kenneth (1999) *Homer's Secret Iliad*, London: John Murray.

12.
A way forward

Wisdom remembered

There is nothing new – it is as old as history – for the older generation to despair of the younger generation. We find fault with school pupils for their lack of the basic skills of mathematics, language, general knowledge and inability to write correct English, we criticise university students – architects and art students in particular – for their apparent ignorance of history, art, philosophy and the heritage of mankind. Today we learn from archaeological explorations, books and museums about people of the past, their buildings and objects. And now, the Internet rather than the library or personal field study is the major source of research. (According to a recent survey, the majority of students spend more money on drugs and alcohol than books.)

But the problems are not necessarily due to the young students – they are the product of parents, adults, teachers, university lecturers and politicians who insist everything is done with 'political correctness' and nothing must curtail the freedom of expression. Self-discipline, personal responsibility, a broad grounding in the appre-ciation and understanding of the classics, art and sciences and any hint of the meta-physical dimensions of nature and human beings are judged by the elders to be over-taxing, too rigorous and dangerously close to upsetting the imagined sensitivities of anyone in the university or those who may be 'not so bright'. Every subject is compartmentalised: branches of the arts, sciences, philosophy and spirituality are fragmented and never taught as a comprehensive whole. Standards are 'dumbed down' to the lowest common denominator; we investigate nothing deeply and every-thing is reduced to time and space and quantity. In other words, there is no *why* of living.

Look at an average modern office building, hospital and school: take away the signage and they are indistinguishable. The only clue that a building is an office is its imposing portals whereas many hospitals and schools have such an obscured entrance it is difficult to find a way into the warren of corridors. The similarity of appearance maybe a clear indication that business, healing and learning are all based on the same materialistic, mechanistic and organisational principles whether you want financial advice, a heart bypass, need to acquire sufficient information to pass an examination or get a degree. It is all 'laboratory' high-tech work. The hospital does not welcome us into a place of holistic healing of the body and spirit – it is a technical laboratory. The school is not a treasure house of knowledge and wisdom – it is a database for information to be absorbed rather than for education. *Education* stems from the word *educari* meaning 'to draw out' inner knowledge rather than to 'cram in' information. Plato held the view that everyone is gifted with total wisdom and knowledge – all we have to do is seek out the teachers who will help us to *remember*. Teaching is an act of remembrance.

Global business activity and politics have shaped the architecture and 'universal' (same) design appearance of many cities throughout the world. London has planned ten new skyscraper office projects in an attempt to retain its status as the financial centre of Europe. In response Frankfurt, London's principal competitor, intends to build thirty-five new skyscrapers over the next ten years in a bid to take over the leading role. The disastrous postwar local authority high-rise residential tower blocks that quickly became unhealthy slums and dens of delinquency and dysfunctional behaviour were demanded by the political 'priests' of modern socialism. The architects designed concrete boxes stacked high for people to live in – some blocks even won awards – but the buildings could have avoided becoming crime-infested ghettos had the planners and architects had a deeper appreciation of the full spectrum of our needs and human nature. In many instances, not even the elementary materialistic requirements for a healthy, dry, wind- and weather-tight shelter were satisfied.

So-called 'progress' and technical advances that continue to shape our lives have brought unforeseen disasters such as Chernobyl, Bhopal, over-intensive farming, over-fishing, pollution, global warming and weapons that can readily wipe out all life on Earth within hours. Despite being victims of both self-created and natural disasters, the human race now numbers 6 billion people (in 1900 the world population was 1.6 billion) and continues to be the most successful species on the planet. But for how much longer? The Green crusaders' banner 'Save the Planet' may not be the most effective slogan. Firstly, 'the Planet' is too vast for anyone to encompass as an idea that an individual may have power to do anything about; secondly, the Planet, in some form or other, will definitely survive. We may gouge things out of the surface, scar the landscape, pollute the oceans and atmosphere but in time the Earth will heal itself and keep turning. It is we human beings, together with other living creatures and plants, who may not survive. If the banners pointedly stated that it is ourselves and our children who are seriously at risk the campaign might have an improved chance of success, but first we must curtail our one-sided materialistic attitudes and worship of 'market forces'. Materiality obscures the human soul.

A philosophy of materialism is not a new concept. As early as the fourth century BC Democritus put forward a mechanistic theory of nature and the universe he called Atomism, which incidentally coincided with Hippocrates breaking away from the holistic healing therapies and medicine. Nevertheless, the mystical concept of a unified, interconnected, harmonious cosmos embracing the whole of existence persisted and continued through to the Renaissance until the eighteenth century when Newtonian science and physics became disassociated from philosophy and metaphysics and the idea of the universe as a living, vibrating energy was transformed into a lifeless, mechanistic mass. This worldview brought about our current mindset that human beings and all living organisms, including the planet Earth, consist of a body with no soul or spirit to the point where, even now, orthodox human psychology does not recognise either the soul or higher consciousness.

We are a sublime creation with the most extraordinary facilities to be true to ourselves, to clearly see a *divine plan*, to be able to dream a dream, and yet we devoutly believe only in actuality and devote our time and efforts towards acquiring success, power and the control and manipulation of nature and natural resources:

> Only after the last tree has been cut down
> only after the last river has been poisoned
> only after the last fish has been caught
> only then will you find that money cannot be eaten.[1]

The story of Easter Island contains a salutary lesson for us as a metaphor in miniature of what we are doing to our own life-sustaining environment. The story begins thousands of years ago when a violent volcanic eruption in the south Pacific Ocean threw up 165 square kilometres (64 square miles) of rock, now known as Easter Island. The Polynesians inhabited the island and evolved a religious culture which created the 600 vast prehistoric stone carvings which vary from 3.5 to 13 metres (10 to 40 feet) high. Until about three or four hundred years ago, they also carved beautiful elongated wood figures, a few of which were brought to Europe by Captain Cook in the eighteenth century and can now be seen in the British Museum, in London, and in St Petersburg. At one time, the island supported a thriving population. The indigenous species of tree provided wood for fishing boats and sea voyages. As the population expanded, more and more trees were cut down to make land available for growing crops. When all the trees had gone, the islanders were left without materials for building boats to catch the fish or make wood carvings. Today, the barren island landscape is marked only by the majestic sculptures – monuments to the thriving culture of a bygone age. The few inhabitants now survive on fruits, vegetables, the export of wool, and tourism.[2]

In earlier chapters we saw how, despite its many benefits, technical progress has created environmental conditions that are potentially detrimental to our well-being. We have already passed the point where our ingenuity can 'fix it' in the hope of inventing even more technology to counter the previous technological problems because technology tends to exacerbate rather than resolve the difficulties. Our faith in materialism, technology, consumerism and market forces has not brought us any nearer to our goal of health, happiness and prosperity.

The world has never been short of wise sages and fundamental spiritual teachings but we have been too caught up in materialism to heed their wisdom. Instead of searching for meaning and understanding the purpose of life, our destiny and the mysteries of death, we expend our preciously short time and energy on trying to discover new transient things to distract our thoughts away from the transcendental. 'The real killer in life,' said the great late American philosopher and anthropologist Joseph Campbell, 'is when you find yourself at the top of the ladder and realise it is leaning against the wrong wall'.[3] He went on to say that this deep sense of dissatisfaction, this lack of fulfilment feeling like a gaping, black hole in the stomach, happens when we devote our lifetime to acquiring material wealth to overcome insecurities and avoiding troublesome thoughts of our own mortality without also taking care of our spirit or higher consciousness.

If we are going to reverse the trend it can only come about by an 'alchemical' transformation of human beings and the reawakening of our holistic relationship with nature. Prosperity, inner security and the healing process will materialise when we change to self-understanding.

> The time has come to think not only in terms of natural laws, but also in accordance with planetary laws that affect us as threefold beings of body, soul and spirit. By doing so, we attune ourselves consciously to cosmic rhythms and feel related to the cosmos as well as to our earthly environment. When we see the disorder Man is creating, it is encouraging to know that order does exist in the cosmos. We can be sure that the sun will not rise a minute or even seconds late. In proportion to our recognition and application of cosmic laws, order will be restored in individual lives and in earthly affairs.[4]

Spiritual wisdom – everything we need to know – is there ready to be revealed to the serious student. The library of Alexandria, founded in the third century BC, is said to have contained about three-quarters of a million treasures of the worldly knowledge, philosophy and wisdom of mankind. It suffered several fires and was eventually destroyed by the Arabs in AD 696. However, not all the writings were lost. Largely through the oral teachings handed down from generation to generation, sacred knowledge and perennial wisdom have been preserved to this day by written works and the few guardians who are present and ever ready to teach anyone who is a serious enquirer and humble listener intent upon 'the right use of knowledge'. According to Vitruvius: 'As for philosophy it makes an architect high minded and not self-assuming'![5]

Much as Vitruvius recognised a decline in the teaching of perennial wisdom and the general standards of education of architects 2,000 years ago, we have witnessed over the past 100 years a similar downward trend and loss of direction in both design, philosophy and understanding that has produced buildings and new towns that are not only soulless but have also proven to be bad for our health and well-being. The power of one individual, Caesar Augustus, as patron and client, presented Vitruvius with the opportunity to relatively swiftly bring about change (see Chapter 8 page 174). Today we can only rely upon the will, power and influence of the wider public – we, the so-called 'ordinary people' – who are the users and occupiers of buildings. It is for us to demand that the fundamental principles that create good, healthy buildings be understood and exercised by the architects, other professionals, property developers and indeed all those in the private and public sector who commission buildings. The built environment is produced collectively by the clients and their architects to serve the people who live, work and play in the buildings: once they have commissioned, designed and built the building, they move – often literally – to 'pastures green' and rarely revisit the project let alone occupy it.

It was Frank Lloyd Wright who made the profound statement: 'The principles of architecture are simply the principles of life'. He went on to explain:

> Just as a house built on makeshift foundations cannot stand, so life set on make-shift character in a makeshift country cannot endure. Good and lasting architecture gives or concedes the right to all of us to live abundantly in the exuberance that is beauty – in the sense that William Blake defined exuberance. He did not mean excess. He meant according to nature, without stint. A good and lasting life must yield that right to all of us. And the only secure foundation for such life is enlightened human character, which will understandingly accept and not merely ape the organic relation between the welfare of one and the welfare of the whole. Only that sort of character is fit for and able to create a permanent and universal well being. To put it concretely again, architectural values are human values or they are not valuable. Human values are life giving, not life taking. When a man is content to build for himself alone taking the natural rights of life, breadth and light and space away from his neighbour, the result is monstrosity like the pretentious skyscraper. It stands for a while in the business slum formed by its own greed, selfishly casting its shadow on its neighbours, only to find that it, too is dependent upon their success and must fail with their failure. Trained imagination and true thought are our human divinity. These alone may distin-guish the human herd and save it from the fate that has overtaken all other herds, human or animal. All this leads to the realisation of a new civilisation with an architecture of its own, which will make the machine its slave and create nobler longings for mankind.[6]

Presently in the West we are re-examining all spheres of existence – from both human and spiritual standpoints – in a totally unprecedented way. This re-examina-tion is a desire (both conscious and unconscious) to reconnect with the spiritual dimension of our being, and presents the wider public and ourselves, individually, with an opportunity to become 'informed clients'. The surge of interest in Feng Shui, even at its most superficial level, indicates that we have come to accept that non-materialistic, unseen forces or hidden energies may influence our daily life; the public's voice against genetically modified foods has demanded a response from complacent politicians and business organisations. Undoubtedly, modern medical science is miraculous but the extensive use of alternative medical care (valued at several billions of pounds and dollars a year in the UK and US alone) is another significant pointer towards a demand that embraces a holistic approach to the treat-ment of human beings. Increasingly, the necessity for intrusive surgery and the auto-matic prescription of drugs is being questioned or refused by discerning patients. Doubts are being voiced, challenging the medical establishment's total dependency on allopathic remedies.

Medical schools in the US have now responded to the controlled evidence from extensive studies that spiritual healing practices are proving to have very positive effects when combined with allopathic treatments. The 1997 journal of the American Medical Association reported that three years previously, only 3 out of 125 US medical schools taught courses on religious or-spiritual issues, which had since increased to 30. Now nearly 60 medical schools have developed courses and may others intend to do so.[7]

Further evidence of this spiritual dimension has come from a most unexpected quarter – the scientific community itself that for so long has focused exclusively on the physical and discounted any metaphysical dimension to nature and reality. Largely the trend has been, perhaps inadvertently, reversed in the later half of the twentieth century by those physicists who have searched for fundamental particles and the elusive 'Theory of Everything'. In 1999 Professor Brian Greene's publication *The Elegant Universe* set out his 'string' (superstring) theory to unify the existence and behaviour of everything from the smallest particles to galaxies. Inside quarks, gluons, photons and neutrinos are tiny 'strings' that vibrate in patterns as if, according to Greene, the cosmos were a 'shimmering aeolian harp' where each electron plays one note and the quark plays another.[8] Are these 'notes' a continuum of Pythagoras's Music of the Spheres?

Physicist Professor David Bohm of University of London proposed theories that appear to account for all paranormal and spiritual experiences: 'Relativity and, even more important, quantum mechanics have strongly suggested (though not proved) that the world cannot be analysed into separate and independently existing parts. Moreover, each part somehow involves all the others: contains them or enfolds them. In this sense, a common language may be said to have been established, and a common set of basic concepts, for this is the one point on which all mystics have agreed. This fact suggests that the sphere of ordinary material life and the sphere of mystical experience have a certain shared order and that this will allow a fruitful relationship between them'.[9]

The elegant mathematics of fractal geometry is another twentieth-century metaphor that re-establishes a philosophy of modern holistic science concerning the scale of apparently chaotic irregularities in the geometry of a structure – for example a vast coastline that beautifully replicates itself as it is scaled down to the infinitesimally small inlets and pattern changes of the beach. Even chaos operates to a mathematical formula that expresses an order – cosmos. IBM scientist Benoit Mandelbrot's book *The Fractal Geometry of Nature* illustrates the extraordinary, mystical patterns of star constellations, islands, mountains and snowflakes, and the growth of organisms from the macro- to the microcosmic scale appears to be governed by repeating elementary laws of geometry.[10]

Alfred North Whitfield said that science was blind because it dealt with only part of the evidence of human experience and there was much more to the world of atomic matter. Max Planck concluded that beyond the subatomic realm yet another world of reality existed beyond our present world of sense, and according to Werner Heisenberg in the atomic (material) realm, atoms are more than 'things'. In other words there is something else which proves there is no distinction between matter and energy. The sensory world is made up of atoms constructed of protons and electrons.

The discovery of anti-protons by Professor Segre and Dr Chamberlain means that the universe consists of normal atomic matter, but within the atom exist subatomic particles comprising protons which have mass – touchable matter – and anti-protons which have no mass. As with light and colour – a non-mass world interpenetrating and interacting with a world of matter. This tells us that the cosmos is in a state of being (now) and a state of non-being in the physical world. Einstein proved that although protons exist they do not exist in time but have an infinite life. When physicists attempt to describe the realities from the infinitesimally small world of subatomic particles to the infinitely vast realms of astrophysics the words are far more reminiscent of the language of the metaphysical poets, transcendental philosophers and the esoteric teachings of perennial wisdom. Concepts of non-linear time, infinity or a sixth dimension can be as incomprehensible as the hidden realms of the occult, paranormal world or notions of the mind, the psyche, heaven and the soul. The universe is a paradox and scientific enquiry, at its highest level, is dependent upon spiritual insights in the same manner as the strivings and discoveries of the alchemists. Theoretical physicists have a profound sense of mysticism where 'reality' is transcendent, impermanent, but entirely interrelated and interconnected by a whole spectrum of realities from the gross physical world to the subtle metaphysical realms. Why does our current mindset recognise only a material world of the senses?

As human beings we have constantly struggled to come to terms with our spiritual nature – the conflict between reason and inner knowingness; between logic and intuition; between religion/spirituality and science; between the sacred and the profane and our relationship and interconnectedness with nature and the cosmos. This is especially so now.

> The whole of creation exists within you, and everything that is within you also exists within creation. There is no boundary between you and quite nearby objects, just as there is no distance between you and very distant objects. All things, the smallest and largest, the lowest and highest, are present in you as co-equals. A single atom contains all the Earth's elements. A single movement of spirit encompasses all life's laws. In a single drop of water is to be found the secret of the boundless ocean. A single manifestation of yourself contains all life's manifestations whatever.[11]

Can our perception of the universe and our relationship to it be expressed in our modern society and the built environment? It appears that throughout history human beings have endeavoured to make this connection: from the architects/priests of the pyramids of Giza and the Mayan temples, to the master builders of Chartres cathedral, to Palladio and other great masters of the Renaissance and twentieth-century architects such as Frank Lloyd Wright, Professor Keith Critchlow or Rudolf Steiner and many other lesser known professionals. All of these have continued the tradition of designing buildings according to the fundamental principles of the sacred arts and sciences to create architecture to symbolise a spiritual, mystical concept expressing man's relationship with nature, the cosmos and the divine world.

Architects and developers cannot be depended upon to take the initiative because all they do is to reflect the demands of the consumers. It is we, the society of 'ordinary citizens', who must look beyond the mundane – the profane – and place materialism and actuality in their proper context in terms of holism. We must have the vision to respect and co-create with nature and have a passion to manifest an architecture that expresses the principles of goodness, beauty and truth. If we subscribe, live and breathe the ancient perennial precepts it can result only in the desperately needed changes to accelerate a shift in consciousness that may have already begun.

According to the 5,000-year-old Hindu tradition, the souls of both the architect and the donor (the client) were inseparably involved in the success of the final form of a building. That form had to be sufficiently geometrically accurate (sacred) for the gods to be compelled to be present. Whether a private dwelling or a commercial or public building the architect alone cannot produce a sacred vehicle for the expression of a 'spiritual presence and a space for the heart' without the client and users of the building understanding and sharing that same vision. Whenever we approach and enter a building designed according to the universal laws or canon, all the vibrations created by the earth energies, the geometry, the colour and sound will resonate with the whole of our being. Subliminally, our senses and every part of our body will see, hear and feel these vibrations and at the most subtle level, our psyche will respond to the occult wave patterns. Physically, biologically, intellectually, emotionally, spiritually and joyfully, we will be reminded of our 'common bond' with nature. We will feel healed and the building, whether it be humble or grand, will be a temple of the soul.

A mystery school for today?

Do mystery school teachings have any relevance to the Western civilisation of the twenty-first century, and if so, are we interested? We know there is more to life than simply earning a living, keeping ourselves and our family physically sustained and continually striving to satisfy the senses. When we go inside a building or arrive at a particular location, human beings commonly experience intuitive insights; we experience sensations, either enjoyable or uncomfortable. We can also recognise the sudden lightening flash of truth and an understanding that it has awakened a part of us that, deep down, has always been known; we listen more to the quiet inner voice – our psyche – that speaks within us. Instinctively we sense the hidden meanings of allegorical myth and metaphor, yet we are frustrated to know how to remove the veil of illusion, self-deception and the fear of the unknown and the unknowable.

Since science repudiated the existence of the spirit of the human soul because it could not be analysed or dissected under a microscope, only the physical body has been addressed. Neither does orthodox science recognise the subtle multi-dimensions of human beings and all living organisms, including the planet Earth. We now lead a secular life completely cut off from our spiritual existence because we do not understand our relationship with nature nor the universal laws nor the inner meaning of existence. Every aspect of our lives is compartmentalised into an incomprehensible isolation and separation. Increasing public awareness for holism, heightened consciousness, clarity of mind and purpose and even spiritual nurturing are human necessities that orthodox religions seem unable to satisfy. Self-awareness and our relationship with the Earth goddess, Gaia, is a universal tenet, but the standard religious elders and priesthood appear to be so steeped in dogma that they are ill-equipped to teach the mysteries and break the code concealing the ancient, perennial wisdom.

The present system of religious ritual does not allow the sacred knowledge to be revealed. Only by a gradual process of study and initiation into the symbols, metaphors, traditions, ceremonies and writings can we begin to understand the essential doctrines of ancient teachings that have always been kept alive throughout history. Unfortunately most of the time the teachings have had to run along narrow channels, but now we are entering a period when there is a strong need and desire to widen the stream of consciousness.

Today the masters who have the knowledge are still with us and ready to teach those seekers who strive for external truth, beauty and harmony. Professor Peter Kingsley, author of *In the Dark Places of Wisdom*, says: 'We have in our hands astonishingly powerful meditation techniques, written in mesmerising poetry two and a half thousand years ago, which provide simple and effective methods – not for turning our backs on this world of illusion but for seeing right through it, to its roots…[which is]…literature produced by people who originally shaped and created the Western culture that we live in'. [12]

In other words, we are not short of the material and the teachers: all that is needed is the demand to change – to counter the one-sided mechanistic functionalism and 'soul-lessness' that is expressed in modern buildings. Whether we are professional architects or from any other walk of life, we need to understand the fundamental realities of the universe and how we relate to it. The underlying laws or canon of nature; the web of vibration and how we interact with the earth energies, cosmic forces, electromagnetic fields, light, colour, sound; the study of the 'seven liberal arts' and the philosophy, physics and metaphysics of life; divine harmony; the inner meaning of symbolism and metaphor – all these could/should be the teachings at a modern mystery school.

At the moment these subjects are being appropriately taught in only a fairly fragmented manner, but when the demand reaches a critical mass the opportunity to create a comprehensive mystery school academy will be presented. Kairos, a nonsectarian organisation founded several years ago by Professor Keith Critchlow, which operates in both Britain and the US, would be a firm foundation on which to base such an academy.

Many other small groups and organisations that have sprung up in Europe and the US have dedicated teachers supported by private individuals who are serious students. Books covering the whole range of 'mystery school' subjects are available in abundance but personal tuition and oral teaching is needed for in-depth study.

Living a life of integrity, encountering the divine and understanding *why* we are living may begin to appeal to a much wider public. This may lead to the mystery school teachings becoming a formalised academy and included as an important factor in the curriculum of the schools of architecture.

References

1. Red Nations quote in *Kairos Quarterly Update*, June 1997 (p. A).
2. BBC1 TV programme, 'Lost Gods of Easter Island, David Attenborough turns Detective', 24 April 2000 and 4 January 2001.
3. Joseph Campbell quote from lecture.
4. Beredene, Joelyn (1981) *Citizens of the Cosmos*, New York: Continuum.
5. Vitruvius (1960) *The Ten Books of Architecture*, Book I, Chapter I, Paragraph 7, New York: Dover Publications.
6. Source unknown.
7. *Journal of the American Medical Association* (1997) 278(g): 792–3. Article by Levin, J. S., Lawson, D. B and Puchalski, C. M., 'Religion of spirituality in medicine'. Reported in Larry Dossey, 'Integration of spirituality and medicine', *Scientific & Medical Network Review* 70, August 1999, Sante Fe, New Mexico, p. 19.
8. Greene, B. (1999) *The Elegant Universe*, New York: W. W. Norton.
9. Bohm, D. (1983) *Wholeness and the Implicate Order*, London: Ark Paperbacks.
10. Mandelbrot, B. (1982) *The Fractal Geometry of Nature*, New York: W. H. Freeman & Co.
11. Gibran, K. Quotation from his play 'Iram That Al Imad'.
12. Anne Baring's interview with Professor Peter Kingsley, author of *In Dark Places of Wisdom*, Dorset: Element Books, 1999. Reported in *The Scientific and Medical Network Review* 70, August 1999, p. 19.

Contacts

Organisations referred to in the main text are listed in this section, along with the addresses of many useful bodies.

UK professional organisations

Building Research Establishment (BRE)
Bucknalls Lane, Garston, Watford, Hertfordshire WD2 7JR

Chartered Institution of Building Services Engineers (CIBSE)
222 Balham High Road, London SW12 9BS

Health and Safety Executive (HSE)
Caerphilly Business Park, Caerphilly, Wales CF83 3GG

Institution of Planning Supervisors (IPS)
Heriot-Watt Research Park, Edinburgh EH14 4AP

Royal Institute of British Architects (RIBA)
66 Portland Place, London W1N 4AD

Royal Institution of Chartered Surveyors (RICS)
George Street, London SW1P 3AD

Educational organisations

Kairos
An educational charity specifically founded to promote the recovery of traditional (perennial) values in the arts and sciences. Studies are focused on the unity of being, the fundamental interrelatedness of all things and the Quadrivium (arithmetic, geometry, music and cosmology). Kairos offers worksheets, seminars, talks and personal study.

UK	US
Amanda Critchlow-Horning	David Yarbrough
4 Abbey Cottages	PO Box 117
Cornworthy, Totnes	Crestone
Devon TQ9 7ET	Colorado 81131

Rilko (Research into Lost Knowledge Organisation)
An organisation covering a wide range of subjects of the occult (hidden) mysteries. Rilko regularly publishes a magazine, promotes the publication of books and arranges monthly lectures in London.
Contact: George Jarvis
             43 Dorchester Avenue
             Palmers Green
             London N13 5DY

The Scientific and Medical Network Review
Contact: Gibliston Mill
             Colinsburgh
             Leven
             Fife
             Scotland KY9 1JS

Live Water Trust
Contact: Hawkwood College
             Painswick Old Road
             Stroud
             Gloucestershire GL6 7QW

A list of publications on sustainable architecture, renewable energy, and pollution control can be obtained from:

             James & James Ltd
             Waterside House
             47 Kentish Town Road
             London NW1 8NZ

Watchdog organisations

The following organisations cover environmental pollution, geopathic stress, VDUs, power lines and safety guidelines.

Coghill Research Laboratories
Ker Menez, Lower Race, near Pontypool, Gwent NP4 5UF
www.cogreslab.co.uk

Electromagnetic Hazard & Therapy including *Powerwatch News,* published bi-monthly on subscription (previously *Electromagnetic News: Electromagnetics & VDU News*).
Editor Simon Best MA; Consultant Alasdair Philips BSc.
PO Box 2039, Shoreham by Sea BN43 5JD
Email: simonbest:em-hazard-therapy.com. www.em-hazard-therapy.com.

Powerwatch Network Newsletters
Alasdair Philips BSc
2 Tower Road, Sutton Ely, Cambridgeshire CB6 2QA
www.powerwatch.org.uk

Scientists for Global Responsibility
Unit 3, Down House, The Business Village, Broomhill Road, London SW18 4JQ

International Institute for Bau-Biologie & Ecology Inc
PO Box 387, Clearwater, Florida 34615, USA

Microwave News
(Bi-monthly publication)
PO Box 17989, Grand Central Station, New York 10163, USA

Dowsing organisations

Europe

The British Society of Dowsers
The General Secretary
Sycamore Barn, Tamley Lane, Hastingleigh, Ashford, Kent TN25 5HW

The Irish Society of Diviners
Theresa Lydon
8 Thomas Clarke House, Dublin 3, Eire

North America

The American Society of Dowsers
Danville, Vermont 05828, USA
Tel: + 1 (802) 684 3417
Fax: + 1 (802) 684 2565

The Canadian Society of Dowsers
Dorothy Donovan
PO Box 26102, Nepean, Ontario, Canada K2H 9R6

Australasia

Dowsers Society of New South Wales Inc
PO Box 391, Lindfield NSW 2070, Australia

Dowsers Club of South Australia Inc
PO Box 2427, Kent Town 5071, South Australia

New Zealand Society of Dowsing & Radionics Inc
PO Box 41-095, St Luke's, Auckland 3, New Zealand

North Tasmania Dowsing Association
PO Forth, Tasmania 7310

South Tasmania Dowsing Association
PO Box 101, Moonah, Tasmania 7009

Radon

Building Research Establishment
Garston, Watford WD2 7JR
Tel: (01923) 664707 (radon hotline)

National Radiological Protection Board (NRPB)
Chilton, Didcot, Oxon OX11 0RQ
Freephone (0800) 614529 (for advice on radon in homes)

The Radon Council Ltd
PO Box 39, Shepperton, Middlesex TW17 8AD
Tel: (01932) 221212

Householder's Guide to Radon
(Free booklet)
Department of the Environment, Room A518, Romney House, 43 Marsham Street,
London SW1P 3PY

Environmental Protection Agency
Section: Air & Energy Engineering, Research Laboratory
Triangle Park North Carolina NC27711, USA
Tel: + 1 (919) 541 7865

The British Geological Survey
Tel: 0115-936 3143 (for geological information for UK post codes)
www.bgs.ac.uk

Index